TRAILS AND TRIALS
OF A
TEXAS RANGER

TRAILS AND TRIALS OF A TEXAS RANGER

BY

WILLIAM WARREN STERLING

ⱦ

DRAWINGS BY BOB SCHOENKE

UNIVERSITY OF OKLAHOMA PRESS: NORMAN AND LONDON

ISBN: 0-8061-1574-2 (paper)

LIBRARY OF CONGRESS CATALOG CARD NUMBER: 60-17900

*To every man whose
devotion to duty has brought
or will bring honor to
that unique breed of men . . .
The Texas Rangers*

General W. W. Sterling

CHAPTERS

ILLUSTRATIONS

PHOTOGRAPHS

DRAWINGS

PREFACE

"You ought to write a book." This challenging thought has often been expressed by friends and acquaintances who have known me throughout the years. Now that I have passed the three score mark, which is more than twice the age predicted by observers of my early career, the suggestion has become imperative in tone. "You MUST write a book," is the mandate of former comrades, relatives of the great captains and numerous other pioneers. My span of life bridges the gap between horseback days and the modern era. Realization of this fact prompts me to put into writing some of the interesting incidents that have happened during my lifetime, plus others recounted to me by actual participants in those stirring events.

This work is in no wise a history of the Texas Rangers. My good friend, Walter Prescott Webb, has written what my equally good *amigo,* J. Frank Dobie, correctly called, "the beginning, middle and end of Texas Ranger histories." My aim is to give a Ranger's eye view of the Service, and to deal with aspects that cannot be fathomed by hearsay or research. Material and data did not come to me secondhand, but were obtained by intimate knowledge of every Ranger station, from the most remote camp on the Rio Grande to the headquarters in Austin.

While holding every grade in the Service, from Ranger to Adjutant General, I had an unequaled opportunity to study my subject. Therefore, this book will be a commander's consideration of the organization, which includes administrative and political phases. The uninformed and often misled public is entitled to enlightenment on the essentials of a genuine Texas Ranger. By the same token, citizens should be apprised of the sinister influences that destroy his usefulness.

My endeavor here is to relate some of the unheralded deeds performed by good Rangers whose names seldom appeared in print, but who lived and sometimes died upholding the best traditions of the Service. The constructive, benevolent and peaceful acts of Rangers will be dwelt upon rather than the amount of gunpowder they have burned. Probably more than any other group of men, oldtime Rangers drew a sharp line of demarcation between producers and non-producers. They were eager to help substantial citizens, but they had short patience with tinhorns, would-be badmen and other frontier wastrels.

Several Texas counties are named for Rangers. In conferring this honor on such leaders as Hays, Walker, McCullough and Brooks, the legislature gave perpetual recognition to the contributions Rangers have made to the progress and welfare of our state. Ex-Rangers have become successful stockmen, bankers, lawyers and statesmen. The achievements of empire builders on the outposts of civilization were possible largely because their lives and property were protected from desperados who respected no rights or laws save those backed up by Rangers. They have patrolled every major oil field since Batson's Prairie in 1904, holding in check the hordes of parasites and thugs who flock to the boom towns. This Ranger protection has been of incalculable value to the petroleum industry and the oil fraternity. Rangers were the mainstay of Texas ranchmen, with whom they have always been closely allied. Stockmen leaned heavily on these sharp-eyed riders and depended on them for protection against rustlers and brand burners. Railroads and industrial plants call on Rangers to preserve order when agitators and labor racketeers incite strikers to overstep their right of peaceful picketing and commit unlawful acts. Rangers take the lead in the prevention of mob violence and their efforts in this direction have been so successful that not a lynching has disgraced our state in many years.

Second only to the Alamo, the Texas Ranger is the best known symbol of the Lone Star State. Most Texans hold that the Rangers are an innate part of our heritage. The organization of this strictly Texas institution antedates the battle in which Travis, Bowie, Crockett and their comrades set a pattern for courage and valor. When the Rangers were under my command, I strongly impressed upon each man his obligation to carry on this integral part of the Texas tradition in a manner that would make the Service a source of pride to every good citizen.

Business Headquarters of the McGill Ranches in Alice, Jim Wells County, Texas.

Under the title "Trials" it is fitting and proper to include chapters on Texas governors. They are commanders in chief of the State's armed forces. Their oaths require them to "cause all laws to be faithfully executed." The prime function of the Rangers is to act as the strong right arm of the governor in carrying out this provision of the constitution. Prior to 1935, governors were vested with full appointive powers, and one of their major responsibilities was the maintenance of high standards in Ranger personnel. When the chief executive's office was held by a statesman, Texas had good Rangers, but when demagogues came into power, either in their own names or by proxy, the Service sank into the mire.

Thanks to the present generation of McGill Brothers, I am able to write this book in a congenial setting. Their business headquarters is a spacious building of early mission architecture. It was erected by the late H. F. McGill as a memorial to his brother, J. Claude McGill. These devoted brothers were co-founders of the vast ranch properties that bear their name. This office is a favorite gathering place for old timers, and contains an excellent library of Texiana. Adorning the walls are pictures of early-day cattlemen who made a sizeable portion of Texas livestock history. As a youth I knew many of these patriarchs and in cow camps have listened to numerous legends about others who rode to the Last Roundup before my day. Under their silent scrutiny and still piercing eyes I am spurred on in my efforts to write in a manner that would merit their mark and brand of approval. Each one of these sturdy rancheros was a strong believer in Rangers.

Additional background for my book lies in the fact that it is being written in Alice, Jim Wells County, Texas. This town, once the largest cattle shipping point in the United States, was named for a daughter of Captain Richard King, who founded the world's most famous ranch and gave prodigious support to the Rangers. The county bears the name of the illustrious James B. Wells, wise counselor and staunch defender of all worthy Rangers. I was blessed with the friendship of both these noble people, and received many kindnesses from each of them.

I have endeavored to get not only the hearts of Rangers into this work, but also their ties of kinship. Many widows, daughters, sons, relatives and veterans have given me their unselfish assistance in my effort to emphasize the finer qualities of a real Texas Ranger. Never did one man owe so much to so many. To the following friends I express my undying gratitude:

John Lipps, Miss Corrine Brooks, Sam Fore, Mr. and Mrs. Val Bennett, Miss Amelia Ochoa, J. R. Farmer, Tom B. Darst, Miss Jane Laseter, Col. T. McF. Cockrell, Charles A. Stewart, Mrs. Katie Smith Welder, Juan Salinas, Mrs. Alice Borden Savage, Dan Kilgore, Ben Ligon, W. T. Neyland, Mrs. Patricia Pittman Light, Will T. Wright, Dan Culver, Miss Eleanor Baker, Truman M. Gill, W. R. Montgomery, D. W. Grant, Mrs. Virgil McGee, Miss Caroline Davy, Gillespie Baker, Mrs. Frank Hamer, James Scott, Mrs. Sarah Eckhardt Lott, J. E. Petty, L. H. Purvis, Reverend J. Barcus Moore, Col. S. J. Houghton, Mrs. Lucile Rogers Reeves, Oscar Perron, Dr. A. C. McCullough, Manuel Benavides, Ross Boothe, J. B. (Dick) Hervey, Mrs. Isabel Sterling Rendall, Argyle McAllen, Mrs. Jesse Sterling Campbell, David Young, Mrs. Mary Sterling Ferguson, Fausto Yturria, T. T. East, Jack Douthit, W. E. McAnnaly, Mrs. Mary Lou Brey, Mrs. Elizabeth Airhart, Mrs. Zora Wright Fore, Dogie Wright, Miss Jane Bryan, Judge Tillman Smith, Judge S. Lamar Gill, Stanton Delaplane, Miss Caroline Duffield and George J. Lacy.

The sustaining friendship of Mrs. J. R. Dougherty, Church leader, Gold Star Mother and gracious lady, has enabled me to surmount many of the obstacles encountered in the production of this book. For the faith they had in me, I express my gratitude to Messrs. William H. Bauer, William A. Dial, Fred M. Golding, Earl C. Hankamer, William H. Hawn, Homer S. Head, Charles W. Hooks, Alvan A. Moore, Walter G. Sterling and Benjamin F. Vaughan. Especial thanks are due my former comrade William A. Dial, president of the Texas ex-Rangers Association. I am grateful to A. C. Jorns for his expert work in reproducing numerous old and faded photographs, and to Ed Bartholomew for permission to use several pictures from his rare collection.

To any helpful friends whose names may have been omitted through a faulty memory, I offer my humble apologies.

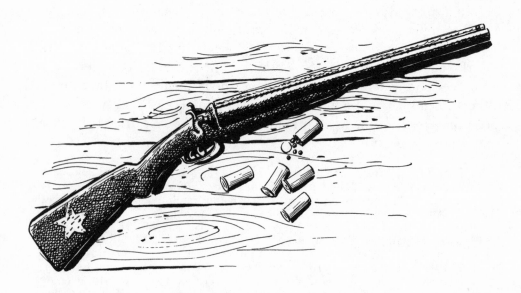

PART ONE

Chapter 1

EARLY LIFE

I WAS born near Belton, Bell County, Texas, on the 27th day of April, 1891. My mother was the former Mary Chamberlain. Her father operated a Confederate mill in Cherokee County, Texas, during the Civil War. Two of her brothers are buried there. After the cessation of hostilities, my grandfather moved to Atlanta, Georgia, where my mother was born. While she was still a child, her family moved back to Texas. She received her early education at the old Thomas Arnold High School in Salado, which was also known as the Salado College. My mother later attended Southwestern University at Georgetown. In 1885, at the laying of the cornerstone of the new capitol, she was among the students brought to Austin to take part in the ceremonies.

My father, Edward Arthur Sterling, was born on a farm in Ohio. As a youth he learned telegraphy, and came to Texas as "front" operator during the construction of the Santa Fe Railroad. When they built their branch from Temple to San Angelo, he found a spot to his liking and became their agent at Belton. The Santa Fe had been unable to acquire a right of way to the central part of town, and were obliged to build their station on the outskirts. In order to compete with the rival railroad,

Birthplace of W. W. Sterling. Bell County.

they picked up and delivered all freight shipped over their line. My father took the contract to perform this extra service, and it proved to be very remunerative. A large number of wagons and teams were required to handle the business. He was a good judge of livestock, and would pay almost any price for a fine mule. Nothing but the best would satisfy him. Among local dealers and horse traders, a mule owned by Sterling became synonymous with a piece of silver labeled "Sterling."

Belton was the home of a unique organization known as the Women's Commonwealth. Local residents, particularly the men, called it the Sanctified Sisterhood. This cult attained nationwide notoriety, and owned some valuable properties, which included the Central Hotel. The founder and moving spirit, who claimed to have received in a divine revelation the idea of her new religion, was Mrs. Martha McWhirter. She was one of the most remarkable women who ever lived in Texas, and to call her an iron-willed individualist would be a gross understatement. She bestowed Biblical names on many of the townsmen. My father was always in a hurry. His favorite buggy team was a pair of matched white Spanish mules, and he usually travelled

4

in a dead run. From his furious driving, Mrs. McWhirter dubbed him "Jehu". She would never call him by any other name.

He bought a tract of wooded land north of Belton. By building an extensive set of improvements on his new purchase, he turned it into a combination stock farm and suburban home. The barn was the largest in Bell County. On the place was a beautiful grove. Towering above the other trees was a giant Spanish oak, which could be seen for miles around. Carved high on the trunk of this landmark were a number of arrows, crosses and similar symbols. Old timers believed that they were signs of nearby buried treasure. This idea was given added credence by a circumstance that became a semi-authenticated legend in our family.

My father made a showplace out of the grove. He had it cleared of underbrush and had rustic seats built around the larger trees. It was then enclosed by an elaborate lumber fence, similar to those found in the bluegrass region of Kentucky. For this job he employed two professional fence builders. The ground was very hard and rocky. While digging one of the postholes, the workman's crowbar dropped out of sight. He and his partner worked the next day as though nothing unusual had happened. Late in the night they returned. An elderly aunt of mine declared to her dying day that she saw a man working and a light moving around the spot. In any event, the pair were never seen again in that part of the country. They did not even come back to get their wages.

Another crew was hired, and the fence completed. It was topped with wide boards, nailed lengthwise from post to post. This made a fine walkway, and we children used it on countless occasions. Upon reaching the section over the mysterious posthole, even our slight weight would cause it to sag. This invariably called for a repetition of the story of the buried gold.

In the early days of Belton, the railway station, or depot, was one of the busiest spots in town. It also served as the gathering place of hack-drivers, teamsters and a large bunch of loafers. Many of those in each category posed as "badmen," and they were often involved in serious brawls. For protection against holdups, the Santa Fe Railroad and the Wells Fargo Express Company furnished their agents with sawed off shotguns. They were double barreled, ten gauged and cylinder bored. When loaded with chilled buckshot, and in the hands of a determined man, these old spatterguns took the fight out of many a pistoleer. Express guards were armed with them when they rode shotgun on stage coaches, and this practice was continued on into the days of the iron horse.

My father had a picturesque vocabulary and a voice like the Bull of Bashan. On numerous occasions he used these natural weapons, together with his piece of Santa Fe equipment, to break up fights on company property.

When my father resigned from the railroad, they gave him this blunderbuss. It stayed around the ranch for many years. During the wildest days of early El Paso, ex-Ranger James B. Gillett served that turbulent pueblo as city marshal. He frequently used one of these young cannon to subdue the local badmen who were bent on exterminating each other. In 1932, I presented the old shotgun to him, and he pronounced it the genuine article. After Captain Gillett passed away, his daughters graciously returned me the valued relic. It is now in the collection of Charles Schreiner III.

My father owned a ranch in La Salle County. It was sold while I was still a small boy, but I have always loved the Cotulla country. He also fed a large number of cattle at the cotton oil mill in Temple, and had a feed lot on Bird's Creek. The Chamberlains were cattle people. With my father as partner, they operated the Chamberlain Ranch near Davilla in Milam County. I must have inherited my love for livestock from both sides of the family. My nature is strictly pastoral. Since earliest childhood, I have cherished the life of a ranchman and ranger. In describing my bloodlines, my father once said, "His mother was a saint. His daddy was a wild Irishman."

In common with most Texas boys, I learned to ride at a very early age. As soon as I was strong enough to hold on, I rode behind my father. A few years later he bought me a burro. Being too small to get on by myself, I had to improvise a way to mount. A favorite morsel in a donkey's diet is the scotch thistle, and they grew in profusion on our place. I would lead him to one of them, and when he put his head down to eat it, I climbed on his neck. When he raised up, I slid on his back and was ready for my ride.

When I was about eight years old, my father gave me my first pony. For some time I rode bareback, and then advanced to a surcingle with stirrups. This little known and long forgotten apparatus was made from a wide girth or cinch. Sewed to it with stout harness thread were two straps, and attached to these were the stirrups. This was the lightest and cheapest form of riding equipment. Children's saddles were unknown, but I was sometimes permitted to borrow a man's outfit, and put my feet in the leathers on top of the stirrups. At the age of eleven I acquired my own saddle. Ever since I can remember, I have loved to rope. My father was a good rider and a fair roper, while my uncles were experts in both lines. They gave me my early instruction in roping, and found me to be an eager pupil. I spent a great deal of my spare time in practice, with fence posts, dogs, milk pen calves and playmates serving as targets for my busy loop.

While I was still a small boy, my father took a contract to build a large reservoir for the Santa Fe at Temple. When it was completed, he suggested that it be named for the railroad president, Lucius J. Polk. He moved the family there, and rented a large two-story house in the south part of town. It was near a clump of hackberry trees. One day a well dressed young gentleman knocked at our front door. His clothes were disheveled and one hand was badly scratched. My mother went to the door, with my sister and me half hiding behind her skirt.

"Madam, do you have a gun or a pistol in the house?" he asked.

My mother did not know him and was nonplussed. "Why, yes," she said, "my husband has a pistol in the closet. What do you want with it?"

"A vicious horse has run away with me, and torn the buggy to pieces," he replied. "I am going to destroy him."

"Oh, don't do that," my mother advised. "Can't you do something else with him?"

"I could easily trade him off," was the rejoinder. "He is a very fine animal. I paid $250 for him only yesterday. I was badly fooled. But I am not going to let some other horse trader sell him again and get an innocent person killed. I am not angry, but believe that it is my duty to prevent another runaway."

His manner was so sincere that my mother gave him the six-shooter. He led the horse to the grove and shot him. When he returned the gun, he thanked her and said, "I am Dr. A. C. Scott. I have just moved here from Gainesville to become surgeon for the Santa Fe."

From that time until his passing, he was one of our dearest friends. A short time after this episode he performed an operation on my mother at our home. Later in life he used to tell that she was his first patient. She outlived him by many years. Under the name of Scott & White, he founded in Temple the most famous hospital in the South. Dr. Scott was never too busy to perform a civic service. He was once appointed a member of the Texas Prison Board. On his first inspection of the penitentiary, he did not mince words in condemning the disgraceful conditions that he found. Some of the guards employed there considered themselves gunmen, and made threats about the good doctor. His reply to them has always been a source of pride and satisfaction to me. He said, "One of 'my boys,' Bill Sterling, is a captain in the Rangers. He will back me if I need any help." Dr. Scott was just paying a compliment to his old friend. He was not afraid of anybody.

Chapter 2
BEAUMONT

WHEN oil was discovered in Beaumont in 1901, my father, who was always energetic and restless, joined the rush. Sometime later he sent for the family.

At the age of eleven, I took a job delivering the old Beaumont *Journal*. From a pair of stout canvas bags wrapped across the fork of my saddle, I threw over two hundred daily papers.

This job kept me on the streets every weekday afternoon, and although not an eyewitness, I learned a lesson that stayed with me throughout my service with the Rangers. Ras Landry, sheriff of Jefferson County was a handsome, dark complexioned man of French descent. With his raven black hair, flowing mustache, and mounted on a spirited horse, he made a colorful figure.

On one occasion, a Negro killed a policeman at the intersection of two principal streets. He fled into the piney woods, where he procured a rifle. The sheriff rode after him, armed only with his six-shooter. The fugitive took shelter behind a tree, and before the officer came within pistol range, threw down on him with his Winchester. The sheriff persuaded his captor to give up. He agreed to do this, but exacted a promise that he would be protected from mob violence. On the way to jail, the prisoner was shot and killed. Opinion was divided as to who fired the fatal shot. Some said it was the sheriff, others claimed that he was killed by a Confederate veteran. In my school of experience, this part was beside the point. The lesson I learned was the worthlessness of a pistol in a long range fight.

Many Texans have the erroneous idea that cattle country exists only in the western part of their state. The last open range was in Southeast Texas. It started at the Sabine River and extended to the Trinity, with portions reaching the Brazos. Many big cattlemen operated in this area. They included the Whites, McFaddins, Cades, Jacksons, Taylors and others. Several of these ranches are still held by descendants of the original owners. White's brand is probably the oldest iron in Texas to be registered by an American. The wire grass, or salt grass, as it is variously called, that grows in the marshes extending from Sabine Pass to Bolivar Point provided winter range for thousands of cattle. I liked no part of the oil business, and spent all my spare time riding the prairie. Thousands of cattle and horses roamed the coastal plain. The money I made delivering papers went to buy me a good saddle. Several neighborhood boys would ride out a few miles from home and rope calves. This practice was frowned on by most of the stockmen. One of the large owners was the late Henry Langham. He was a splendid horseman, very kind to all of us, and was one of my boyhood heroes.

Among the visitors at our spacious house was a remarkable man. He exerted a weighty influence over me, and all that I learned from him was good. His name was Edwin M. Ketchum. He had been a captain in the Union Army, and was chief of police in Galveston during the destructive 1900 hurricane. He had come to Beaumont with a dirt moving outfit, and was engaged in building earthen storage tanks. He had an erect, military bearing, wore cowboy boots, was a crack shot and would fight a circular saw.

He took a contract to build some reservoirs in Sour Lake. All of his mule skinners were Negroes. After a few warnings that they could not stay in Hardin County, a mob formed to run them out. Captain Ketchum heard something about this, and sent a man post haste to town after several boxes of cartridges loaded with buckshot. Before the messenger returned, the mob converged on his camp. The captain took

Captain Edwin M. Ketchum and watch presented to him by citizens of Sour Lake.

his shotgun, and ordered them to halt. When they continued to advance, he cut loose on them with birdshot. The crowd scattered and raced to safety.

Captain Ketchum came to our house the next day, where he related each detail of the episode. He said that faint hearted men sometimes become frozen with fear, and that one of the Sour Lake mob was seized with that malady. When the shooting started and they began to run, this fellow couldn't move. When he looked around, he was standing alone. The captain quickly reloaded and threw down on the straggler. "Hit the grit," he ordered, but the mobster's legs still refused to function. The veteran of many battles in the Civil War lowered his gun, and burst out laughing. This broke the spell, and unfroze the coward's running gear. When he was out of shotgun range and in the shelter of the piney woods, he sought to retrieve some of his lost ego. He yelled back at the captain, "You go to h-e-l-l."

Conditions were bad in Sour Lake. Nobody had yet thought of asking for Rangers. Many meetings were called in the name of "Law and Order." The only tangible results they achieved were in the form of wild bursts of oratory. At one of these gatherings, a patriot arose and declared, "We are going to have law and order here even if we have to raise hell to get it."

Captain Ketchum's vigorous action in dispersing the mob was widely commended. Citizens presented him with a handsome watch. It bore the inscription: "To Edwin M. Ketchum for your stand in defense of human rights on the night of July 9, 1903, at Sour Lake." He gave me pictures of both sides of his watch, and a full length photograph of himself. The example he set on this occasion became the pattern for my future attitude toward mobs.

Like most brave men that I have known, Captain Ketchum had a keen sense of humor. His exploit was carried on the front pages of many newspapers. They proclaimed that the mob was stopped by a "Confederate" veteran. At that time and in that country, editors could not conceive of anything good being done by a Yankee. He enjoyed many laughs over this error. While receiving congratulations from friends and admirers, he proudly wore in his coat lapel the emblem of the G.A.R.

In 1905 my father moved the family to Houston. We had a summer home in Seabrook, on Galveston Bay. There were many cattle and horses on the open ranges of that area. The principal owner was the late Sam Allen. His son, "Little Sam," and his son-in-law, Walter Williams, were usually with the outfit. Both of these great cowmen treated me with marked kindness, and taught me many lessons about the cattle business. My chief riding partner was Tom Dow.

The fall of 1906 saw me ready to go to college. I had not yet reached the minimum age of sixteen years, but as I was six feet and three inches in height, my parents decided to try for a special dispensation. Houston had not yet adopted the coldness of a city, and people were far more informal. My mother and another lady were seated at a table in a downtown drug store, drinking a soda. They were discussing colleges and universities, as both had sons ready to enter. My mother, who was an alumna of Southwestern University, said, "I naturally want my son to go to Southwestern, but he is eager to go to A. & M. I am not too happy about it. I hear that A. & M. is a pretty tough place."

W. W. Sterling at the age of 17 while
a cadet at Texas A. & M. College.

A distinguished appearing gentleman, with a red imperial beard was
seated at the next table. When my mother concluded, he arose and
addressed her. With great politeness and dignity, he said, "Madam, I
did not intend to eavesdrop, but I could not help hearing your remark
about the A. & M. College. I am Dr. J. Allen Kyle, and I want to
correct your erroneous opinion of my school."

She replied, "Dr. Kyle, there must be good reasons for such loyalty.
My son will go to A. & M."

I entered A. & M. in the fall of 1906. At that time. Skeeter Bill
Robbins had gained notoriety as a Western outlaw. The College then
fronted on the railroad, and the students walked up from the station.
I had on a big black hat. When I approached the first group of old
boys, one of them called out, "Yonder comes Skeeter Bill." The name
stuck. It used to nettle me, but now I would give almost anything to
merit the appellation. I did not get to graduate, but was vastly benefited
by my two years' stay at Aggieland.

In 1909 my father decided to move to Tulsa, Oklahoma. I later joined the family and for one term attended Henry Kendall College, forerunner of Tulsa University. My principal aim was to play on the baseball team. The late E. E. Baldridge of Fort Worth summered a large string of Texas steers nearby, and I rode some for him. Ex-outlaw Emmett Dalton had a moving picture that he showed at one of the local theaters. At the end he would deliver a short lecture. We became well acquainted and I never forgot his admonition. It was the 1910 version of "Crime does not pay." Emmett would say in solemn tones, "The wages of sin is death. Mind your mother, boys, and don't drink whiskey."

Another celebrity who worked on the other side of the law was ex-Deputy United States Marshal Bill Tilghman. He was a fine looking man, with clear blue eyes and a square jaw. It did not take too much discernment to tell that he would play for keeps. He also had a picture show, and gave a lecture. It dealt chiefly with the capture of the Doolin gang. I enjoyed talking to him, and he gave me an insight into the deadliness of their operations. He said, "We used shotguns for night work. I loaded my own shells, and filled the spaces between the buckshot with mustard-seed shot."

Chapter 3
COWMAN

Ionly stayed in Oklahoma a short time, and at the first opportunity I returned to my native state. Landing at Corpus Christi, I met one of my former roommates, the late William Heuermann. He owned some land in San Patricio County, near the present town of Odem and he had some fine neighbors. Among them were the Willises, the Humphries and the Hursts. Each of these families later furnished one or more Rangers.

I was now twenty years old and wanted to get in the Service. Lon L. Willis shared this desire, and we made plans to enlist. The sheriff of San Patricio was an outstanding man, the late Dave Odem. He said he would be glad to recommend us. He did not know me very well, but declared that if Lon's father, the late J. D. Willis, said I was all right he would bank on his judgment. Captain J. J. Sanders' company was stationed in Kenedy. It was decided that I was to go first. The captain was out of town, but his sergeant, Earl Yeary, told me I would have to wait until I was twenty-one. Lon Willis went up later, and Captain Sanders enlisted him.

From this beginning, Odem became known as a Ranger town. Lon L. Willis, who later became a captain, George Hurst, who became a sergeant, Cleve Hurst, Ed Heuermann, Chris Willis and O. C. Humphries all entered the Service. Each one of them served faithfully and well.

When Willis was a captain, the administration changed. A politician came into power, and wanted to give the captaincy to one of his favorites. He said to Captain Willis, "If you will take a reduction in rank, you can stay on. We will make you sergeant." Lon replied, "My mother taught me that if I ever took a step, to take a forward one." I am glad to be numbered among the boys from Odem.

After being declared too young to join the Rangers, I went to Falfurrias. The county had just been organized, and was named for our old family friend, Captain J. A. Brooks. I also knew the Rachal family, Postmaster W. W. Sloan and several other people in the new town. The founder and largest land owner was the late Ed C. Lasater. His ranch contained nearly a half million acres, and he ranked with the biggest stockmen in Texas. In every sense of the word, he was a cattle king. Mr. Lasater gave me a job as *segundo,* or second boss of his cow outfit. This consisted of fifteen *vaqueros,* and a *remuda* of over three hundred saddle horses.

The wagon ran the year around, and most of the time was on the move. We would leave one watering early in the morning, noon at another and make the third campside for the night. There was neither highway nor railroad south of Falfurrias, and the pastures were very large. Most of the country was covered with scrub oak. Also found in these *encinales* were numerous large oak trees. The terrain was very sandy, which made heavy going for all vehicles. Six mules were required to pull the chuck wagon. The foreman of the ranch, James T. Maupin, had carefully selected his team. They were perfectly matched both in size and color. Each one was a *bayo coyote,* or buckskin dun with a black stripe down the back. The crowning feature and reigning queen of this hitch was the bell mare. She looked exactly like them. Jim Maupin, a cow boss of the old school, had the sense of humor so often found among his kind. He delighted in telling ranch visitors that she was the dam of all six mules.

Vehicles used in the white sands had to be equipped with wide tires. For rapid transit, the big cattlemen of that region used two wheeled carts. They were drawn by fast trotting horses and relays were often stationed at convenient locations. It is doubtful that this type of conveyance was ever found in any other part of the country. They skimmed lightly over the sand, but were very rough riding.

When rain fell in the spring, it was a beautiful country. Red, blue and yellow wildflowers completely covered the ground. Every variety of chaparral put on sweet blossoms, and the mild gulf breeze was laden with perfume. The soft, golden bloom of the huisache and the white buds of the cat-claw led their thorny companions in fragrance.

Numerous colonies of bees swarmed in the wooded area. They made their hives in the hollow trunks of the larger oaks. The discovery of a bee tree was hailed with delight, and the boys lost no time in committing legitimate robbery. One good deposit would furnish enough wild honey to last the camp a week, and it made a welcome change from our standard dessert of molasses.

The *encinales* abounded with wild turkeys. I had never cared to hunt, and did not kill a one of them. We were too busy with the cow work, and I enjoyed riding the good horses much more than shooting game. When the *vaqueros* craved a variation in their diet of beef, they went out and brought in two or three gobblers. These did not even have to be shot. The hunters simply waited until they caught a flock in the middle of a large glade. They would then put spurs to their horses and make a

dash for the quarry. The heavy birds were too fat to fly very far, and soon gave out. The riders killed what they needed for meat with the doubles of their ropes.

In the heavy brush country of Southwest Texas, practically every large ranch used lead steers. The selection and training of these useful animals would begin while they were still calves. One with a great deal of white on him was preferable, as older steers are attracted by that color. He would then be gentled like a work ox, have a bell put on his neck and be treated like a pet. When his owner had a bunch of steers gathered, he would be turned loose with them for several days and nights. By that time they were well acquainted with him and accustomed to the sound of his bell. When ready to move a herd, he was caught and led in the desired direction. The other steers would follow him, and less herding was required.

The lead steer owned by Mr. Lasater was a splendid specimen of his kind. He was over sixteen hands high, black and white in color and had long horns. When I was with the outfit, he was about ten years old and had gotten very irritable. On one occasion we were shipping steers from Realitos, in Duval County. The old ox was tied to the fence inside the railroad pens. Garland M. Lasater was a small boy. He wanted to get a closer view of the black paint steer. I picked the youngster up in my arms and walked over toward the animal. When we got within about ten feet of the old rascal, he lashed out at us. I jumped back and the vicious kick did not reach its mark.

In a number of bare spots around Falfurrias, the shifting sand has formed large dunes or *medenos*. On windy days the air is heavy with flying grit. This scourge not only irritates the eyes and nerves of the inhabitants, but it is also the subject of many tall tales. One of them deals with a drover who was trailing a herd through that part of the country. He put his cattle in a large corral and during the night a storm blew up. The story goes that the sand filled the pen to the top of the fence, and in the morning all the cattle were gone.

Another ranchman in the vicinity decided to have a small pasture plowed up to use as a field. When his men began to sow the seed, a large flock of blackbirds converged on the new ground. A strong wind was blowing and it swept away everything that was loose. The owner was at his office in town, and somebody told him about the menace

Captain John A. Brooks. Picture taken at
Alice in 1900. Reproductions were sent to
close friends on his eightieth birthday.

to his crop. He sent for the foreman who was an old cowman with no relish for farming. "Joe," asked the boss, "are the birds eating up our seed?" "No sir," he replied. "They can't fly fast enough to catch them."

After leaving the employ of the Lasater ranch, I became well acquainted with Ed Rachal. He is truly a remarkable man. Scion of a pioneer family of ranchmen and trail drivers, he exemplifies my concept of a genuine Texas cowman. He is one of the best ropers in the country, a consummate horseman and a fine judge of livestock. He has handled as many cattle as any living man. With all these attributes of a frontiersman, he is a polished, cultured gentleman. In speech I have never heard him make a grammatical error, nor have I heard him utter an oath. Mr. Rachal is not a large man in size, and he never carried a pistol. He has lived in cow camps with some of the toughest men in Texas and the Indian Territories. His sincerity, dignity and fair dealing commanded their respect, and he never backed down from any of them. He does not use tobacco, drinks little or no liquor, and makes no show of being deeply religious. If he wanted a drink, however, I am sure he would take one. He has exerted a great influence on my life.

Mr. Rachal was just getting started in the ranching business for himself, and I went to work for him. On the Fourth of July, 1913, he, my brother, Edward A. Sterling, and I drove a *remuda* of horses from El Barroso, near Falfurrias, to Monte Cristo in one day. The distance is about seventy miles, and most of the way was through deep sand. We rode at a long trot, and arrived at the Sterling Ranch a half hour before sunset. We changed horses many times during the trip. When we passed through a gate, one of us would rope a fresh horse, saddle him and then catch up with the bunch. I have read of long rides, but believe that this one will compare favorably with many of them.

Brooks County was created in 1911, and held its first election in 1912. At that time I cast my first vote. E. R. (Newt) Rachal was the first tax assessor of the new county. His son, the late Frank C. Rachal, and I were chums. Like his brother, Ed, he was a fine cowhand, and he had also gone to business college. His father turned the office over to Frank, and I agreed to help him. Together we made up the first tax roll of Brooks County.

Chapter 4
BANDIT WAR

Iɴ 1913, my father acquired an interest in twenty-four thousand acres of land in Hidalgo County. In the first Valley land boom, an attempt had been made to cut it up into farms. The idea was many years ahead of its time, as it was too high to irrigate from the canals, and too dry for farming. My father took over the management, and I leased the pastures. I added fifteen thousand acres more, and built up a good start of cattle. The 1915 drouth teamed up with the Bandit War to give me a setback. Monte Cristo had been a noted harboring place for smugglers and cow thieves. Just before we got there, the Rangers and customs inspectors had made a concerted drive on them. At one time, they had twenty prisoners chained to mesquite trees near the ranch. Many people advised my father to take his family out of there before they were all killed. To these warnings he simply replied, "We live here."

No comprehensive account of the so-called Bandit War, that raged in Cameron and Hidalgo Counties, has ever been written. More than forty years have elapsed since the termination of that inter-racial conflict, but to this day, much of it has remained an unpublished mystery. A few sketchy attempts have been made to relate some of the highlights. I am the only surviving participant who has endeavored to write about the background, cause and history of the uprising. Hearsay evidence on the subject is either biased or prejudiced, depending on the sympathies of the witness.

Prior to the coming of the railroad in 1904, the lower valley of the Rio Grande was virtually terra incognita. Fully ninety-five per cent of the population were Latins. They had few, if any, tangible reasons to regret the outcome of the Mexican War. The fact that the soil on which they lived now belonged to the United States did not alter their way of life. Spanish continued to be the universal language. The inhabitants retained all their old ideas and customs.

They could not properly be classed as adopted citizens. The fortunes of war rather than voluntary migration had made these quasi-orphans residents of the United States. They lived under one flag, but spoke the language of another nation. To fit their unusual situation, many localisms were employed. They often referred to the territory between the Nueces River and the Rio Grande as *Medio Mejico* (Half Mexico). They coined their own term of disfavor for the few Anglos who had strayed down into their country. From Mexico to Cape Horn, Americans are known as *Gringos*. In the idiom of the lower border, they were called *Bolillos*.

A large horse was known as a *galon,* with the accent on the last syllable. For a long time this word had me puzzled. I consulted both the Spanish and the Spanish-English dictionaries, without finding it listed. On numerous occasions, I had heard a *vaquero,* on seeing a big horse, exclaim, *"Que galon de caballo"*. I finally found the answer by consulting our good neighbor, the venerable Don Macedonio Vela of Laguna Seca. This Spanish-Irish *caballero* is generally credited with planting the first orange tree in the Valley, and was a thoroughly reliable historian. He explained that the term dated from the period immediately following the Civil War. Many Union cavalrymen were stationed at Fort Brown and at Ringgold Barracks. Their mounts were very tall. The soldiers clucked to them, and in a nasal twang would say, "G'long, g'long." Observant natives, who are great mimics, began to call all large horses *galons*, and the word was added to the local vocabulary.

The value of *Medio Mejico* and the wisdom of having acquired it by conquest was sometimes questioned by weary horsemen who traveled across the hot sands. They wondered if it was an asset or a liability. One sultry August day I was riding from Santa Anita, which was owned by John Young, to San Juanito, owned by his half-brother, James B. McAllen. My companion was a middle aged cattle buyer from Central Texas. His horse shied at the warning buzz of a rattlesnake, and he was almost unseated.

This sudden jump caused him to rub against a giant cactus. His leg was filled with thorns, his soul with bitterness and his mouth with profanity. The pilgrim mopped his brow with a red bandana and said, "So we fought the Mexicans and took this God-forsaken land away from them. I am in favor of fighting them again and making them take it back."

When the St. Louis, Brownsville and Mexico Railroad extended their line from Harlingen to Sam Fordyce, many new towns sprang up along the route. The branch roughly paralleled the Rio Grande, and traversed the heart of the Valley. Northern land men and colonizers quickly grasped the potentialities of the undeveloped region. They recognized the value of its fertile soil and semi-tropical climate. Home-seekers were brought in by the trainload. These pale faced people, particularly the older ones, were eager to escape the rigorous winters of their homeland. Texans had overlooked the resort in their own back-yard, and wealthy vacationers from our state went to California or Florida. In 1918 my family attended a picnic near Sharyland. Among the crowd of several hundred persons, we were the only native Texans.

Parties of "prospects" in overcoats, caps and earmuffs, were arriving daily in the Magic Valley. They liked what they saw. The warm sunshine melted the ice in their blood and broke down their sales resistance. Real estate agents experiencd little difficulty in persuading them to take their life's savings out of cold storage and invest them in raw land. These transactions brought on a sudden and tremendous increase in the Valley's population. The newcomers, or "snowdiggers," were totally unlike the natives. They were full of business and had little or no patience with the dilatory customs of this "land of *mañana*." In language, appearance and habits, the two peoples were as far apart as the poles. Distrust and misunderstandings between them were inevitable.

On April 22, 1914, American warships bombarded Vera Cruz. Sailors and marines landed and our flag was raised in the city. This occupation caused great indignation among the inhabitants of both sides of the river. It also provided more ammunition for the agitators and they used it freely. Tension continued to mount, and the ones who knew the people best felt that an outbreak was imminent. The Mexicans seemed to believe that the Japanese could handle us as they had done the Russians, and would hint that they were counting on them to right the wrongs of 1836 and 1847.

Secretary of State William Jennings Bryan's vacillating policy and "peace at any price" attitude were contributing factors in the events leading up to the Bandit War. Nowhere in their history have people of Spanish extraction had any respect for weaklings. This trait in their character and the value of the iron hand was demonstrated during the long regime of Don Porfirio Diaz. Each new gesture of appeasement merely added to the audacity of potential bandits. Protests over the mistreatment of Americans in Mexico only served to make our State Department an object of ridicule. From Washington, Bryan dispatched countless "notes" that were treated as mere scraps of paper.

All over the Valley, incensed citizens held a series of mass meetings. "Whereas" became the watchword. Resolutions condeming our policy in Mexico and on the border were passed amid yells that literally made their adoption viva voce. During one of these gatherings, a patriot arose and said, "Mr. Chairman, I move that we wire Secretary of State Bryan to go to hell." They indulged in an orgy of eloquence and oratory, but their contribution to the suppression of the bandit trouble was purely verbal. Out of the hundreds of able bodied men who attended, few ever rode out in the chaparral to encounter the invaders. This service was performed by less than five per cent of the early Valley settlers.

The casus belli of the Mexican War was the territory that lies between the Nueces River and the Rio Grande. By 1915, a large number of Americans had settled on the southern edge of the disputed strip. The malcontents looked on this shift in population as an "invasion". German and Japanese agents in Mexico aided and abetted their efforts to injure the United States. They promised the support of their governments.

The center of activity and the favorite gathering place in McAllen for people of Mexican extraction was the general store of D. Guerra and Sons. The head of this firm was a former sheriff of Starr County and one of the Valley's best citizens. Don Deodoro rode many miles through the chaparral with us during the bandit trouble, and rendered valiant service in its suppression. On January 19, 1915, Tom S. Mayfield went to the Guerra store and arrested Basilio Ramos, alias B. R. Garza.

This foreigner had been banished from his native Mexico by the Carranzistas, because he was a Huertista, or supporter of Victoriano Huerta. Upon landing on this side of the river, he made his way to San Diego, Duval County, Texas. Here he found some kindred spirits, and also secured employment as local agent for a Kansas City brewery. His gratitude to the nation that offered him asylum was repaid by fomenting a plot to cause its overthrow. After another attempt to get into Mexico, he was arrested and thrown into jail at Monterrey. His fellow countrymen again deported him to the United States, and he landed in McAllen. When arrested there by Tom Mayfield, he had in his possession the incredible document known as the Plan de San Diego. It was written in Spanish, and was signed by eight men. Among them were a saloon keeper and a lawyer.

The Plan de San Diego provided that on February 20, 1915, at two o'clock in the morning, the Mexicans were to arise in arms against the United States and proclaim their liberty and their independence of Yankee tyranny. At the same time they would declare the independence of Texas, New Mexico, Arizona, Colorado, and California. The army would be the "Liberating Army for Races and People"; and the red flag with its white diagonal fringe would bear the inscription "Equality

and Independence". Funds would be provided by levies on captured towns, and state governments would be set up in the state capitals.

Every North American man over sixteen would be put to death as soon as his captors could extract from him all his funds, or "loans"; every stranger found armed should be executed regardless of race or nationality; no leader should enroll a stranger in the ranks unless he were Latin, Negro, or Japanese. The Apaches of Arizona and other Indians were to receive every guarantee and have their lands returned to them.

The five states were to be organized as an independent Mexican republic, which at an appropriate time would seek annexation to Mexico. When success had crowned the initial effort, six more states north of those named—evidently Oklahoma, Kansas, Nebraska, South Dakota, Wyoming, and Utah—were to be taken from the United States and given to the Negroes who were to select a suitable banner for their republic. This buffer Negro state would lie between the Mexicans and what one of the signers of the plan called "the damned big-footed creatures" of the north.

Tom S. Mayfield, who exposed the plot, is one of the greatest officers who ever served on the Rio Grande. Born in Gonzales County, he came to the Valley before the first canals were built in Pharr. He handled the large grading crews with a firmness and tact that attracted the notice of Sheriff A. Y. Baker, who soon made him a deputy. His work in this capacity was outstanding. Ex-Ranger Baker leaned heavily on Mayfield in keeping peace and order among the large number of Latins who resided in Hidalgo County. He spoke their language fluently, and his fair though stern treatment of them won their respect.

Border Latins are hero worshipers, who admire strength and valor. Their highest form of praise is to call a man *Puro Hombre*. They often try a new officer by fire, either openly or from ambush. If one or two of the attackers are killed in the trial, his reputation is established and he usually has no further trouble. The former enemies often become good friends. Tom Mayfield did so well along this line that many of the natives named their fighting bulldogs and game roosters "Myfeel". This is the way they pronounce his name. He was also commissioned as a Texas Ranger, and did more than any living man to suppress the Bandit War.

Two separate and unrelated elements appeared in the Bandit War. One had to do with the stealing and smuggling of livestock, while the other was a bizarre plot to regain lost territory. I was well acquainted with the master mind of the rustlers. He had entirely too much intelligence to waste his talents on wild schemes, or to believe that any land would be taken from the United States. Furthermore, he was well content to remain safely in the background while his henchmen preyed on the herds of the large ranches. He fled the country soon after the start of the trouble, and until it subsided, he stayed in Mexico.

The Plan de San Diego was written by someone who had more education than Basilio Ramos. Several well informed border residents claimed that a politician who later held a high position in a State agency had a hand in its composition. This schemer had suffered at the hands of Mexicans while living in their country, and was eager for revenge. I also knew him more than casually. He brought no credit to the organization he represented, and was not above committing the offense with which he was charged.

In my opinion there was no pre-arranged agreement between these two groups. Both were composed of bandits, but their interests were not the same. Apparently, it was coincidental that the killing of cow thief Donaciano Sanchez occurred almost simultaneously with de la Rosa and Pizaña's attempt to carry out the Plan de San Diego.

The area of large ranches north of the railroad was known as the "back country." Newcomers seldom if ever ventured into that land of giant cactus and diamond backed rattlesnakes. It was the happy hunting ground of numerous *ladrones*. These hard riding centaurs made their living by stealing cattle, horses and mules. As a diversion from this predatory pastime, they turned to smuggling livestock from Mexico. For their base of operations, they would use some small ranch near the river, the owner of which was generally their leader. He registered a brand in Texas, and used the same iron across the Rio Grande. This ruse made it difficult for the United States Customs Inspectors to spot the "wet" stock.

These rustlers were highpowered desperados, and were anything but cowards. Their main knowledge of English was the declaration: "We no gottie scare for nobody." They lurked in the brush like half wild creatures. Peaceful *paisanos* described them as men who "lived with a

carbine in one hand and a rope in the other". These were tools of their trade, and they would use either of them at the slightest provocation. Their only weakness as top fighting men was their poor marksmanship. While shooting deer or other game, they never missed, but when the chips were down, they became rattled. This was particularly true when their adversaries were the dreaded *Rinches*. Many of us have escaped unscathed from various border skirmishes because of their erratic aim while under fire. These freebooters welcomed the opportunity to engage in any form of outlawry. It would be doubly attractive if the deviltry smacked of patriotism, or if it would serve to harass the hated foreigners. They formed an important nucleus of the bandit movement.

James B. McAllen was a descendant of Juan Jose Balli. This *caballero* was the original owner of the Spanish land grant designated as San Salvador del Tule. Mr. McAllen was our neighbor, and as a boy he

remembered the Red Ride. This bandit exterminating scout was conducted by a company of Rangers under Captain L. H. McNelly. He
also recalled that during the Catarino Garza revolution in 1891, Captains
Brooks and McNeel's men had killed a number of undesirables. As a
friend, he warned the current crop of border bravos that the next purge
would be even more drastic. They scoffed at his advice, and continued
to prey on his herds.

In 1913 I was placed in charge of a bunch of cattle in a back country
pasture known as Los Indios. It later became a part of Richard King's
Santa Fe Ranch. The cattle belonged to the late George W. Armstrong, who subsequently gained wide notoriety as a white supremacy
advocate in Mississippi. There was no highway from the valley and
no automobile could pull the heavy sand. The entire region was isolated,
and I saw only one Anglo during my sojourn. There was neither house
nor other shelter on the place. My saddle blanket and slicker served
to keep me warm and dry. A large, sandy field had been cleared on
the adjoining ranch, San Esteban, and it was crudely farmed by share
croppers. One of the renters was Donaciano Sanchez.

He had three sons about my age, who did all the work. They
were very friendly to me, so we made our camp together and pooled our
scant rations. Their father was a large, formidable looking man who
rode a fine horse and always carried a Winchester. This attracted no
particular attention, as it was a custom of the country. He only came to
see his sons occasionally, and always rode in about sunup. After sleeping most of the day, he would ride away as mysteriously as he had
arrived.

When the Bandit War opened in 1915, the first man killed was the
father of my camping companions. Cattle stealing and not territorial
disputes however, caused his death. Sanchez and another notorious cow
thief were taking some calves out of the Mula pasture on the King
Ranch near the Mesquitine windmill when they were discovered by
Frank Martin.

Martin was foreman of La Andrea. He suspected one of his *vaqueros*
of being in league with the men who were stealing cattle. One day
he ordered his buggy hitched up, stating that he was going to Raymondville. Martin drove a few miles through the brush, then went
back to the ranch. The suspect had saddled his best horse and gone

to notify the rustlers that the coast was clear. Martin then rode out to the Mula pasture where he encountered Sanchez and the other man. He was armed only with a pistol, while the two rustlers had Winchesters, so Martin put spurs to his horse and burnt the breeze with the bandits in hot pursuit. They had the advantage both in number and weapons. Frank emptied his pistol, shooting back as he ran. One lucky bullet hit Sanchez in the head and killed him. His accomplice gave up the chase and lit a shuck for Mexico. To my knowledge, he stayed on the other side for nearly forty years before returning to Texas.

Sheriff A. Y. Baker, George Linesetter, Deodoro Guerra, Ernest Horn, and Lee Welch.

Later, when talking to Frank Martin about this incident, he said to me, "Bill, I was riding one of the fastest horses on the ranch, but it seemed to me like he was crawling until that chance shot stopped Sanchez."

Several days after the killing, Ramon Guerra was riding in his father's pasture. The young man saw a flock of *totaches,* a variety of vulture found in Southwest Texas, circling over a mesquite thicket. He went to the spot and found seven dead King Ranch calves that had been tied up with rawhide thongs, ready to be branded by the thieves. When Sanchez was killed and his *compañero* fled, the animals were left to die.

In the spring of 1915, groups of twenty or thirty armed Mexicans were seen in the northeastern part of Cameron County. They began stealing saddles, horses and cattle. They not only robbed ranches belonging to Americans, but looted those whose owners were Mexicans. This "army" also pillaged some isolated stores. They took part of the groceries and all the ammunition. The names of Luis de la Rosa and Aniceto Pizaña were frequently heard in connection with this brigandage. They were referred to as "generals" and were reported to be the leaders of the "revolution".

On July 17, a young man named Bernard Boley was killed by the bandits. He became the first casualty among the Americans. During this month some half dozen incidents occurred. These included the burning of a railroad bridge south of Sebastian. At Los Indios ranch a Mexican was killed. This would indicate that some of the bandits had used the "war" as an excuse to carry out private vengeance. Tension was now at a fever pitch and all rural residents prepared for serious trouble.

Early in August the Bandit War began in earnest. Several Rangers and Cameron County deputies rounded up a ranch near Paso Real, on the Arroyo Colorado. They charged the house and killed two men. Several of them went inside. Desederio Flores was hiding under a bed. Ranger Joe Anders, who afterward became a captain, started to look under it. Flores shot at him with a 44 calibre English bulldog pistol. Anders had a very large nose, which earned him the nickname of "El Narizon". He received a powder burn on this distinguishing part of his face, which left it scarred for life. Charles W. Price, who subsequently served twenty-six years as sheriff of Jim Wells County, participated in this incident. He was at that time a Ranger.

Ex-Ranger Joe (Pinkie) Taylor jerked the mattress off the bed and Flores was riddled with bullets. Taylor was a member of a pioneer family in Goliad County, and made a fine record in the Rangers. He married, settled down and became a Valley farmer. His family objected to pistols. Shortly after he discarded the familiar weapon, the enemies he had made in the Service killed him and mutilated his body. He was a crack shot, and if he had been armed, the assassins would not have ventured within the range of his six-shooter.

On August 6, fourteen bandits rode into Sebastian, a small town in the northern part of Cameron County. They robbed a store, and then went to a corn sheller, which was being operated by A. L. Austin and his son, Charles. These inoffensive farmers had recently moved to Texas from Montgomery, Missouri. The outlaws captured the unarmed Austins and held them prisoner until young Elmer Millard drove up in a wagon. They put the Austins in it and forced Millard to drive them to a spot near their home. The Austins were then killed by a fusilade from the bandits' rifles. Millard was released. A saying on the border is that when coyotes howl in the daytime, it portends either bad weather or bad news. When Mrs. Austin heard the shots and saw Millard returning without her menfolks, she rushed to the scene. As she bent over the dead bodies of her husband and son, the coyotes in the nearby brush set up a wail. The story told by the gentle lady from Missouri steeled the hearts of many men in the Valley.

Two Americans were wounded by bandits on successive days. The outlaws shot into an automobile near Los Fresnos, and they wounded the night watchman at Lyford, both of these points being in Cameron County.

Late in the afternoon of August 8th, a bunch of bandits attacked the old Norias Ranch. They had arrived at Los Cerritos, southeast of Norias, at two o'clock in the morning. Pedro Longorio, Luis Solis and Macario Longorio were watching for wild cattle when the cavalcade rode up on them. The bandit leaders forced the three *vaqueros* to help water their horses and threatened to hang them all if they told anyone of their presence on the ranch. Pedro took advantage of the opportunity and got an accurate count of the bandits, who numbered fifty-two.

Ranch house on the Norias Division of the King
Ranch as it appeared during the Bandit War.

Ranger Captains Henry Ransom and Monroe Fox, with detachments
of their companies, had been to Norias, but were out scouting at the
time of the attack. The Rangers lacked leadership. Both captains were
from the interior of Texas and the adjutant general, who came down to
take personal charge, was a native of England. After numerous parleys,
plans and counter-plans, they decided to ride out in search of the enemy.
The scouting party passed within half a mile of the bandits, who laid
low and were not discovered. As soon as the officers were out of hearing
the bandits took roundance on them and made their attack.

The ranch house was a large, two-story wooden building. Present at
the fight were Lauro Cavazos, Frank Martin, George Forbes, Gordon
Hill, Joe Taylor, Marcus Hines, Portus Gay, a squad of soldiers under a
corporal, Albert the colored cook, several women and maybe another
man or two. The terrain is flat and the railroad made only a low
breastwork. The soldiers, armed with 30-06 Springfield rifles, were
very accurate in their marksmanship, especially from the prone position.

Marcus Hines was a huge man, who weighed over three hundred
pounds. Like most big fellows he was jolly and could enjoy a joke on
himself. In speaking of the fight, he said to me, "When the bandits came

I thought they were the Rangers and started toward them. When they began to shoot, I returned the fire. The other men said I showed great bravery in advancing on them, but I did not realize that they were the bandits." I have been on numerous scouts with Marcus Hines and can personally testify that he was fearless.

The raiders were under two leaders, Antonio Roche and Dario Morada. The *vaqueros* at Los Cerritos reported that they quarreled a great deal on the day of the fight. The bandits carried a big red rag that they used as a flag. The battle lasted over two hours. Forbes, Martin and two soldiers were wounded and Manuela Flores, wife of a railroad employee, was killed in the section house. Ten bandits were killed and an unknown number of wounded were carried away by their comrades.

At the time of the Norias fight, Chon Cantu was nine years old. His father worked on the ranch and they lived about half a mile from the headquarters. When the shooting started the family thought it was only the Rangers having target practice.

After the battle, the bodies of the dead bandits were placed in one pile. The Rangers and cowboys used the only means at hand to accomplish this task. They pitched their ropes on the legs of the fallen attackers and dragged them up to the heap. During this process, a photographer arrived on the scene. The pictures he took were widely circulated. Several years later, at a Texas Senate investigation, one of the legislators expressed horror and indignation at this treatment of human beings. Lon C. Hill, whose son participated in the fight, told the committee: "Gentlemen, those horses and those ropes were nothing but the Norias hearse. No regular funeral equipment was available."

Shortly after the attack on Norias, a bunch of thirty bandits crossed into Texas at Los Ebanos, in western Hidalgo County. A posse led by A. Y. Baker and Tom Mayfield struck their trail, which was headed for our ranch. They telephoned me from Sam Fordyce, and told me to have fresh horses ready. The invaders made a circle around the headquarters, and passed through our north pasture. When Baker and Mayfield arrived, we had their mounts in the corral. I joined them at this point and we followed the bandits' trail for three days. Alf Truitt, ex-foreman of the Wells Ranch, and later city marshal of Mission, did the trailing. After going about forty miles to the north, they turned east. They completely circled Edinburg, the county seat, and headed back for the Rio

Grande. The site of the present town of Weslaco was a thick brush pasture, and the bandits crossed the railroad at that point. Sheriff Baker was a heavy man and his horse gave out. He told me to stay with him, and Mayfield took the posse to the river. Henry Carlisle found the flag that the bandits had used on this raid.

On one of these chases, a man met us in a Ford car. He brought the message that I was urgently needed in Mission. The occasion was a baseball game for the championship of the Valley League. Sheriff Baker was an ardent baseball fan. He gave me permission to go, and said for me to join them at a place where he planned to camp that night. I dropped out of the grim work of bandit hunting for half a day, played my ball game and then rejoined the pursuit.

A description of life on a ranch during the Bandit War would be unbelievable to a present resident of that peaceful and productive region. Practically no fence riding was done, and when it became necessary to grease the windmills, a couple of Rangers would have to escort the cowboy assigned to that job. If more men were available, they went along under the principle that there was safety in numbers. Very little automobile traveling was done at night. In passing through a gate, the lights were turned out and the opening approached with great caution. Sentries were posted at night, and everything was in a state of armed preparedness. My mother was of pioneer stock, and had no fears for herself. She was only concerned about her two sons, who were constantly guiding parties of deputies, Rangers or soldiers. Our services were in frequent demand. We were familiar with the heavily brushed country, and could speak Spanish. My parents held family prayer at the ranch every night, in which any wayfarers who happened to be there participated. Rangers, soldiers, cowboys and house servants joined in these devotions. Ex-Ranger Levi Davis, one of the most dangerous gunfighters I ever knew, used to spend several days at a time with us just to listen to my mother's prayers. It was claimed that he never relaxed vigilance, but with us he was at ease. He was accustomed to the rough fare of a Ranger camp, and one morning at breakfast my mother offered him some oatmeal. Levi looked up in surprise and said, "Why, Miss Mary, I'm not sick." He thought that cereals were only for invalids. My mother was a remarkable woman, outstanding in any company. She said to me, "Son, I am enveloping you in a mantle of prayer.

Taken at Pharr, Texas during the height of the bandit trouble Left to right: Tom Mayfield, W. W. Sterling, and Ranger O. D. Cardwell. In the background is Lucius J. Polk.

Memorize the Ninety-first Psalm. 'The Sword of Robert Lee' is a great poem; treat your pistol as if it were the sabre of the Peerless Leader. Always think of me before you draw it." No mother was ever more loyal to her sons, and to me she frequently quoted the passage, "Thy gentleness hath made thee great."

On September 4th, a detachment from the Third Cavalry under Captain Frank R. McCoy joined Sheriff A. Y. Baker, Deputies Tom Mayfield and George Edwards in trailing a bunch of bandits to Cavazos

Crossing. The day before, they had looted the village of Ojo de Agua. The Mexicans crossed the river ahead of their pursuers. Upon reaching the other side, they opened fire on the Americans and a pitched battle ensued. More than a dozen of the enemy were killed, and thirty or forty were wounded. The sole American casualty was one wounded soldier.

During the skirmish, the reflection of a glass in the sunlight could be seen across the river. It was high up in a tree. Captain McCoy trained his binoculars on the shining object, and stated that it was a man with field glasses directing the enemy fire. Turning to Sergeant Shaeffer, who was later killed near the same spot, the captain said, "Sergeant, the range is nine hundred yards, practically no wind. Try a shot." The sergeant assumed a prone position, wrapped his sling around his shoulder and squeezed off a shot. The man tumbled out of his observation post. The next day, the commander at Reynosa protested that one of his officers had been killed while on a "peaceful" mission.

The revolutionists were armed with a wide variety of guns. These had been acquired by purchase, capture or theft, as the opportunity presented itself. Their most popular rifle was the light, handy, 30-30 Winchester carbine. It was designed strictly for sporting purposes, and would quickly overheat from rapid fire. Many bandits used the Mauser, which was the official rifle of the old Mexican Army. One of them had come into possession of a 405 calibre Winchester, designed especially to kill elephants. The Rangers made various jocular remarks while under fire. On one occasion, several of them were lying behind the partial shelter of a sand bank. Bullets from across the river were flying overhead. The fact that Mexicans habitually shoot high was evidenced by the numerous water tanks riddled by bullets during their revolution. Ranger Joe Davenport, who afterward became captain of the United States Customs Inspectors, declared that each missile sang its own song. He explained, "When a bullet from that old elephant gun goes over, it moans in deep bass tones 'C-U-I-D-A-D-O' (Look out, or beware!). The pointed Mauser bullet whines and screams 'G-r-i-n-g-o'."

The bandit trouble was in full swing when Dodge automobiles came out. We bought the first one sold in the Valley, and I proudly drove it home. When I arrived there, my father met me at the gate. "Son," he said, "hurry to the McAllen Ranch. A bunch of bandits has attacked it, and the fight is still going on." Several outlying ranches were on

Ranchmen and Rangers as they travelled in Hidalgo County during the Bandit War. Left to right: Lloyd David, W. W. Sterling, A. H. Reed and Ranger Paul West. In this 1915 Dodge car, one of the first owned in the Valley, I rushed Captain Henry Lee Ransom and a squad of Rangers to the McAllen Ranch, which was under attack by bandits.

the same telephone line. Two miles south of McAllen's it forked, the other branch going to Guadalupe el Torero, owned by Lane and Cantu. Sam Lane called my father and said, "Get Bill and the boys to come as soon as possible. I saw the bandits going to San Juanito and now the shooting has started. I am heading for the rock quarry." He was an old frontiersman, and from his natural fort could have stood off a whole troop of bandits.

Captain Ransom and two of his Rangers were just starting out on horseback, and were delighted at my arrival in a new automobile. It was eighteen miles to the ranch, and when we arrived, the fight was over. There was plenty of evidence that a desperate battle had taken place. Directly in front of the house, a bandit and his horse lay dead in a single heap. Another dead man was found near a rock outbuilding. Mr. McAllen was gone, and the only person in sight was a Mexican woman who had been acting as cook and housekeeper. She told us that after the fight, *el patron* had gone to the brush. I climbed the windmill tower and as loudly as I could shout, called to Mr. McAllen. He recognized my voice and came back to the house.

Maria de Agras had been a *soldadera* in Mexico. She furnished us an account that was more than a witness's version, for she was an active participant in the battle. Fresh from the revolutions in her native land, she was inured to the sight of bloodshed. During the attack on the ranch, she had no intention of remaining a passive spectator. When the bandits arrived, Mr. McAllen was taking his siesta in the front room of the one story ranch house. It had four large windows, which were covered by wooden shutters, painted green. The chief rode to the front door where he was met by Maria. He ordered her to tell the ranchman to come outside. She saw at a glance that they meant to kill him.

The *soldadera* awakened her employer, handed him a glass of whiskey and told him about the heavily armed men at the doorstep. Mr. McAllen picked up his ten gauged shotgun which was loaded with buckshot, and fired both barrels through the closed blinds. The leader and his horse were killed instantly. This was the most deadly blast from a shoulder gun that I have ever seen. The death dealing weapon was a fine imported fowling piece, made by W. W. Greener. Shotguns made by this celebrated English gunsmith were the favorite arm of express messengers, frontier marshals and others charged with guarding treasure or suppressing riots. Mr. McAllen's salvo proved to my entire satisfaction that the legends I had heard about Greener shotguns loaded with buckshot were well founded.

The sudden death of their leader made the surviving bandits realize that Mr. McAllen would put up a desperate fight. They scattered to the shelter of the smaller buildings. These were grouped around the main house in the traditional plan of a Southwest Texas ranch. They were out of shotgun range, and he started using his 30-30 Winchesters. Several of these handy rifles were always kept within easy reach in that part of the country. The bandits sniped at him from their hiding places, and he returned their fire. Maria reloaded his rifles and lent him words of encouragement. He killed another bandit outright and wounded three more. Two died a few days later. These casualties caused the marauders to give up the fight.

Knowing that Mr. McAllen was alone, they thought that he would be an easy victim. His determined resistance had been fatal to several of their number, and they also knew that help would soon arrive. When Mr. McAllen came back to the scene, he showed no signs of fear. His emotions appeared to be a mixture of disgust and regret. "Bill," he said to me, "this is the first time I have been forced to do anything like this." Later he said, "Let's go look at the dead man." He had not been moved, and his gray horse was still lying half on top of him. The dead bandit was a *guero* and had many freckles on his face. Mr. McAllen looked down at him and exclaimed, "You dirty dog, you tried to murder me on my own doorstep." He started to stomp the dead bandit with the heel of his boot, but I restrained him.

The main ranch house had many bullet holes in the walls. True to form, the Mexicans shot high. I took Mr. McAllen to his city home in Brownsville. From that time on, he always came to our ranch and got me to accompany him to San Juanito. I stayed with him until he looked over the cattle and attended to his other business. These trips usually took two or three days, and I continued this practice up to the time of his death. I visited Mr. McAllen in Brownsville a short time before he died. He was pale from being indoors, but looked well and talked about future visits to the ranch.

The outrages continued during the latter part of September, and they showed no signs of abating in October. On the 18th day of that month at Olmito, six miles north of Brownsville, the bandits perpetrated one of the most dastardly crimes of the war. Under the cover of darkness, they wrecked the southbound passenger train of the St. Louis, Brownsville and Mexico Railroad. With fiendish cunning, a bunch of bandits removed the spikes from a rail, which they left in place. Then they tied a long wire to it, and hid in the dense brush along the right of way. When the train approached, they jerked the loosened rail. The engineer had no chance to stop and the locomotive and two cars were overturned. He was killed and his fireman was badly scalded by steam.

Seated in the smoker were four unarmed soldiers who were returning to Fort Brown after being absent from duty on furlough. Two State officials, Dr. E. S. McCain, Deputy State Health Officer, and District Attorney John I. Klieber were in the car. Harry Wallis, a former Ranger, was also a passenger. When the train came to a stop, four bandits entered the car and began shooting the occupants. One soldier was killed instantly and two others badly wounded. Judge Kleiber was on the floor with one of the wounded soldiers, who bled profusely. The blood partially covered his clothing, and the bandits apparently thought that both were dead. Wallis and Dr. McCain hid in the toilet. The bandits fired a number of shots through the door, hitting the doctor in the abdomen and Wallis in the hand. Dr. McCain died the next day and Wallis recovered. A Mexican passenger on the train told the bandits about the secreted men. I knew both Klieber and Wallis very well. The

Train wrecked by bandits 10 miles north of Brownsville in 1915.

unbelievable part of the whole affair was that no one on the train was armed. Wallis told me that he would have had his pistol if he had been traveling by automobile, but thought it would not be needed on the train.

News of the wreck spread like wildfire. Ranger Captain Henry Ransom and several of his men arrived on the scene and began a search for those implicated in the tragedy. Personal belongings of the victims and other loot from the derailed train were found in the houses of several suspects. One was identified as the man who told of the men hidden in the toilet. Another had a piece of cloth torn from his shirt. The missing patch was found where the bandits stood when they pulled the rail from under the engine. This proof of his participation in the train wreck served as his death warrant. He and three others equally as guilty were summarily executed. The wrecking of the train was the work of a band numbering over sixty men, and was supposed to be under the personal command of the two "generals," Luis de la Rosa and Aniceto Pizaña. Yet during the entire Bandit War, they did not essay to attack a company of Rangers, who never exceeded ten or twelve in number.

On the night of October 27, a band attacked an outpost of Troop G, Third Cavalry and a unit of the Signal Corps at Ojo de Agua, about nine miles from Mission. A crude wireless outfit was set up for communication with the troop headquarters. The first volley was fired at the instrument, putting it out of commission. This act proved that someone with more intelligence than an ordinary bandit was directing the movement. The total number of American soldiers was fifteen, and the night attack took them by surprise. Captain W. J. Scott, with twelve men, was camped for the night at Peñitas, two miles away. On hearing the firing, he hurried to Ojo de Agua, and assisted in driving off the enemy. The Americans lost three killed and eight wounded. The Mexican loss was seven killed and seven or more wounded. Among the dead was a Japanese.

By this time everyone realized that spasmodic efforts would never end the bandit trouble. Business was at a standstill, with many citizens selling out and leaving the Valley. At night farm people were coming into towns where armed patrols were on twenty-four-hour duty. By a fortunate circumstance, Captain Frank R. McCoy, one of the outstanding Army officers of all time, was stationed in the Valley. He was the right man at the right place and at the right time, an unusual combination on the Mexican border. McCoy afterward was made a major general, and if his time had been a little earlier or a little later, he would certainly have been a full general. His tact, ability and personality were unsurpassed.

Brigadier General James Parker took command of the Brownsville District on May 18, 1916. As a young lieutenant in the Apache Indian campaigns, his hard riding had earned him the nickname of "Galloping Jim." He was the first general officer I ever knew. By training and temperament, he was well suited for his present assignment. As his chief of staff, the new commander selected Captain Frank R. McCoy. During the border disturbances, I had served as his scout, interpreter, and confidential adviser. He used me in a similar capacity at Fort Brown.

After observing the situation for a few weeks, General Parker formed a plan to stop further invasions from Mexico. He warned the commander at Matamoros, General Alfredo Ricaut, that, notwithstanding the policy of Secretary of State Bryan, he would not let the international boundary stop his soldiers in their pursuit of raiders. Ricaut promised

Texas Rangers, Company D, left to right: Mason Rountree, Bert Veale, C. D. Cardwell, Cleve Hearst, Almond Sheeley, Captain Henry L. Ransom, and J. J. Edds.

to do his best, but stated that he was practically helpless. The bandits had gathered an army of nearly five hundred men, which rode up and down the Rio Grande, in defiance of his orders.

On June 16, a band crossed the river about ten miles west of Brownsville at a place called Ranchito. They headed northeast and ran into a detachment of American soldiers, who opened fire on them. One bandit was killed and the rest turned back toward Mexico. General Parker ordered Lieutenant Arthur D. (Hook) Newman with fifty men from Troop H of the Third Cavalry to pursue the invaders.

The detachment left Fort Brown at midnight, and several hours later struck the bandits' trail. They followed it to the river, and then crossed into Mexico. The water was deep enough to swim their horses. Newman overtook the enemy at Rancho Pedernal, and had a short running fight with them. At least two were killed. The Americans suffered no casualties.

Lieutenant Arthur D. Newman was a young New Englander who had recently graduated from West Point. He loved the Cavalry and border duty, and was very popular with the Rangers and cattlemen. I had left our ranch in charge of my brother. A matter came up requiring my presence at home. Upon General Ricaut's promise not to permit any more raids to this side, it looked like a quiet time and I secured a few days leave from Captain McCoy. I had just left the command the day before Newman invaded Mexico, and therefore missed the expedition. Upon receipt of the news that they had crossed the river, I hurried back to Fort Brown and my friend Newman was jubilant over receiving his baptism of fire. The untimely death of this

45

fine officer in an airplane accident just prior to the First World War cut short what would unquestionably have been a brilliant military career.

On June 17, four troops of the Third Cavalry, a detachment from the Fourth Infantry and a unit of the Signal Corps crossed the Rio Grande about ten miles above Fort Brown. They marched toward Matamoros, and camped for the night at Rancho Pascuala. The American troops were within seven miles of their objective when they were recalled by orders from Washington. Captain William S. Wells of Troop G of this expedition and several other Third Cavalry officers had been frequent guests at our ranch. I secured the details from them.

During the recrossing of the river, Carranza soldiers fired on the rear guard of the Americans. Colonel Robert Lee Bullard of the Twenty-sixth Infantry was the senior officer on the scene. He was a fiery Southerner, and ordered the Cavalry to chase the Carranzistas as long as they could keep up with them. The country was in the midst of a devastating drought, and the dust kicked up by the Mexican cavalry made an effective smoke screen. In this pursuit, two Carranzistas were killed, while the Americans suffered nothing worse than inflamed eyes from the dust. In the First World War, Robert Lee Bullard commanded the Second American Army in France, with the rank of lieutenant general. One of my most prized possessions is his book, *American Soldiers Also Fought,* presented to me by the general.

General Parker's firm stand and vigorous action broke the back of the Bandit War. His demonstration of the fact that he would not hesitate to order American troops to pursue the invaders into Mexico took the fight out of border bravos at all levels. They found that dealing with a veteran frontier general was vastly different from thumbing their noses at a pacifist Secretary of State. Furthermore, the twenty-four-hour occupancy of their territory by American troops, plus the flight of the Carranzistas before the Third Cavalry, proved to be a salutary lesson. General Ricaut promised to summarily *fusilar* any Mexican who attempted to cross the Rio Grande at any point other than a regular port of entry.

I enjoyed my stay at General Parker's headquarters. He was a large man, a strict disciplinarian, and the young lieutenants stood somewhat in awe of him. To me he was kind and considerate. When his charming wife visited Fort Brown, he presented me to her in these words: "Dear, this is the hard riding Texan who has been such a help to us." His splendid book, *The Old Army,* occupies an honored place in my library.

One of the principal figures in the first phase of the Bandit War was Ranger Captain Henry L. Ransom. He was a native of Fort Bend County, and had served as chief of police in Houston. While in this capacity, he killed a noted criminal lawyer who resided there. During the Philippine Insurrection, he enlisted in the Thirty-third Regiment of Volunteers, which was composed almost entirely of Texans. General John A. Hulen was a captain in this outfit, and former Ranger Captain Lee (Red) Hall was a first lieutenant. Ransom's early life around the Brazos bottom prison farms and his service in the Philippines had caused him to place small value on the life of a lawbreaker. On one occasion I guided his company on a scout through western Hidalgo and eastern Starr Counties. We met a troop of Cavalry from Fort Ringgold who were also looking for bandits, and made a night camp together. The Army captain had served in the Philippines, and after supper he invited Captain Ransom to his tent for a visit. I went along and listened to their conversation. The tales they told about executing Filipinos made the Bandit War look like a minor purge.

We had been accustomed to Ranger captains like Brooks, Rogers and Hughes. When the press announced that Captain Ransom was coming in to help put down the bandit trouble, the news was most welcome. Many of his men had been convict guards who were trained to shoot fleeing convicts with buckshot. After I became adjutant general, I would never enlist a man of this background. Captain Ransom held the belief that he was an instrument of justice, and that he had a definite mission to perform. He said, "A bad disease calls for bitter medicine. The Governor sent me down here to stop this trouble, and I am going to carry out his orders. There is only one way to do it. President Diaz proved that in Mexico." He compared the suppression of organized crime to a game of tenpins. "Knock the kingpin and you get all of them," he said. "That's what I did to that lawyer in Houston." He used this philosophy throughout the Bandit War.

As far back as 1854, bandits raided the towns of Roma and Rio Grande City, or Rancho Davis. They were pursued by United States troops, who captured the two leaders and hung them from mesquite trees. Apparently, it had long been the custom along the Rio Grande to make quick disposition of bandits. The Army hung them, while the Rangers shot them.

I only went on two scouts with his company. He said that anybody who had guilty knowledge of crimes committed, or anyone who harbored bandits, should be killed. We drove up to the Santa Anita Ranch just as the cow outfit was starting out. Ransom said, "Those fellows look like bandits to me, and we ought to get rid of them." I was only a kid, but said, "No, Cap, that would never do. They are only ranch hands. I know all of them personally." On several other occasions I made similar pleas, thereby saving the lives of more than one *hombre*.

Captain Ransom had a soft side. He earned my mother's undying friendship by saying, "Miss Mary, I wish I could take the place of your boys in their trouble." Many substantial citizens, while decrying his drastic methods, reaped the benefit of his work. They had to admit that he was the right man for the unpleasant job of ridding the country of business-paralyzing bandits. Several years later Ransom was killed in a hotel in Sweetwater, Texas. Sam McKenzie was present, and he told me the circumstances of his death. Two men were shooting at each other in the long hall on the second floor. The Rangers were spending the night there. Ransom ran out of his room and ordered them to stop the shooting. He was struck by a stray bullet and instantly killed. One Houston newspaper, in an editorial on the death of Ransom, used the verse, "He who liveth by the sword, shall die by the sword."

The most important military figure in the Bandit War was Captain Frank R. McCoy. He was the best liked Army officer who ever served on the lower border. Captain McCoy was a native of Pennsylvania and a graduate of the United States Military Academy at West Point. While stationed in Mission with the Third Cavalry, he won the friendship and confidence of the Hidalgo County sheriff, his deputies, ranchmen and Rangers. During horseback scouts in the chaparral, he would arm himself with a service rifle and ride stirrup to stirrup with us. He was always immaculate in appearance, and could maintain his neatness under the most rugged conditions. His service included a tour of duty on the General Staff, and an assignment as military aide to President Theodore Roosevelt. He often entertained us with intimate stories of the Rough Rider. Captain McCoy spent a great deal of time at our ranch, and always referred to my mother as "The Mother of the Gracchi."

Unlike some other Army officers, Captain McCoy realized that to be effective in guerilla warfare, regular troops must be supported by men who are experienced in brush fighting. For this exacting duty, no force has ever equalled the Texas Rangers. He had made a careful study of the Mexican War. From it he learned that the victories of the Americans under Taylor and Scott would not have been possible without the aid of Rangers under Hays, Walker and McCullough. Captain McCoy cooperated to the fullest extent with Sheriff A. Y. Baker, who received his training in the Rangers.

While scouting with the Cavalry, we had a good opportunity to observe and compare them with the Rangers. The peacetime cavalrymen of that day were mostly men who came from cities in the East. They complained bitterly about the hardships of the trail. Our boys made a lark out of these scouts. We kept up a running conversation of jokes and other light talk to make the miles seem shorter. Walton (Lupe) Edwards was a great mimic. He used to repeat the soldiers' wail, imitating their army talk which was strongly flavored with Brooklynese. They called the brush covered country "the chaps" from the chaparral, and every civilian knows that army food is called "chow." To them it was a tragedy when they had to postpone a meal. Lupe would whine through his nose, "all day in the dusty chaps, without a bite of chow." The cavalry horses were also used to having their feed on time. They suffered greatly from the varied terrain, rocks a few miles, deep sand for a while and heavy brush all the way. The city bred soldiers, although using the lighter McClellan saddles, did not ride like the Rangers. Army mounts could not stand the hardships like native ranch horses. There is a border saying that a cowboy can ride a horse twenty miles farther than a soldier and that an Indian or Mexican can ride the same animal ten miles after he has been bedrocked by a cowboy.

We were all horseback raised and inured to long rides without food or water. In pursuing bandits or other dangerous game, several things happen to a man. First, he learns to appreciate his horse more than ever, even though he is a natural horse lover. The faithful animal, in addition to carrying a rider with saddle, rifle and ammunition, soon gets into the spirit of the chase. His ears will point his master to a hidden enemy as surely as any hunting dog points a covey of quail. His heart is so much in the chase that it will beat a warning tattoo that his rider can feel and use as an alarm. Rangers who have trailed bandits through brush or mountains will contest anybody who claims that a dog is man's best friend. This exciting work will make hunting a tame and boring business to those who can't get a thrill out of game that does not shoot back.

About three years after the main trouble was over, a bunch of bandits appeared in Jim Hogg County and raided the San Antonio Viejo Ranch. Among those held in temporary captivity in the main house was the late Claude McGill. He was one of those rare individuals who could enjoy a laugh, even at his own expense. The State Senate conducted an investigation of the Rangers, the bandit activities, and conditions generally prevailing in Southwest Texas. Numerous citizens were summoned to appear in Austin. My father and I were among this number. Mr. McGill was on the stand, being questioned by a senator who was small in stature but large in pomp and dignity. The ex-captive stated that the bandit chief punched him in the stomach with his Winchester and said, *"Pica le. Pica le."* (Roughly translated, this means "Get along. Get along.") The senator then asked, "And what did you do, Mr. McGill?" Slowly puffing on his ever present pipe, the genial cowman replied, "I picaled." Those in the audience who understood Spanish roared with laughter.

I was in Goliad for some dental work when news of the foray reached me by telephone. Our ranch was eighty miles away, but I hurried to Hebbronville. When the owner, Tom T. East, returned to San Antonio Viejo for the first time, Tom Mosely and I went with him. I am the only surviving member of this trio.

Shortly after returning from the Pancho Villa expedition, General John J. Pershing made an inspection trip to Forts Brown and Ringgold. The late Caesar Kleberg and I accompanied him. While driving up the Valley, he made a remark that I have never forgotten. The general said, "Some day this will all be a garden spot of fruits and flowers. The people of Mexico and the United States will live side by side in peace. This will be like the Canadian border. There will be no need for forts or army posts." Several times he spoke in this vein. I told him he would make a fine land salesman for one of the developers of the Valley. It is a long way from the Rio Grande to Washington, and many years elapsed before I saw him again. In 1931, when he was General of the Armies and I was a student officer at the Army War College, I was privileged to renew my acquaintance with the Commander of the American Expeditionary Forces.

In 1919 Legislator J. T. Canales of Brownsville asked for an investigation of the Rangers. He charged that the organization was honeycombed with intriguers and incompetents, and that they were at the top level. Representative Canales did not want to abolish the Rangers, as his enemies charged. His family had long been the friends of worthy members of the organization. Captains Brooks, Rogers and Hughes stopped on many occasions at La Cabra, his father's ranch in what is now Jim Wells County. While serving as captain of Company D, I rode a horse presented to me by his brother, the late Albino Canales. Many members of the House and Senate knew the charges brought by Mr. Canales to be true, but they believed that the Rangers could be saved by a good housecleaning. The adjutant general was to blame for the low grade personnel. I always supported the position taken by Judge Canales.

The end of the Bandit War was a great relief to all citizens of the Valley. However, ranchmen and travelers in the back country continued to carry Winchesters and six-shooters for many years after actual hostilities had ceased. In my opinion, the three men who contributed most to the suppression of the trouble were McCoy, Baker and Mayfield.

Estimates of the number of Mexicans killed have been placed as high as three hundred. Probably less than half that figure would be more nearly correct. The American dead, including soldiers, totaled around fifty. If prompt and drastic action had not been taken, the casualties on both sides would have been greater. This is particularly true of isolated ranches owned by Americans.

I was with that pioneer Valley settler, Lon C. Hill, Sr., at the Ranger investigation in Austin. A member of the Texas Senate said to us, "I cannot conceive of a condition existing in our state that would justify such extreme measures." Mr. Hill replied, "No, Senator, from the security of your North Texas home you could not. We residents of the Valley realized that perfectly. For this very reason we acted promptly, instead of waiting for those cutthroats to carry out their Plan de San Diego."

For several years after the Bandit War, we maintained constant vigilance around the ranch. One night, I was detained by cow work at an outlying camp and did not get home until after dark. The kitchen and dining room were in a separate building. As I walked toward it, the *caporal,* Florentino Salas, spoke to me in a low tone. He was standing in the shadows, and he had his Winchester. *"Que pasa?"* I asked. (What goes on?) *"Quien sabe, Patron,"* he replied and pointed to the table in the dining room. An elderly man was seated there, and my wife and one of my sisters were bringing food to him. They were relieved when I arrived, and we soon pieced the story togther. The old gentleman was a victim of amnesia, and he had walked all the way from Mission. I called the telephone operator there, and she told me that practically everybody in town was searching for him. Florentino only knew that a strange man had gone in the house, and that the ladies seemed to be disturbed. He was standing guard on the outside, and if the intruder had attempted to harm my womenfolk, he would have shot him. One of Florentino's brothers had fallen into bad company, and would have been killed in the bandit trouble if I had not rescued him. The faithful *vaquero* was prepared to go to any length to show his gratitude.

Chapter 5
NEW YORK
NATIONAL GUARD

ON June 19, 1916, President Woodrow Wilson ordered the entire National Guard of the United States to mobilize on the Mexican border. The Chief Executive accomplished a twofold purpose when he ordered this unprecedented movement of citizen soldiers. It served as a show of strength to Mexico, and also demonstrated to our own people that modern wars could not be won with militia. Students of military science know that it is imperative to use only highly trained and seasoned troops. The long haired politicians who opposed an adequate Regular Army were wont to shout, "We can whip our enemies with squirrel rifles," and cite the War of 1812. These outmoded ignoramuses, in order to get votes, would permit our brave volunteers to be slaughtered. The General Staff and the War Department realized that we would be drawn into the European conflict. President Wilson had acted on their advice and counsel.

Troops from fourteen states were sent to the lower Rio Grande Valley. Early in July, the New York contingent arrived in McAllen and Mission. Not a drop of rain had fallen in Hidalgo County for eighteen months. Practically all of the cattle had starved to death. Simultaneously with the arrival of the soldiers, it began to rain. They would not believe that we had been in a prolonged and devastating drought.

I soon met the division commander, Major General John F. O'Ryan. He represented the highest type of National Guard officer, and his chief concern was for the welfare of his men. The supply of drinking water in the two towns came from irrigation canals. Illness began to appear among the soldiers, and several of them died. Included in this number was a brother of Grover Whalen, long a prominent figure in New York. On our ranch northwest of Mission were two deep wells. They furnished an abundance of pure water, which was lifted by air compressors. I showed them to General O'Ryan and introduced him to our family. He has been our staunch friend from that day forward.

54

The general was looking for an artillery range and a maneuvering area for the division. I found both of them for him, and he used the ranch as his base of field operations. It soon became a favorite rendezvous for all the officers. Chaplain John Henri Sattig of the Fourteenth New York Infantry presented us with a guest book. It contains the names of several hundred New Yorkers. Among them are many famous people. We witnessed the amazing spectacle of a brush country ranch transformed overnight into an active Army camp that sometimes contained more than ten thousand men.

Among the prominent names in our guest book was that of Major Cornelius Vanderbilt. On one occasion I took him to Santa Anita, which is among the oldest established ranches in Texas. It was owned by the late John J. Young, a descendant of Juan Jose Balli who received the land from the King of Spain. Mr. Young was a typical Southwest Texas ranchero, and he immediately ordered his *mozo* to serve coffee. After the first sip, Major Vanderbilt said, "Mr. Young, this is the best coffee I ever tasted. It must be some special blend that you have imported." Our host smiled and replied, "No, Major Vanderbilt, it is peaberry coffee and it costs fifteen cents per pound. One of the women on the ranch roasts it in a dutch oven." The New Yorker was still puzzled, and asked, "Then what gives it this delicious flavor?" Don Juan answered, "It could be that it comes from an old border custom. We like our coffee strong and we always add some boiled goat milk."

My mother presided over the social life of the ranch. Her efforts to welcome the strangers inspired a treasured inscription in our guest book. It was penned by Author Rupert Hughes, who was serving as a major in the "Fighting Sixty-ninth" Regiment of Infantry. It reads: "To Mrs. Mary Sterling of Sterlings Ranch Texas. One of the South's noble women whose hospitality was large enough to entertain an army. From her admiring well wisher, Rupert Hughes."

General William (Wild Bill) Donovan was a young lieutenant in the same outfit. With that name he could belong to no other. I saw him in Washington just before Pearl Harbor. He said, "The best drink I ever had in my life was a glass of ice cold buttermilk. It was given to me one hot summer day by your lovely mother."

When the tropical hurricane of 1916 struck Texas, the Seventy-first Infantry Regiment was camped for the night at our ranch. Most of the soldiers were young boys fresh from the city and their only shelter was provided by pup tents. The storm lasted nearly twenty-four hours, and the camp became a scene of wild confusion. The men suffered greatly from exposure and many of them collapsed. Like most South Texas ranches, our kitchen and dining room were in a separate building. This was turned into a first aid station. It had a large open fireplace which was kept going full blast. One of the soldiers was Norman Selby, known to the prize fighting world as "Kid McCoy." He performed heroic service by working all night and resuscitating a number of exhausted soldiers.

We made many lasting friendships among the members of the New York National Guard. Everybody who had any part in the mobilization profited by the experience. Some of the Nation's wealthiest men had dropped their personal affairs in order to perform their share of military service. Numerous employees were on leave from their jobs. Most of them were urgently needed at home. They welcomed the order terminating their service on the Mexican Border. These patriotic men would have less than a year to prepare for the forthcoming war "to make the world safe for Democracy," and "to end all wars." Most of the New York Guardsmen remember the Sterling Ranch.

Chapter 6
FIRST WORLD WAR
AND BRECKENRIDGE

THERE were two boys in our family, both unmarried. My brother was twenty-three years old and I was twenty-six. When the First World War was declared, we hurried to town and offered our services. The medical officer was Lieutenant James A. Simpson, who in later years became a member of my staff. He gave us a thorough physical examination. At the conclusion, Doctor Simpson said, "Ed, they will take you, but Bill can never pass." I had suffered a powder burn in my eyes, and was otherwise bunged up from riding rough horses. The medico called Captain McCoy, and together they gave me this advice. "The Germans and Japanese are very active in Mexico, and they are going to harass us on the border. With your experience, and knowledge of Spanish, you can be most valuable to the war effort by serving here." My brother immediately volunteered, and became the first young man from his county to go.

Two troops of the Third Cavalry were stationed in Mission. One of them was commanded by Captain Fitzhugh Lee, Jr., son of the famous Confederate and Spanish-American War general. The other was under Captain Frank R. McCoy. Both of them had served in the White House as military aides to President Theodore Roosevelt. The Rough Rider hoped to organize a division for service in the forthcoming world war. He had selected Captain McCoy to be his chief of staff. The captain showed me his correspondence with Colonel Roosevelt, and assured both my brother and me that we would be given commissions in the outfit. The War Department knew that there was no place in modern warfare for individually raised components, and the proposed Roosevelt Division did not materialize.

The ranch work had to go on, and my father was getting along in years. He never learned to speak much Spanish, and had a great deal of trouble with the hands. Everybody told me that I was doing my bit raising cattle and guarding the border. The draft board classified me as 5-G, totally unfit for military service. I did not feel right out of uniform, and sought a way to get in the Army. The State was authorized to raise a regiment of infantry "for immediate overseas service." I went to Temple at my own expense and was examined by my old friend, Dr. A. C. Scott. He said, "I'll patch you up so you can get in," and that is what he did. I was commissioned a second lieutenant in the Ninth Texas Infantry. Some of the most prominent men in the state were in this outfit. In some way the papers were fouled up in the Texas Adjutant General's Department. We were told that on a certain day we would be federalized. Postponement followed postponement. We became the lost regiment. The Armistice found my company drilling on the banks of the Arroyo Colorado near Harlingen.

In the years immediately following World War I, the cattle business suffered one of the worst slumps in its history. The impact of this calamity on stockmen was reflected in an address delivered before a convention of the Texas Cattle Raisers Association. At the annual meeting in Fort Worth, President James Callan said, "Gentlemen, most of us are broke and know it; others are broke and don't know it. Only a fortunate few are solvent." Will Rogers was just beginning to attract national attention as a humorist, and oil had just been found on Waggoner's Three D Ranch. Will wisecracked, "Mr. Waggoner is the smartest cowman in Texas. He has an oil well for each cow."

The circumstances depicted by Callan and Rogers compelled me to follow many other ranchmen to the oil fields. My destination was Breckenridge, in Stephens County. Here I hoped to recoup my losses, and go back to raising livestock. There will never be another field like that fabulous place. Conditions similar to those found there will not be seen again. The price of oil was $3.50 a barrel and many of the wells could produce ten thousand barrels per day. There was no proration, and the income tax was in its infancy. The news of easy money had filled the town with a milling throng, and crime was rampant.

I had resided in the county barely long enough to qualify as a juror when District Judge C. O. Hamlin appointed me as foreman of the grand jury. After examining a few witnesses, it was apparent that the sheriff and several of his deputies were taking bribes by the wholesale. They had placed their graft on a business basis. In exchange for official protection, the local "laws" maintained a fixed scale of prices. The degree and form of each underworld activity governed the amount demanded. To me this was a revolting disclosure. Among the Rangers and border officers with whom I had served, bribery was unknown. Their good name was not for sale, and they valued honor above their lives. I was appalled at the corruption that existed in the sheriff's department.

In those days of prohibition, the worst beverage sold in the oil fields was a mixture of jamaica ginger and creek water known as "jake." The monetary profit in this devil's broth was enormous. By copious dilution, dealers made over a thousand dollars out of a five-gallon can of the pure stuff. Those who drank this fiery potion contracted a peculiar jerking in their limbs. It was known as "jakeleg." The ghastly discoloration of their faces further marked the victims, and turned them into pitiful specimens of humanity. The only remedy ever found that would in any way help these unfortunates was a serum developed by a veterinarian. He probably proceeded on the theory that nothing but a dumb brute would drink jake. The sheriff was interested in several so-called drug stores. These jake joints kept a few bottles of patent medicine on their shelves to serve as a blind for their real purpose.

The grafters became so bold that a group of the best citizens asked me to run for sheriff. I had already sent my wife home, and wanted to get back to South Texas, but finally consented to make the race. Shocked at the disclosures of corruption heard in the grand jury room, I decided to make a statement that could not be misunderstood. Included in my platform was this announcement: "The first man who offers me a bribe will land in the emergency hospital." I thought that the church people would share my views about graft and get solidly behind me. This was not the case. The minister of the largest congregation in town preached a sermon against me. He referred to me as a "border gunman" and termed my forthright statement as "braggadocio". His top paying parishioner owned a lot of real estate that was bringing high rentals for questionable purposes. I learned a sad but valuable lesson in that campaign. When some of the psalm singing hypocrites are hit in the pocketbook, they vote with the grafters. I made this proposition to the people of Stephens County: "Just ascertain which candidate the crooks are supporting, and get on the other side." The bums will always stick together and vote in a solid bloc. The good people frequently divide. On election day, the king bootlegger, the vice queen of the county, and the preacher were all electioneering for the jake seller. Hundreds of the largest land owners were astounded to find that they could not vote in their native county. They had changed their legal residences when moving to other cities. These substantial citizens made up my strongest group of supporters. I was defeated in the run-off. My opponent was sent to jail for bootlegging about the time I was sworn in as Adjutant General of Texas. I relate the above not for the purpose of crying on anybody's shoulder, but because I had promised a clean oil field if elected. My opponents claimed that such a thing was an impossibility.

During the Breckenridge boom, many amusing incidents occurred. After the first wild rush, the seething mass of fortune hunting humanity began to simmer down. The local courts, both civil and criminal, were swamped with cases. The litigation that always follows the discovery of a new oil field, as well as the lucrative criminal practice, attracted numerous lawyers to Breckenridge. Young attorneys, hanging out their first shingle, old heads who had not been overrun with clients back home, and a few natives made up the bar of Stephens County. To relieve a badly congested docket, the legislature created another judicial district. The sole function of the new court was to handle cases in the oil field county.

In an effort to curb the local crime wave, the Governor decided to appoint an outstanding man as district attorney. After canvassing the field, he selected the late Claude McCaleb of Fort Worth. This able prosecutor had a keen sense of humor, great wit, and was never bested in an exchange of repartee. In one of his cases, the attorney for the defense made an impassioned plea for the acquittal of his client. He urged that justice be tempered with mercy, and declared, "It is better for ninety-nine guilty men to escape, than for one innocent man to suffer." His effort made a deep impression on the jurors. When McCaleb arose to present the state's closing argument, he made a wry face, took a chew of tobacco and said, "Yes, my friends, I agree with counsel for the defense and subscribe to his theory. BUT, gentlemen of the jury, in this county, the ninety-nine have already escaped. It's high time that ONE was convicted."

A noted Stephens County case involved religious law instead of the secular variety. One of the brethren was about to be churched. He was charged with the heinous crime of dancing. The culprit owned a small piece of land. By dint of unceasing labor, he had eked out an existence for his family. Fortune finally smiled on him, and several good oil wells were found on his farm. Now everybody called him "Mister" and the ones seeking loans bestowed on him the title of "Colonel."

After receiving a few royalty checks, he moved to Mineral Wells. His waking hours were spent in playing dominoes and lounging around the spa's water dispensing pavilions. He had always been a staunch Baptist, faithfully adhering to the tenets of that exacting denomination. Ease, idleness and luxury soon caused his downfall. Now he had to face an ecclesiastical tribunal. When the trial was opened, the culprit asked permission to say a few words in his own behalf. The request was granted, and he made his plea in these words: "Brethren, if you all will forgive me this time, I'll promise never to do it again. I never danced before in my life, and I wouldn't have been dancing then if I hadn't been drunk."

On a trip to Fort Worth with an oil rich citizen of Stephens County, we decided to eat dinner in a rather pretentious restaurant. In order to impress *hoi polloi* and justify their high prices, the menu was richly garnished with words printed in French. One of the listed items was "braised leg of filet". "What's that?" asked my dining companion. When the waiter pronounced it, he exclaimed, "What kind of joint is this? Do you think I'm going to eat the 'bruised leg of a filly'?"

When the Ranger oil boom was at its height, a fellow described by the newspapers as "picturesque" was appointed chief of police. He may have been in the Rangers for a short time, but he did not last. This grafter boasted that he was going to "get his," and that he already had $50,000 in various banks. Less than a year later, I was driving into Breckenridge with a deputy sheriff. We met the Stephens County convict truck, and the erstwhile chief was in it. I remarked to my companion, "That man has gone a long way down the scale. A year ago he was rich. Now he is guarding convicts." The deputy replied, "He is not a guard. He is a prisoner on the chain gang."

My campaign was exciting, and at times became rough. The opposition resorted to one of the crudest and most transparent tricks in the history of county politics. The sheriff took his car out in the country and shot several holes through the windshield. He parked it on the courthouse square, and claimed that he had been ambushed. They circulated the rumor that I had fired the shots. I scotched these innuendos by declaring that no man with a sense of proportion would use a gun on such a specimen. "If anybody went out to kill him," I stated, "the only fitting weapon would be a Flit gun and a can of insect powder."

I was glad when the election was over, and felt no sorrow over being defeated. Many who had urged me to run failed to furnish their promised support. I longed to get back to Southwest Texas. A new oil field had opened near Laredo, and it offered many opportunities. After bidding farewell to a few real friends, I cranked up my Model T Ford, and drove to Webb County, on the Rio Grande.

Chapter 7
MIRANDO CITY

THE first oil field in deep Southwest Texas was opened in 1921, about fifty miles from Laredo. Several small gas wells had been found earlier at Reiser, in Webb County, and the Jennings gas fields of Zapata County dated from 1919. Oil had been known to exist in one shallow well at Piedras Pintas in Duval County, since the Civil War. A similar one was located on El Tecolote ranch near Charco Redondo, in Zapata County. For many years oil drawn from these two wells had been used to grease wagons and windmills. Neither of them was of enough importance to warrant the designation of "oil field."

Oliver Winfield Killam, native of Missouri but more recently a State senator and grain dealer in Oklahoma, drilled the discovery well. It was located in the Mirando Valley of Zapata County. Shortly afterward, he laid out a townsite on the Texas-Mexican Railroad, at a point twenty-eight miles east of Laredo. With more optimism than regard to size, he named the project Mirando City. It was situated west of and below the Reynosa Escarpment. This geological phenomenon cut off all formations that would produce fresh water. None could be found at any depth in the new town.

This obstacle did not daunt the city founder, nor did it stringhalt his plans for development. Taking a cue from the neighboring pueblo of Aguilares, he arranged with the Tex-Mex to supply the necessary water in tank cars. These were side-tracked at the intersection of the railroad and the main street. Here they served as both city water works and town pump. For domestic use, the villagers toted the precious fluid in buckets. A barrel of drinking water was worth more than a barrel of crude oil and baths were at a premium. The pioneer settlers of Mirando City were both rugged and strong.

New oil production was found south of the young town. Gas fields were opened to the north and east. The Killam interests laid a pipe line to the railroad and began moving oil in increasing amounts. Most of it was shipped in tank cars to Port Aransas, there to be loaded on coastwise tankers. The Carnahan Company also built a shorter pipe line from the Schott field to their loading racks on the railroad. By 1922 the boom was on, and the usual conglomeration of adventurers flocked to the new field. Some were solid, upright people destined to go far in the petroleum industry. Others were boomers who depended more on luck and circumstances than on integrity.

The oil business was still in its infancy when the Mirando field was discovered. There were few geologists or petroleum engineers, and a good drilling rig could be bought for around twelve thousand dollars. If an operator happened to be lucky, mud would do for brains. A Laredo plaza philosopher summed it up in these words: "There is only one difference between a gentleman and a son of a gun in this oil game. The gent gets an oil well, while the s.o.g. gets a dry hole. Two men can go out under identical circumstances. If one strikes oil, they will call him 'Mister' and elect him president of the chamber of commerce. If he gets a dry hole, they will call him a bum, and say that he ought to be in jail." In his long search for petroleum in paying quantities, one wildcatter of my acquaintance had almost starved to death. He finally hit the jackpot. The new found wealth called for a trip to the Mayo Hospital. He was given a thorough examination which included an analysis of his blood. It tested ninety-five per cent chili.

John A. Valls, who for twenty-eight years served the Forty-ninth Judicial District as prosecuting attorney, was a unique individual. His counterpart will never again be seen. If there ever was a "natural" or a man made to order for the time, place and conditions of his office, it was John A. Valls. He knew the people, the country and the law.

To him duty was the most sublime word in the English language, and throughout his official career, he lived up to that precept. An entire book should be written about him. Every page would make fascinating reading.

Joe Condren, a blustery Irish railroad man from New York, had moved to Texas as a young man. He was a conductor on the Texas-Mexican railway, which runs between Corpus Christi and Laredo. From the large size of his head, the Latin Americans, who made up fully ninety per cent of his passengers, nicknamed him *El Cabezon*. True to his racial instincts, he had entered politics, and when the Mirando oil fields were opened, he was chief deputy sheriff of Webb County. I had ridden with him many times, and we were good friends.

Condren was extremely good natured and had a fine sense of humor. His ready wit served him well. It brought him through several tight places during his railroading days. Most of his customers carried pistols, and some of them when returning from *parandas* in Corpus Christi or Laredo, became very belligerent. He calmed them down with his unfailing smile and endless supply of yarns. These were spun in three languages, English, Spanish and Irish.

He had many amusing experiences during his long career as a slow train conductor. One of these left an indelible impression on his memory. On an unusually hot day, even for the semi-arid country traversed by the Tex-Mex, his passengers included a large, fat colored woman. She was nursing an extremely well fed baby. The ample sources of supply made it apparent that nourishment for the infant did not need to be supplemented by a bottle. The child had long since reached the saturation point, but the mother urged him to take a little more. She was about to give up, when Joe came walking down the aisle. "You better finish your dinner, chile," warned the buxom mother. "If you don't, I'm gonna give it to the conductor."

The sheriff of Webb County and most of his deputies were Latin Americans. They were good men, but many of the roughnecks and drillers, fresh from the interior oil fields, resented being handled by them. Mirando was the first oil strike on the border, and it presented many law enforcement problems. Governor Pat Neff told me that on hearing of it, he feared he would have to send all the Rangers and half the National Guard down there to maintain order. Deputy Sheriff Joe

Fierros said to me one day, "Those crookednecks are the worst people I ever saw." What he meant, of course, was roughnecks, but the fact remained that they did not like the local officers.

Judge Valls and acting Sheriff Condren were deeply concerned over the situation that confronted them. The sudden influx of strangers into their bailiwick had created an emergency for which they were unprepared. The officials had been unable to find a man satisfactory for the assignment in Mirando City. Several deputies had been bluffed out by the oil field toughs.

On my arrival in Laredo, the first acquaintance I met on the plaza was Captain Allen Walker. He had won the Congressional Medal of Honor, and was presently employed as a deputy United States marshal. We were old comrades, having served together farther down the Rio Grande. After greeting me warmly he asked, "Where are you going, Bill, and what are you doing?" I replied, "I am moving to Mirando City, and I hope to make some money there." The captain was an austere, reserved person but he exclaimed, "You're just the man we've been looking for. Let's go see Judge Valls." I protested that my present aim was to recover financially from the slump in the cattle business, and that I did not want to serve as an officer. "I won't take 'no' for an answer," he said. We went by the United States marshal's office in the Federal Building, and then on to the county courthouse. The conference was held in the district attorney's office. Judge Valls, Sheriff-elect Condren, Deputy United States Marshal Walker and I made up the group. The district attorney opened the meeting with the declaration that "a state of anarchy exists in the Webb County oil fields." He stated that in addition to the newly arrived criminals, several of the worst border characters he had ever dealt with were now living in Mirando. It was plain to see that he was very much in earnest in all that he said, and his voice trembled with emotion as he explained the situation to me.

I finally agreed to accept the proffered commission as a deputy under Sheriff Antonio Salinas. It was understood that I would be free to attend to my private affairs when not engaged in official business. Before leaving the courthouse, Judge Valls called me back in his office for a few final words. He started the conversation by saying, "Mr. Sterling, you have a good face, and I firmly believe you are the man we need

to cope with these scoundrels." He told me about several hard cases harboring in Mirando. "You will probably have trouble with one of them. He is one of the most dangerous men I have ever known." The good judge continued in his kindly voice and fatherly manner, "If that killer starts anything, don't hesitate to defend yourself. I will see you through any court action." This is probably the only time that Judge Valls ever gave such advice to anybody.

This badman gave me no trouble. The only time I had to handle him, he was meek as Moses. Maybe he knew that he was already "paid for." I was always grateful for Judge Valls' attitude, and we remained the best of friends throughout his life. One of my most treasured souvenirs is an autographed picture of him with the inscription "To my friend and protector" on the margin. The title "protector" emanated from a famous murder case that was tried in Laredo. He prosecuted it with great vigor and I served as his bodyguard.

After I arrived in Mirando City and surveyed the situation, it was plain to see that Judge Valls had not made an overstatement. There were a number of fights and other disturbances. When the word got around that a new "law" (to oil field people, all officers are "laws") had arrived, quite a few wagers were made as to how long I would last. Many oil workers hold a justified animosity against professional oil field "laws." These highbinders prowl from one boom town to another, following oil discoveries like a pack of wolves. They prey on the honest people, and are worse than any other class of criminals found in a new field. These slickers try to convince the gullible sheriff that he needs assistants who have had oil field experience. He is told that without them it will be impossible to handle the incoming crowds. No local officer ever succumbed to the wiles of these badge flaunting crooks without coming to grief. He would either rue the day he deputized them, or become corrupt himself. As soon as these scoundrels got set in a new oil field, they started a series of outrages. Their sworn duty was the last thing they had any idea of performing. To them, an official position was simply a blind from which to carry on their pay-offs and other forms of graft. In more than one instance these oil field "laws" were known to be highjackers, who robbed oil workers at the point of a gun. Many of them were vicious and trigger happy. Pistol whipping of a roughneck was a common occurrence. This lengthy explanation is interpolated to show the distrust in which most officers in an oil field were held. With a full realization of these facts, I was able to lay plans for better relations between officers and citizens. My first step was to gain their confidence.

There were numerous lawless characters in the Mirando fields, upon whom kindness was lost. They had no intentions of changing their ways, and resisted any attempt to make them earn an honest living. My approach to this problem was direct and effective. "If you miss the first train out of town, Mister," I told each one of them, "you better overtake it." I would not let the criminal element harbor on me, and the word soon went out over the underworld grapevine that they would be very unhappy in Mirando City.

In 1922 there were not enough jobs to go around, and when many of the boys hit town they were dead broke. I told all of the local restaurants to give any working man who needed it a five dollar meal ticket, and to charge any unpaid ones to me. This small act of kindness made me many friends among the roughnecks. Not a single working man beat his bill. Only twice was I called on to pay. Both of these meal tickets were taken out by members of prominent families. One of their relatives held an exalted position in national politics, and another occupied a high place in religious circles. They were just a couple of black sheep who brought no credit on their people. The renegades suffered by comparison with the oil field boys.

A strong point in my favor was the fact that I did not drink. Alcohol and pistols will not mix, especially when the liquor is in the stomach and the six-shooter in the hands of a law enforcement officer. The men quickly found that there would be no graft of any kind. Most of the boys accepted me as a friend and protector rather than an enemy or a man to be avoided. I organized a baseball team and we built a good ball park with a full-fledged grandstand. Several church groups got together and held Sunday school in one of the public buildings. The oil and business men started to bring in their families, and it was at last proved that an oil field could be made a good place in which to rear a family.

The first justice of the peace was a sickly doctor, who also owned the drug store. He was not interested in anything but his fees, and in making a stake big enough to move away. As soon as I had been in the county and precinct long enough to qualify, the commissioners court of Webb County appointed me justice of the peace for Precinct No. 5. My bailiwick covered the southeastern portion of the county, and included all the oil fields. I had to make a surety bond, and two of the wealthiest land owners in the county volunteered to sign it. They were Amador E. Garcia and ex-Ranger S. V. (Pete) Edwards. Both of them had refused numerous requests to go on bonds, but they seemed happy to accommodate me.

Under our Texas laws, a justice of the peace is an ex-officio notary public. I made pretty good money out of my notary fees. Some unscrupulous lease hounds, however, soon dispensed with my services. When they sought to get a lease from a man who did not understand English, and there was any question of their good faith, I would always advise the lessor in Spanish to consult his lawyer before he signed. This practice cost me several notary and interpreter fees, but it earned me the undying gratitude of the rancheros.

Among my varied experiences as an *alcalde,* one encounter I had with a game warden could be classed as outstanding. It was a glaring example of the lack of common or horse sense on the part of some officers. I was not surprised when he killed a good man shortly after being moved out of our county. An unpainted pine shack served as a combination justice of the peace and real estate office. Spread on the floor was a badly shot up deer hide. It was easily identified and its history well known to everybody in the community. The buck from which it was taken had been killed by an elderly man who shared the office with me. He belonged to several sportsman's organizations and was a stickler for rigid enforcement of all game laws. This aged gentleman's eyesight was very poor, and he could not use a rifle. He was forced to do his hunting with a ten gauged shotgun. One warm autumn day he stumbled on an old buck, fast asleep in the shade of a big mesquite. When the startled animal jumped up and started to run, the equally surprised hunter cut loose with both barrels of his young cannon. It was loaded with buckshot, and he literally blew the rear end off the deer.

The blast badly disfigured the hide, but the oldtimer was so proud of his trophy that he had it tanned. He brought it to the office where all might see, and we used it for a rug. A refinery near Mirando kept us supplied with a paraffine floor oil. To keep down the dust and sand tracked in by our roughshod visitors, we made free use of this product. The game warden made our office his headquarters.

One day he cocked his eyes at the hide, took out his pocket knife and scraped some greasy substance from the flesh side. The sleuth smelled the scrapings in the most approved Sherlock Holmes manner, and solemnly declared that it was an illegal hide, killed in the summer. He further stated that he was going to send it to Austin, and have it analyzed in the laboratory. I informed him that he could not take the hide anywhere without the owner's consent. He did not choose to dispute this ultimatum. The deerslayer, however, was eager to test the accuracy of the game department's laboratory, and cheerfully gave the required permission. In due time, the exhibit was returned, together with the results of the analysis. It showed that the warden's fancied "summer tallow" was not even animal fat, but that it was mineral floor oil. The physical facts and circumstances would make this instantly apparent to anybody but an overbearing officer. If I had not intervened, he would have deprived an old man of his constitutional rights.

During the era of prohibition, the Rio Grande became a unique river. It was dry on one side and wet on the other. This fact, as much as the low cost of drilling shallow wells, attracted numerous operators to the Mirando field. Laredo also became the point of no return for many traveling men and representatives of interior firms. The border police received countless wires from business houses, inquiring about these truants. They were last heard from in Laredo. After they had spent all their money, and with Texas sized hangovers, these otherwise respectable men would drag themselves back to the American side. They were forced to wire the house for funds, or borrow from sympathetic lodge brothers. In all the local fraternal orders, the distress sign was badly overworked.

The road between Laredo and San Antonio was much narrower in 1922 than the present day highway. Most of it was unpaved and both sides were lined with chaparral. A tour of Southwest Texas towns was being made by a small circus. Their menagerie consisted of an ancient elephant, and they traveled overland. During the Mirando boom, they showed at Encinal, and were moving to Laredo. They started before daylight. A number of oil men who had visited Nuevo Laredo the night before were driving back to San Antonio. In the cold gray dawn, their wondering eyes beheld, walking down the road, an elephant. He was not pink, but several of the *crudos* thought it was time to sign the pledge.

One of my cases involved the civil rights of a lowly citizen. As had happened before, a browbeating peace officer was the reason for this wrangle. The incident may possibly demonstrate to the parlor reformers and other remote control uplifters how far a conscientious Texan will go to protect the most humble member of a minority race. We render them this aid, not because of prodding from pressure groups, but simply as a matter of justice and sense of duty.

A blustering braggart had succeeded in getting himself elected constable of our precinct. He occupied this office not on account of any merit he possessed, but because nobody else would have the job. This fellow had a Wild Bill complex, and did his best to dress the part of that famous cow town marshal. He wore the biggest black hat this side of Mexico, kept it pulled down over one eye and swaggered around the street in a manner calculated to strike terror in the hearts of all who beheld him. The "constabule" was the antithesis of everything a good officer should be, both in looks and deeds.

One day he notified me that he had an important criminal case to try, and asked me to convene justice court for the hearing. I was busy loading some oil cars at a railroad siding about a mile out of town, and told the counterfeit gunfighter not to bother me unless he really had a case against the accused. He assured me that it was one of the worst crimes he had ever handled. Pursuant to this declaration, I washed up, took off my greasy overalls and donned my best judicial garb, which consisted of a clean blue chambray shirt and khaki trousers. The next step in getting ready for the trial was to pick up my copy of the Revised Statutes and stick a six-shooter under my shirt. I was then prepared to function in the dual capacity of judge and sheriff. Upon my arrival at the building used for holding court, I found that quite a crowd had gathered to witness the trial. I opened court in the prescribed manner and told the officer to state his case.

The constable had arrested a Negro, and charged him with stealing some mechanics tools from a white man. The latter was born and reared in the North. When he first arrived in Texas, he had been one of the most militant and vociferous champions of the downtrodden colored man. He was particularly bitter about the way his dusky friends were treated by the Southern whites. Since coming to Mirando, he had spent most of his time in the Negro section of our village. After the complaining witness had taken the stand, I asked him the statutory question, "Did the defendant take those tools without your knowledge and consent?" His answer was, "No, I sold them to him on credit. When he did not pay for them on time, I had him arrested." It was readily apparent what had happened. The torch-bearing seller had enlisted the aid of the awe-inspiring constable, who was delighted at the opportunity to bully an humble Negro. I told the defendant that he was free and the case dismissed. The bad lawman then jumped up and demanded that the Negro pay him for the time and effort spent on his case. He threatened to pistol whip him if he failed to do so. I quickly arose and without drawing my own weapon, took the bully's gun away from him. After maneuvering him into the proper position, I applied the toe of my boot where it would do the most good. The erstwhile badman attempted to save face by telling the roughnecks that he was going after his Winchester. He would be right back and retrieve his lost reputation. The rifle must have been extremely hard to find, for he started after it over twenty-five years ago and has not yet returned. He was just another sample of the characters I had to deal with in the new oil patch along the Tex-Mex.

In the height of the boom, when the oil field boys sought drink and entertainment across the river, many owners of saloons and honky-tonks in Nuevo Laredo received a liberal education in American business methods. They also learned about hot checks from the Mirando City residents who had partaken of their commercialized hospitality. One day an automobile loaded with denizens of the dives from south of the border drove up in front of the justice of the peace office. A spokesman for the litter came in with a sheaf of checks that had been given to the keepers of the various dens of iniquity. There was nothing remarkable about the checks themselves, for they bore the usual mark of "no account," when presented at the Laredo banks. The notable features were the formidable array of signatures they bore. Among the names signed to these dishonored drafts were John D. Rockefeller, Cornelius Vanderbilt and many other wealthy people. This sort of deception and wholesale forgery caused the hardworking inhabitants of Nuevo Laredo to issue a sweeping manifesto, "cash on the bar, no more checkies".

Some eminent anthropologists maintain that the skull of an African is no thicker nor different in structure than that of a Caucasian. Nevertheless, there must be something about the heads of Negroes that enable them to withstand blows that would crush a white man's cranium like an egg shell. A demonstration of this theory took place in a dirt contractor's gang, while building a fire wall around some oil tanks near Mirando. An Afro-American fixed up an elaborate variation of the old time "fool killer". It was to be used to slug his rival for the affections of a dusky belle. The intended victim and the jealous suitor were mule skinners working on the same job. This bludgeon was made out of a piece of steel pipe, an inch and a quarter in diameter and about five feet long. It was deadly enough in its natural state, but he made it heavier and more rigid by painstakingly filling the hollow part with clay, and packing it down with a ramrod. Holding the cudgel in both hands, he slipped up behind his enemy and dealt him a terrific lick on the head. A colored teamster testified that he heard the sound and thought it was made by a mule kicking a scraper. When the witness looked around, the victim was standing on his head, so great was the force of the blow.

I was talking to some friends in town when a frightened, bareheaded Negro ran up to me and said, "Cap'n, (I was not a captain at that time, but to old time colored folk every man who carried a pistol was

'Cap'n') a nigger knocked me in the head a while ago." "Who did it and where is he now?" I asked. He replied that his assailant was at the dirt moving job about a mile from town. I told the injured man to go on to the doctor's office and that I would take the guilty one into custody. He declined the medical attention, however, with these words: "No, suh, I wants to go with you and see you arrest him. He said that he would kill any law who tried to take him." The poor fellow insisted on going back with me. He apparently hoped that his attacker would try to carry out his threat, and get killed in resisting arrest. The fact that this wounded Negro, after having been stood on his head by a blow from a stuffed iron pipe, was able to get up and walk to town in the hot sun should be ample proof of the thickness of his skull. The wielder of the fool killer reconsidered his plan to kill the arresting officer and was soon securely chained to a telephone post, pending transfer to the county jail in Laredo.

Judge Valls was immensely pleased with my administration of the affairs in Justice Precinct No. 5 of Webb County. He expressed great relief that the condition he had previously described as "anarchy" had ceased to exist. I was introduced around the courthouse as "the man of the hour in Mirando City" and was most gratified when the district attorney told the grand jury that "Sterling is the best justice of the peace in Texas."

At that time, justice courts operated under the iniquitous fee system. Neither the arresting officer, the county attorney nor the judge received any compensation unless the defendant was convicted. This relic of barbarism often worked a grave injustice. In addition to my row with the "constabule," I had several other clashes with deputies who thought I ought to fine everybody they haled into court. One of them asked, "Are you trying to starve us to death, and do you yourself want to work for nothing?" My answer was, "I need the money as bad as any of you, but I will not find an innocent man guilty just to collect a fee. That infamous practice breeds disrespect for all law enforcement."

Never having done any sordid, routine police work, I knew very little about family fights and rows of that nature. It is the general belief, however, that if anybody, especially an officer, interferes in one of these brawls, both the woman and man will jump on the peacemaker. My sole experience in one of those marital disturbances took place in one of the cheap wooden hotels in Mirando City. One evening just before sundown a girl about twelve years old ran to my home and cried breathlessly, "Please come quick. Papa is killing Mamma." I ran home with the child and saw that the man had a hammerlock on the woman's arm. She was in great pain from the twisting. I wound up and knocked him sprawling on the floor with my fist, putting some extra steam into the blow as part payment for the husband's cowardly act. Instead of the proverbial resentment toward me for hitting her spouse, the lady appeared to be most grateful for my timely though vigorous aid. She also sarcastically reminded him that there was a lot of difference between fighting a man and beating a woman, as had just been demonstrated. I locked him up in a boxcar on the Tex-Mex side track, which was used in lieu of a calaboose. Next morning he would be transferred to the county jail. Along about midnight, his wife came to my house, with her arm still in a sling. In her other hand she held a pillow. She informed me that her husband never could sleep well without his favorite headrest. Would I please unlock the car so she could take it to him?

My justice court trials soon came to be known as great attractions. They were held in a sort of community hall, and a large audience was usually on hand. Most of the members of the Webb County bar practiced before my tribunal at one time or another. Quite a few amusing incidents took place. In one case that was being tried, Attorney C. B. Neel referred to his client as a "gratuitous bailee." I stopped Mr. Neel, who is still my good friend, and solemnly warned him not to use profanity in my court. The joke backfired on me, however, when the elderly attorney who represented the other litigant arose. In a kindly, learned and patient manner, he explained to the Court that the expression I objected to was a legal term, and that the counsel was not using swear words.

Chapter 8
LOS OJUELOS

Just south of Mirando City lies a picturesque and historic ranch. From the existence of several underground springs, it is called Los Ojuelos. It would be more fitting to reverse the names, for Los Ojuelos antedates the upstart oil town by more than a hundred years. The houses at the rancho are built of solid rock, although some people erroneously refer to them as adobes. The *ojuelos,* or small springs, are the only natural water below Laredo, between the Nueces River and the Rio Grande. During the Civil War, numerous wagon trains and ox carts laid over here for water and rest while hauling baled cotton to Mexico. After these caravans crossed the Rio Grande, they proceeded down the river on the Mexican side to Bagdad. From this Gulf port, the cotton was loaded on British and other foreign vessels. All Confederate ports were blockaded by Union warships, but they had to lay idly by while the money crop of the South was shipped from Mexico to the European markets.

The *hacienda* of Los Ojuelos was owned by Don Eusebio Garcia, a courtly gentleman whose wife's ancestors had been granted the land by the King of Spain. Title to this property was based on this original Spanish land grant, and had never passed out of the hands of the family. He and I became fast friends and he offered me the use of a good rock house on the ranch. I promptly and gratefully accepted. The dwellings were built for the Southwest Texas climate, their thick walls and high ceilings making them cool in summer and warm in winter. We spent nearly three years at this hospitable ranch, and have nothing but pleasant memories of our Latin American neighbors. During the entire time, not a single unpleasant incident happened.

At one time, most of the salt consumed in northern Mexico came from a lake in Hidalgo County, Texas. It is called El Sal del Rey. Wooden wheeled *carretas* were used to transport this necessary commodity, and they were drawn by multiple yokes of oxen. For convenience and protection, they traveled in groups of a dozen or more. Going and coming, they stopped at Los Ojuelos. The bull-whackers used long, heavy whips, made of plaited rawhide. All were experts in the art of popping them, and the reports sounded like cannon shots. They vied with each other in making the loudest noise. Don Eusebio told me that when he was a youth, this practice greatly annoyed the ranch people. They would send a rider to meet each incoming wagon train. The boss would be warned that if his men persisted in cracking their whips, they would be denied the privilege of watering at the springs.

One warm spring morning when our baby daughter was a little over a year old she was in a jump swing on one end of the front gallery. She appeared to be fascinated by something on the floor, and was kicking at it with her tiny knit slipper. Her mother was horrified to discover a rattlesnake coiled under the swing. It had crawled up on the porch to bask in the sun. My wife, who comes from pioneer stock, including an ancestor in the battle of San Jacinto, maintained her presence of mind in this grave emergency. She did not scream or run toward the child, but called to Juan Flores, who lived across the narrow street. He slipped to the gallery corner and caught the snake by the tail, jerking it away before it could strike. This episode is a fair sample of pioneer life on the border and of the fealty of our neighbors.

The only other Anglo-American residents of Los Ojuelos were William W. Allen and Joseph S. Morris. They occupied a rock house across the plaza from our home. Mr. Allen was a drilling contractor, a bachelor and altogether a rugged character. He wore a large Stetson hat, uncreased after the manner of early Texans, and nearly always

Joseph S. Morris (in car) and W. W. Allen on
Main Street, Mirando City, during the oil boom.

carried a Colt forty-five single action six-shooter. His fearlessness had
earned him the distinction of being selected as the first driller to take
a rotary rig to California. Cable tools were used exclusively in that
state, and with them it took a long time to drill an oil well. Employment on one of these protracted jobs was often referred to as "home-
steading." The native sons met the importation of rotary rigs with
open hostility. By comparison, it made their method look inferior. No
love was lost between the exponents of the two methods. The cable

tool men called the rotary crews "swivel necks" and the rotarians called their competitors "rope chokers." Mr. Allen had several other picturesque and descriptive names for them, but they are all unprintable.

Joseph S. Morris was a much younger man. A native of Tennessee, he had started in the Somerset field as a roughneck, and now worked for Mr. Allen as head driller. By dint of industry, ability and integrity, he became a member of the firm. He spent many evenings at our house. On one of these visits he discussed with me the advisability of asking his employer for a partnership. I urged him to take this step, and pointed out that it would be a case of a worthy young man teaming up with a good older one. Such a combination was bound to succeed. My opinion has been vindicated. Mr. Allen passed away several years ago, and today the junior partner operates the superb drilling company under the name of Allen and Morris. A younger brother, Will Crews Morris, spent his vacation in Los Ojuelos. He often performed K. P. duty for Mrs. Sterling, taking his pay in pies and cookies. After graduating from the University of Texas Law School, he became the firm's general attorney.

Don Eusebio Garcia's best friend and most emulated idol was Thomas Atlee Coleman. He was a native of Goliad County, a third generation cowman and one of the really great cattle kings. Don Tomas was *muy simpatico*. This trait plus his magnetic personality and courtly bearing carved for him an exalted niche in the esteem of the Latin American rancheros. His vast influence was felt in both State and National politics. When in his company, I always felt that I was in the presence of a big man.

When T. A. Coleman's star was at its zenith, the talk of oil development in Southwest Texas was a mere rumor. Nevertheless, he and Don Eusebio Garcia once made an oral agreement. While driving over one of the Coleman ranches, the two *compadres* fell to discussing their chances of finding liquid gold. Half jokingly Don Tomas spoke of the ups and downs of the cattle business, and the desirability of having a few oil wells to tide over a broke cowman. Turning to his companion he said, "Eusebio, if oil is found on my ranch, I'll give you a good forty acre lease, and if production is brought in on Los Ojuelos, you can assign me the same deal, what do you say?"

"Hecho," replied Don Eusebio, which is equivalent to saying "Done," in English. The great slump in the livestock business that followed World War I caught beef baron Coleman over extended. His mighty cattle empire crumbled and fell. Geologists had for many years been interested in the *ojuelos,* or subterranean springs, on the Garcia ranch, and the Reynosa Escarpment that divided Don Eusebio's land. Both these phenomena proved to be good markers, and an oil field was brought in on the Garcia property. This windfall came almost simultaneously with the collapse of the cattle business. Don Eusebio was a man of his word.

In 1923, I had one of the most heart warming experiences of my life. I drove Don Tomas Coleman and his faithful friend, Don Eusebio Garcia, out to look at the Coleman oil wells on the Garcia land. It was most touching to hear those two patriarchs exchange regards and compliments. Don Tomas said that the money he and his family were living on at the time came from the wells that he owned through the word of a friend. It reminded me of a text I once heard an old time preacher use in a sermon. The good man said, "In those days there were Giants." Both of the old *companeros* seemed to sense that it would be their last drive around any ranch together. It was a great privilege for me to be the one selected to accompany them. A few months after our ride, Don Tomas went to the Last Roundup.

Don Tomas Coleman's ranch brand *El Cometa,* the comet, was a well known livestock symbol on the ranges of Texas and Mexico. Horses wearing this famous iron were in high favor with the Rangers. They were also preferred by contest ropers whose work demanded mounts with speed, stamina and cow sense. One of these *Cometa* horses figured in an incident that made a lasting impression on Will Rogers.

The citizens of San Antonio formerly staged an elaborate event called the International Fair. In addition to various other attractions, they invited the top cowboys of the cattle country to meet there for a series of steer roping contests. These events provided the setting for a coined-on-the-spot term, which was quickly added to the roper's glossary. The method used at these old fairs in tripping an animal, or "busting" him so hard that he can easily be hogtied, is still known to veteran cowmen as "fairgrounding."

The climax of this wild and woolly sport was reached in the fall of 1902 when two teams of three men each met for a matched roping. Large sums were wagered on the outcome. One outfit was sponsored by **Don Tomas Coleman**. Because all the boys were from the cactus country, he named them Coleman's Pear Eaters. They were Dr. **Lew Blackaller**, **Jim Proctor** and **Jack Hill**, with several alternates. The other team was called the Friscos. They were the proteges of **Colonel Zach Mulhall**, livestock agent of the St. Louis & San Francisco Railroad. It was composed of **Clay McGonigal** and **Ellison Carrol**, who alternated for several years as world's champions, with **Jim Hopkins** making the third member. Clay McGonigal was asked by a newspaper reporter to give the requisites of a good contest roper. He laconically replied, "Just a race horse and a dern fool." When the total time was figured, the Pear Eaters had won by five and one-fifth seconds.

Each contestant roped three steers. The last one drawn by **Jack Hill** made a wild dash and jumped over the fence. Everybody in the crowd thought that this tough break would lose the match for the Pear Eaters. He was riding a sorrel *Cometa* horse and was only a step behind. Jack did not hesitate. He jumped the gallant horse over the fence, roped his ox and tied him on the outside.

In 1927 when Will Rogers passed through Laredo on his way to Mexico, several of us met him at the early morning train. We went to a local hotel where one of the civic organizations had prepared a breakfast in his honor. Several other sightseeing tours were planned, but he wanted to do as little of this as possible. Calling me to one side he said, "Let's get away from this. I would like to see some of the Rangers and cowboys."

He told me that in 1902 he was just starting out as a rope spinner under the "nom de lasso" of The Cherokee Kid. He continued, "I went to the International Fair in San Antonio with Colonel Zach Mulhall's bunch. A man from this part of the country pulled off the best piece of roping I ever saw." He then described Jack Hill's fence hurdling feat, without omitting a single detail. "That man is one of my best friends," I told Will. "He lives in Laredo now. Let's go see him." He replied, "That's fine. I had rather see that old timer than all the chambers of commerce in Texas."

We drove out to Jack Hill's home. I introduced the two ropers and

Ranger Camp at Los Ojuelos in Webb County. Left to right-Ranger Ed Harrel, Sergeant (later Captain) Light Townsend, Mrs. W. W. Sterling and daughter Inez, Ranger Hays Wallis, Ranger W. A. Dial, Ranger Chel Baker and W. W. Sterling. Inez had her experience with the rattlesnake on the gallery of this old rock house.

they had a wonderful conversation. Will was especially interested in the fence jumping incident. "You are absolutely right about every part of it, Mr. Rogers," said the old brush popper, "but I can't seem to remember you." The Great American replied, "You had no reason to remember me, Mr. Hill. You were the star of the roping contest, and I was only a punk kid."

The Garcias were glad to furnish a camp house for the Rangers, as well as corrals for their horses and pack mules. The presence of Rangers and a justice of the peace at the ranch was a guarantee that all predatory people would keep their distance.

The house next door to ours was used as the headquarters of Captain Wright. Members of his famous Company D included Sergeant Light Townsend, Rangers W. A. Dial, Ed Harrel, Hays Wallis, Lake

Webb and Chell Baker. We did not see a great deal of them, as they spent most of their time on long horseback scouts. When not engaged in this duty, the boys paid us frequent visits. Our year and a half old daughter was very fond of them. One day my wife wanted to call on some friends in town. She would be gone about an hour. The Rangers offered to keep the baby, provided they could take her to their camp. The next day one of them inquired, "How did the baby sleep last night, Mrs. Sterling?" "Fine," she replied, "why do you ask?" "Well," the Ranger explained, "that poor little thing seemed to be so hungry that we gave her some *frijoles* and coffee." This differed somewhat from the formula and carefully selected diet her mother prepared for her, but she suffered no ill effects from the crude Ranger fare.

Rangers scouting in the warm climate of Southwest Texas traveled light. Notwithstanding this fact, it was necessary to take along a few essentials. The camp equipment and spare ammunition of Company D were transported on pack mules. Only a man who has spent hot, weary days keeping these ornery hybrids in motion can appreciate their perverse natures or imagine their laziness. Captain Wright cherished the sluggish animals, and would not permit his pets to be belabored. Lake Webb had the misfortune to draw the assignment of prodding the beasts of burden, and of making them keep pace with the horses. This was a discouraging task, but the resourceful lad finally found a way to increase their speed. Out of an old inner tube, and a natural mesquite fork, he fashioned a stout slingshot. When one of the long eared loafers lagged, the muleteer, who was bringing up the rear, surreptitiously pelted him with a missile from his rubber weapon. When one of the pack mules was thus aroused and hightailed it to the front of the column, the captain declared. "The heel flies sure are bad in this part of the country."

Los Ojuelos was the most strategic point from which to intercept the numerous pack trains engaged in the profitable enterprise of transporting tequila. Before any of my red nosed friends contract a mild case of D.T.'s at the thought of Rangers enforcing liquor laws, an explanation of their activities along this line might be in order.

Apprehending violators of the eighteenth amendment was always a distasteful duty to the Rangers. They were never interested in the cargoes of pack trains, as such. Other serious factors were involved in the movement of this illicit liquor. Too often they escaped the notice of an uninformed and thirsty public. The tequila bearing caravans, convoyed by rifle escorts, constituted an armed invasion of the United States. They had to be dealt with as foreign enemies, and not as ordinary domestic bootleggers. Furthermore, the cattlemen of Southwest Texas were engaged in the eradication of fever ticks. This program had strained their credit to the limit and severely tried their souls. In the heavy brush pastures preferred by the *tequileros,* it was impossible for the ranchmen to gather and dip one hundred per cent of their herds. This was a Government requirement as well as a biological necessity. The cattle had to be dipped every fourteen days in order to arrest the life cycle of the prolific parasites, and any interruption of this schedule resulted in untold trouble to the ranchmen. After a cowman had been credited with several dippings, or had partially cleaned his pastures by vacating, it was most disheartening to find that a bunch of ticky horses and mules had re-infested his premises. The depredating rum-runners cut any fence that happened to be in their line of travel, as they sought to avoid leaving telltale horse tracks in the gates. This further hampered tick eradication efforts for it allowed the cattle from an infested pasture to mix with those in a clean one. The captured horse stock of the bootleggers were immediately driven to the nearest vat and dipped, but every place they touched became an exposure, if not a re-infestation. In several instances, cowmen had to build many miles of otherwise unneeded fence as a result of pack trains passing through their country.

A more serious reason for the Ranger's warfare on these freebooters was the fact that the *tequileros* would not hesitate to kill anybody who happened to cross their trail. The victims might be ranchmen on whose land they were trespassing, geologists and oil men prospecting in the border country, or innocent tourists who just chanced to be opening a gate when the invaders rode up. Gregg Gibson, only son of pioneer cowman James Gibson, ran the Barreneño Ranch in Duval County. This splendid young man, while riding his own pasture and attending to his own business, was murdered by a pack of foreigners, who were in our country breaking our laws. Gregg Gibson came by Los Ojuelos to see me only a week before the tragedy and I was deeply saddened by his death. My heart went out to his father, who had been my friend for many years. This description of the conditions as they existed in the days of tequila running should show that the Rangers were protecting life and property in the border counties. They were not scouting to deprive some thirsty toper of his firewater.

The method used by the Rangers and the United States Mounted Inspectors of Customs, practically all of whom were ex-Rangers, was to ride a course roughly paralleling the Rio Grande until they cut the sign of a pack train. The customs men, being Federal officers, were interested in the smuggling aspect of both liquor and livestock illegally brought into the United States. The Rangers wanted the bandits because they were violating many State laws. They cut fences, infested pastures with ticks, and jeopardized the lives of Texans. The men in both Services were first of all Americans, and they combined forces to repel the invader. Regardless of where their individual interests or duties lay, the Rangers and mounted customs inspectors worked in perfect harmony. The only rivalry or friction emanated from some of the higher-ups who were political appointees.

After picking up a trail, the Texans followed it until the pack train was overtaken, and then a battle, usually a running one, would take place. Sometimes the bootleggers would attempt to make a stand, but the first volley from the Rangers generally put the survivors to flight. While tracking a tequila pack train, we could always tell how much of a fight they would put up, by the number of empty bottles found along the trail. If the bootleggers drank a good deal of their own product, they would do a lot of shooting before they checked out. On the border it was believed that if a rabbit got a drop of tequila, he would spit in a bulldog's eye. That was the way it affected the rumrunners. By way of compensation, if the fiery liquor improved their valor, it did not help their already bad marksmanship. The considerable number of shallow and unhallowed graves along the old tequila trail give mute testimony to the superior skill of the American rifleman. As justice of the peace, I was called upon to hold inquests over several of these permanent residents. One of the boys, as an impromptu epitaph, wrote on the headboard this self-explanatory couplet: "Here lies the body of a rumrunning stranger. He tried to kill a Texas Ranger."

A new low in diplomatic relations between the two countries was reached when the Department of State, or its equivalent, in Mexico made a claim against our Government for the lives of their citizens who were killed in this country, while engaged in bootlegging. The collector of customs in the Laredo district called on me for some facts to give our State Department. The data supplied needed to be written on asbestos paper, so hot was my reply, but it must have had the desired effect, for they never called on me again.

The next step was to gather the captured bottles into one pile, and dispatch a man to the nearest ranch house. He reported the seizure by telephone and called a justice of the peace, if there were any candidates for an inquest. The liquor was destroyed on the spot, while the horses, mules and saddles were sold at a customhouse auction. The only good that I ever knew tequila to do anybody was when poured on the scalp to kill dandruff. Used in this manner, it makes a crude but effective germicide.

A larger number of these pack trains succeeded in keeping their rendezvous with upstate bootleggers, and making delivery without interference. Their high percentage of success was due in a large measure to the fact that the liquor runners closely resembled the natives both in appearance and language. This racial similarity, plus a generous local distribution of the lucrative profits, greatly hampered the efforts of both Rangers and custom inspectors. The smuggled bottles were transferred to high powered automobiles, which were waiting in and around Duval County. From this base the wet goods were forwarded to the interior. The cultural center of San Diego, in addition to its other claims to notoriety, became the tequila capital of Texas. The number of *mescaleros* infesting that vicinity may be imagined from a story that went the rounds in those spirited days. An enterprising denizen of San Diego promoted a baseball game between the bootleggers and the consumers. The latter were not able to complete their nine locally. They were compelled to send to Alice for reinforcements. Here they experienced no difficulty in making up the required number, with a goodly supply of substitutes in reserve.

In addition to other hazards that confronted pioneer Texas ranchmen, a sinister menace threatened them in Austin. Lurking around the General Land Office like a flock of vultures were a group of greedy promoters known as vacancy hunters. Each newly discovered oil field opened a happy hunting ground for their operations. The legitimate land owner was their natural prey. A former employee of the Land Office, William Sydney Porter, made a careful study of the frauds perpetrated in this important State department. Under the nom de plume of O. Henry, Will Porter wrote two heart rending stories about the injustices practiced by land sharks, using the knowledge he had gained by actual experience. In describing the claim jumper's dealings in the General Land Office, the king of short story writers declares, "The trail of the serpent is through it all."

A group of these people discovered some excess acres in the original Spanish land grant of Los Ojuelos. This happened immediately after oil had been found on that ancient domain. In the litigation that followed, Don Eusebio Garcia, with his attorneys, witnesses and interpreter went to Austin. I accompanied him on this trip. The jurisdiction in Land Office cases lies in Travis County. While the Garcia land case was being heard in the civil District Court, another trial was going on across the hall in the criminal court room. The young district attorney, Dan Moody, was prosecuting two Mexicans for robbing some railroad cars. He needed a Spanish interpreter and I was selected to act in that capacity.

At the conclusion of the Ojuelos land grant case, our party left the Travis County courthouse, and started walking south on Congress Avenue, where we met a parade. Marching in it were a group of citizens from Williamson County. In the van were two men carrying a wide banner bearing the legend "Dan Moody for Attorney General." Having just met the candidate and being deeply impressed by him, I deemed it a fortunate circumstance to be in Austin at the launching of Moody's career as a statesman.

The unjust law covering vacancies had not been repealed at the time of the Ojuelos suit, and the land grabbers were awarded title to their booty. When we got back to the ranch, Don Eusebio's wife chided him about the deal he had gotten in Austin from the Americans. The elderly don replied, "Yes, I lost the lawsuit. But in the United States they only took a piece of my land. In Mexico they would have taken it all."

At Los Ojuelos the ranching operations were in the hands of Amador

E. Garcia, only son of Don Eusebio. He was the apple of his father's eye. The younger Garcia was every inch a cowman, and a worthy pupil of the fabulous Tom Coleman. He ran cattle in vast numbers over the brush lands of Southwest Texas and northern Mexico. He always supplied me with top saddle horses. His carefully selected *remuda* was made up of the finest horseflesh that careful breeding, good judgment and ample money could secure. Amador put on some excellent rodeos, or *jaripeos,* in Laredo. This was back in the days before they became too commercialized for genuine ranchmen. He brought the most skillful *charros* from Mexico and the top cowboys from the United States together. In friendly rivalry they competed for rich prizes. Dick Shelton of Tilden, the greatest steer wrestler or bull dogger the world has ever known, received his first pay for this daring act from A. E. Garcia. I was Amador's assistant in this cowboy-*charro* contest and in later years flagged Dick Shelton in many big time rodeos.

My reputation for harmonious relations with Mexicans was gained by according fair treatment to people of all classes. Upon taking over in the Mirando district, I made it clear that the Mexicans were not going to be blamed for everything bad that happened in that vicinity. By the same token, if a Mexican was guilty of any wrongdoing, he would be fittingly punished. The overworked custom of pointing the finger of guilt at Mexicans on general principles was definitely ruled out.

A noted border tragedy that occurred a few days before I arrived in Mirando City was the killing of United States Customs Inspector Robert Rumsey. It happened near the old town of Torrecillos, which is now named Oilton. Rumsey was an ex-Ranger and a terror to smugglers. On many occasions they had conspired to kill him. He finally became a victim of overconfidence and failure to attend to the vital details of protecting himself and his comrades.

Rumsey, Frank Smith and Bill Musgrave were patrolling the Corpus Christi road about thirty miles east of Laredo. Rumsey was in charge. Smith and Musgrave were young men, just starting in the Service. They naturally depended on the senior officer for leadership. It is a well-established fact in brush fighting that rifles are the essential weapons. Six-shooters are worthless at the longer ranges. For a border

Robert Rumsey, killed by rum runners near Mirando City in 1922.

officer to be caught away from his Winchester has always been regarded as a fatal error. Ex-Ranger Bob Rumsey was thoroughly schooled in all phases of his profession, and this is probably the only time he ever strayed from that rule.

They were scouting in Rumsey's car. Besides their six-shooters, Smith and Musgrave were armed with Winchesters. Bob Rumsey, in addition to a brace of pistols, carried a double barreled shotgun. The inspectors met two trucks carrying tequila, which they stopped and seized. Rumsey placed Frank Smith in one of them and Bill Musgrave in the other.

He ordered them to drive toward Laredo while he followed behind in his car. The senior inspector did not instruct the two recruits to take their Winchesters. He kept them in his car, and was thus in possession of all the long range weapons.

The procession reached a point on the old gravel road just under the escarpment, or *el bordo*. Here they met an automobile going east, and in it were five heavily armed rumrunners. They had been sent to convoy the two captured loads of tequila. After they had passed the trucks, Rumsey, who was bringing up the rear, stopped his car. He started to get out and flag them down. When he was about half-way out of the car, the bootleggers opened fire and killed him. They took possession of the dead man's automobile, with the rifles and the shotgun. Smith and Musgrave, being armed only with their pistols, emptied them at the killers and were forced to take to the brush. Frank Smith believes that he hit one of them with a long range shot from his six-shooter.

This encounter took place about three miles from Mirando City, and caused great excitement in the new oil town. I arrived there a few days later, and was appointed a deputy sheriff for Webb County. I had no part in the fight, but summoned many witnesses in the case to the grand jury. I subsequently rode on numerous scouts with Frank Smith and Bill Musgrave. Both were men of unquestioned courage, and Frank Smith was the best trailer in Southwest Texas. It is regrettable that a fine man like Bob Rumsey had to lose his life in this manner. No experienced border officer blamed Smith and Musgrave for their action during their baptism of fire. Frank Smith especially, exacted a heavy toll from the smugglers in later fights.

Captain W. L. Wright and Sergeant Jack Webb were on duty in a railroad strike at Cleburne. I was visiting them when we read about the killing of Bob Rumsey in the Dallas *News*. The Captain had scouted nearly every foot of that country, and was deeply moved by the death of his friend. While holding the newspaper in one hand, he jerked out his pistol and exclaimed, "Wish I'd a been there, boom, boom."

Numerous species of cactus, both great and small, are found in profusion around Los Ojuelos. Prominent among these is the peyote. It is a rare variety of the spiny family, which thrives in the semi-arid climate of that region. This drug-producing plant is highly prized by certain tribes of American Indians. They like to use it in their rituals and ceremonials. In former years, barrels filled with dried peyote buttons could be seen on the station platform at Aguilares. From there it was shipped to Oklahoma and other states with a large Indian population.

The Government finally declared it a narcotic, and forbade further shipments by common carrier. This order resulted in an annual motorcade into Southwest Texas. Many Indians, traveling in the most expensive automobiles, came after their cherished peyote. Most of the cars were equipped with every luxury, which even included electric fans. Numerous Latin residents of the area spent their entire time hunting peyote. They tried to keep a supply dried and ready for the wealthy Indians. It constituted an important money crop.

Members of the Osage tribe are reputed to be the richest people, per capita, in the world. One of their chiefs, Isabel Dinna, always came by our house for a visit. He was saddened by the prohibition imposed by the Government, and lamented their action in these words, "My friend, they have taken our land away from us. Why can't the Government leave us the medicine of our fathers?"

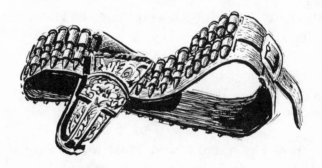

Chapter 9
LAREDO

THE Rangers suffered in morale, and lost much of their prestige under the Fergusons, even in the first administration of Ma. One day in Laredo I met a charming lady, wife of a Chicago railroad executive, who was stopping over on her way to Mexico. Her first words to me were, "I have just had a childhood illusion shattered. I've always wanted to meet a real Texas Ranger and on his native soil. I've just seen the captain stationed here. Imagine my disappointment and chagrin when I met, not the tall, tanned rider I had always visualized, but a flabby, pasty faced bartender." I hung my head as any good Texan would and tried to explain to the disillusioned lady that he was a Ferguson Ranger, and a typical representative of that administration.

During the first seige of proxy government, the Governor's husband announced that he was going to carry in the wood and water for his wife. It soon became apparent, however, that he dictated and she signed on the dotted line. His illegal activities in the highway department, the textbook board and his commercialized clemency were beginning to come to light. People wondered who was the real governor.

This confusion set the stage for an amusing incident that I witnessed in Laredo. It occurred under circumstances usually cloaked with great dignity and decorum. A group of aliens, seeking to become naturalized American citizens, were being examined by Federal Judge Joseph C. Hutcheson. While testing one applicant's knowledge of the United States he asked, "Who is governor of Texas?" The reply was "Ferguson." The Court continued, "Which one?" Consternation seized the anxious foreigner, and he had visions of being denied admission into the Land of the Free. He finally managed to answer, "I don't know." His relief knew no bounds when the habitually austere judge smiled and said, "Neither do I."

Dan Moody was duly elected attorney general. His accession to that high office was most gratifying to me and a boon to the people of Texas. It soon became apparent that a large portion of his time would have to be expended in curbing the forays on the highway and other departments by the impeached former governor. The young attorney general performed his duty with such vigor and skill that many ill-gotten dollars were recovered from fly-by-night road contractors.

After a year of unparalleled irregularities in the Governor's office, an outraged citizenry clamored for the termination of their regime. It had caused our State to be the laughing stock of the Nation. Voters demanded that Dan Moody, scourge of the Fergusons, become a candidate for governor. I actively supported him and, with Representative Robert Lee Bobbitt, went to a statewide gathering of his friends in Dallas. This huge meeting was attended by most of the prominent civic and political leaders of Texas. It was called after the first primary as a protest against the Fergusons' failure to keep their promise. Every student of Texas politics remembers that the Fergusons had agreed to resign if Moody led by one vote in the first primary. When he polled around a hundred thousand more, they welshed out of the pledge.

The old grandstand at the State Fair Grounds, forerunner of the Cotton Bowl, overflowed with people, and many stood on the field. A galaxy of eloquent speakers addressed the assembled throng, and each in his turn cited specific derelictions of the Fergusons. Two of these speeches made a lasting impression on me, and I have never forgotten them. One was delivered by former Governor William Pettus Hobby, and the other by the late John Boyle of San Antonio, prominent Catholic lay leader. Concluding his timely statements, Governor Hobby said: "Dan Moody has Jim Ferguson right where I had him in 1919. When the votes are counted after the second primary, it will be found that history has repeated itself."

Attorney Boyle was one of the most noted orators in Texas. He painted a vivid word picture of a case that involved a fiend in human

Governor Dan Moody

form who was pardoned by the Fergusons. (To borrow an expression from the radio and television, "neither names nor places will be disclosed, to protect the innocent.") Judge Boyle was particularly bitter about the treatment accorded a group of mothers who tried to see the Governor personally to protest the pardon of this monster. They were told by a secretary, "You will have to see Governor Jim." The audience was spellbound, and they listened to the speaker with rapt attention. During his excoriation of the Fergusons, one could almost hear the drop of a pin.

Attorney General Moody was elected governor by an overwhelming majority. The following January, I attended his inauguration in Austin. Robert Lee Bobbitt, one of the best friends I ever had, was elected Speaker of the House of Representatives. He threw his weight behind my application for a captaincy in the Rangers. Speaker Bobbitt urged that the first order of business be a housecleaning in the Service. However, Governor Moody had seen so much corruption in the highway department that he decided to give his first attention to that looted agency. Other sanitary improvements that always follow a Ferguson administration occupied so much of his time that it was not until April that Governor Moody got around to giving me my commission. It always gives me a great deal of satisfaction to acknowledge my debt of gratitude to Robert Lee Bobbitt for his powerful support in securing for me this appointment. The friendship of this distinguished jurist and statesman, formed in the early Mirando days, is one of my most treasured possessions. It has weathered the vicissitudes of many stormy years. This relationship includes his splendid son, Robert Lee Bobbitt, Jr., who served with distinction in World War II as an officer in the United States Navy. Robert Lee Bobbitt III and Galloway Calhoun Bobbitt are the namesakes of two illustrious grandsires. They make up the third generation of my friends, the Bobbitts.

My gratitude to Governor Dan Moody is deep and undying. He knows that I will always be his supporter and backer in any matter that may arise, be it personal, business or political. One of my most cherished customs, which has endured for many years, is sending him a greeting on June 1. This is Governor Dan's birthday.

During my Mirando City service, I did not once draw a pistol.

Chapter 10
BORGER

I WAS appointed captain of Company D, Texas Rangers on April 15, 1927, by Governor Dan Moody. Honorable Robert Lee Bobbitt, who at that time was Speaker of the Texas House of Representatives, sponsored me for the position. My boyhood ambition had been realized, and I was deeply grateful to those who made this possible. I was gratified even more twenty years later when Governor Moody told me that he had never regretted making the appointment. The other field captains in his administration were officers of rare ability, experience and integrity, each of whom was a credit to the Service. I was indeed fortunate and proud to serve with such an outstanding group of Ranger commanders.

Adjutant General R. Lamar Robertson immediately dispatched me to Borger, a new town that had sprung up in the Panhandle. Here the wildest oil boom in history was going full blast. It had gotten entirely out of control. Borger presented a new and unprecedented problem in the maintenance of decency and order. Unlike other oil fields heretofore found in Texas, it had no backlog of old timers to form a nucleus of good citizenship and law enforcement.

The promoter of the place, who named it for himself, had simply laid out his townsite on the Staked Plains, bringing all new people

Robert Lee Bobbitt

with him. He imported a bunch of professional oil field "laws" from Oklahoma, and these jackals were headed by a chief known as "Two Gun Dick." He even brought his own doctors and undertakers, the latter being paid $100 for interring paupers.

It was claimed that they would knock a drunk man in the head and bury him for the fee. The town had the dubious distinction of being the only one in the world with two names, Borger by day and "Booger" by night. Word quickly got out over the underworld grapevine that the town was wide open. "Anything goes in Borger," became the theme song of the biggest bunch of assorted criminals who ever congregated in an oil field. All of them proposed to cash in on the bonanza.

At this critical time, Texas had a chief executive whose record showed that he would not permit such conditions to flourish under his administration. Governor Moody began his official career as county attorney of Williamson County, and was soon advanced to district attorney. His outstanding service in this office attracted statewide attention, and he was elected attorney general of Texas. In each of these positions his actions proved that he regarded a public office as a public trust. As governor, Dan Moody would not hesitate to use all forces under his command to suppress lawlessness in any part of the State.

Several of his boyhood friends who then lived in Amarillo went to Austin and apprised him of the intolerable conditions existing in Borger. As a result of their visit, Boyd Gatewood, his private secretary, was sent to make an on-the-ground survey of the situation. While this report was being studied, three officers were killed there in three days. Governor Moody decided that the time was ripe to use the Rangers. He ordered Captains Frank Hamer and Tom Hickman, with detachments from their respective companies, to move into Borger.

I arrived at the boom town on Easter Sunday of 1927, and found the cleanup in full swing. Captain Hamer greeted me by quipping, "Judging from the time it took you to get here, you must have made the trip from Laredo on horseback and led your pack mule." The concern of the other two captains over my slow arrival soon became apparent. Their presence was required in places far removed from Borger. The departure of Hamer and Hickman left me in sole charge.

Several newspapers had sent special correspondents to the field, and they were always eager for hot news. Tom Caufield of Waco was the

Visitors at the Adobe Walls Monument in the Texas Panhandle during the first Borger Cleanup. Standing, left to right, Wesley Bryce, Captain W. W. Sterling and Captain Frank A. Hamer. Seated, Deputy Sheriff Jack DeGraftenreid and Ranger (later Captain) Hardy Purvis.

one I remember best, as he and I were particular friends. The gentlemen of the press asked me what tactics would be employed by the Rangers under my command. I replied that we were simply going to reverse the customary Borger procedure. Where the criminals had been killing officers, we were going to kill off some of the crooks.

This statement had a good psychological effect, and we did not have to shoot anybody. The exodus of crooks and parasites, which had started with the arrival of the first Rangers, was given added impetus by this announcement. They were strung out along the highways in droves, some in cars and trucks, others afoot. Outbound trains, both passenger and freight, also did a land office business in transporting these undesirables.

The Salvation Army had moved a unit into Borger shortly before our arrival. True to form, they were doing a great deal of good. We co-operated with them in every possible way, realizing that while our methods were different, our objectives were the same. The numerous slot machines we seized were taken to a vacant lot near the police station, where they were destroyed by blows from axes or sledge hammers. Many spectators came to witness the destruction of these one-armed bandits. Working men would step out of the crowd and say, "Let me use that axe awhile, Captain. I've always wanted to beat one of those mechanical hijackers. This is the only way it can be done." Some of the machines were of the two-bit variety, and the money they disgorged amounted to a considerable sum. All funds taken from them were publicly turned over to the Salvation Army.

Local cleaning and pressing establishments reported that they had on hand several hundred gaudy silk dresses which had been left behind by their owners. I informed them that we were not a part of the vice squad, and that the sudden departure of the unfortunate women was simply a case of the wicked fleeing. I suggested to the laundry men that they give the abandoned garments to the Salvation Army.

Numerous establishments known as "emergency hospitals," flourished in Borger. These sinister places housed many activities that would not be tolerated in a legitimate institution. They were almost without exception operated by doctors who had left their former abodes on account of the readiness with which they prescribed narcotics. These quacks would construct large, barn-like buildings out of cheap lumber, cut them up into small rooms, and recruit some "nurses" of the same stripe. Then they were ready for business. The unfortunates who fell into their clutches should have been called victims instead of patients. Many complaints were received from injured men who had been thrown out of these places after being robbed of their valuables.

Owing to the nature of their occupation, oil workers frequently received severe burns. I knew that nothing could be more soothing to them than alcohol rubs. On one occasion we captured a large truck load of pure grain alcohol that had been smuggled in from Mexico. It seemed a pity to pour out such a fine remedy. I sent a five-gallon can to several of the hospitals, hoping the contents might be used to alleviate pain and suffering. Along about midnight a riot call came from one of these institutions. Using our contribution as a base, the nurses had made up a batch of bathtub gin. All hands, from doctors to patients, were in a state of belligerent intoxication. That ended my noble experiment, and some worthy cases were no doubt deprived of the good alcohol can do when applied externally.

The corruption in Borger and vicinity was due largely to the fact that certain local officers were hand in glove with the criminals. One notorious resort was in full operation some ten miles from town. It had an intricate system of cellars and underground hideouts. These secret passages had baffled the half-hearted efforts of local officers, when they tried to get incriminating evidence against the proprietress. The real reason for her immunity from prosecution was that one of the powerful local politicians was under her influence.

I was seated in a Borger drug store one day when a Western Union messenger came up and handed me a letter. It was from a woman who said that her daughter had been enticed into this place, and it also contained a plan of the entire layout. The sorrowing mother appealed to us for help in breaking up this den of iniquity. She said that her only hope lay in the Rangers. The map was correct in every detail, and by following it we were able to make the biggest catch of liquor and gambling paraphernalia in the history of the Panhandle.

The Hutchinson County grand jury was in session, and the next day we were summoned to bring our evidence before them. The first witness called was Ranger Jim McCoy, one of the best men in the Service. He was asked to give them the name of the person who had told us about the raided place. McCoy replied that the only one who knew was the captain, and that they would have to ask him.

I went into the grand jury room, and was astounded to see the divekeeper's devoted friend sitting at the head of the table. He was serving as foreman of the body whose sworn duty was to investigate all forms of crime. After administering the oath to me, his first question was, "Who gave you the information about the place you all raided?" Obviously, the foreman was not concerned about the violation of the law that had taken place in his county. He only sought to identify the informer, so that he or she could be punished in the manner of the underworld.

My contempt and disgust knew no bounds. "The Rangers make it an inviolable rule," I told him, "never to divulge the source of our information." Before propounding the next question, the foreman assumed his severest official manner. "Captain," he said, "do you realize that if you refuse to answer a grand juror's question, you are liable to be remanded to jail?" "That law only applies to honest grand juries," was my rejoinder, "and if anybody gets locked up, it will be you. You are recreant to your trust as a grand juror, and are responsible for a lot of the crookedness in this county." He knew this to be the truth and was glad to excuse me from further questioning. This was probably the only time a witness appearing before a grand jury threatened to put the foreman in jail. It could have happened only under the conditions that existed in Borger.

After the cleanup had gotten well under way, Adjutant General Robertson asked me if we could use any additional men. I told him that we did not need any more Rangers, but that to handle our legal matters, we could certainly use a good lawyer. The man who came to Borger in response to this request was First Assistant Attorney General Galloway Calhoun. He had formerly served as district attorney in his home town of Tyler, and was a prominent Methodist lay leader. His Sunday school class was one of the largest in the Nation, and he also occupied a high station in the Masonic Lodge. He subsequently became Imperial Potentate of the Nobles of the Mystic Shrine.

His advent into the Borger campaign was an immense contribution to its success. This Christian gentleman not only handled the legal side in a masterful manner, but his moral and spiritual influence on everyone with whom he came in contact was of incalculable value. We were in Borger on the Sunday designated as Mother's Day. On that Sabbath morning, one of the most unique and touching religious services in church annals was held. Mr. Calhoun's father was a Methodist minister. The son could also fill any pulpit on short notice.

We rounded up a bunch of nondescript characters, both male and female. They were herded into a barn-like structure that was used as the public meeting house. Galloway Calhoun preached them a sermon that neither the motley crowd nor I will ever forget. The silver-tongued orator, with a fervor inspired by the sight of so many depraved people, delivered the best Mother's Day message anybody ever heard. There was scarcely a dry eye in the audience. I sat up on the rough lumber

Galloway Calhoun

rostrum behind the speaker with my pistol concealed but scout belt showing, and was as much enthralled by the spectacle as any hijacker in the house. This meeting did as much for the uplift of Borger as the combined efforts of a dozen officers.

Among the milling throngs on the streets and sidewalks of Borger were many human derelicts. I found one of these in a most unexpected place. Adjoining the police station, a large wooden building served as the jail. This insecure building had a huge chain fastened to the main floor beam. Prisoners charged with the more serious crimes were shackled to it. The inmates dreaded this barbarous but necessary fetter, which from the multiple prisoners it held, was known as the "trotline." One night I happened to walk by the jail door just as it was opened to admit a new occupant. I was shocked to see on the trotline a man who had been one of the most successful teaming and trucking contractors in the oil fields.

I told the jailer to bring him to the office. He consulted the register and informed me that it would be impossible to comply with my request. The one I wanted to see was a Federal prisoner and therefore not under the jurisdiction of State officers. Because of my acquaintance with the man, and as a personal favor to me, the turnkey consented to let me talk with him privately. When he was brought in, I exclaimed, "Great Goodness, Mr. Blank, what on earth has happened? How did you ever get in this shape? I would like to help you if it is possible to do so under the circumstances." With head hung in shame, he replied, "Bill, there is nothing you or anybody else can do for me. I thought there was a lot of easy money in oil field drug stores, and bought several of them. Before I knew it, they had me on dope and now I am addicted. They have me dead to rights." The only thing I could do for this former good man was to get the jailer to take him off the trotline until he was picked up by the Federal authorities. He died a short time afterwards but for many years his name continued to be on the equipment as a partner in the firm. Few, if any, of his former friends knew the story of his tragic end.

We handled a noteworthy case that illustrates the law-abiding natures of most early Panhandle settlers. Shine Popejoy, the king bootlegger of the Borger district, had an immense whiskey still across Bugbee Canyon in Moore County. We captured both the outfit and its owner and took

Texas Rangers at Borger, Texas April 17, 1927. (1) Not identified, (2) Private Hickman, (3) W. W. Taylor, (4) A. P. Cummings, (5) Captain Tom Hickman, (6) Capt. Bill Sterling, (7) Capt. Frank Hamer, (8) Mayor Miller, of Borger, (9) Charles Davis, Standing behind; (1) Pvt. Purvis (2) Pvt Ballard. Jail in the background contained the dreaded "Trotline."

the man to the county seat, where charges were filed against him. Upon our arrival in Dumas, we were astounded to find that there was neither courthouse nor jail in the town. The docket book was in the store of a local merchant and upon examination we found that this bootlegger's case was number eight on the list. Moore County at that time was thirty-six years old, and there had been less than a dozen criminal cases filed since it was organized. We took our man to Sherman County and also found that it had no adequate jail. The same was true of Hartley County. We finally landed him in the Dallam County jail at Dalhart. Sheriff Alexander, who received our prisoner, was killed by a jail inmate a short time after we were there. Before oil was discovered in the Panhandle, these sparsely settled counties had little use for jails or court-houses.

The Matt Kimes gang of bank robbers had been operating in and around Borger, swooping down from Oklahoma at frequent intervals. Ray Terrill's name was always connected with the gang, but I learned later from Ray himself that this was a mistake. Hardly a day passed that several "positive" tips did not come to us, that either Kimes or Terrill had been seen nearby. These false rumors caused us to make many dry runs.

The Kimes outfit, in a display of criminal bravado, set out to equal the record made by Jesse James. They robbed two banks simultaneously at Beggs, Oklahoma. The outlaws killed City Marshal McAnnaly, and to add lustre to their achievement, they shot up the town. One of their wild bullets killed a lady undergoing treatment in a dentist's chair. The gang separated, and two of them holed up in a rooming house on the Canadian River near Borger.

Captain Tom Hickman and I, Rangers Hardy Purvis and M. T. Gonzaulus, Deputy Sheriff Jack De Graftenreid, with several others, rounded up the place. We arrested Blackie Wilson and Hawk Whitehead. Part of the bank's money and some jewelry they had in their possession were recovered. The following letter is self-explanatory, the only inaccuracy being that Captain Hickman was the senior captain present at the capture. On the stationery of the First National Bank of Beggs, Oklahoma, dated December 3, 1927, it reads:

Governor Dan Moody, Austin, Texas. Sir: I am enclosing a copy of the Judgement and Sentence on Plea of Guilty of one Roy (Blackie) Wilson, who was captured in Borger, Texas by your Rangers led by Captain W. W. Sterling. I will appreciate it greatly if you will have this paper forwarded to Captain Sterling with the request that he make formal application to the Governor of Oklahoma for the reward which was offered for the apprehension and conviction of this bank robber. I told the Captain that I was going to make every effort to secure this reward for him and his men when I was in the Panhandle to identify Wilson, and I am doubly anxious that he receive it now. The arrest of Wilson and his subsequent confession made possible the rounding up of the worst gang of bank robbers this state has ever known. I am sending this letter to your office for the reason that I have no other way of getting in communication with Captain Sterling. If he will make application and inform me of his claim I will do everything that is necessary here. Very truly, (Signed) Glen E. Leslie, Vice-President, First National Bank.

Matthew Kimes and Raymond Doolin after their capture in Arizona.

We were informed that before the Beggs robbery, Kimes and his accomplices had taken what they called the "blood oath." In a finger pricking ceremony, each was reported to have sworn that if any member of the gang landed in jail, the others would get him out or die in the attempt. Taking them at their word, I thought maybe we could catch some of the other Beggs robbers by using our prisoner for bait. We took Wilson and Whitehead to a little wooden lockup in Pampa. It was not even a county jail, and we threw them in like they were petty bums. This was done without showing the slightest deference to the eminent position they occupied in criminal circles. Our indifferent attitude was a heavy blow to their ego, and they were a completely dejected pair.

Deputy Sheriff Larry Laramore of Creek County, Oklahoma, Glenn F. Leslie, vice-president of the First National Bank of Beggs, and young McAnnaly, son of the slain city marshal, came to Pampa to identify the robbers. The Oklahomans poked all manner of fun at the bandits. Deputy Laramore said, "I wouldn't have believed that such high powered bank robbers could have been held for three days and nights in such a flimsy jail." The prisoners were so disgusted with their accomplices that they confessed, waived extradition and disclosed the whereabouts of the others. Matt Kimes was captured in Arizona, at the Grand Canyon.

Wilson and Whitehead did not know that adequate steps had been taken to deal with any friends who might come to their rescue. Stationed at each corner of the cracker-box calaboose was a Texas Ranger. If the promised jail delivery had been attempted, there would have been some interesting developments.

Several years later I went to the Oklahoma penitentiary in McAlester, for a visit with Matthew Kimes and Ray Terrill. I was accompanied by Warren (Rip) Collins. This former Texas A. & M. football star and major league pitcher had forsaken athletics to become a Ranger. The bank robbers were confined in different parts of the prison. We had friendly chats with both of them. Terrill was working in the kitchen, and he offered to cook us a good steak for dinner.

Ray Terrill branded as false all the notoriety given to the so-called Kimes-Terrill gang. "We never did work together," he declared. "I was a burner. Matt was a daylight stickup man. He had that kind of nerve." By "burner" Ray meant that he opened bank vaults at night with electric or acetylene torches. Matthew Kimes, who was in the stockade reserved for life termers, was also very friendly. He enjoyed a good laugh about the dry runs we made after him. "I left Texas the day I heard the Rangers were ordered to Borger and never did go back," he said. He reminded me of a caged grizzly bear as he paced to and fro in his enclosure. Kimes had the most perfect pair of criminal eyes I ever saw, with one exception. These are owned by a notorious South Texas politician.

The city of Borger bought a new patrol wagon, and as the first phase of the cleanup began to slow down, the Rangers helped to break in this piece of municipal equipment. They would ask a suspicious looking loafer what he did for a living. The answer would usually be, "I am a working man." If an examination of his hands showed callouses or other evidence of honest toil, he was free to go about his business. But if he had the soft, white hands of a gambler or other parasite, the hoodlum wagon gained another passenger. By this simple method, we picked up many wanted men. The hand test proved to be almost infallible.

The only pleasant interludes during my otherwise drab service in Borger were the visits I made to the Hutchinson County division of the 6666 Ranch. Wherever brands and their origin are discussed, some cowboy will solemnly declare that Captain S. Burke Burnett, founder of the cattle empire bearing his name, won a fabulous pot in a poker game by holding four sixes. The narrator will further state that the lucky captain took his money and started in the cattle business. To show his gratitude to Dame Fortune, he adopted the winning hand as his brand. I have no authentic information on the matter, but can truthfully state that it was a lucky day for me when Sam Elkins, the foreman, and Matt Roberts, local manager, took me to the ranch. Matt said that they had been watching me for several days while driving around town, and could tell that I was a cowhand who needed to breathe some air that was free from gas fumes. The first good rest I had been able to get in a long time came to me that night. The quietness of the ranch and the clanking of the old fashioned Eclipse windmill soon made me forget the grim work at Borger. Those wooden mills pumped water with a rhythm that was music to the ears of a weary cowboy, especially when it brought memories of the same kind of *papalote* on the home ranch along the Rio Grande.

I had been accustomed to the ranches in Southwest Texas, where all the cow work was done by *vaqueros*. The 6666 was the first one I visited in the Panhandle, and all their hands were Americans. One of the favorite pastimes of the cowboys was to "hooraw." Just as soon as we became better acquainted, they started in on me. Boots worn in that part of the country were made with low tops, while the riders in the brush country prefer the high topped style for protection against rattlesnakes. One night as I started to bed, several of the boys came to my room. "Captain," said their spokesman, "will you do us a favor?" "Certainly," I replied, "what is it?" "Well," he continued with great solemnity, "we are going to take the hounds out tonight for a hunt, and we want to borrow one of your boots to tree the wolf in."

Working on the ranch were a dozen or more cowboys, one of whom was married. His wife had charge of the kitchen. I wondered how one woman could cook for that sized crowd, and it cost me a fine to learn the answer. After finishing my first breakfast there, I arose and thanked the lady for a good meal. The boys greeted this gesture with a burst of laughter and she said, "Captain, you're fined two bits." She had a rule that each man must carry his own dishes to the kitchen and deposit them in the "wreck pan." All who failed to do this were assessed the penalty. Ignorance of the custom was not accepted as an excuse. I thought the idea a splendid one, and later introduced it on a ranch in Arizona. The men there almost mobbed me for putting such fool notions in the heads of their womenfolks.

Sam Elkins was a Panhandle cowman of the old school and his entire life had been spent on the Staked Plains. In 1928, I attended the convention of the Texas and Southwestern Cattle Raisers Association in Amarillo, and he drove over to see me. When the old timer came up to my room at the hotel he told me that although past sixty years of age, this was the first time he had ever ridden in an elevator.

Late one night I received an emergency call from Amarillo. The excited speaker stated that a man on horseback had attempted to hijack a prominent local oil operator. The alleged holdup was supposed to have taken place about half way between Borger and Panhandle. The story did not ring true, as the day of mounted bandits was long past. I told the informant that the case would have our prompt attention, and that I believed it could be quickly solved. Without leaving my hotel room, I put in a call for Sam Elkins. He answered the phone and sleepily asked, "What in the world do you want with me at this time of night?" "Are the Four Sixes holding a herd in the lane near Panhandle?" I inquired. "Yes, we're trying to, but the dern oil men don't have enough sense to drive slow through the sleeping cattle. They keep on honking their horns. The whole bunch will probably stampede and be gone before morning." The ranch had always used that lane for a bed ground to save night herding. Sam had not taken into consideration the constant flow of traffic resulting from the oil boom in Borger.

111

I drove out next morning and talked to the cowboy who was on guard at the head of the lane. He said that when the Amarillo man came down the road at a high rate of speed, he simply tried to tell him to slow up. The oil tycoon thought he was being hijacked, and was afraid to stop. He and the horseman had quite a race, as well as a galloping cussing match. That was the whole story. Earl Callaway was an associate of the oil man. To show his appreciation of our work in Borger, he presented me with an unusual pair of boots. The tops were made of ostrich skin, and they invariably attracted attention among boot fanciers, both male and female.

My Ranger territory was the southwestern part of the state. It included several hundred miles of the Mexican border. Most of our work was along the Rio Grande and on ranches in that area. The Panhandle was in Captain Tom Hickman's district. He and Captain Hamer of the headquarters company handled the second Borger cleanup which also involved martial law. I had no part in it, but was deeply interested in the facts surrounding the murder of District Attorney Holmes. This assassination was the principal reason that Governor Moody invoked military rule in Hutchinson County.

When I was a Ranger captain there in 1927, Holmes represented many criminals. Apparently, when he changed to the other side of the law, one of his erstwhile clients killed him. The late district attorney tried to have me cited for contempt when I could not produce a badly wanted felon that he was trying to release on a writ of habeas corpus. His action in this case was the indirect cause of a new law being added to the civil code.

Under the old statute, a county sheriff was the sole custodian of his jail. He was responsible on his bond for every person who was put in it. If a case of mistaken identity occurred, or if for any other reason the wrong man was even temporarily locked up, he could be sued. The sheriff of Potter County asked us not to use his jail at Amarillo, because several suits had already been filed against his bondsmen. Reluctance of sheriffs to accept prisoners forced the Rangers to use other methods to hold men who were wanted in distant places. In order to thwart the criminal lawyers, they would take those charged with felonies out on "canyon parties." Only by this means could fugitives from justice be held and delivered to the proper authorities.

After my Borger experience with sheriffs who were afraid to put our prisoners in their jails, I determined to do something about it if the opportunity ever presented itself. Soon after being appointed adjutant general, I got my former schoolteacher, Representative A. P. Johnson of Carrizo Springs, to put a bill through the legislature that corrected this inequity. It may be found in Article 6866 of the Texas Civil Statutes. The measure relieves sheriffs from any liability that may arise from the placing of a prisoner in their jails by a State Ranger.

My last Panhandle oil field service was performed in a raid that demonstrated the lengths to which depraved people will go in order to avoid honest labor. It netted two typical Borger underworld characters, and rescued an innocent child from their clutches.

One day an oil worker came in and reported that a notorious dive was operating in the bed of a canyon near his lease. The owners were a hard looking man and a harder looking woman. Many criminals and thugs used the place as their hangout. He was afraid to pass it on his way to work. Finally, he had decided that the only way to get rid of the nuisance was to make an appeal to the Rangers. Our informant further stated that he had seen a nice looking little boy on the premises. In appearance he was so unlike the evil couple that they could not possibly be his real parents.

The party who went with me to investigate this resort was made up of Rangers Hardy Purvis, Jim McCoy, Sugg Cummings, and maybe one or two others. When we drove up to the building and got out of our car, a typical Oklahoma bootlegger ran out of the door and headed up the canyon slope. We ordered him to stop, but he paid no attention to the command and only increased his speed. The Rangers fired several shots to scare him, and I aimed one at a rock a few yards ahead and let go with my 30-06 Winchester. The bullet kicked up a lot of gravel, and some of it powdered the fugitive's face. Ranger Purvis, who subsequently became a captain, was right on his drag and made the capture. We asked the divekeeper why he did not stop at the first shot, and he explained that he thought we were local "laws." He was paying them a weekly bribe, and ever so often they would put on an act for the sake of appearances. The owner would run and the crooked officers would fire a few shots to give it the appearance of a bonafide raid.

The woman partner in crime looked, talked and acted worse than the man. We took the lad, who was about ten years old, outside and asked him where he lived. It was easy to see that there was something sinister in his story. He told us that he had been reared in the Presbyterian Orphans Home in Amarillo, and that the couple we had just arrested had adopted him a short time before. We found out that they had done this to give the place an air of respectability.

There was a huge trap door in the floor with a cellar underneath and this was full of corn liquor and slot machines. We immediately destroyed both of these illegal commodities, took the man and woman to jail and the boy to our hotel. He declared that he was now a Ranger, and that he was going to take the name of Bill Moody, "Bill" for the captain and "Moody" for the Governor. Jim McCoy took him in charge, and he soon became a great favorite with all the company.

We went to the orphan's home and reported the incident to the superintendent. He was dumbfounded at the way he had been hoodwinked by the male and female criminals. They had made a statement to the home declaring that they were Christians, and that their residence was within two blocks of a church and three blocks from a school. The superintendent assured us that in the future he would exercise a great deal more care. The good man said that he did not know such terrible people existed.

Shortly after this episode an order came from Adjutant General Robertson sending me back to my own Company D, which was stationed in Hebbronville. I was glad to have had a part in the first cleanup of Borger, the like of which will never be seen again. However, three months of rugged oil field service plus a thorough sand blasting by the Panhandle monsoons made the message most welcome. I had formed some lasting friendships in that region, particularly in Amarillo. Here I made up my Rotary attendance, being a member of the club in Laredo. I thanked all those who had helped me, and took my departure for the Rio Grande.

Chapter 11
CAPTAIN OF
COMPANY "D"

I WAS delighted to take over my own Company D which still did a great deal of scouting on horseback, and was rich in tradition. It had been commanded by such famous captains as Dan W. Roberts and John R. Hughes, both of whom I knew personally. The company had been under Captain Hughes longer than any other man, and his leadership enabled it to establish an unsurpassed record. After he retired I frequently sought his advice and counsel. Governor Moody had just purged Texas of a Ferguson administration, in which the Ranger Service suffered more than any other State agency, with the possible exception of the highway department.

My predecessor as captain was a tallow faced ex-bartender whose principal experience in riding had consisted of straddling beer kegs. The Fergusons had appointed so many incompetents of his type that some wag suggested arming their Rangers with bung starters instead of six-shooters. In the company at that time were two good men, Sergeant Light Townsend, who later became a captain, and Warren Smith of Frio County, but they were handicapped by the lack of a leader. I was determined to do everything in my power to restore the good name of the company.

Hebbronville, Jim Hogg County, was our station. At that time it was the largest cattle shipping point in the world. This region is one of the finest livestock countries in America. Its nutritious grasses include the prized tallow weed or *monogote,* which, in good seasons, will fatten cattle like a feed lot. Many wealthy ranchmen made headquarters there, and when drouth or low prices threatened to break most of them, oil was discovered on their lands. No scientist engaged in the improvement of cattle breeds has been able to excel the cross of oil wells on mortgaged cows. Many cattlemen were saved by this process and Hebbronville developed into a petroleum center as well as a cow town.

A noted landmark in the southwestern part of the county is the ancient and picturesque Rancho Randado. Its buildings are made of stone, though they are often erroneously referred to as adobes. It is a typical example of the early Mexican settlements found on both sides of the Rio Grande. The inhabitants built their houses close together in these ranchos for protection against Indians. Jim Hogg County was organized in 1913 and Randado, which had formerly been in Zapata County, became a part of the new one. When informed that his ranch was no longer in Zapata County, Don Bernardo de la Garza, owner of Randado exclaimed, *"Valgame Dios!* They have taken me out of the shoe and put me in the hog." *Zapata* means "shoe" in Spanish.

Hebbronville has successively been in Duval and Jim Hogg Counties. It has always been a law abiding community, where very few crimes of a serious nature were committed. The old time cowboys, however, considered it their inalienable right to play saddle blanket poker. Some of the civic minded ladies decided one time that inasmuch as Hebbronville was now a county seat, this pastime must be stopped. They turned over several likely names to the grand jury. Mike East was called before that august body for questioning. The district attorney had a wide reputation for getting information out of reluctant witnesses but Mike insisted that he was guilty of no wrongdoing. "What were you playing?" asked the prosecutor. "Cards," was the reply. "And what were you playing for?" was the next question. "Chips," answered the cowboy. "Aha," said the D. A., who figured he had trapped the card player, "and what was done with the chips after the game?" "I don't know, Judge," quoth Mike. "I didn't have any."

In 1927 I went to Atlanta, Georgia, with the eminent sculptor Gutzon

116

Borglum. Some years previously he had started the Confederate Monument on Stone Mountain. Factional strife among the patriotic organizations had caused the commission to be taken away from him and given to a second rate sculptor who was unable to finish it. Several prominent citizens invited Mr. Borglum to Atlanta for a conference, in the hope that arrangements could be made for him to complete the memorial. Included in the group were leaders of both the Daughters and Sons of the Confederacy, Editor Clark Howell, and the Venable family, owners of the mountain. The story of this ill-fated project is one that brings nothing but sorrow to the hearts of every Southerner, and is too long to be told here.

In addition to his talent as a sculptor, Mr. Borglum was a civil engineer. He had planned to utilize this science in following the natural contours of the huge monolith. Mr. Borglum made a full-scale model of his masterpiece which he alone could follow. When the committee of politicians dismissed him, it was destroyed.

Mr. Borglum maintained that the model was his personal property, but a powerful enemy succeeded in getting the grand jury to return an indictment against him. One of the local newspapers carried a front page picture of the sheriff holding up a pair of handcuffs that he said would be put on Gutzon Borglum when and if he came to Atlanta. I held him in high esteem, and we had many friends in common. They felt that he should not return to Georgia alone, and it was not hard for them to persuade me to go with him. His son, Lincoln, at that time a lad about fifteen years old, was the third member of the party. We took the train to LaGrange, Georgia, where we spent the night. Mr. Borglum registered at the hotel as "G. de la Motte," which was his middle name, and I signed as "William Warren," this being two-thirds of mine. This was the only time I found it expedient to use an assumed name.

The following day we went to the Venable home in Atlanta, where we spent several pleasant days meeting Mr. Borglum's friends and supporters. He decided to look over the work of his successor, even if it had to be done at long range. For this purpose, he procured a pair of binoculars.

I was standing at his side when he saw that the figures he had carved had been blasted away. His denunciation of that act of vandalism was made in classic language. Lincoln and I made a trip to the mountain, where visitors were taken on tours of inspection by professional guides. We agreed on a plan that would let us hear first hand what Mr. Borglum's enemies were telling the public. I was to play the part of a Texas tourist, and do all the talking. Lincoln was to remain silent, regardless of what might be said. He carried out his part perfectly.

I asked the guide why Mr. Borglum had not been permitted to finish the monument. This hireling replied that Mr. Borglum was a German, and they wanted a sculptor who was a native American. I informed him that he was entirely wrong, and that Mr. Borglum was an American of Danish descent who had been born in Idaho. The guide replied that he was simply following instructions from the management in making this statement. He did not know that he was talking to young Borglum. Lincoln, while clenching his fists and turning red in the face, showed remarkable self control in letting the falsehood go unchallenged.

Mr. Borglum was deeply interested in the history and traditions of the Rangers. He was eager to make a statue that would be a source of pride to Texans and reflect credit on the Service. He was born on a western ranch, and shared with his sculptor brother, Solon, the ability to carve the best horse figures in the world. This fact was demonstrated in numerous statues, from Gutzon's classic *Mares of Diomedes* to Solon's plunging spectacle, *The Stampede of Wild Horses*. The most observant and critical ranchman cannot detect a single flaw in the horse sculpture of either one of the Borglums.

It was a decided loss to the State when he could not carry out his plan for the statue, for the Rangers would never have been able to establish their world wide fame without the aid of good horseflesh. Mr. Borglum was kind enough to select me as the model for one of his Ranger figures. This choice was no doubt made on account of my six-feet-four-inch height, and he told me he liked the erect, easy way I sat in the saddle. The politicians and the depression combined to prevent the consummation of this dream.

I enjoyed my association with this great man, who had a magnetic personality and a keen sense of humor. He told me his method of trapping dilettantes who persisted in talking a good game. He would lend them a big book on the subject with which they professed to be familiar, and it would contain a large number of uncut leaves. If these

DRAWN BY LINCOLN BORGLUM
FROM A DESIGN BY GUTZON BORGLUM

pages were still intact, and he said they usually were, when the volume was returned after a "careful" reading, he would enjoy a quiet chuckle at the borrower's expense. Lincoln Borglum, now a thorough Texan, serves the South Texas Hereford Breeders Association as its president. He and I are still staunch friends.

The trip to Georgia kept me out of Texas about ten days, and shortly after my return, a most unusual incident occurred. The more a person knows about horses, the more astounding it becomes. Trainers in circuses as well as on ranches agree that all animals, whether wild or domestic, can sense fear in a man, and that they act accordingly. This theory was proved to my entire satisfaction by a young tenderfoot and an outlaw horse.

One day a pale faced boy got off the Tex-Mex train and walked to the Ranger camp, which was not far from the station. It was dinner time and we invited him to share our meal of beef, beans, *panoche* and coffee. He said that his home was in Pennsylvania and that he had come to Texas for the express purpose of joining the Rangers. While sympathizing with his ambition and adventurous nature, we were forced to tell him that he was a trifle young for our Service.

I told him, however, that I would give him a job on a ranch, where he could learn the work of a cowboy. He gratefully accepted the offer and I took him to a pasture I had leased about thirty miles from Hebbronville, called El Macho Bayo (dun mule), which was stocked with six hundred cows. It was in late August or early September when Southwest Texas is subjected to long periods of calm. In these times there is not enough wind to turn the windmills, and stockmen are forced to pump water for their cattle with small gasoline engines. Our pilgrim was a good mechanic and we promptly appointed him chief engineer, although he was eager to ride, rope and shoot.

Will McMurray, who subsequently served for six years in the Rangers as captain of Company D was at that time ranching in Jim Hogg and Starr Counties. He presented me with a fine sorrel horse that stood sixteen hands high and weighed around twelve hundred pounds. Captain McMurray said that he wanted me to ride a mount big and strong enough to carry a man of my size. Unfortunately, through bad handling, this horse became "spoiled" and threw everybody who tried to ride him, including some of the best *vaqueros* in Southwest Texas. We had given up trying to make a useful saddle animal out of him and turned him out in the big pasture. Here, from lack of work, he got fatter and meaner.

After installing my boy in camp, I went back to Hebbronville, telling him I would return in a couple of days, and would bring more gasoline for the engine. On my arrival in town, I found an emergency order sending me up the river on a five-day scout. After the second day I began to worry about the cattle and to wonder what they would do for water, but I stayed on the trail until our mission was accomplished. When at last I got back to Macho Bayo the engine was running and the cattle had all been watered. I asked the lad how he had gotten the needed gasoline and he replied, "I saddled up a horse and brought a can full from the store."

That Eastern boy, who had not ridden half a dozen times in his life had caught the outlaw horse as he came in for water, because he was the biggest and fattest one in the bunch. He then put a saddle on him,

Captain Will McMurray, now a prominent cowman of Southwest Texas. His unsurpassed knowledge of the country and people along the Rio Grande was gained by making countless scouts through the chaparral on horseback. A natural leader, his good judgment and command of the Spanish language eminently qualified him to serve six years as Captain of Company "D"

and mounted up with the five-gallon gasoline can in his hand. Resting the can on the saddle horn, he had ridden five miles to the store, filled it with gasoline and brought it back. No cowboy could have done this nor would one have attempted such a thing. The men who knew the horse and who heard the story were dumbfounded. The only explanation I can offer for this phenomenon is that the boy did not know enough to be afraid, or that the horse took a liking to him. It could even be that the day of miracles is not past.

Chapter 12
FALFURRIAS

IN 1928, Company D was moved from Hebbronville to Falfurrias. This hospitable town, situated at the crossroads of several main highways and gateway to the Rio Grande Valley, offered an ideal location for our headquarters. Upon reaching my majority in 1912, I had cast my first vote for Woodrow Wilson and Captain Brooks. It was the first election held in the newly organized county bearing Brooks' name. I had many old friends in Falfurrias, and welcomed, as did the other Rangers, the change in station. Our payroll amounted to a substantial sum for those pre-oil days, and when the customs and immigration officers moved in, the combined salaries made a considerable addition to the town's economy.

The late J. R. Scott, son-in-law of Frank S. Rachal and president of the First National Bank, told the boys to spend as much of their spare time around his institution as was possible. He felt that the presence of Rangers there would be a sure deterrent to bank robbers who were so active in other parts of the state. We placed our children in the fine public schools, entered into the various civic activities and soon became a contributing part of the town's life. There was no work for Rangers to do in Falfurrias, and it was merely used as a base of operations.

One of the most noted murder trials in the history of Karnes County resulted from the killing of a man in Kenedy by the city marshal. It was a private affair, in no way connected with law enforcement or the marshal's official duties. These men had grown up together in a community where the inhabitants seemed bent on killing. The man on trial had killed a near relative and the dead man's family record was almost as bad. In his preliminary remarks, District Attorney C. S. Slatton made a forthright statement. He said, "Heaven knows that Karnes County has a bad enough record for killings, but it is only fair to say that the feud which resulted in this one was imported from another county."

The reputation formerly held by Karnes County was the subject of a joke told during the Spanish-American War. At that time communication facilities were limited, with radios undreamed of and only a few long distance telephones. Somebody started a wild rumor and it soon spread all over Southwest Texas. The Spanish Fleet had been sighted in the Gulf. It was about to land an army near Corpus Christi. This force was going to march on San Antonio, and destroy everything in its path. A mass meeting was called in Floresville to devise means of defending the town and repelling the invaders. Before a single orator had a chance to make the eagle scream, a Hebrew merchant got up and asked to be heard. In a few well chosen words, he told the assembled citizens, "Shentlemens, there is nothing for us to worry about. The Spaniards will never get through Karnes County."

I was sent to Karnes City with Ranger W. R. Smith and another man to maintain peace and order in the court. At a previous trial, the witnesses had staged a shooting scrape in the courthouse yard. It was also alleged that the defendant had bought a machine gun for the purpose of killing the sheriff. District Judge William O. Murray was determined that this one should be conducted properly, hence the request for Rangers. During the trial we slept in the jury room with the jurors. This was the first time, as far as I have been able to ascertain, that Rangers ever performed this service or acted as guards for jurors.

In this case an occasion arose that required me to use all the tact and judgment I had learned through years of experience. A fine old timer who was a member of the most prominent family in the county had been in a number of fights and was not afraid of anybody. He had always been justified in his shootings, and had never hurt any man who didn't need it. This patriarch would not go anywhere without his pistol, nor had he ever given it up. Due to the nature of the people in attendance at the trial, Judge Murray ordered us to search everybody who went in the courtroom. The old warhorse did not want to miss a single session of the proceedings. Everybody wondered what would happen if he were asked to give up his six-shooter.

Both he and his son, who was at that time a county official, were warm personal friends of mine. We were drinking coffee together just before court opened and I said, *"Tio,* will you do me a favor?" "Sure, Bill, I'd be glad to," he replied. "Well," I continued, "as you know, the judge has ordered us to search everybody before they go in the court-room. Will you please go by your son's office and leave your pistol?" He scratched his head and asked, "What if a fight starts?" "In that case," I told him, "I have two guns and you can have one of mine." "Fine," he laughed and said, "I'll do it." The result was accomplished without any fanfare or trouble.

The people in Karnes City are most friendly and congenial. When not engaged in my official duties, I played bridge with the local club and generally enjoyed my stay in that open hearted town. I have always believed that a Ranger captain should be a man who could fit into any civic or social activity. By doing this he is able to get the confidence of substantial citizens, and to command a respect from them that cannot be gained by the mere use of his six-shooter.

The men were great practical jokers and would do almost anything to set the stage for one of their pranks. During this trial, it was necessary to send Rangers after an important witness who lived in Gonzales County. I invited that prince of good fellows, Marvin Butler, ex-Ranger and former A. & M. football star, to go with us. He was delighted to accept, but said he would like to take along a local minister. This young man had just been sent to Karnes City. When we arrived in Nixon and parked on the main street, Marvin got out and started circulating through the people on the sidewalk. Pretty soon quite a crowd gathered around our open car, and I was puzzled at the source of the attraction. Marvin didn't say much on the way back, but when we got to Karnes City he gathered the boys and told them what happened on the trip. They laughed loud and long. While the car was parked in Nixon, he had pointed to the preacher and whispered to several people on the sidewalk, "See that fellow the Rangers have in their car? He is a notorious bank robber they have just arrested." The prankster declared that one man in Nixon looked intently at the parson and said, "You can tell by that fellow's face that he has cracked many a safe."

The defendant was found guilty and sentenced to thirty years in the penitentiary. This marked the first time a white man had ever been convicted for murder in Karnes County. Marcus Ryan, who at that time lived in Runge, is now my neighbor in Corpus Christi. He was foreman of the jury that rendered the verdict in this case. In spite of veiled threats and attempted intimidation, he performed his stern duty in a manner that should be emulated by all citizens who serve as jurors.

Chapter 13
DEMOCRATIC CONVENTION

THE Democratic National Conven-
tion of 1928 was held in Houston. Many notables attended and several
unscheduled activities were staged. Publisher Amon G. Carter of Fort
Worth cut loose with his pistol in the lobby of the Rice Hotel. Senator
Carter Glass became annoyed at what he termed "gross inefficiency"
on the part of the hotel elevator starter. Despite his size and age, the
gentleman from Virginia took a swing at the overgrown bellboy, and
knocked him down.

One-eyed Connely, the famous gate crasher, was on hand. He had
been arrested by every other law enforcement agency in North America,
and wanted to have his picture taken handcuffed to a Texas Ranger.
Never having owned a pair of the manacles, I was unable to participate
in this publicity stunt. Colonel Edward Halsey, who afterward became
Secretary of the Senate, was sergeant-at-arms of the convention and
deputized the Rangers as assistants.

Virtually every nationally known newspaper man and many of the
columnists covered the convention, among these being Will Rogers. A
championship rodeo was in progress at the Rice Institute football field,
and I served as one of the judges. During a lull in the convention, Will
brought several of the writers out for an afternoon performance. When

the cowboy-humorist arrived at the rodeo, he immediately became the center of attraction. He enjoyed introducing the cowhands to his friends, among whom was Samuel G. Blythe. This eminent writer began asking questions. His first one showed the concept held by some Easterners of what it takes to make a genuine Westerner. He did not ask who was the best rider, the fastest roper or the greatest bulldogger in the rodeo. "I have always wanted to see a cowboy roll a cigarette with one hand," he said, "and now is my chance." In the group standing around the visitors were the top rodeo performers and the three judges. These included Captain Tom Hickman of the Rangers; Reese Lockett, cowboy mayor of Brenham; Lewis Jones, champion roper; Bob Crosby, permanent holder of the Roosevelt trophy for the best all around cowboy; Turk Greenough, champion bronc rider; and me. Rogers, who did not smoke, looked around for somebody to demonstrate the silly stunt, but on taking a poll of the group, he found that none of them were victims of the habit. Blythe shook his head in mock sadness and said, "Another childhood illusion shattered. I wanted to see a cowboy roll a cigarette with one hand, and these fellows don't even smoke."

One night many years later I was a guest of General George Smith Patton, Jr., on his schooner yacht, the *When and If*. I had told him this story while we were attending the Army War College in Washington, and he asked me to tell it to his son. We were anchored for the night near the mouth of the Potomac. Seated in the cockpit of the schooner, I did my best to comply with my host's request. While he smoked cigars, he disliked cigarettes, and wanted his son to hear the Will Rogers-Sam Blythe tale. It was evidently registering with young George, for his father kept nudging me in the ribs, and none too gently. Patton was, at that time, colonel of the Third Cavalry at Fort Myer. He took part in all forms of athletics from polo to boxing, and was one of the strongest men in the Army. He compiled a history of the Third Cavalry. As a scout, I had served with that famous regiment during the Mexican Bandit War of 1915. I was able to supply a good deal of first hand data and to lend him some valuable reference books. One of my treasured possessions is a copy of his work with the inscription: "To General W. W. Sterling, from one sailor to another," and signed "George S. Patton, Jr., Major, Third Cavalry," which was his rank at that time. Having been reared on the Texas coast, I belong to a breed which has been described by the late Richard Kleberg as "half cowboy and half sailor."

During the tick eradication program in Texas, I had an official encounter with a cattleman who was known as Wharton County's most bull headed citizen. Those who knew him best warned that he could not be handled without a fight, which they predicted would result in bloodshed. However, by the use of ordinary horse sense combined with the proper amount of firmness, his cattle were dipped without gunplay.

Forrest Damon came from a pioneer Texas family, and had some admirable traits of character. He was a bachelor and lived alone on his ranch about two miles west of the Colorado River. In other days he had figured in several rough-shod affairs, which included stopping construction of a State highway through his land. He did this by threatening the road workers with a Winchester, and his past history further revealed a readiness to use a gun in the settlement of controversies. He was a large red-muzzled man who wore a broad brimmed, uncreased hat which made the average cowboy sombrero look like a golf cap. When angry, which was at least half of the time, he would pop his teeth like a wild hog and, altogether, presented a formidable picture.

All stockmen are familiar with the war waged by the Bureau of Animal Industry on the fever tick, but to those who are uninformed on the subject, a few words of explanation will be in order. Dr. Mark Francis, of Texas A. & M. College, discovered that ticks were the carriers of so-called Texas fever, and that it was not transmitted through bodily contact, as many people formerly believed. Texas cattlemen lost millions of dollars annually from the ravages of these bloodsuckers, and on account of them, could not bring in purebred animals from the North. These obstacles could be overcome only by the complete eradication of fever ticks.

The magnitude of the undertaking can be measured by taking into account the geography of the state. Texas has about a thousand miles of Mexican border, adjoins Louisiana and Arkansas for several hundred miles, and millions of its acres are covered with brush and woods. The task appeared to be hopeless. Many livestock owners refused to cooperate. In some instances resistance to dipping was climaxed by dynamiting the vats.

The Texas Livestock Sanitary Commission took over the program, and tick inspectors were appointed for each county. A compulsory dipping law was passed by the legislature. It was necessary to dip all cattle or the other herds would soon be re-infested and the work given a setback.

Forrest Damon not only failed and refused to dip his cattle, but he defied anyone to make him do it. He announced that he did not believe in the law. Damon also threatened violence against the tick inspectors if they even dared to set foot on his land. After exhausting their efforts and patience, the local authorities called on Governor Dan Moody for Rangers. Captain Frank Hamer was dispatched to protect the tick man who made the first inspection. He had little patience with the ranchman, as he disliked the overbearing type, and wasted no time trying to mollify him. Hamer told Damon to sit down and be quiet until the inspection was over, and that any monkey business on his part would get him a good booting. Ticks were found on the cattle and a dipping order was duly issued.

On the date set to dip the cattle, I was sent to Wharton to see that the order was carried out. Quartermaster Aldrich, who telephoned me the Adjutant General's message, was an imported product and knew very little about the character of Texans. He told me that in all likelihood I would have to kill Damon before the cattle could be dipped.

Accompanied by Ranger W. R. Smith, I left our station in Falfurrias at two o'clock in the morning and six hours later we arrived at the dipping vat. It was in the woods about a mile from the ranch house, and several cars of inspectors were waiting for us. They had placed their automobiles in the form of a hollow square, and looked like they were better prepared to repel invaders than to dip cattle. I left Bob Smith at the vat, and told them to go ahead with their work. The chief inspector said, "No, sir, we are not going to do a thing until you have Damon in custody."

Instructing Smith that if I did not return in half an hour to proceed with the dipping, I drove to the ranch house and stopped at the front gate. Damon was standing in the doorway. His great bulk filled it so completely that I could not see his hands. I got out of my open car, called a pleasant good morning to him, and started walking toward the

gallery. He had a small arsenal in the house, with shotgun, pistol and Winchester within easy reach. I wore a short brush jacket and my holstered six-shooter was in plain sight. I did not give any indication that the situation called for gunplay.

The absence of rough talk or drawn pistol disconcerted and puzzled him. It was not the approach he had anticipated. I stated my name and business. Damon growled, "You're the gunman the Governor sent down here to kill me, ain't you?" "No," I replied, "I'm not here to kill you. We're only going to dip your cattle." "You can't dip them," he blurted out. "We're already dipping them," I informed him. "Sit down and be quiet, and we'll get along fine." He stared at me in amazement. We went into the room that served as his office and sleeping quarters, where there were some rawhide bottomed chairs.

In performing my duties as a Ranger, I always tried to explain to a man, if he showed any signs of intelligence, the reason for handling him, rather than to carry out my mission solely by force. "Mr. Damon, you appear to be a good citizen," I said. "Why did you bow your neck against tick eradication?" "Well, for one thing," he replied, "I don't like to be MADE to do anything." He further complained that a little Yankee from the United States Department of Agriculture had angered him by threatening to send him to the Federal penitentiary, and by flashing his official badge. He would imitate the agent by saying, "You see my 'baadge,' you see my 'baadge'." The ranchman was particularly infuriated by the nasal twang. When informed that I had never owned or used a badge, it seemed to please him. His attitude changed and he became more friendly. But his next statement almost floored me, and its line of reasoning accounted for his peculiar behavior. He said, "Those ticks you are killing belong to me. I pay taxes on them and they are mine. I can do as I please with them." I was astounded by this weird argument but finally managed to say, "Suppose you had smallpox. They would also belong to you, but you would not be permitted to scatter them all over the country, would you?" This seemed to register with him, and nothing more was said about dipping.

There was a large bed in the room. I told my unwilling host that on account of living in the Mexican country so long, I had to have a siesta. I then pulled off my boots and slept for almost an hour. When I woke up he looked at me in wonderment and asked how I knew that he wouldn't kill me. I told him I knew he was too good a man to do that, and therefore, had trusted him. Ranger Smith came in with the report that the cattle were dipped. I introduced him to Damon and said that we were ready to start back to Falfurrias. The ranchman told us to wait a minute. He called to an old Negro and said, "Mose, can you tell a ham from a shoulder?" "Of course I can, Mr. Forrest," he replied. "Well, go to the smokehouse and get the captain the best ham you can find. I want him to have something to remember me by."

Having spent his entire life on a Colorado River bottom stock farm, where all the laborers were Negroes, Forrest Damon was able to fathom their innermost thoughts. If a colored man committed an offense which in his opinion deserved punishment, he would utilize his knowledge in bringing the culprit to justice. On one occasion, a Negro murdered another one and threw his body in a deep lake. The case remained unsolved for several years. The authorities had been unable to produce the corpus delecti. During a long drouth, the water dried up, and neighbors discovered the victim's skeleton. Damon was positive that the guilty party was a man who had married the widow of the deceased. The new husband denied all knowledge of the crime, and the officers were baffled. Damon volunteered to help them provided he was allowed to use his own methods. The offer was accepted, with the understanding that no physical violence would be used. The suspect was arrested and placed in the county jail. Damon then put some of the dead man's bones in a cotton sack and hung the gruesome bundle in the adjoining cell. Along about midnight the prisoner screamed to the jailer, "Take them awful bones away. I'll confess."

Forrest Damon and I became good friends after the tick episode. He told me frankly that he had made up his mind to shoot it out with the next man who attempted to dip his cattle, even though he might be a Ranger. The old timer believed that his rights had been violated. He was all riled up after the encounter with Captain Hamer. When I came to his house, he had been brooding over his fancied wrongs for a week, and was in a desperate mood.

His numerous enemies hoped that he would put up a fight, and they did a lot of ribbing on both sides. We were warned that Damon was a very dangerous man, and he was told that the Rangers sought to kill him. This accounted for the remark he made when I drove up to his house. Malicious gossip of this sort only strengthened my determination to dip his cattle without hurting him.

The last time I saw Forrest Damon was at a restaurant in Wharton. Over a cup of coffee, we discussed our first meeting. "When you came up to me smiling," he said, "it took me by surprise. I couldn't seem to get started with what I aimed to do." He had expected a lot of loud talk, threats and swearing. When I approached him in a friendly, good natured manner, it spoiled his plan of battle. A short time before his death, Damon killed a man he caught hunting in his pasture.

Chapter 14
HIDALGO COUNTY
AND A. Y. BAKER

HIDALGO County, in the fabulous Lower Rio Grande Valley, for many years was a hotbed of stormy politics and bitterly contested elections. The one held in 1930 was particularly hard fought, as it was almost like a battle between the old and new settlers. Violence and bloodshed appeared likely to occur on election day, so my company was sent there to preserve order. Possibly ninety per cent of Valley residents at that time were from the North, and they had moved down to escape the cold weather. Through the efforts of high powered land salesmen from their own part of the country, they had discovered the Magic Valley long before its potentialities were realized by most Texans.

Natives living in the counties farther up the state would find it impossible to visualize the tumult and confusion of these elections. Neither could they picture in their minds the antics of the voters at the polls. Men and women formed in long lines just outside the distance markers and jeered at everybody in sight. They kept this up in relays and when one gave out of breath, another took his or her place. Ranger Tom Heard watched with particular interest a loud mouthed woman who had a harsh, rasping voice. She never seemed to come up for air. He was a bachelor, and he engaged in some good natured repartee with this amazon.

134

Tom told her that he had never married just because women talked too much. He then inquired how long she had been in Texas and where she had formerly lived. The woman replied that she had moved down from Chicago about a year ago, but already felt fully qualified to straighten out the affairs of her adopted state. The Ranger then asked her why she hadn't straightened out Big Bill Thompson and Company before leaving the Windy City. He further stated that her long residence in that center of civic virtue and clean politics should eminently qualify her as an uplifter. She kept up her tirade until Heard finally asked her if she had been vaccinated with a phonograph needle.

These newcomers, or snowdiggers, as they were called by some, had no concept of the authority granted by law to the Rangers. They thought we were empowered to take charge of the polls and exercise all the functions of election judges. When we explained that all we could do was to protect life and property, they were keenly disappointed. They seemed to think we had the Kaiser-like power to "lay waste to the village and levy a tax."

When the polls closed, a report came to us that a mob had formed in Mercedes and that they were going to capture the ballot boxes. The election judge there appealed for Rangers to escort the ones from his precinct to the courthouse in Edinburg, as the law directs. Captain Hamer and I answered this call, and on arrival found the town in a state of wild excitement. The presiding officer advised us to take the boxes out through an alley, but we declined to use a back exit. The regular way to move them was by the front door, and we had no intention of using any other route. We advised the mob leaders to seek their remedy in court instead of by violence and warned them that any attempt to take the boxes would only result in some killed or wounded rioters. Hamer and I had previously agreed that in the event it became necessary to shoot we would aim low and stop them by shooting their legs and feet. Fortunately, we were not forced to fire a shot.

The trip to Edinburg was made without any untoward incident taking place, but on arrival at the courthouse, we found another hysterical bunch, who screamed that they were going to take every one of the boxes. Hamer never did lose his sense of humor and said to me, "The gee whiz. I thought all the people in the world were in Mercedes. Where did they find enough left over to make up this new gang?" In order to save possible bloodshed, I made them a proposition that seemed to appeal to their sense of fairness. Having made quite a study of mobs, I knew that if their attention could be diverted to something reasonable or humorous, they would often turn from their purpose. I told them that they were not about to get any boxes, but if they were determined to try, the only sensible thing to do would be to put the two leaders of their party in the vanguard. The ones in the front row began to look around and sure enough, the two principal agitators were conspicuous by their absence. Following up their temporary hesitation, I continued, "They are not here, but both of them are probably at home under the bed, while you poor dupes are going to get shot." Then, concluding to try a little stockyard humor on them, I patted the stock of my Winchester and said, "This rifle will shoot through fifty inches of wood. Don't be a bunch of blockheads. Go on home." They laughed and took my advice. The ballot seeking mob soon dispersed.

One of the greatest human tragedies in the history of Southwest Texas was enacted in Hidalgo County. The man who played the leading role was brave, generous and public spirited, yet his last years were clouded. A. Y. Baker had been one of the most outstanding Rangers who ever served his native state. He was absolutely devoid of fear. I have known men who, through sheer will power and devotion to duty, would face any danger without flinching, but who freely admitted that they were not immune to the emotion. They were like Field Marshal Ney, of Napoleon's Old Guard. When a comrade chided him because his knees were shaking before a battle, he said, "If they knew where I am going to take them today, my knees would be shaking even more than they are now." This brand of courage was totally foreign to the nature of A. Y. Baker. He would go into action with a laugh. The boys called his battle smile the "graveyard grin." This characteristic is the infallible mark of a truly dangerous fighting man. I had rather go up against a whole corral full of men who fly into a rage than one who regards a gunfight as a laughing matter.

The political wars in the strife torn county were the result of the numerous bond issues that had been voted, the consequent raise in taxes and alleged graft in the sales of the securities. It is a pity that A. Y. Baker should be remembered for his participation in these affairs rather than for the many good deeds he performed. He spearheaded

Ex-Ranger A. Y. Baker

the first phase of the development in the Rio Grande Valley. To my certain knowledge, for I accompanied him many times, he rode on horseback countless miles through the dense chaparral during the Bandit War of 1915. The campaigns ridded his county of the organized marauders who were bent on murder and pillage. Through his efforts the newcomers were enabled to work in peace and safety. They soon converted the brushland into citrus orchards and the open spaces into thriving towns.

One of the leaders in the so-called Good Government League was fined in Federal court for perpetrating a fraud on a home seeker. It was alleged that he sold a piece of land to his victim by showing a canal running through the property. The "canal" did not even connect with the source of water supply, which was the Rio Grande. I was present at the Governor's office in Austin at a later date, and heard another one of the leading spirits of the league say to the Chief Executive, "A. Y. Baker was so much better than the crowd who succeeded him that we ought to put flowers on his grave every day of the year."

A. Y. Baker had initiative and originality of thought, as well as a keen sense of humor. One of the early Valley land promoters owned a private railroad car and used it as his business office when in Texas. Somebody had obtained a judgement against him, which was transferred to Hidalgo County and placed in the hands of Sheriff Baker for execution. He went to the siding where the car was parked and chained it to the track. The judgement was immediately paid off.

On another occasion Baker was a witness before the Texas Senate in a case that involved a contested election. The loser had been attorney for one of the canal companies that had more land under their system than they could properly irrigate. He was a good man and it was not his fault, but when water failed to arrive in time to save their crops, the farmers became desperate. One day an irate group of them attempted to take both the law and the lawyer into their own hands. At the hearing in Austin, a State senator asked, "Isn't it a fact Mr. Baker, that the gentleman has a large following in the Valley?" "Yes, sir," the sheriff replied, "I saw about a hundred men following him one time, with a rope."

When Author Walter Prescott Webb was gathering material for his book, *The Texas Rangers,* I showed him my photograph of A. Y. Baker. He remarked, "That man had the forehead of a Supreme Court Justice." I served as a deputy under Sheriff A. Y. Baker when he was first appointed, and learned many lessons from him. One of the most valuable of these was his method of dealing with "bad" or dangerous men. He said, "It is just like a lion tamer handling wild animals in a cage. If you are not afraid, you are as safe as you would be in church, but if you ever weaken, they'll kill you." Hays, McNelly, Gillett, Brooks, Hamer and many other famous Rangers died peaceably in bed. The fact that none of these warriors had on boots at the time of their passing should bear out Baker's theory.

A large portion of the inhabitants on both sides of the Rio Grande believed that A. Y. Baker bore a charmed life. Many of the *valientes* aspired to kill *El Panadero*. He was often marked for slaughter, and several wealthy enemies had offered heavy rewards for his scalp. However, the opinion held by prospective collectors of these bounties was unanimous. All of them agreed that overwhelming odds existed against their surviving any attempt on his life.

On countless occasions, Baker proved his remarkable coolness under fire. A couple of noteworthy examples will be recounted here. Early in the present century, A. Y. and his partner, Ranger Lonnie Livingston, rode out from their station at Alice to Palito Blanco, which was in the southwestern corner of Nueces County, near the line of Duval County. It is now in Jim Wells County. Their mission was to arrest an outlaw of Mexican extraction. This *hombre* not only refused to surrender, but he barricaded himself in a house and opened fire on the Rangers with a Winchester. Baker's rifle jammed, and this predicament literally left him in a jam. In recounting this incident Lonnie said "Old Bake just grinned and started whistling a tune. He calmly got out his pocket knife and used it as a screwdriver to fix his gun." The redoubtable Livingston, who grew up in Cotulla, did not bother to say that he saved Baker's life by killing their adversary. Palito Blanco was a noted rendezvous for bravos and *valientes*. Its more prominent citizens included the Mexican revolutionist Catarino Garza.

The second instance happened during the skirmish at Cavazos Crossing, heretofore described in the chapter on the Bandit War. After reaching the densely wooded south bank of the Rio Grande, the bandits were joined by a number of soldiers from Reynosa. Apparently they had been dispatched there to cover the retreat of their comrades. The Mexicans concealed themselves in the heavy, semi-tropical undergrowth and opened fire on the Americans, who had broken off the pursuit when they reached the river. Baker decided to employ a ruse to bring some of the bandits out in the open. He walked out on a sand bar in plain sight of the enemy, in order to draw their fire. At the first volley, he fell to the ground, and they thought he had been hit. Many of the exultant *hombres* rushed out of thickets with *gritos* of delight. In their minds, they had killed *El Panadero*. Their joy was short lived however, for when they exposed themselves, the Americans opened up on them with a deadly fire. A Mexican string band came to the river, and lent encouragement to the *bandidos*. When Baker feigned his wound, they struck up a lively tune.

Ex-Ranger Baker had a contempt for those who constantly watched everybody around them and had the mannerisms of men who maintained constant vigilance or who lived in dread that somebody would get the drop on them. They would not let anybody get behind them, nor would they turn their backs on a door. In restaurants or hotel lobbies, these wary fellows would never take a seat that did not face the entrance. There was none of that in the makeup of A. Y. Baker, or "Bake" as he was called by his early Ranger comrades. On many occasions I have seen him seated on the curb of a border town, happily chatting with friends. Especially on Saturday afternoons, a stream of people from both sides of the Rio Grande passed by on the sidewalk behind him. In the throng were numerous *hombres* who would love to see him killed. He did not even cast a glance in their direction.

Our Mexican friends love a game rooster, and many of their sayings are influenced by these stout-hearted birds. Border folk borrow these expressive idioms and use them constantly. When they say a man is extra good at anything requiring prowess, they say that he is a *gallon,* pronounced "guy yown." A game rooster will crow anywhere, while the Dominicker will only strut in his own barnyard. The most scathing epithet that A. Y. could apply to any man was to call him a "Dominicker." Regardless of what might be said by his traducers, he was *Puro Hombre* and my friend. Peace to his ashes.

From the time the Rangers ceased to be Indian fighters and became preservers of the peace, it has been a well defined principle that they are most efficient in localities where they have few, if any, acquaintances. This is especially true where feuds and elections are involved. I had ranched in Hidalgo for many years and knew all the old timers, including practically every Latin American citizen. I requested the adjutant general to send a captain from one of the other districts, and excuse me from election duty in my former home county. I had no desire to escape an unpleasant job, but knew that it had always been the best Ranger policy to use strangers, who had no friends on either side.

The general's National Guard training had not fitted him for the finer points in Ranger administration, however, and he took the position that a captain should handle all matters within his district. The newcomers made great capital out of the fact that my old Latin friends came up to shake my hand, and give me the *abrazo*. They chose to think that my pleasure in seeing these *compañeros* and good people meant that I was taking part in the election, when the only interest I had was to preserve order.

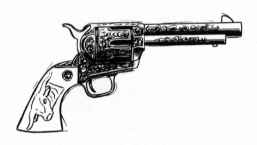

Chapter 15
PROTECTING LIFE
AND PROPERTY

I N 1928, the American Legion held their national convention in San Antonio. The Alamo City, with characteristic hospitality, put on the big pot and the little one for the visitors. Entertainments of all kinds were provided for them. Legionaires composing the local committees vied with each other in insuring that there would be no dull moments for the veterans of World War I. Colonel W. T. Johnson was staging a World's Championship Rodeo at the old ball park on Josephine Street. He named me as one of the three judges. I was a member of the Legion and, accompanied by my family, had hoped to make the occasion a sort of vacation.

It was only ten years after the signing of the Armistice. The delegates were still filled with the joy of living. They proposed to take full advantage of the various forms of amusement offered by their hosts.

The local gambling fraternity hoped to reap a rich harvest from the delegates, and to use the convention as an excuse for plying their trade. A group of them rented the Tapestry Room in the old St. Anthony Hotel and started their high powered games. After a number of visitors had been fleeced, somebody telephoned the governor in Austin.

Adjutant General Robertson was a delegate to the convention, and Captain Hickman had recently arrived in San Antonio. Late one night

I was asleep in my hotel room, when a telephone call came from the general. He told me to meet him right away, in the lobby of the St. Anthony. When I arrived, several other Rangers were already there. General Robertson explained that our mission was to close the gambling den, and that he would take personal charge. After mapping our plan of action, we converged on the Tapestry Room. From the number of bottles in evidence, a more appropriate name for it would have been "Tap Room." It was filled with a boisterous crowd, and games of all kinds were running wide open. Our commander announced that the Rangers were taking charge. He ordered us to seize all gambling paraphernalia. The professional gamblers expressed great indignation at the raid. They claimed to have bought from the entertainment committee, a "concession" that included immunity from arrest. This was the basis of a subsequent investigation by the local Legion Post.

Most of those bucking the games were half drunk, and with each loss, they became more belligerent. One big, swarthy fellow was particularly hostile. He did not hesitate to express his resentment of the intrusion by the Rangers. While approaching a gambling table, Captain Hickman had brushed by him, and his feelings had been ruffled. He walked around muttering threats, and otherwise working himself up to make an attack. Eduardo Neri was head porter and general factotum at the St. Anthony. He was not very happy over the raid, but we had been friends for many years, and he felt no resentment toward me. Captain Hickman's back was turned to the man he had jostled, and Neri was observing the crowd. Suddenly he called out to me in Spanish, *"Cuidado con el Indio. Trae navaja."* (Look out for the Indian. He has a knife.) Thanks to this timely warning, I was able to keep the tall, dark stranger from using his weapon. He was a convention visitor in Texas, so the only injuries he suffered were to his pride and property. He lost his knife. We turned him over to his buddies, who were most grateful for our leniency. They promised to keep him in their hotel for the duration of the convention.

In 1929, the American Legion Post of Falfurrias decided to put on a genuine cow country rodeo on the Fourth of July. The town is ideally situated for this kind of roundup, as it is in the center of a great livestock region. I was elected chairman of the rodeo committee, and we planned to stage a celebration that would exemplify the spirit of pioneer Texas. Hospitality was to be the keynote and theme song. We invited the cowboys from the surrounding country to come a few days ahead and get used to the local grounds. Everybody in Falfurrias pitched in to help make it a success, and the Southern Pacific Railroad loaned us their splendid brass band for the occasion.

The featured event was a quadrille on horseback. It was coached and directed by that grand pioneer, Ed Rachal. The dancing couples were Mr. and Mrs. Percy Hunter, Mr. and Mrs. Jim McBride, Mr. and Mrs. George Sorenson, Mr. and Mrs. C. F. Hopper, Ranger Tom Heard and Miss Katie Smith, ex-Ranger John Hinnant and Mrs. Bill Sterling. These were all home town people. The figures were executed at a gallop and the spectators greeted the performance with loud applause. Several of our fine partners in the set have crossed the Great Divide but those of us who remain will cherish their memory as long as we live. I had hoped that the sons and daughters of this group would carry the Falfurrias Quadrille into the second generation. It could not be duplicated anywhere in the world. The ownership of more cattle was represented by the crowd who attended this rodeo than could be found in any other grandstand in America. It is a pity that the Falfurrias Fourth of July celebration was allowed to degenerate into a mediocre affair, then finally die out.

Among the throng who came to Falfurrias for the festivities was a trouble hunting character who claimed to be a pugilist. He had created disturbances at public gatherings all over Southwest Texas, and his reputation for truculence had earned him the nickname of "Rowdy." After the street parade was over, I took my little daughter up behind me and we rode to the town's main restaurant. Facing the crowd congregated there was this plugugly, who screamed defiance at the officers and challenged any man in Falfurrias to a fist fight. Ranger Bob Smith, a medium sized man, was trying to quiet him down without being forced to use his gun. We had agreed to be as lenient with unruly visitors as circumstances would permit, thereby sustaining the community's reputation for hospitality. Rowdy scorned the plea that he behave himself, so I told Bob to lock him up. He glowered at me and shouted, "Why don't you try it yourself?" I took my little girl around the corner out of sight, got off my horse and came back. The bully put up his hands in the most approved boxer fashion and ran at me like a

Producers of the 1930 rodeo staged in Beeville for Student's Loan Fund of Texas A. & M. College. Top row, left to right: Pryor Donald, Col. Jack Forgason, Mrs. W. W. Sterling, L. A. Pierce, E. E. McQuillen, Emerson Sain. Bottom row: Graves Peeler, Eugene Reagan, Dick Scott, Captain W. W. Sterling, unidentified. Captain Sterling is wearing the original Texas Aggie boots. He presented them to Aggie Football Great Joel Hunt.

Brahma bull. Instead of the haymaker he expected from a yokel, I hit him with a straight left, turning the wrist just as my fist connected with his jaw. He went down like a poll axed ox, and his Fourth of July exhibition came to an abrupt end. The sheriff arrived on the scene and took the fallen gladiator to the Brooks County jail. He moaned that the Ranger captain had knocked him down with a six-shooter, and his head probably felt like it. The lengthy account of my Falfurrias fisticuff is related because the lick that flattened Rowdy was destined to become an American byword.

While the New York soldiers were on the border in 1916, Norman Selby, known to all prize ring fans as Kid McCoy, spent considerable time on our ranch. I had always been a devotee of boxing and after becoming well acquainted, I asked him to show me the technique of his famous punch, which was known at that time as the "McCoy corkscrew." He was glad to oblige his Texas friend and gave me a thorough demonstration, without, of course, actually hanging one on my chin. It was a blow of concentrated power that started in his toes and carried all the strength of hip, shoulder and arm. Just as it landed, he would snap down his wrist and fist. This slight turn added more force to the punch and gave it the name of "corkscrew." Selby's instruction stood me in good stead on many occasions, especially in the oil field cleanups. I have never hit a man with a gun in my life. One poke with my educated left hand has always been enough to cool the hardiest ruffian. Keeping in top physical condition has enabled me to get full benefit from these lessons. What Rowdy believed to be a lick from a long barreled pistol was only a well coached left fist, but it was literally "the real McCoy."

Several years later, while occupying the office of Adjutant General of Texas, I was happy to join Will Rogers, Al Smith and a group of prominent Americans in petitioning Governor James Rolfe of California to grant clemency to Norman Selby. He was serving a long sentence in San Quentin penitentiary for the alleged murder of a woman. I have the Kid's letter telling me his side of the unfortunate affair. He said that they were out on a wild Hollywood party and claimed that the shooting was accidental. He finally received his pardon, and died several years later in Detroit, where he was employed by Ford.

While stationed in Falfurrias, I was elected president of the Association of Former Students of Texas A. & M. College for a term which began in 1929 and ended in 1930. I was deeply grateful to my fellow Aggies for thus honoring me, and felt that their action proved that a good Ranger could qualify for leadership in any field.

The presidents generally came from the larger cities, where they had the support of big A. & M. Clubs. Editor Dickey was kind enough to say in the *Facts,* "The election of Captain Sterling has brought another honor to Falfurrias." This position required me to travel all over the state for meetings with the various A. & M. Clubs. It enlarged my extensive circle of friends and altogether was a most interesting experience. With E. E. McQuillen, secretary of the association, and Madison Bell, head football coach, I made a good will trip that covered most of East Texas and ended in Shreveport, Louisiana. The present stature of the association is largely due to McQuillen's untiring efforts and outstanding ability. Madison (Matty) Bell is recognized as one of the nation's foremost football authorities, and now serves Southern Methodist University as director of athletics.

I also met with the New York A. & M. Club in that city, during my term as president. My financial contribution to the association was made in the form of a rodeo I put on for the benefit of the Students Loan Fund. It was staged in Beeville, and largely through the cooperation of several Southwest Texas Aggies, the event turned out to be a huge success. Colonel Jack Forgason, Graves Peeler, Dickie Scott, Pryor Donald, Eugene Reagan, Emerson Sain and L. A. Pierce made up this group. Secretary McQuillen came down from College Station to handle the fiscal matters, and was delighted to find that the proceeds of our A. & M. roundup amounted to a tidy sum.

In 1929, oil was discovered in Bee County at Pettus. True to the established pattern, several police characters from other fields arrived close on the heels of the new strike. One of these from Borger opened a drug store. Among other illegal activities, it was used to house a bunch of slot machines. The late George Ray, a prominent ranchman who had been my friend for many years, wrote me that the peaceful little town was rapidly being overrun by criminals. I promised him to make an official call on the troubled spot and assured *Tio* George that he would be able to note a marked improvement in conditions after our visit.

Rangers Bob Smith and Tom Heard accompanied me on this mission. The trip was made in an open touring car, and except for those rare occasions when it was raining, we always traveled with the top down. At that time the highway was very narrow, and as we rounded one of the numerous curves, a *paisano,* or chaparral bird, with outstretched wings tried to cross the road ahead of us. He flew squarely into the front fender and was killed, but he did not fall off. We left him there and drove on to Pettus. When we stopped in the oil field section of the town, people began to crowd around our car. They looked at the dead road runner and naturally supposed that one of the boys had shot it with his pistol. Several shrugged their shoulders and muttered, "Those Rangers sure can shoot." We did not bother to correct their impression. After destroying the slot machines and issuing several "sundown orders," we took our departure. Lawlessness in Pettus was stopped before getting out of hand, and through the cooperation of the fine old time residents, it remained a peaceful oil field.

Chapter 16
DEER HUNTING

I N 1929, a party of deer hunters consisting of Governor Dan Moody, Attorney General Robert Lee Bobbitt, President H. E. McGee of the M. K. and T. Railroad, Colonel Murrell Buckner and several other gentlemen arrived in Hebbronville on Mr. McGee's private car. General Bobbitt had arranged for them to hunt on the George Edds ranch in Jim Hogg County. Several of my Rangers and I joined them to act as guides and otherwise assist in making the hunt a success. I never did care to kill game, but went along just to enjoy the fellowship of camp life in the company of our distinguished guests.

Many young or inexperienced hunters, upon first sighting a deer in the open, are struck by a chill known as "buck ague." They shiver and shake, and their trigger finger refuses to function. On our outing in Jim Hogg County, one of the railroad men suffered an attack of this malady. This man's hunting rifle was a long barreled Winchester that held eight or nine cartridges. His guide showed him a big buck standing broadside under a mesquite, and told him to shoot. He pointed the gun in the general direction of the deer and feverishly started working the lever. He pumped all the shells out of the magazine but never could pull the trigger.

Governor Moody was a fine shot, and always brought in his share of the game. He was also greatly interested in the Rangers, and took advantage of this opportunity to observe our work in the ranch country along the Rio Grande. On the second day of the hunt, Light Townsend, Bob Smith, and Tom Heard met me at a pre-arranged spot at noon. They did not expect much to eat in the middle of the day, so they only had coffee and several boxes of ginger snaps. All Rangers are good foragers and mine were no exception. They planned to get fresh meat later that afternoon, and they would make up for their postponed midday meal with a big supper.

When the Governor and I drove up to the camp, they were drinking coffee and eating their cookies. We joined them in a cup of coffee and he asked if that was all they had to eat. They answered in the affirmative, and when we were leaving, Governor Moody said that he intended to do something about it when he returned to Austin.

Several months later the following article appeared in the state newspapers, and it was captioned:

GINGER SNAP DINNER RAISES PAY OF RANGERS. Austin, Texas, March 22—Governor Dan Moody will approve the bill increasing the pay of State Rangers, he said today, and revealed the story behind his favorable action. Last winter while hunting, the governor came upon an encampment of four Rangers in the wild border country along the Rio Grande and was their guest at the noonday meal. "Black coffee in a tin can and a few boxes of ginger snaps," he said, "ccnstituted that meal." The present rate of pay, the governor said, justified but little more than the meager meal. The four men slept on the ground sheltered by only two blankets apiece. The bill which the governor will sign increases the pay of privates from $90.00 to $150.00 per month, of sergeants from $100.00 to $175.00 and of captains from $150.00 to $225.00. The present allowance for subsistence, $3.00 a day when on duty away from their base and $1.00 when at their base remains unchanged.

"It's been a long time coming and it's badly needed," Adjutant General Robertson commented when informed of the Governor's intention. Attorney General Bobbitt's deer hunt was not only a pleasant one, but proved most beneficial to the entire Ranger Service.

R. S. Sterling, who had been appointed chairman of the Texas Highway Commission by Governor Dan Moody, owned the Chupadero Ranch in Webb and Dimmit Counties. He and the late Dolph Briscoe, his associate in the cattle business, entertained many large hunting parties there. I was a guest on several of these hunts. They invariably proved to be both pleasant and instructive. The Governor was usually present, which afforded the opportunity for State officials at all levels to meet in the informal atmosphere of an outing. Gathered in the ranch house living room around a cheerful open fire, the evenings were profitably spent in the discussion of our mutual problems. The incense of burning mesquite wood, which has always been my favorite perfume, seemed to sooth all the guests into a peaceful state of relaxation.

On one of these trips, I went with Bob and Luther Snow, the lion hunting brothers who have been my friends since boyhood. Bob is an ace of the Texas Game and Fish Commission, and Luther is now, and has been for many years, sheriff of Willacy County. Both of them are tried and true friends of real Rangers. They gave us a demonstration of their methods and technique in capturing wild animals without the use of guns. One morning their dogs bayed a bobcat, and everybody in the party hurried to the scene. They simply pitched a rope on the kitty, jerked him down, put a booted foot on his neck and trussed him up with the other end of the rope. They didn't get a scratch and handled the wildcat like they were playing with a pet.

Sam Anderson had been foreman of the ranch for many years, and was a noted character in Southwest Texas cattle circles. Like most old time cowmen, he had small patience with hunters. He looked on them as nuisances, claiming that they always got in the way and obstructed his ranch work. One of these sportsmen, before starting out for the day's shooting, asked Sam to give him some directions. "Well, young man," said the cow boss, "go about five miles west, then turn south. Go across an arroyo and walk carefully through a prickly pear flat. Then go up on a caliche hill until you come to a burnt mesquite stump. When you get there you are lost. Wait until night and build a fire. I'll be tired out after a hard day's work, but will have to come get you."

Ab Blocker, most noted of those stalwart foremen who bossed herds of Texas longhorns up the Chisholm Trail, spent many years at the Chupadero, working for his equally famous brother, John. Ab originated the XIT brand, which he drew on the ground with the toe of his boot, for the three million acre Capitol Syndicate Ranch. Being a consummate cowman, he knew that brands formed by straight lines would not blotch. "Barbecue" Campbell, manager of the huge but brandless outfit, immediately ordered his blacksmith to make a number of irons after

this pattern. As a reward for his idea, Ab Blocker was permitted to burn the XIT on the first cow that ever wore that renowned bovine trademark. Brother Johnnie, as he was invariably called by Ab, has his name perpetuated in a noose that he always built big enough to encircle the widest spread of horns. All over the cow country, in rodeos and whenever cattle are roped, it is known as the "John Blocker loop." His son, William B. Blocker, told me one time that his father used a big loop even when roping calves. He said the elder Blocker could always jerk it up before the animal ran through. Few, if any, present day ropers can accomplish this feat.

Many stories have been written about Ab Blocker's quaint sayings and doings. One of these had its setting on the ranch formerly owned by Governor Sterling. During World War I, airplanes from Kelly and Brooks Fields in San Antonio began to make cross country flights to Army posts on the Mexican border. The present generation could scarcely realize the amazement and near consternation caused by these strange machines as they roared over the heads of excited natives. The alarm caused by these flights is illustrated by an incident that

W. W. Sterling guarding one of the first airplanes to make a cross country flight. It landed on the Sterling ranch in Hidalgo County.

occurred farther down the Rio Grande. I rode the first one of those old jenny biplanes that came to the vicinity of Fort Ringgold, and it landed on our ranch in Hidalgo County.

The plane had passed over a nearby settlement and Joe Lane, who was a noted character in that part of the country, came to see me the next day. He declared that he was going to file a damage suit against the Government. "When that infernal thing flew over yesterday," he said, "my kids nearly butted their brains out running under the house."

According to the spinners of this yarn, Ab Blocker and his cow outfit were holding a bunch of cattle on a *guajillo* hill when two military planes flew over them in a westerly direction. The boss and all his cowhands forgot about the herd and lit out after the pair, hoping to overtake them. John R. Blocker had brought a buyer out to look at the cattle and found them scattered all over the pasture. When the riders returned, they were wild eyed with excitement and their horses were lathered with sweat. The elder Blocker was amazed at his brother's conduct, for in the handling of untold thousands of cattle, neither stampedes, storms nor hostile Indians had been able to make him desert a herd. When pressed for the reason, Ab is reported to have replied, "Well, Brother Johnnie, two dern fools flew over awhile ago riding pear burners, and I wanted to see where they were going to light." Pear burners are all too familiar to Southwest Texans, but to others it might not be amiss to explain that they are used to singe the thorns off prickly pears so cattle can eat the leaves. They work on the pressure principle of blow torches, and make a roaring noise that sounds somewhat like the exhaust of an airplane engine.

The best deer hunting in Texas is found in those counties that comprised my Ranger territory, and when high State officials came down for a vacation, I was happy to join them. Governor Dan Moody, Attorney General Robert Lee Bobbitt, the late Claude Teer, chairman of the Board of Control and the late Murrell Buckner of Dallas made up a party to hunt on El Sauz, at that time a division of the King Ranch. It is no longer a part of that cattle empire. The late lamented Caesar Kleberg, grandson of a San Jacinto veteran and one of the truest friends I ever had, was our host.

Many articles have been written about this great man, and his life deserves to be the subject of an entire book. He exerted a vast

influence for good over the lives of many younger men in Southwest Texas, and I am honored to be included in that number. The Austin hunters came down in a private car, which was parked on a switch east of Raymondville. Judge S. Lamar Gill and Ranger Sergeant Light Townsend came out the next day to do their part in entertaining the distinguished visitors.

The hunters bagged several deer and turkeys, as well as their limit of quail. Governor Moody killed a reddish colored hog, and everybody in the party wondered if it could be a freak javelina. I assured them that such was not the case, because from my personal knowledge these half wild red pigs were of domestic origin. In 1911, I was bossing a cow outfit for the late Ed C. Lasater of Falfurrias. He turned several hundred head of Tamworth hogs loose in his Zacahuistal pasture, which subsequently became a part of the Encino division of the King Ranch. The Tamworth breed was developed in an attempt to get a hog that would produce the maximum amount of bacon, and they were slab sided, long legged animals, with rambling dispositions. Mr. Lasater had his men put bells on some of the sows, and they tried to herd them like sheep or goats. My old *companero* Romulo Rodriguez was in charge of this operation, and the other *vaqueros* teased him unmercifully about being a *porquero,* or swineherd. The ungainly

154

porkers with the long running gear could not be restrained, however, and they scattered all over the *encinales*. It was one of their progeny that fell to the Governor's rifle on El Sauz.

Some people in private life may wonder what high public officials talk about when they are relaxing on hunting trips. On this one, Governor Moody and General Bobbitt discussed a fine legal point related to wild life. The conversation dealt with nature's balance among game and predatory birds. Some expert figured that a hawk will eat fifty quail a day, which is far above the legal bag limit. Hawks were the attorney general's favorite target and he said maybe it would be equitable to permit a hunter to kill fifty quail for every hawk. After giving the matter due consideration, both State officials agreed that no such rule or law should ever be enacted.

The party moved up to the Norias division of the ranch, where "Mr. Caesar," as he was affectionately known, made his headquarters. The late Tom Tate, who had made a fine record as a Ranger, was one of Mr. Kleberg's most trusted men, and he helped entertain the guests. Sam Chesshire, also an ex-Ranger, is one of the most noted residents of Norias. At the age of eighty-two, he still carries on. He is a natural born humorist and for years has kept everybody around him in good spirits. I always referred to him as "the jester," for he reminds me of Wamba in Scott's *Ivanhoe*.

Everybody looks alike to Sam, and he never had the slightest feeling of awe in the presence of "big" people. Railroad officials, industrial magnates or financiers who visited the ranch were often targets of his keen wit. They loved to engage him in rough and ready verbal tilts, in which he gave them as good as they sent. I once heard a prominent railroad president tell a story at the old Norias ranch house dinner table. From his seat at the other end, Sam called out, "You know good and well that you are telling a dern lie." These business tycoons doted on his sense of humor for they knew that like all old time Rangers, he would not "hooraw" with anybody he didn't like. Not long ago I spent the night at the new Norias ranch as a guest of the late Richard Mifflin Kleberg. I was both touched and flattered to find my picture in Sam's room. We have been close friends for well over forty years, and I hope they have to take him out and kill him on the Judgement Day.

Chapter 17
JUDGING WORLD'S CHAMPIONSHIP RODEOS

O<small>N</small> one occasion Adjutant General R. Lamar Robertson summoned me to Austin on a matter he felt should have special handling. It concerned a recent election in a Gulf Coast city that had the usual aftermath of a bitterly contested political campaign. Charges of fraud were made by the losing faction and they had prevailed upon the Governor to order an investigation made by a Ranger. The chief of police was named as the main object of their complaint. The city in which the alleged violations occurred was not in my territory, but I was selected for the assignment.

The general was most specific in his instructions. He told me to use tact and discretion, but to leave no stone unturned in my efforts to secure the full facts. Pursuant to this order, I went to the city in question and the next day was back in Austin ready with my report. My superior was dumbfounded and informed me that the type of investigation he wanted would require a long time to complete. I replied that mine had been carefully made, and the accused man was innocent. When asked how I arrived at that conclusion, I told him that it was only necessary to examine the election returns. The boxes controlled by the underworld went solidly against the chief. This fact was an infallible criterion. The good citizens often divide, but the crooks do not. My findings were vindicated by a further and fuller investigation.

Numerous large ranches, including the most famous one in the world, were located in my Ranger territory. A large number of its inhabitants were Americans of Mexican extraction. The fabulous Lower Rio Grande Valley with its cosmopolitan population was in my district, which also contained several major oil fields. There was a wide diversity of interests between the citizens that made it difficult to protect the lives and property of each individual without being accused of partiality. I had grown up in the cattle business, knew something about oil and spoke the Spanish language. Furthermore, I understood the temperaments of the people with whom I had to deal, and enjoyed the widest acquaintance of any man in the region. These friendships were of untold value in carrying on the Ranger work.

I have always believed that the cause of justice could be served best and society benefited most by applying the ounce of prevention in law enforcement. This does not mean that I advocate the sacrificing of a single principle or allowing criminals to go unpunished. An officer who possesses the knack of keeping down trouble is worth more to the state than ten others whose only aim is to make glowing reports and send somebody to the penitentiary. The moment a man is sentenced there, he becomes a liability on the state. If there was an honorable way to save him from this fate worse than death, I always tried to use it.

On account of the large number of Federal, State and county officers residing and working in my district, a sizable portion of the citizens were men who carried sidearms. It was my custom, when hard feelings had arisen over elections, lawsuits or any kindred activity, to go into those communities and quietly stay around until tempers cooled down. Both factions knew that we would discharge our duty with strict impartiality. The presence of Rangers in those tense situations always had a soothing effect on the warring parties, and in more than one instance spelled the difference between peace and bloodshed.

The purchase and issue of ammunition was one of the prime functions of Quartermaster Aldrich. Rifles used by my company were Model 1895 box magazine lever action Winchester carbines, chambered for 30-06 cartridges. These old muskets have never been surpassed for rugged and trouble free service, especially when this duty is performed on horseback. They are particularly well suited for scouting in the sandy country along the border, as well as in other remote regions where a Ranger rides without benefit of gunsmiths. No Texan or other Westerner ever fancied the bolt action piece as a saddle gun, for in addition to being unhandy, it would not fit snugly under the rider's knee.

Competing manufacturers constantly strive to develop more speed and power in their ammunition. In this stepping-up process, the breech pressure is greatly increased, and these super shells are unsafe for lever action rifles. Factories protect the public by printing on each box the specific type and model to which their new product is adapted. On one occasion, the quartermaster shipped my company a case of these high velocity cartridges.

Fortunately for us, Ad Toepperwein, probably the greatest professional shot of all times, was giving an exhibition in Falfurrias. He was an authority on matters pertaining to firearms, and we always enjoyed his visits to the Ranger camp. I showed him the case of shells that had just arrived from Austin, and after one look, his face paled. "Captain," he said, "these cartridges were never intended for lever action rifles. They are liable to blow up. I would not shoot one of them in your gun for any amount of money."

In 1928, I served as a judge in the World's Championship Rodeo in Chicago. It was held at Soldier's Field, the largest stadium in the United States. Bob Dow, a cowboy of the old school and attorney general of New Mexico, furnished legal as well as technical advice to the judges. Our first official duty did not concern a cowboy contest, but dealt with a promotional idea emanating from the fertile mind of the greatest rodeo producer of his time, Tex Austin. To stimulate interest in his show, he had placed several professional rope artists in Chicago's playgrounds. They gave instructions in rope spinning to a large number of boys, who took to the sport with great eagerness. The ten lads showing the greatest proficiency were to be given a two weeks' vacation on Tex's ranch in New Mexico.

Picking the top ten out of several hundred competitors was a heart rending task. They looked so pale to us who were from the Southwest. Their hands and faces were grimy from coal smoke. One little fellow attracted my attention and aroused my sympathy at first glance. He was spindle legged, pigeon breasted and appeared to be undernourished, but his smile was the brightest of them all. He couldn't get the hang of a lariat, was usually tangled up in his loop and, as cowboys say about clodhoppers, he couldn't throw a rope down a well. As the eliminations progressed, I kept cutting him in the bunch with the winners. My partiality was so obvious that one of the other judges remarked that in his opinion better ropers were being passed. "That may be true," I told my colleague; "he certainly is no great shakes as a roper but he needs the New Mexico air and sunshine worse than any of the others. I am going to give it to him even if I have to fight all concerned, which can include the other two judges." In all my rodeo judging, this was the only time I ever favored a contestant.

Hoot Gibson, who ranked next to Tom Mix as the best movie cowboy of the era, used Tex Austin's show as the setting for a picture titled "King of the Rodeo." I had never seen one in the making, and like all country boys, was glad to have a small part in a movie. The hard work and stunts were performed by doubles. The star would get on a bronco in the chute, screw down and wave his sombrero while yelling,

Cowboy star Hoot Gibson in Soldiers Field, Chicago. Left to right, Deaf Scott, Hoot Gibson, Tex Austin, Captain W. W. Sterling.

"Let 'er go," even though the pictures of that time were silent. Then they would stop the camera until a cowboy could mount and make the ride on a bucking horse. When the whistle blew, the camera would again be cut and the hero showed panting from exhaustion. In justice to Hoot Gibson, however, it is only fair to state that he was a good rider, having won prizes at the Pendleton, Oregon, Roundup. He was kept out of rough work because an injury to him would have resulted in putting many people out of employment, as well as delaying the production.

Tex Austin decided to send some representatives from the rodeo to visit a local hospital. The crippled children had asked to see a moving picture cowboy and a Texas Ranger. As we entered the first large ward, the youngsters pointed at me and shouted, "Hello, Hoot." They paid no attention to the star, for in height he barely came up to my shoulder. I kept pointing down at him and telling the kiddies that this was the movie hero, but they only gave me the Bronx cheer, "G'wan. G'wan," they jeered. "We know who you are." I excused myself and ducked out, knowing that publicity was the breath of life to actors. Obviously, the youngsters liked their heroes big, and their cowboys Texas size.

In October, 1929, I judged the New York Rodeo, which was held in Madison Square Garden. Tex Rickard was the promoter and the proceeds went to the Broad Street Hospital. Will James, the cowboy artist-author, and Will Rogers were honorary judges. James had just finished one of his best books, titled *Sand*. I bought a copy and asked him to inscribe it for me. The matinee performance had been concluded and the hands were bringing the bulldogging cattle back from the arena corral. One old steer threw up his head and snuffed. Will drew a picture of him on the flyleaf of my book, and wrote some nice lines with his autograph. The hospital sponsors gave a dinner to the rodeo judges and a group of New Yorkers who were Western enthusiasts. I sat next to Arthur Chapman, and heard him recite his own composition, "Out Where the West Begins."

Irving S. Cobb, the Kentucky humorist and author, was a frequent visitor at the rodeo, and he soon became a great favorite with the cowhands. When he arrived at the Garden, we always took him backstage, where his wisecracks about the men and horses kept everybody near him in a hilarious state of merriment. We had many friends in common, and he was particularly devoted to three distinguished Texans. These were Will and Mike Hogg, sons of Texas' first native born governor, and Hal L. Mangum, owner of Hacienda La Babia, in Coahuila, Mexico. Cobb visited La Babia several times and his picture occupies a prominent place on the walls of the ranch. It adorns a room in which I have slept many nights, and it was easy for me to visualize the great man as I saw him last in New York. Many years, as well as many good friends, have passed since we were together in Madison Square Garden.

Don Hal Mangum, famous in two nations as the perfect host, wanted to make certain that his guest killed some game. The hacienda abounds with wild turkeys. The Kentuckian could not tell the difference between these birds and their domestic cousins. *El patron* had a *vaquero* stake a tame turkey close to the road, in a clump of huisaches. The yarn goes that Irving Cobb fired and missed the gobbler but the bullet cut the cord in two and let him get away.

We were in the middle of the New York Rodeo when the 1929 stock market crash occurred, on what has become known as "Black Tuesday." The next day we had a free afternoon, so my wife and I went to see Eddie Cantor in the matinee performance of "Whoopee." He ad libbed about the crash all through the show. One wisecrack I recall was about guests registering in the New York hotels. Cantor quipped, "When a man asks for a room in these times, the clerk inquires, 'Do you want it for sleeping or jumping?'"

The concluding event of the Madison Square Garden rodeo was a mad scramble known as the wild horse race. In it a bunch of loose bronchos are herded into the arena where they are saddled and ridden to the finish line at the other end. This spectacle is probably the most exciting part of any cowboy show. The contestants work in pairs. When the starting whistle blows, it becomes a scene of mad confusion. The judges find it most difficult to spot the winners, especially for third place. By the time he crosses the finish line, the arena is filled with rearing, plunging runaway horses, many with the saddles turned and dragging underneath.

We judges alternated in our assignments and on this particular night it was my turn to catch the third rider. I was mounted on my black

General W. W. Sterling up on Zarco.

paint horse, Zarco. He was given this name by the Mexican who broke him because one of his eyes looked like glass. The New York and Brooklyn boys who hung around the rodeo could never master the Spanish pronunciation of this name, so they called him "Sockko." Zarco was the best pinto I ever saw but was nervous and highstrung, with predictions often made that some day he would break my neck. He bore the Diamond Bar brand of the late T. T. East. Zarco showed marked quarter horse breeding, and was extremely wide between the forelegs.

Near the conclusion of the wild horse race, my eyes and attention were firmly fixed on the finish line. Two big Wyoming broncs had thrown their riders and were hung together by stirrup leathers. While running wildeyed around the arena, they hit us from behind, knocking my horse to his knees and me to the ground. A loud groan went up from the crowd, as everyone in the Garden, including myself, thought I would be trampled to death. Zarco was wiry as a panther and he quickly freed himself from the clumsy bronchos. He got on his feet and I crawled between his widespread forelegs, thereby saving myself from serious injury. He was a very spirited animal, but did not move until the cowboys got us untangled. A wealthy New Yorker had offered me a fabulous price for Zarco, the figure being many times his market value. Money was scarce and I had been tempted to sell him. After the heroic exhibition of loyalty to his master in Madison Square Garden, I announced that he was not for sale. His action there vindicated my opinion, which is shared by all true horsemen, that among animals, man's best friend is a good horse.

Having used one of them for many years, I had always cherished the desire to see where Colt pistols were manufactured. Through the kindness of Mr. Fletcher Montgomery, at that time president of the Knox Hat Company, I was permitted to gratify that wish. At the conclusion of the New York Rodeo, he had his chauffeur drive my wife and me to Hartford, Connecticut, home of the Colt Patent Fire Arms Company. He also telephoned them and made arrangements for us to have a personally conducted tour of the plant. The officials extended every courtesy to their Texas visitors. They placed a guide at our disposal and he showed us each step in the manufacture of a six-shooter. We watched one start from a slab of steel and followed it

through the various stages until the finished product was given the firing test on the indoor range.

In talking to several veteran employees, I was amazed to find that their knowledge of pistols was confined to the part on which they worked. They knew nothing about the alterations made by Rangers and other frontiersmen in smoothing up the action of their favorite weapon. Men whose lives often depended on a split second found it profitable to spend their spare time figuring out ways to increase speed. There are various methods to improve on the factory job and several fine Western gunsmiths specialized in working on Colt single action six-shooters. In my opinion, the best of these was the late J. D. O'Meara of Lead, South Dakota. He tuned up all my pistols. One of the last guns he fixed before his death was a long barreled forty-five with checkered ivory stocks, that I presented to Robert J. Kleberg, Jr., of the King Ranch. He is one of the finest shots I ever knew.

The factory men examined my pistol with great interest and carefully noted the changes that had been made in its mechanism. The six-shooter I showed them is one of my most treasured possessions. It ranks high among the finest presentation Peacemakers ever turned out by Colt. The engraving work is finished in black with gold inlays, and it was presented to me by the late John J. O'Hern of Laredo, Texas. "Capt. W. W. Sterling" is overlaid on the backstrap in gold letters, with "Texas Ranger" inlaid at the top. The stocks are made of Colt Medallion ivory with the Texas steer head on one side and my cattle brand, Cross L, on the other. Old time Rangers held a strong aversion against pearl handles on pistols. This was not merely a superstition but was on account of their fragility. One veteran told me that every dead man he ever saw had been armed with a pearl handled pistol when he came out loser in his final duel.

The crowning event of our Hartford excursion was the visit to the Colt Museum. The priceless items found within its walls were of vital interest to me for I was both a Texan and a Ranger. Much of our early history is interwoven with the saga of the Colt. Gazing at the Walker Model cap and ball pistol, I tried to visualize the meeting between Captain Samuel S. Walker of Texas and Samuel Colt, which took place in New York around 1839. Walker had all the essentials of a great Ranger captain. He was richly endowed with intelligence, initiative and originality. He did not hesitate to show the inventor the weak points in his product, nor to tell him how these defects should be remedied.

Colt's mechanical mind readily grasped the soundness of the warrior's ideas and he incorporated them in a pistol of new design which he named the Walker Model. The Ranger and the genius became staunch friends, and their combined talents produced the best hand weapon of its day. When Sam Walker was killed in the Mexican War, he died with his own model of Colt's pistol in his hand. When Sam Colt went on to found the arms empire bearing his name, he took out patents on the improvements to his invention that were thought out by Ranger Captain Walker.

Most all of the taxes, in the counties that comprised my Ranger territory, were paid by stockmen. For this reason and others, I felt that they should be entitled to first call on the services of Company D. Their lands were situated in the semi-wild area which seldom, if ever, was patrolled by urban officers. The Texas Rangers had originally been organized for the protection of life and property on the range. We did a great deal of our scouting on the ranches, and as my men had grown up in the cattle country, they were well suited for this type of duty. Each one was a good horseman, trailer and brand man who had been picked for his skill in these essentials of a border Ranger. When one of our ranchmen worked his cattle, we threw in with the outfit and made regular hands. I also wrote to the late E. Berkley Spiller, secretary of the Texas and Southwestern Cattle Raisers Association, and told him that we were always eager to cooperate with their brand inspectors.

Our presence on these ranches at roundup time was a deterrent to stealing and also had a strong moral effect on potential cow thieves. They never could tell at what hour of the day or night they might meet up with a Ranger. Constant vigilance of this kind kept would-be rustlers guessing, and they were never able to get organized for any serious depredation. Service of this sort brings lasting benefits to cowmen and other citizens, but does not get into the official records. Nevertheless, it is worth more than a double row of filing cabinets full of reports.

On one occasion I was ordered to Hemphill in Sabine County. The murder of a prominent lumberman and various other lawless acts had prompted the request for a Ranger. My arrival in that Louisiana border town marked the first time a Ranger had been there on official business since Captain Will Scott's company was ambushed by the Conners in 1887. I chanced to meet an old school friend on the street, and asked him to give me a confidential report on the murder case. "The man's wife is the main suspect," he said, "and the sentiment among townspeople is divided, fifty-fifty." "What do you mean by that?" I inquired. "Fifty per cent of them believe she killed her husband," he replied, "and the other fifty per cent believe she had it done." The state did not succeed in proving either charge.

To show his contempt for the local officers, a bootlegger who operated on both sides of the Sabine River announced that he intended to sell a barrel of squirrel whiskey on the courthouse steps. The county attorney, who was a vigorous and fearless prosecutor, took a dim view of this proposal. He had no intention of permitting the temple of justice to be used as a corn liquor dispensary. The adjutant general instructed me to render him every assistance, and pursuant to that order,

I remained in Hemphill to repel the invader. The rumrunner's boast was apparently the result of imbibing his own product, as he did not show up, and I went back to my station in Falfurrias.

My return trip was made by automobile as far as Lufkin, where I could catch a west bound train. It was not due for several hours, and I spent part of this time in a visit to the sheriff's office. Here I met Homer Garrison, Jr., who was just beginning his law enforcement career as an Angelina County deputy sheriff. He is now director of the Texas Department of Public Safety.

Chapter 18

JOHN A. VALLS

I HAD a great many dealings, both personal and official, with the late District Attorney John A. Valls, of Laredo. He was one of the most remarkable individuals who ever lived on the Mexican border. All county, State, and Federal officers held him in the highest esteem, and he was particularly friendly toward Texas Rangers. Judge Valls was born in Bagdad, a town that was situated near the mouth of the Rio Grande in Mexico. It is now gone, but during the Civil War it was a flourishing seaport. Confederate agents shipped countless bales of their cotton from Bagdad when all Texas ports were blockaded by Union warships. At the christening of young John Valls, General Porfirio Diaz, who subsequently became President of Mexico, was his *padrino,* or godfather. He always cherished his godson, and was most devoted to him as long as he lived. Judge Valls has shown me letters from *El Presidente,* and in these he invariably called him *"mi hijo"* (my son).

John Valls' parents were Spanish, and after the war they moved across the river to the United States. The boy attended parochial schools in Brownsville and later went to Spring Hill Academy near Mobile, Alabama. Here he was taught by the beloved Father Abram Ryan, Poet Laureate of the Confederacy. Judge Valls told me that the influence of these two great men, General Diaz and Father Ryan, had been the greatest factor in the molding of his character.

168

District Attorney John A. Valls of Laredo. Admiring friends observed his birthdays by filling his office with flowers.

He was one of the ablest prosecutors in Texas and the people of his district held him in high esteem. The fear of running afoul of Don Juan kept hundreds of wavering *hombres* on the straight and narrow trail. While he had as much moral courage as any man I ever knew, it always seemed to me that he lived in constant dread of assassination. A case in point will show what I mean.

Judge Valls was a bachelor and a man of fixed personal habits. It was his custom, when the weather permitted, to take long walks around Laredo. Most of the time he went alone. On these strolls, which were his only form of exercise, he always carried a cane. His *baston* not only served as a walking aid and dog repeller but it completed the picture of a cosmopolitan gentleman. As he strode briskly along, his erect carriage and austere bearing presented an impressive figure of official dignity. One afternoon his route took him down a side street to the banks of Arroyo Secate. Here he heard the drone of a flying bullet and naturally believed it had been fired at him. He hurriedly left the scene and went to the sheriff's office, where he reported the incident. Deputy Sheriff Refugio (Cuco) Carrejo and I made a careful investigation of the affair. It turned out that several small boys had been shooting at a target they had set up on the streetcar bridge. One of the 22 calibre bullets had ricochetted off a timber and the noise it made was the cause of his alarm.

While Judge Valls was somewhat embarrassed over these findings, he lost none of his aplomb. During a long tenure of office, he had prosecuted numerous criminals who resided on both sides of the Rio Grande. He also had political enemies in Mexico as a result of his loyalty to General Diaz. The district attorney frankly admitted his apprehension and stated that he could never be sure that one of them would not some day or night take a pot shot at him.

While Duval was not in his district, Judge Valls knew a great deal about what went on there. He once remarked to me, "When the authors of the Texas Constitution framed that document, they did not contemplate any such conditions as today exist in Duval County."

That widely publicized domain adjoins Brooks County, in which my Ranger company was stationed. It has always posed a difficult law enforcement problem to State officers. Duval County has often been called "a cancer on the body politic" and if this statement is too extreme, I can personally testify that it was a thorn in the flesh, or rather a black spot, in my Ranger territory. Under the laws of our state and the existing circumstances there, I found it very hard to work out a plan of action which would be practical.

Residents of other sections were wont to ask, "Isn't Duval County in Texas and subject to our laws?" Or, "Why don't you crack down on them?" The answer is found in the observation made by Judge Valls. When a violation of the law occurs in Texas, the only place the accused can be indicted is in the county where the offense was committed, and by a grand jury composed of citizens of that county. Neither the governor nor any other State official can indict or cause an indictment to be returned. On one occasion we had arrested a bunch of gamblers and divekeepers. The late State Senator Archer Parr, political dictator of Duval County, asked me, "What do you want to arrest those fellows for? We won't indict any of them." Efforts of the most conscientious officers are futile when good citizens fail to do their duty on either grand or petit juries.

The old law governing the disposal of gambling paraphernalia was a good one. It stipulated that the owners had no standing in court nor could they sue any officer who destroyed this illegal equipment. Acting under this statute, we would go into Duval County and break up slot machines as soon as they appeared. By this means we hit the gamblers in the pocketbook, even if it was impossible to get a conviction in court. This law has been replaced by a much weaker one.

Our methods were most obnoxious to the politicos as they deprived them of a considerable part of their graft. At a San Diego fiesta, my Rangers seized a roulette wheel that was operating on the plaza, and turned it over to the sheriff. He kept it at the jail a couple of days, then returned it to the owner who was probably assured that the Rangers had only made a token raid. This time we made sure that the gambling wheel would never again make a revolution. We took a saw and cut it in two. One piece and the brass axle were sent to Austin while the other half was made into pistol handles. By this act I incurred the displeasure of a notorious politician who, for a percentage, permitted all forms of vice to run in Duval County.

The late Senator Archer Parr was a kindly man who loved to joke with people, especially around the capitol. One day I saw him in the Austin railroad station, waiting his turn at the window. The Reverend Atticus Webb, head of the Texas Anti-Saloon League, was just ahead of him in the line. Senator Parr noticed that the ticket was being paid for in nickles, dimes and quarters. He said, "Say, Atticus, you must have taken up a collection among the brethren to pay for this trip." Webb was most unpopular in San Diego, and about this time Justice of the Peace George F. Lotto of that bootlegging center officially declared the Volstead Act unconstitutional.

Chapter 19
PATROLLING
MY TERRITORY

O<small>N ONE</small> occasion the sheriff of Cameron County called me at the Falfurrias Ranger camp and requested help in arresting three men for whom he held warrants. He declared that each one of them was double tough. They lived on a small ranch situated in the eastern part of the county, just south of the Arroyo Colorado. This region could well be called a dark and bloody ground, for in the past it had been the scene of numerous ambuscades, skirmishes and wholesale livestock raids. One of the most celebrated and sanguinary battles in Ranger annals took place nearby, when Captain L. H. McNelly and his company wiped out an entire band of marauders. Many descendants of these slain *bandidos* resided in the vicinity, and their way of life ran true to bloodlines. One of its native sons was the bandit leader, Aniceto Pizaña.

A substantial majority of the Cameron County voters resided in La Feria, Harlingen and San Benito, many of them being newcomers to Texas. They decided that the cause of law enforcement could best be advocated by placing a sheriff in office who would give them a "business administration." On this issue they had defeated a veteran border officer and elected their favored candidate, who was a very personable man. He succeeded in giving the citizens exactly what they had voted for, but he showed a marked reluctance to have any dealings, either personal or official, with desperados. Hence, the appeal for Rangers. His county was in our territory, and we willingly responded

172

to the call. Accompanied by Rangers Bob Smith and Tom Heard, I hurried to Brownsville.

Upon arrival at the border city, we went directly to the courthouse and reported for duty. After exchanging greetings, the sheriff lost no time in giving us the bloodstained history of the wanted *hombres.* He warned that they could not be taken without a battle. A deputy United States marshal who was a native of Cameron County had known them all their lives. He agreed with the sheriff. This man had earned a reputation along the lower Rio Grande for being a "ribber," or one who abets a fight in which the shooting is done by others. I had seen several evidences of his handiwork, and therefore was on my guard. From the trend of their conversation, it was apparent that both of them would prefer that we kill the men named in the warrant rather than bring them in alive.

I was fully cognizant of the fact that a prime function of Rangers is to render aid and assistance to county sheriffs. In the present case I was particularly eager to take the men into custody, as they had openly flaunted their deviltry in the face of the local officers. But, I was determined to do this in a manner prescribed by law, and did not propose to shoot them unless they resisted arrest. The present duty was to us just a routine scout. We were not concerned with the savage natures of the accused, nor were we impressed by their reputations.

The automobile used by Company D was a Model A Ford touring car and the top was always down. Tom Heard shot his rifle from the left shoulder while I did my shooting from the right one. For this reason, I always sat on the left side of the back seat and placed him on the right. By this arrangement, both of us could shoot our Winchesters from natural, unstrained positions. We were thus able to utilize the fire power of our rifles in the same manner that a warship delivers a broadside. Bob Smith was an excellent driver, and he could use his pistol effectively even while at the wheel.

With the sheriff and a deputy riding in their own car, we started out on our mission. They pointed out to us the ranch owned by the wanted men, and we immediately closed in on it. Nobody was at home except a boy, who said that the others had left in their car a short time before we arrived. He told us that they had gone to see a friend who lived on the north side of the arroyo.

At top speed we drove to Paso Real, a noted crossing on the Arroyo Colorado. For many years a ferry had been in operation on this reddish tidewater stream. Paso Real has a long and violent history. Early day travelers always breathed easier after they had passed the bandit infested spot. On more than one occasion, the entourages of Captain Richard King had been ambushed at this pass. Stage coaches between Alice and Brownsville ferried across the arroyo at Paso Real. They continued to do this until 1904, when the overland route was outmoded by the Saint Louis, Brownsville and Mexico Railroad. We knew that when they returned, our men would have to cross on the ferry, and that there could be no better place to intercept them.

Just as we arrived, the fugitives drove off the boat, and sped away to the south. It looked as though another shooting would be staged at Paso Real, but I was still determined to delay this as long as possible. The sheriff and his deputy drove their car on the ferry and crossed to the other side of the arroyo, thus separating themselves from us and the prospective fight. They did signal us that the wanted men were in the southbound automobile.

The speed of our Ford was stepped up by the use of ethyl gasoline, which had recently been put on the market, and it did not take Ranger Smith long to overtake the fleeing car. At my command it stopped and the occupants threw up their hands, thereby ending our present business in Cameron County. We then returned to the headquarters of Company

174

D in Falfurrias. Our assignment had been carried out and the mission brought to a successful conclusion, without expending a single round of ammunition.

When the nature of Ranger duties, our border territory and the type of men we were called upon to handle are taken into consideration, I may have gone too far in my efforts to avoid bloodshed. There were reasons and background for my attitude.

Situated as it is on an international boundary, the Valley was the natural headquarters of many men whose vocations required them to carry sidearms. Texas Rangers, United States Customs Inspectors, border patrolmen, Army officers, sheriffs, constables, marshals and innumerable "pistol deputies" congregated in the border towns. Their number was augmented by rancheros from the back country. These pioneers would consider themselves half undressed without their six-shooters. Strangers from interior points were justified in their astonishment, when they first saw this array of walking arsenals.

Hundreds of homeseekers from the northern states were moving into this semi-tropical, snowless region. Colonizers brought them down by special trainloads. One of the leading developers deemed it expedient to go ahead of his "land drives" and request all pistolians to stay out of sight until they passed through town. He feared, and probably with good reason, that the spectacle of so many armed men might terrify his prospective purchasers. Furthermore, it could cause them to hide their checkbooks.

One day a motorcade of these land buyers stopped on the main street of Mission. In order to oblige my real estate friend, I had retired to the interior of a cold drink emporium. An elderly, distinguished appearing couple managed to escape from their guide and conductor. They came up to me, and with a benevolent smile, the lady said, "I feel so safe down here, when I see a tall man like you carrying such a big revolver." These words were most gratifying. Sombrero in hand, I thanked her profusely. The gentleman was a New England capitalist. It is barely possible that he owned stock in Colt's Patent Firearms Company of Hartford, Connecticut, manufacturers of my 45 calibre Peacemaker.

The various Mexican revolutions, which began in 1910 with Francisco I. Madero's rebellion against President Diaz, had created a state of unrest on both sides of the Rio Grande. Straggling *insurrectos* dodged back and forth across the border. They transferred their allegiance to each new *jefe* who set up a provisional government in Mexico. It was practically impossible to keep up with the different "istas," whose names were derived from their leaders. Maderistas, Carranzistas, Huertistas, Zapatistas and Villistas all had their day. One newcomer in the Valley became hopelessly confused by the unfamiliar Spanish appellations. He referred to members of the two leading factions as "Canceritas and Villians."

Doroteo Aranga, known in revolutionary circles as Pancho Villa, operated principally in Chihuahua, Sonora, and adjoining Mexican States. He sent only one expedition to the lower Rio Grande. Neither Pancho nor his *dorados* accompanied this army, which was commanded by General Jose Rodriguez. The Villistas attacked the heroic city of Matamoras, but were repulsed with heavy losses by the Carranzistas under General Emiliano Nafarette.

Villas' ragamuffin forces brought along their famous marching song, "La Cucaracha." The populace on both sides of the border quickly picked it up. Dozens of verses have been improvised for this martial air, most of them unprintable. Captain Lon L. Willis, who grew up singing Mexican songs in San Patricio County, mixed both languages and composed a stanza of his own. He dedicated it to the Rangers and it goes like this:

> *Ye se van los Carranzistas,*
> *Ya se van pa' Torreon,*
> *Me dijo un amigo,*
> Better let the *Rinches* alone.

The Sterling Ranch in Hidalgo County, where I spent my early manhood, was in the middle of the 1915 Bandit War. It was also the cattle shipping point of many large ranches. They included Rincon de en Medio, owned by Judge James B. Wells. San Juanito, owned by James B. McAllen, and Laguna Seca, whose *patron* was Don Macedonio Vela. Mission was the border rendezvous of gunmen from various parts of Texas, Montana, California and Kentucky. A sizeable portion of these battlers was also made up of retired Army personnel.

Before reaching the age of twenty-five, I had been called on to do a great deal more than my share of shooting. Instead of becoming hardened in these trials by fire, the prayers of my mother and the good advice of Judge Jim Wells caused them to have the opposite effect on me. I resolved that in my future dealings, both personal and official, I would go as far as was humanly possible to keep from killing anybody. My sainted Methodist mother used to say, "My sons never hurt anybody who didn't need it awful bad."

A few months after my first daughter was born, she began putting her tiny arms around my neck, and all thoughts of violence took wings in the trusting gentleness of her embrace. These were the influences that governed my actions, and they stayed my hand on more than one occasion. I was given assignments that ranged from the Rio Grande to the Sabine and from the Gulf to the Panhandle. In carrying them out, I neither swerved an inch from duty nor took a step in retreat. During my service in the Rangers, I had a number of opportunities to shoot men under circumstances that would have been justified legally. The fact that my orders were executed without a single fatal shooting has always been a source of pride and satisfaction to me. I hold the firm belief that this would not have been possible without the prayers of my family.

The late T. H. (Chub) Poole of Cotulla was one of the greatest Rangers and sheriffs of all time. He served many years in a county that at one time had the reputation of being the deadliest in Texas. The hardiest ruffians were as meek as lambs around him, and nobody even dreamed of trying to run anything over him. Yet he never killed a man. Not all officers can be as fortunate in this respect as Sheriff Poole, but it is a well known fact that men with the most nerve are the ones who are least likely to become trigger happy.

Most of the children in Falfurrias had saddle ponies, and our little girl was especially devoted to horseback riding. The Ranger camp became a center of the juvenile mounted activities. I was keenly interested in finding the best type of children's pony. Some of the youngsters who had learned to ride on burros seemed to develop a tendency to beat on the sluggish animals. I once sent a burro by railway express to a nationally known tire manufacturer who wanted a gentle mount for his young son. Those who know donkeys can understand why this lad asked his father, "How do you make him begin?" Burro riding was the earliest form of "beating your way."

Shetland ponies are favored by many parents but some of them become headstrong and stubborn, especially after they grow older. The ideal children's mount is an undersized Spanish pony. These grand little animals are intelligent, trustworthy and have fine dispositions. My own daughters learned to ride on mounts of this kind, and through the years I have presented a number of them to other children.

While scouting along the Rio Grande with a group of mounted inspectors of United States Customs, my boys assisted in the capture of a pack train loaded with tequila. Among the beasts of burden seized on this occasion was a sturdy little brown pony. Though only about twelve hands high, he was able to carry as many bottles of the contraband liquor as any of the larger horses. A single glance at him convinced me that he would bring a great deal of riding happiness to some lucky child. I bought him at the government sale of smuggled goods and gave him to my daughter, who promptly named him Bootlegger. My judgement of horseflesh was fully sustained, for he proved to be one of the best ponies in Texas. The newspapers gave him wide publicity because of his unusual background.

Chapter 20

GOOD NAME

WHEN Governor Dan Moody took office in 1927, the Texas Highway Department was in a disgraceful condition. This agency had grown into a huge business that handled millions of dollars annually, and the Governor was determined to place at the head of it the best available man. The highest powered political pressure could not turn him from this purpose. He appointed as chairman of the Texas Highway Commission a successful Houston business man, Ross Shaw Sterling.

Early in the present century an oil boom was going full blast in Sour Lake. Heavy rains soon turned the unpaved main street of the town into a quagmire. On one occasion a wagon was bogged down in the middle of a block. When four mules could not budge it, the irate teamster began to beat them with a club. Two men ran from opposite sides of the street and reached the scene at about the same time. Each of them ordered the mule skinner to stop or they would give him a dose of his own medicine. After it was over, the two humane men shook hands. "I admire the stand you took in this mess," said one; "what's your name?" "Sterling," was the reply. "So is mine," said the other, and thus my father met the future Governor.

Sterling is a rather uncommon name. While not related, the philosophy of life and habits of our families were very similar. The Governor enjoyed teasing me in his good natured way, and I considered this a compliment, as I knew that he would not joke with anyone he didn't like. He once asked, "Bill, what kin are we?" I replied, "Well, Governor, if it's all the same to you, I had much rather be a good friend than a poor relative." This remark seemed to please him, as he quoted it on several occasions. I visited in his home many times. They treated me like one of the family, and I was particularly close to his son, Walter Gage Sterling.

When R. S. Sterling announced for governor, I naturally supported him with every resource at my command. In the first place, I would have gone all out for him on account of friendship and the knowledge that he would give my native state an honest administration. In the second place, he was running against the Fergusons who always paid the criminal element for their support by crippling or destroying the Ranger Service.

After Mr. Sterling was elected, I did not see him for several months. One day in Austin, he asked me why I hadn't been around. I told him that I did not care a thing about getting in on the shouting, as my work had been done in the campaign when it was needed. He then said, "The A. & M. College is a military school, and I believe the Adjutant General of Texas should come from there. You look around for a qualified Aggie and I'll appoint him."

This unusual, and as far as I am able to ascertain, unprecedented offer was a great tribute to my Alma Mater. The incumbent, Robert Lamar Robertson, was an A. & M. man, and the college had turned out numerous others who would make excellent adjutant generals. After carefully going over the field and considering a number of good men, I decided to recommend Colonel William C. Torrence of Waco. He had made a splendid record in both Mexican border service and in the First World War. He possessed every qualification for the office. After making this decision, I went to Houston to report my findings to the Governor-elect.

The details and results of this conference between Governor Sterling and me were widely publicized at this time, both by word of mouth and in print. As the surviving participant, I am glad to write a true

Governor R. S. Sterling

account of the meeting. The Governor's private office was situated on the twenty-second floor of the Post-Dispatch Building. It was impressive and magnificent. His desk occupied the center of a large room under a dome. This was decorated by murals depicting his various properties and interests. Despite the grandeur of the setting, there was no hint of haughtiness in the demeanor of the owner. His kindly gaze dispelled any tenseness, and made me feel perfectly at ease.

He opened the conversation by asking, "Well, how did you come out in your hunt for an adjutant general?" "Fine," I replied, "I would like to submit the names of a couple of good men." Adjutant General R. L. Robertson had been very kind to me and we were schoolmates at A. & M. In a gesture of loyalty I asked if he had a chance for reappointment. "No," said the Governor-elect. "He is a good man and his brother-in-law is a past state commander of the American Legion, but he is not the aggressive type I want in my administration." "In that case," I continued, "the man I want to recommend is Colonel William C. Torrence of Waco." "I have heard a lot of good things about him," said the Governor. "Edgar Witt, who has just been elected Lieutenant Governor, also says that he is a fine man, and wants me to appoint him."

Then Governor Sterling said, "Here is the way this thing shapes up. General Hulen of the Thirty-sixth Division has a candidate for adjutant general; General Wolters of the Fifty-sixth Cavalry Brigade has one; the Legion wants Robertson and you and Edgar Witt want Torrence." He paused and I said, "Well, Governor, each of the gentlemen you have mentioned is a friend of mine; I can get along with any of them." "You won't have to do that, Bill," he said with a twinkle in his eye. "I am going to appoint you."

To say that I was astounded would be an understatement. I had not applied for the position and did not dream that I was being considered. Upon recovering from my surprise, I thanked the Governor profusely and told him that I was deeply grateful for the honor he had bestowed on me. I then said, "Governor, you already have my unqualified support. Wouldn't it be good policy to use this appointment to please one of those powerful organizations?" "There will be no politics used in my administration," he declared. "I am going to put the best man I can find in every position, big and little. There may be some confusion about my appointing another Sterling, but there is no use penalizing a man just because he has a good name. I want the laws of Texas enforced, and believe you are the one who can get that done." Because I got the appointment, I did not let Colonel Torrence down. Upon taking office, I made him State Service Officer which carried the same salary as the adjutant general, with a great deal less grief.

After Governor Sterling told me that I was to be his adjutant general, he cautioned me not to mention it until he made the official announcement. I followed his instructions to the letter. The Ranger captains were always greatly concerned over a change of administration, and were particularly interested in knowing as soon as possible the identity of the new general. One of them suggested that inasmuch as I was close to the new Governor, I might be able to get from him a hint about the matter. I turned a deaf ear to all these appeals, with the explanation that I was not in a position to ask that kind of question.

Only to Captain Will Wright did I give any information, and that was done without violating my trust. His son-in-law, Blake Fore, of Kenedy, is one of my best friends, and I saw him a few days after my conference with Governor Sterling. Captain Wright was one of the oldest captains in age, and naturally was concerned about his future standing in the Rangers. I told Blake Fore that while not at liberty to divulge the name of Governor Sterling's appointee, I wanted him to tell his father-in-law that Captain Wright never had a better friend than the new adjutant general.

Chapter 21
ADJUTANT GENERAL
OF TEXAS

Early in the month of January, 1931, I went to Austin to take up my new duties as Adjutant General of Texas. The capital city was bustling with activity and presented quite a contrast to my former station in Falfurrias. Preparations were in full swing for the forthcoming inauguration of Governor Sterling. The Forty-second Legislature was ready to begin its regular session. This biennial assembly, plus the advent of a new administration, had filled the town with eager people. These included members of both Houses with their families, temporary employees, lobbyists, job seekers and visitors.

News of my appointment had appeared in the papers and numerous people sought me out to offer their congratulations. Some of them were sincere well wishers, while others simply played the old political game of professing friendship for one who at the moment was in the saddle.

In relinquishing his office to me, my predecessor was both courteous and considerate. General Robertson carefully explained the details and inner workings of the department. I already knew most of the personnel, having met them while serving as Ranger captain. I joined Major General John A. Hulen, Brigadier General Jacob F. Wolters and Brigadier General R. Lamar Robertson in completing last minute

Members of my old Company who acted as Guard of Honor when I took the oath of office as Adjutant General. Left to right: Sergeant (later Captain) Light Townsend, Ranger Tom Heard, General W. W. Sterling, Ranger W. R. Smith and Captain P. B. Hill, Chaplain.

details. We then proceeded to the south entrance of the capitol, where a temporary platform had been erected. Seated on this structure were many notables. Among them were former Governors William Pettus Hobby and Pat M. Neff, Lieutenant Governor Edgar Witt, Speaker of the House Fred Minor and House Parliamentarian Oveta Culp, who later became Mrs. Hobby. She is my junior by many years but I have long enjoyed the friendship of this illustrious lady. We are both natives of Bell County.

The ceremony was brought to a climax when Governor Dan Moody and Governor-elect R. S. Sterling, followed by Mrs. Moody and Mrs. Sterling, proceeded to the center of the stage. Chief Justice C. M. Cureton administered the oath of office to the new Governor. The inaugural ball and reception took place the same night. My wife and I stood in the receiving line for several hours, where we joined with other State officials and their wives in greeting friends from all parts of Texas.

January 22, 1931, was the date set for me to take the oath of office. The adjutant general's department was at that time located in the east wing of the capitol. On this morning I found the outer office filled with people. These included relatives and friends who had come to witness my induction. Headed by General Robertson, with Chaplain P. B. Hill and members of my old Company D acting as guard of honor we marched to the chambers of the Supreme Court. Standing in the presence of my parents and wife, and holding my little daughter's hand, I was sworn in as adjutant general of my native state. Chief Justice C. M. Cureton, whose father once commanded a company of Rangers, and a friend of the family for three generations, administered the oath. I was now head of all the Rangers, and accepted the responsibility with deep humility.

We took up our living quarters at Camp Mabry, a beautiful wooded spot on the outskirts of Austin. It is a state military reservation, and was formerly used for the annual encampments of the Texas National Guard. The post had practically been abandoned, and most of the buildings were vacant. General Robertson was a bachelor and lived in a downtown hotel. During his administration the United States Property and Disbursing Officer occupied the residence reserved for the adjutant general. The wife of a high officer in the Guard advised

Mrs. Sterling that we had the right to rank Colonel Nichols out of this house. The advance from captain to brigadier general did not affect my sense of fairness, and I had no intention of disturbing a settled family. We fixed up a comfortable apartment in the spacious old hospital building and were well satisfied with our new home. I had a barbecue pit built in a nearby grove, and the long neglected camp became a mecca for picnickers and other visitors.

I shipped a carload of saddle horses from Falfurrias, and riding continued to be our favorite recreation. We had a number of fine animals that had been presented to us by stockmen on whose ranches I had scouted. My famous rodeo horse, Zarco, was given to me by R. H. Welder of San Patricio County. Mrs. Sterling rode a beautiful paint mare named Lady, presented by her cousin, Caesar Kleberg. Our daughter's favorite pony was Bootlegger whose shady past has already been recounted. He soon became popular with Austin youngsters, and a number of them learned to ride on his patient back. Governor Sterling sent his five gaited saddler, Black Gold, to Camp Mabry, and joined us in our rides when he could spare the time. There were many fine bridle paths in the hills around Mount Bonnel, and we used them almost every day.

My first step was the selection of a competent staff. General Robertson had a good organization in the military branch of the department, and it was in a high state of efficiency. Two men who were outstanding in their respective fields occupied the key positions. One of these entails a great deal of responsibility, and the man who fills it was called at that time the United States Property and Disbursing Officer. His accountability in Federal property amounts to millions of dollars, and he is under a heavy surety bond. Lieutenant Colonel Taylor Nichols of Robstown had performed the exacting duties of this office in an excellent manner, and I was happy to reappoint him.

The post of assistant adjutant general was held by Lieutenant Colonel Horace H. Carmichael, of Hillsboro. The Texas National Guard was almost the breath of life to him, and one of his sons was eligible for the Guard appointment to West Point. In the face of some opposition from a high ranking officer in the division I retained him and he did a fine job. Richard Carmichael fully justified the confidence we had in him. After graduating from the Academy, he became a distinguished general officer in the Air Force.

I was fortunate in having the services and counsel of Miss Lucile Phelps, who had practically grown up in the department. Her father, Colonel Edwin M. Phelps, served for many years as assistant adjutant general. She knew every detail of the office. Mrs. Charlene Gregory Wurzlow, whose family and mine had been lifelong friends, was my secretary. The aid and loyalty of these two ladies were of immense value to my administration.

The fact that I was the first adjutant general to be appointed from the Rangers since 1879 caused some speculation about the way I would be received by the National Guard. I had no misgivings on this score. The roster of general officers commanding the major components of the Texas National Guard contained the names of three of my best friends. Major General John A. Hulen of the Thirty-sixth Division once remarked that he "could take five hundred men like Bill Sterling and settle the border troubles, on both sides of the Rio Grande." Brigadier Generals Jacob F. Wolters of the Fifty-sixth Cavalry Brigade and Claude V. Birkhead of the Sixty-first Artillery Brigade had demonstrated their friendship to me in many ways. Former Adjutant General Dallas J. Matthews, assistant chief of staff of the Thirty-sixth Division and a power in the Guard, was a lifelong friend of my family. He had favored me in many ways during his term of office. Numerous guardsmen had visited our ranch when they were serving on the Mexican border, and many others were from my Alma Mater, Texas A. and M. College.

I had been a lieutenant in the Texas National Guard during World War I, and a scout for the Third United States Cavalry in the 1915 Bandit War. Much of my spare time had been spent at Forts Brown, Ringgold and other border posts. Nearly all of our Anglo friends in that region were Army officers. My brother married the daughter of a major general in the Regular Army, who was a graduate of West Point.

When the National Guard was mobilized on the Mexican border in 1916, Major General John F. O'Ryan of the New York Division used me as his unofficial advisor and guide. Shortly before his death in San Antonio, I accompanied General Fred Funston on his last inspection trip to the Valley. I also went with General John J. Pershing when he visited border posts soon after he returned from the punitive expedition in Mexico. Having kept in close touch with military affairs for many years, I did not feel the least bit out of character while serving in my native state's armed forces as chief of staff.

General Robertson desired to continue in the National Guard, and as a vacancy existed in the post of inspector general, I utilized his long experience by giving him this important assignment. He arranged for me to meet with a number of Guard officers at a luncheon in Waco, where they could get better acquainted with the new adjutant general and vice versa. Among my old friends at this conference were Colonel William C. Torrence and Major Horton B. Porter, both of whom had been guests at our ranch. The assembly was well satisfied with my statement of policy, and were convinced that the National Guard would get a fair deal from me, notwithstanding the fact that I had not been appointed from their organization. "I am like a married man who has a place in his heart for his mother and one for his wife," I told them. "Neither will ever encroach on the domain of the other. This is the way I feel about the National Guard and the Rangers. Furthermore, I do not owe my appointment to any group or clique, if such exists in the Guard, and can discharge my duties unhampered by entangling alliances." The meeting was a success, and each officer pledged me his support.

Shortly after my return to Austin, Will Rogers came to the capitol for a visit with me and his other friends among the Rangers. He walked around my desk and said, "I just wanted to see how you would fit in that swivel chair after all those years in the saddle." I replied, "Will, I am going to quit wearing boots, get me a little hat and try to make a city hand." He did not laugh but said in all seriousness, "Don't do that, Bill. Be yourself. That's how I get along." Will and Jimmie Rodgers, the singer, were on a benefit tour raising money for the victims of the Red River flood in Northeast Texas. They were not related and spelled their names differently, but both gave generously of their time, money and talent to relieve the sufferers. They were true friends of the Service, and each held a commission as a Special Texas Ranger.

During my first year as adjutant general, the Rotarians held a statewide meeting in Austin. The home club served as host, and I was named chairman of the program committee. Jimmie Rodgers had just reached the height of his popularity, and I asked him to

Photograph presented to me by Will Rogers and Jimmy Rodgers.

appear as our feature attraction. He responded in these words: "I am ready and happy to obey any order from my superior officer," although I had not intended it to be a command performance. The audience was delighted with his songs, and at the conclusion the artist presented me with the fabulous guitar he had used in making many of his records. It was made by Weyman, whose instruments have become collector's pieces. Inlaid on the neck in mother of pearl letters is "Jimmie Rodgers."

Will Rogers headed a group of cowboys and Special Rangers who gave me a magnificent parade saddle. The cards that accompanied this thoughtful gift read like *Who's Who*. It is one of the finest specimens of its kind, and was designed by a Ranger who had made a lifelong study of riding gear. The tree, which is the most vital part of a saddle, is covered with the heaviest bull hide. Carefully selected leather was used. It came from the best tanyard in California, where the matchless oak bark process is employed to tan packer hides. The stamping is beautifully executed, while the judicious number of gold and silver ornaments display good taste rather than gaudiness. A show saddle, like a pretty lady, can have its looks spoiled by too much glitter. After reaching a certain point, a million dollars in jewels may be loaded on either of them without adding a nickel's worth to their natural beauty. A unique and seldom noted feature in the decor of the saddle is the *hilo de oro* (gold thread) embroidered around the skirts and *rosaderos*. Several yards of this imported material went into these designs. This painstaking needlework, as well as the hand tooling of the leather, reflect the skill and patience of a maestro who learned the art in Mexico. When my rodeo days were over, I wanted this masterpiece to have a good home. Furthermore, I saw an opportunity to show my gratitude to one of those priceless individuals, a faithful friend. For these reasons, and for the pleasure it gave both of us, I presented this saddle, together with my Ranger scout belt and spurs, to Fred M. Golding.

The Red River emergency provided my first official taste of War Department red tape. There was an acute shortage of clothing among the refugees and the Red Cross sent out an appeal for all kinds of wearing apparel. Several thousand woolen uniforms that had been discarded by the National Guard were stored in the warehouse at Camp Mabry. They were obsolete, as the high collared blouse had been replaced by a new style, with rolled collars. These garments were warm, and had a great deal of service left in them. They would never again be used by troops and it cost the State considerable money to keep them in mothballs.

These circumstances presented an opportunity to kill two birds with one stone. They afforded a chance to get rid of a surplus and at the same time put the old suits to good use. I announced my intention of sending them to the flooded area without delay. My subordinates, who were well versed in Army regulations, emphatically stated that it could not be done.

I called my old friend, Horace Booth, a high official of the I. & G. N. Railroad in Houston and asked him if he would furnish free transportation for the shipment. He replied that his company would be happy to make this contribution to the relief program. A boxcar was soon spotted at the warehouse door. Then I obtained an official request for the discarded uniforms from the Red Cross. My assistants were almost frantic, and one of them predicted that I would end up in Leavenworth. He made every effort to get clearance, and sent many messages to Washington. I told him that the uniforms were going out on the next train, regardless of the answer. About an hour before they left, Colonel Carmichael came in with a dispatch from the War Department, authorizing us to donate the items in question to the Red Cross.

Three vacancies existed on the State staff. The lieutenant colonelcy was given to Dr. J. A. Simpson of Laredo. He was an officer of world wide experience with whom I had served on the Mexican border. Colonel Simpson brought a great deal of ability in both medical and military science to the National Guard. I appointed my brother, Edward A. Sterling, Jr., of Laredo, a major. He was a combat veteran of World War I, and a member of the class of 1915 at Texas A. & M. College. I gave the other majority to Paul L. Wakefield, who served as my aide.

When I took over, several rabid Fergusonites were on the State staff. These included a son-in-law of the Fergusons. Believing that the staff should be kept entirely free of politics, I did not disturb them in any way. They were treated with the utmost fairness and shown every consideration. When the Fergusons came into control, they repaid this courtesy by immediately removing my appointees.

The Forty-second Legislature increased the appropriation for the

State Service Office, and authorized two additional officers. The depression had tightened its grip on the country, and competition for these positions was keen. I appointed Lieutenant Colonel William C. Torrence, of Waco, State Service Officer, with William A. Wyatt of San Marcos and Captain Frank Chapa of San Antonio as assistants. At its 1931 session in El Paso, the American Legion approved my slate. My appointees rendered excellent service in furthering the claims of Texas veterans.

While going over the administrative details of the department, I discovered that a policy that was both unwise and dangerous had been pursued by the adjutant general. When he was out of the city, or for any other reason absent from his office, all Ranger matters on which final action had to be taken were handled by the assistant adjutant general. This officer's training did not qualify him to make intelligent decisions in problems of law enforcement. Because of his rank, however, he was required to issue orders that affected the lives and property of trusting citizens. They often proved to be nothing more nor less than shots in the dark.

My decision was based on long experience in the field, plus personal knowledge of many mistakes made by rank conscious officers. I recalled a case in point that took place in 1915. When the bandits attacked the ranch headquarters at old Norias, two companies of Rangers converged on the spot. The adjutant general hurried down to take personal charge.

Not a single qualification for this responsibility was reflected in his background. Born in England, he was State printer in 1892, and thereafter accepted any appointment he could get. By virtue of his rank, any decision he made was final. While the higher command was holdings its council of war, the bandits were camped a few miles away. After refreshing themselves and resting their horses, they made their unmolested way to the Rio Grande.

I took immediate steps to correct this dangerous procedure. Calling in Colonel Carmichael and Captain Hamer, I gave them explicit instructions about their respective duties. They were advised that in my absence, all matters pertaining to the Rangers would be referred to, and handled by, the senior captain. Carmichael exclaimed, "General, I certainly want to thank you for giving this order. I am delighted to be relieved from any connection with the Rangers. I know nothing about their work." In view of his statement my amazement knew no bounds when, several years later, he was named director of the Texas Department of Public Safety.

Throughout my four years' service as captain of Company D, it became more and more apparent that something was radically wrong at Ranger headquarters. I could sense that an unhealthy condition existed there, and it seemed to be getting progressively worse. This sinister influence was undermining the morale of the men, and was highly detrimental to the Service. Most of the trouble emanated from the machinations of the quartermaster, R. W. Aldrich.

Several years before I took over as adjutant general, this synthetic Texan had been allowed to usurp the rank of senior captain. The statute under which the Rangers functioned was specific in both wording and intent. Article 6561 stipulated that: "The headquarters company shall consist of one captain, who shall be designated as senior captain of the Force, one sergeant and not to exceed four privates." Article 6563 provided that: "The Governor shall appoint a quartermaster for the Ranger Force, who shall discharge the duties of quartermaster, commissary and paymaster, and shall have the rank and pay of a captain." The duties of this appointee were clearly defined. His job was strictly clerical. He had no authority whatsoever over the Rangers, nor any right to exercise command.

The laws setting out the duties of the senior captain and those of the quartermaster had been totally disregarded. This violation was particularly flagrant when the statures of the incumbents were compared, or their worth measured in terms of value to the Service. Frank A. Hamer, captain of the headquarters company, was a great Ranger leader. He knew Texas and had a deep insight into the minds and hearts of his fellow Texans. R. W. Aldrich, the imported quartermaster, possessed neither of these essentials. He had obtained his knowledge of the Rangers and "Texus", as he pronounced the name of our state, from copious reading of wild West and pulp magazines. He did not look like a Texan, talk like a Texan nor think like a Texan, for he was not a Texan.

I well remember when Aldrich first came to Captain J. J. Sanders' company in Alice. His advent into that hard riding outfit of Texans created a sensation. When he walked through the gate at the Ranger camp, grizzled old Sam McKenzie, a veteran of Captain Bill Mc-Donald's company, exclaimed, "What kind of varmint is that?" Sam's astonishment can well be understood, for it is doubtful that a comparable specimen ever arrived at a Ranger station. Aldrich wore a sheep herder's hat, and his face was as white as the snow of his native clime. He had on a pair of new, store bought boots, which obviously were the first ones he had ever worn. He cut a ludicrous figure as he essayed to herd his unfamiliar footwear down the wooden sidewalks.

Edward J. Heuermann, who is now a prosperous farmer in San Patricio County, was one of my roommates at Texas A. & M. College. In World War I, he served overseas as a commissioned officer and in World War II, he was a military intelligence agent. Ed Heuermann is one of the few surviving members of Captain Sanders' company. He and Aldrich were in this outfit at the same time. Ed and I recently had a long visit. We talked at great length about old Ranger days, and from him I was able to get some authentic information.

He was amazed at a brochure recently brought out in Austin. Some misinformed writer referred to Aldrich as "a man who had chased bandits on the border." Ex-Ranger Heuermann said, "The only bandits Roy ever saw were the ones in pictures. Each Ranger in the company picked a partner to side him, but none of the boys would pair off with Aldrich. He didn't know what was going on either in camp or in the brush. The few times he was on horseback, he rode like a soldier, rising in his stirrups or posting when his horse trotted. This was particularly amusing to the Rangers. When we were away from camp, Aldrich spent most of his time hunting arrow heads."

Practically all of the old time Rangers hated any form of paper work. Captain Sanders soon saw that the self-styled soldier of fortune was totally unfit for border service, and made him company clerk. Aldrich was well suited for this chore, as he had been a banker in Oklahoma. He happened to be in Austin when the current quartermaster resigned under fire. Aldrich stepped into the vacancy and took up the bookkeeping duties, probably with the grade of sergeant. The captaincy had been promised to Walter I. Rowe, a well qualified Ranger who was recovering from a serious wound received in line of duty. Aldrich talked a good game, was quite a joiner, had some money and an education. With these qualifications he succeeded in undermining a disabled Texan and securing the appointment as quartermaster captain.

Purchasing a house near Austin, Aldrich assembled a menagerie and an extensive library. Many of his books dealt with subjects most Texans do not care to read about, but this class of literature apparently added to his popularity with certain groups of that city.

The newcomer soon developed into a small time Machiavelli. He began to use his wiles and cunning to ingratiate himself with the adjutant general. That officer was persuaded that his duties would be lightened if he would place the quartermaster in charge of the Rangers. With one exception, all adjutant generals had been appointed from the military branch of the state's armed forces. The Texas National Guard, for which my admiration is unbounded, had grown to such proportions that its affairs required almost the entire time of the general. It was not too difficult for a schemer like Aldrich to sell himself as the indispensable man.

By paring the men's accounts, he made a great show of saving money for the State. His thrift was only practiced on the Texans. He dealt most generously with his brother and himself. A case in point was that of car allowances for the field Ranger companies. Each captain received $50 per month for maintenance of an automobile. It was used by the entire company. My district was larger than several eastern states, and this amount did not begin to pay for the mileage. Aldrich allotted himself one of these allowances. His car was not used for State business, but to transport himself from the capitol to his suburban home.

After intrenching himself in the department, R. W. Aldrich accomplished a further infiltration by sending for his brother. Since his advent in Texas, he had been employed by a San Antonio social club. This resort was a notorious hangout for gamblers. Tod Aldrich admitted that the only horseback work he had ever done was to ride a plow mule bareback through a corn field in his native state. When brother Roy told him about the easy pickings in Austin, he followed suit and joined the "Texus" Rangers.

With Roy in the swivel chair and Tod as the fair haired boy, this white faced pair set up a despotism that was a disgrace to Texas and a severe blow to the morale of the Rangers. Their tyranny reached an almost unbelievable point. When a new man joined the headquarters company, one of the old timers would usually give him a friendly tip.

"If you want to do well in the Rangers," the recruit was advised, "the big idea is to get along with the Aldriches." When Governor Sterling placed me in charge of the Rangers, I told them, "Getting along with Bill Sterling is not the main idea. Just be a good Ranger and you will automatically get along with the new Adjutant General."

Captain Hamer and some of his men once decided to find out just how far the Aldriches would go with their intrigues. They had a man in a distant city send a telegram to the Texas Rangers, advising that a bank absconder was hiding out in an Austin tourist lodge. It also stated that a large reward had been offered for his apprehension. The message was addressed to the captain of the headquarters company but the quartermaster took it and read the contents. He did not say a word for a few minutes, then he called his brother out into the corridor of the capitol. Without notifying the other Rangers, the conniving brothers went to the motel to arrest the banker and get the reward. Captain Hamer had rented a room there and gave them the horselaugh.

Aldrich further stringhalted our efforts to maintain high standards in the Rangers, by opposing increases in their pay. For many years those who cherished the Service had fought for adequate salaries. General Hulen, in his 1906 report, made a plea for this needed raise. He declared, "Only by offering suitable wages can we hope to attract a better class of men, and to avoid the enormous turnover in personnel."

The quartermaster made the assertion that he could get all the Rangers he wanted for $75 per month. Captain Hamer's reply to this iniquitous statement voiced the sentiments of a majority of the Texans in the Service. He said, "You could send off seventy-five tobacco tags and get a better Ranger than Aldrich." The Texas Rangers, more than any other organization, is dependent on the quality of its personnel. When made up of good men, it is a wonderful outfit. By the same token, when sorry men are in the saddle, it quickly becomes a disgrace to the state. Aldrich sought to fill the ranks with second and third raters. Only in this way could he continue his domination.

Notwithstanding the fact that numerous evidences of Aldrich's chicanery had come to my personal notice, I approached his case with an open mind. When the matter of his reappointment came up, I was determined to give him a fair hearing and a square deal. His maneuvers and antics during my first days in office were those of a thoroughly confused man. He rushed around in feverish haste, fawned on both generals and danced attention to our orders. The field captains were highly elated over the recognition that had been given to the Ranger Service. Each one of them was glad to see an honor bestowed on one of their comrades.

This is reflected in an excerpt from a letter I received from Captain Tom R. Hickman. On January 2, 1931, he wrote:

> After having heard many rumors as to who will be our next Adjutant General, I was informed by fairly reliable authority today that in all probability you might receive the appointment. Several of the other rumors have been very pleasing to me, but I must say that your appointment to the place would give me great satisfaction. I have always wanted to see some Ranger Captain advanced to the important post of Adjutant General, for I feel that then our organization would get fairer and better consideration than it has ever been given. Personally, I would not want the honor, because it carries entirely too much responsibility when compared to the salary, but if you would consider it, I certainly hope it is offered to you.

These Texans were not afraid to be measured by a true Ranger yardstick; neither did they dread to be commanded by a man who would be hard to deceive in any phase of their duties. Aldrich did not share this feeling. He realized that if a man who knew the requisites of a real Ranger was ever appointed adjutant general, his shameful rule would be ended.

The counterfeit Ranger began his campaign by asking General Robertson to speak to me in his behalf. I showed my predecessor the Ranger statutes, and called his attention to the biennial report he had submitted to the Governor. In the table of organization, Aldrich appeared at the head of the Rangers instead of in his lawful place as quartermaster. The ex-Adjutant General's face paled. In his blind reliance on Aldrich, he had entirely overlooked the regulations. The schemer next sent a business man of the city to see me. This individual made me a startling proposition. He said, "General, you are a cowman, and on occasions trade in livestock. If you need any money to carry on this business, Aldrich has plenty, and will lend you all you want." My reply was in the form of a question, "Wouldn't I be a fine public official if I borrowed money from a subordinate?"

His last effort was one of desperation. There is not a man on earth for whom I have more respect than Governor Dan Moody, nor one whose counsel I would be more eager to heed. A few days after his term of office expired he invited me to ride with him from Austin to San Antonio. En route he said that Aldrich wanted him to talk to me and urge that he be kept in his present position. "Governor," I asked, "If you had served in the same organization with a man for four years, and he was not straightforward enough to come to you and state his case, what would you do?" The ex-Governor asked in surprise, "Hasn't Aldrich been to you?" "No," I replied, "he has only tried to high pressure me through friends like you." "Then you ought to fire him," said Governor Moody.

I am not a hunter and have never enjoyed killing any wild creatures except predatory animals. However, before night hunting became illegal, I sometimes hunted varmints in the brush with a headlight. You can readily tell when you are shining a coyote. These sneaking animals will never come at you straight, but will circle around and show only one eye. This was the approach used by Aldrich. When news got around that he was out, there was great rejoicing among the boys on the border. One company gave a barbecue to celebrate the end of carpetbagger rule in the Rangers.

Aldrich has rated all this space for a specific reason. When I let him out, some misinformed people thought he had received a bad deal. The true facts of his discharge have never before appeared in print.

My next problem with the Rangers had to do with Light Townsend. That gentleman was a member of a pioneer Texas family and had been in the Service for a long time. He had served for the last four years as sergeant of Company D, which I commanded. Any hint of friction between us was a result of the system then in use, and not from personal animosity. The method employed in selecting the two top officers of the Rangers was not conducive to harmony. When a new administration went in, those men who aspired to be captains began their campaigns by making formal application to the governor. These were supported by as many endorsements as could be obtained. In most cases, the recommendations included lengthy petitions.

The governor appointed the men of his choice as captains. The ones next highest on the preferred lists were made sergeants, when vacancies

First Row: General W. W. Sterling, Adjutant General, Governor Ross S. Sterling, Captains W. L. Wright (Co. A), Tom R. Hickman (Co. B), Light Townsend (Co. C), P. B. Hill (Chaplain), A. R. Mace (Co. D), C. O. Moore (Quartermaster), Sergeants J. A. Miller, J. W. Smith, J. B. Wheatley, M. T. Gonzaullas, John W. Sadler, Captain Frank Hamer, Miss Inez Sterling (Sweetheart). *Second Row:* Rangers R. W. Sumrall, Stewart Stanley, Robert G. Goss, M. Burton, Fred E. Griffin, Earl McWilliams, H. L. Johnston, Edgar T. Neal, Harold Slack, Joe W.

existed in that grade. The sergeant often felt that he owed his job to the governor, rather than to the captain. Townsend and I were both applicants for the captaincy of Company D. Governor Moody saw fit to name me. I did not blame the sergeant in the least for wanting to be captain, and assured him that he would be shown every consideration. My company headquarters were in Falfurrias, but in order that he might be his own boss most of the time, I requested the adjutant general to station him in Raymondville. Some of the people who had signed his petition kept telling him that he should have been the captain and in other ways tried to make him dissatisfied with his lot.

When it became known that I was to be appointed adjutant general, Sergeant Townsend felt grave concern about his future in the Rangers. He hurried to Falfurrias and asked Judge J. A. Brooks, of Brooks County to speak to me in his behalf. The sergeant knew this veteran captain to be one of my closest friends, as well as the man from whom I learned to be a Ranger. In refusing to intercede for the sergeant, Captain Brooks did not mince words. "Townsend," he said sternly, "you know that you have never shown the proper loyalty to your captain. You do not deserve any consideration from Bill Sterling."

White, W. A. Dial, A. Y. Allee, Earl B. Franks, O. C. Humphries. *Third Row:*
Ex-Ranger A. B. Coffee (Com. Ex-Ranger Assn.), Rangers, W. E. Young, Thad
Tarver Elbert Riggs, H. D. Glasscock, H. B. Purvis, W. H. Kirby, W. E. Lowe,
Ted Lewis, E. M. Davenport, Tom L. Heard, J. L. Rehm, L. V. Hightower, R. E.
Pool. *Top Row:* Rangers J. P. Huddleston, Arthur B. Hamm, William R. Smith,
B. M. Gault, O. T. Martin, W. D. Cope, George M. Allen, Jim McCoy.

The day after I took office, Townsend sent an emissary to see me.
He was Graves Peeler of Atascosa County, ace brand inspector for the
Texas and Southwestern Cattle Raisers Association, and one of my best
friends. He held a Texas Ranger commission, and I had scouted many
miles with him. A further bond between us was that we both attended
Texas A. & M. College. Peeler began the conversation by saying, "I
guess you are going to fire Light Townsend, aren't you?" "No," I
replied, "I am going to make him a captain." My visitor was astounded
and said, "Light realizes that he was not as loyal to his captain as he
should have been. He expects you to give him a rough ride." "Regardless of that," I continued, "he has been a sergeant a long time, and is
entitled to the promotion. Personalities are beside the point." At a
Ranger conference in Austin, Captain Townsend asked if he might say
a few words. Pointing his finger at me, his voice trembled with emotion
as he said, "Boys, that man gave me the fairest treatment I ever got
in my life. Instead of firing me, as I probably deserved, he promoted
me."

The cases of Aldrich and Townsend proved my deep devotion to
the Ranger Service. I would not use it to reward my best friend nor

to punish my worst enemy. Aldrich had never done anything to me personally, but as he was a detriment to the Service, I discharged him. Townsend had offended me, but as he was the logical man for the place, I promoted him.

My slate of Ranger captains had been screened with great care, and I was now ready to submit it to Governor Sterling for his approval. In character, personality, experience and ability, this list of leaders could not be surpassed.

Frank A. Hamer, captain of Headquarters Company, is the subject of a chapter in this book. The same is true of Captain Will L. Wright, who commanded Company A. Captain Tom R. Hickman, of Company B, is the sole survivor of this splendid staff. Still hale and hearty, he is one of the best known and most popular men in Texas. His life and exploits have been covered in various articles and books. Captain Albert Mace of Company C had received his early training in the Rangers and for many years served as sheriff of Lampasas County. He made an enviable record as chief of police in the oil boom town of Mexia, and was an ideal Ranger commander.

Captain Light Townsend was currently sergeant of Company D. It was deemed advisable to give him command of Company C. He was transferred to Del Rio, where he and Captain Mace exchanged companies. Captain Townsend rendered many years of service to the State. His death from a heart attack, which occurred in 1932, cut short his career as Ranger captain.

After a thorough canvass of the field, I concluded that the best available man for the quartermaster's post was C. O. Moore. He had been sheriff of Falls County before joining the Rangers. Upon the declaration of martial law in the oil fields around Borger, he was appointed sheriff of Hutchinson County. The emergency demanded a strong man for that office, and Moore took over, "on loan" from the Rangers. He was granted a leave of absence, with the understanding that he would be re-instated at the end of his term. When the administration changed, he began to worry about his status with the new adjutant general. Not knowing that he had already been selected quartermaster captain, Moore asked me if there was any chance for him to get back in the Service. "I can't make you a Ranger, C. O.," was the reply, and his face fell, "but there is one thing I can do. I am going

THE RANGER'S PRAYER.

O God, whose end is justice,
Whose strength is all our stay,
Be near and bless my mission
As I go forth today.
Let wisdom guide my actions,
Let courage fill my heart
And help me, Lord, in every hour
To do a Ranger's part.
Protect when danger threatens,
Sustain when trails are rough;
Help me to keep my standard high
And smile at each rebuff.
When night comes down upon me,
I pray thee, Lord, be nigh,
Whether on lonely scout, or camped,
Under the Texas sky.
Keep me, O God, in life
And when my days shall end,
Forgive my sins and take me in,
For Jesus' sake, Amen.

Pierre Bernard Hill
Chaplain Texas Rangers

to make you a captain." His delight over that disclosure knew no bounds. He made an excellent quartermaster. Emmett Moore, his son, is presently warden of the State penitentiary.

The Reverend Dr. Pierre Bernard Hill, pastor of the First Presbyterian Church in San Antonio, had been appointed chaplain of the Rangers by Governor Dan Moody. His worth to the Service and the good influence he had on the men cannot be overestimated. He was a great favorite with all of us. Each company looked on a visit from him as a happy occasion, as well as a spiritual uplift. Dr. Hill can best be described as a friend who was always eager to help a Ranger, either with a prayer or a six-shooter. Compatible with the dignity of his post and the affection in which he was held, I promoted him to captain. In addition to his other contributions to the welfare and morale of the Service, he composed "The Ranger's Prayer." A copy of this inspiring verse blesses the home of practically every old time Ranger.

Governor Sterling notified me, through his secretary, that he was ready to proceed with the appointing of Ranger captains. I went to see him a short time ahead of the men, as there were several matters he wanted to discuss with me before taking final action. A politically powerful publisher nursed a personal grudge against one of the captains, and had opposed his reappointment. I happened to know all about the incident that had caused this animosity, and was able to assure the Governor that the captain was in the right. There was some opposition to another prospective appointee, and my decision in this case was also accepted by the Chief Executive. He remarked, "I know how anxious you are to build up the Rangers. I want the laws enforced. That's why I appointed you. I am going to give you a free rein."

We filed into the private office, where I presented each candidate to the Governor. He was already acquainted with most of the group, and greeted them with a friendly handshake. "Gentlemen," he said, "Bill tells me that you are the ones he believes to be best qualified to serve Texas as Ranger captains. I am going to follow his recommendation. I know that none of you will let us down." In all probability this was the only time a Texas Governor ever allowed one man so much latitude in selecting Rangers.

No applicants backed by the customary endorsements from high powered politicians were given serious consideration. Captains Hamer,

Wright, Hickman and Mace were reappointed. Captain Townsend, Moore and Hill were promoted. In every case my new captains came from the Rangers. The wisdom of this policy was reflected by the high state of efficiency, calibre of personnel and splendid morale that existed in the Ranger Service during the administration of Governor Sterling.

Among the young men who applied to me for enlistment in the Service was Alfred Y. Allee. His family and mine had been friends for three generations. He grew up on a Southwest Texas ranch, spoke good Spanish and was thoroughly familiar with conditions on the border. I knew that he possessed all the requisites of an outstanding Ranger. After giving him the same sort of advice a father would give his son, I had him sworn in. My high opinion of A. Y. Allee has been fully vindicated. In 1947 he was promoted to the rank of captain. His territory includes Duval County. He has handled each new crisis in that strife torn region in a masterful manner.

Before I took office in 1932, the lack of adequate automobile transportation had seriously handicapped the movements of the Rangers. The only provision for car maintenance was an allowance of $50 per month for each company. The rate received by the field captains was set to fit that of the quartermaster, but there was a vast difference in their requirements. We had to travel hundreds of miles each month in carrying out our assignments.

During many years service on the Mexican border, I made a study of the system used by the Federal Government in dealing with the automotive equipment of their mounted customs inspectors. It was a proven success. I knew that a similar plan would improve both the mobility and efficiency of the Rangers. Pursuant to this idea, I had every third Ranger designated as a "car man." He received an allowance of $80 per month for his automobile, and was required to transport two other men. It worked out fine, and everybody in the Service was happy over this innovation.

In order to get this extra money, it was necessary to convince the appropriations committee that it was needed. They looked into all phases of my request, and granted it without a dissenting vote. General Jacob F. Wolters accompanied me on my appearance before the legislators. On the way back to the office, he said, "You ought not to work so hard on the Ranger appropriation. Your salary does not come

Group of Rangers and famous New York theatre owner on east steps of capitol. Bottom row, left to right: Quartermaster Captain C. O. Moore, Adjutant General W. W. Sterling, S. L. Rothafel (Roxy), Captain Frank A. Hamer. Top row, left to right, Ranger Oscar Martin, Ranger George Allen, and Ranger (later Captain) Mannie Gault.

out of it." My reply to this admonition was, "General, I will always do everything in my power to help the Rangers."

After the Republic of Texas entered the Union as a state, protection of its frontiers against hostile Indians became an obligation of the United States. During the seventies and early eighties, most of this duty was performed by the Rangers. Many of these aged veterans were entitled to Federal pensions. Scarcely any of them knew how to put in their claims. Some of the old timers had been exploited by unscrupulous lawyers, who charged them exorbitant fees for handling their cases.

The commander of the Ex-Rangers Association was Major A. B. Coffee. He had rendered a great service to his comrades, by personally forwarding their applications to Washington. The major's resources were exhausted in this worthy cause, and he wrote me that he could go no farther without assistance. His work was also handicapped by the lack of cooperation from the adjutant general's department, where the records were kept. When he saw in the press that a Ranger had been appointed to that office, he immediately came to Austin. I gave him a full time job, an office, and the services of a stenographer. With these facilities at his command, he was able to secure pensions for many deserving ex-Rangers. The old warriors' expressions of gratitude more than repaid me for my efforts.

A number of notables, who for one reason or another came to Austin, found their way to my office. Among these distinguished visitors was S. L. Rothafel, known to the theatrical world as "Roxy." On March 3, 1931, he brought a troupe to the Gregory Gymnasium under the title of "Roxy and His Gang." The featured attraction of his concert was the appearance of Madame Ernestine Schumann-Heink.

Although nearing the end of her career, this venerable prima donna captivated the large audience. This was accomplished not only by the quality of her voice, but by her radiant personality and gracious manner. The entire performance, presented by the Amateur Choral Club of Austin, was received with enthusiasm.

I was amazed at Roxy's extensive knowledge of the history and traditions of our organization. During his stay in the capital city, he spent most of his spare time talking with the men. He expressed a desire to have his picture taken with a group of Rangers, and we were glad to gratify that wish. Available at the moment were Captain Hamer and Rangers Oscar Martin, George Allen and B. M. Gault, all of Headquarters Company. Quartermaster Captain C. O. Moore was also on hand. Roxy and I met them on the east steps of the capitol. He put on my hat and held my six-shooter in his hand. We succeeded in getting a fine photograph. Roxy felt a deep interest in the welfare of the Rangers. Before taking his departure, he said, "General, I would like to come down here some time and put on a show for your pension fund." He was astounded to learn that the State made no provision for veterans of the Ranger Service.

Chapter 22
SERVICE IN AUSTIN

 S HORTLY after getting settled, I was honored by an invitation to join the Town and Gown Club. My association with this distinguished group of educators, authors, statesmen and townspeople was the most pleasant part of the two years I spent in Austin. J. Frank Dobie was my sponsor. His thoughtfulness in this matter added one more item to the debt of gratitude I owe this great Texan. Each new member is required to tell a more or less original story. Mine dealt with a ranchero in Zapata County.

In that semi-arid region, very little wind blows in the early part of September. During this period of dead calm, the stockmen are hard put to water their cattle, goats and horses. There is not enough breeze to turn the windmills. My neighbor, Don Fulano de Tal, had two wells at the home ranch. They were located on opposite sides of a small earthen reservoir. One year the calm lasted so long that he decided to meet the crisis with a desperate measure. He took down one of his windmills, thereby leaving all the wind for the other one.

Accompanied by Colonel Taylor Nichols, United States Property and Disbursing Officer, I went to Washington for a conference of State adjutant generals. The Texas newspaper correspondents spread the welcome mat for us and made our stay in the capital a most pleasant one.

They gave a luncheon in our honor at the National Press Club, and in the afternoon they took us to the American League baseball park. Here we met the owner of the Washington Senators, Clark Griffith. He in turn introduced us to his manager, the peerless Walter Johnson. The "Big Train" called Fred Marberry, Sammy West and Lloyd Brown, the members of his team who were from Texas. We went down in front of the stands for a group picture.

It was featured in the next morning's newspaper. Paul Yates said in his dispatch to Texas:

> Cap'n Bill Sterling routs King of Siam from spot on Page 1. Sterling, six feet four, vies with 98 pound King in Washington.
>
> While the king was keeping a round of engagements, Adjutant General Sterling and Colonel Nichols were having a round of entertainments. Thursday, they are to be received by President Hoover.

Mark Goodwin of the Dallas *News* and Bascom Timmons of the Houston *Chronicle* arranged this appointment, and accompanied us to the White House. Before being shown in, Mark briefed me on the proper way to greet the President. "Don't offer to shake hands with him, until he makes the first gesture," said my sponsor. I was duly mindful of this admonition. When we entered his private office, Mr. Hoover arose, smiled, and welcomed me with a firm handclasp.

The leading Texas dailies carried the account of our visit to the White House under the heading, "Hoover knows Ranger history. Has long chat with Adjutant General Sterling." The story said:

> President Hoover is familiar with the history and tradition of the Texas Rangers, he revealed today in a chat with Adjutant General W. W. Sterling and Colonel Taylor Nichols. The President kept a big crowd of callers waiting while he talked about the Rangers with Sterling, an old time Ranger.
>
> While waiting at the White House, someone suggested that Sterling take a bunch of Rangers to Nicaragua and capture Sandino. Sterling said he had made such an offer to Major General Frank R. McCoy, who was in charge of the United States forces hunting Sandino.

The Associated Press had a photographer on hand, and he took our picture as we were leaving the White House. It appeared in many leading newspapers.

I made a survey of the various jobs in my department, and set up a plan whereby we could give employment to the maximum number of students. If a position paid $150 per month, they were permitted to arrange their schedules so three boys could perform the required service and divide the salary. The depression was on, and $50 often meant the difference between staying in school or being forced to drop out. Young men so employed came from the university, the Presbyterian Theological Seminary and in the summer, several were from A. & M.

Colonel Taylor Nichols was an ardent baseball fan, and Captain John T. Tyson, who had charge of the arsenal at Camp Mabry, was an old league player. These officers organized and managed the Adjutant General's Baseball Team. It was composed of men within the department, many of whom were current college stars. I had been a pretty good amateur ball player all my life, and although forty years old, was given the place of first baseman. My rank doubtless had a great deal to do with this selection, and when the going got too rough, I was glad to relinquish the position to a younger man.

Inmates of the penitentiary at Huntsville had a fine team that year. It was called the Prison Cyclones. I arranged for a game with them, through Colonel Lee Simmons. Their manager called me on the telephone, and was very much perturbed. "General," he said, "large crowds come from Houston and other nearby points to see our Sunday games. We are obligated to our public to put on a first class contest. Do you think your team is good enough to do this?" I finally grasped his point. He thought all our players were men of my age, and that the game would probably be a walkover for the Cyclones. I assured him that we would not disappoint the fans, and the game was played. We won nine to one, much to the chagrin of the manager. Our college boys got one laugh out of the game. When the ball was knocked over the fence, many of the inmates would yell, "Let me go get it."

The first time I came up to bat, I recognized the catcher, and was astounded to see him in the penitentiary. "I've seen you somewhere, pardner," I said. "What's your name?" "Yes, you know me," he replied, and gave me his name. He had been a star on the team of a denominational college, where he was one of the most popular young men in school. "What happened, and how did you get in here?" I asked. "Living too high and looking for easy money," he replied. "I had an automobile agency and was doing fine. Then I got to drinking and gambling. Finally, I got to switching titles and selling mortgaged cars."

During my service as a Ranger captain, I once received a call from the manager of the prison farm at Blue Ridge. He was an old friend, John Lutenbacher, former sheriff of Goliad County. His division of the prison system housed most of the Latin convicts. John solicited my aid in breaking up the use of marihuana among his charges. We found that they had been planting it in flower beds, small patches and other places that would escape detection. Few people could recognize the plant, which closely resembles a harmless weed. I had seen it along the border, and was able to identify it at a glance. We worked for several days, and found enough to fill a cotton sack. The manager had received reports from penal farms in other states, advising him that convicts had been surreptiously growing the terrible *cannibas sativa*. Texas had no law prohibiting its cultivation or sale.

Soon after taking office, I started to work for an adequate law against all forms of narcotics. State Senator J. W. E. H. Beck of the first district was also a physician. I arranged a meeting in my office between the doctor-statesman and the Federal narcotic agent from San Antonio. At this conference we worked out a bill patterned after the Federal statute. Senator Beck was happy to sponsor this badly needed bit of legislation. It was known as Senate Bill No. 171, in the regular session of the Forty-second Legislature. The bill passed the Senate by a vote of thirty-one yeas and no nays, while the House voted one hundred and nine yeas and one nay. It was approved on April 30, 1931. The emergency clause was invoked, and it became effective the same date.

My office became a favorite gathering place for old timers. Included among them were several veterans whose exploits had contributed in a large measure to the fame of the Rangers. During their visits to Austin, Captain J. A. Brooks, Captain John R. Hughes and Captain James B. Gillett always spent a great deal of time with me. Gillett resigned from the Service while holding the grade of sergeant. He was always called "Captain," and to make the title official, I issued him a commission in that rank. The wise counsel and mature judgement of this trio were of incalculable value to me in handling the Rangers.

On a summer day in 1931, I noted that both Captain Brooks and Captain Hughes were among my visitors. The two old comrades just happened to be in the city at the same time. Captain Frank A. Hamer of Headquarters Company occupied the next office. The venerable Dan W. Roberts, oldest living captain of Company D resided with one of his daughters in Austin.

Five Ranger Captains whose service extended from 1876 to 1933. Seated Captain Dan Roberts. Standing, from left to right, Captain J. A. Brooks, Adjutant General W. W. Sterling, former Ranger Captain, Frank A. Hamer and Captain John R. Hughes.

In the presence of these men, I recognized the opportunity to get a rare Ranger picture. It would never come again. Calling a photographer, we drove to the home of Captain Roberts. The old Indian fighter was very feeble in body, but his mind was clear and alert. He gave us a cordial welcome, and seemed delighted to appear in what he knew would be his last picture. We succeeded in getting the photograph of five Ranger captains who served from 1874 to 1933. They were Dan W. Roberts, John A. Brooks, John R. Hughes, Frank A. Hamer and W. W. Sterling. Out of this group, I am the sole survivor.

During the annual homecoming at the University of Texas, all fraternity, sorority and rooming houses decorate their premises. Prizes are awarded to those in each class whose displays are most typical of Texas. Captain Roberts' daughter took roomers at her home, so we went all out to help her win. The headquarters company pitched a real Ranger camp in the front yard. It attracted wide attention, and drew a good deal of favorable comment. Rangers Oscar Martin, Jim McCoy, George Allen and Earl McWilliams worked in relays. They served cowboy coffee, and otherwise entertained the visitors. Seated in a rawhide bottomed hickory chair was the aged Captain Roberts. His snow-white hair and weather-beaten countenance lent additional color to the scene. We were very much gratified when first prize in her division was won by the daughter of this veteran Ranger.

This reunion of ex-students is aptly called the Annual Roundup. When planning the third edition of that gala event, the committee decided to give it a genuine flavor of Texas. They felt that it would be appropriate to use the Rangers. The chairman of the rodeo committee was a student named Allan Shivers. This gentleman completely fulfilled the promise he showed in his youth. As Chief Executive of Texas, he occupied the Governor's Mansion longer than any other man in history. He invited us to take an active part in the festivities, and bestowed on me a title, as well as the responsibilities of, "Chief Wrangler."

I was very happy to accept. The ancient rivalry between the University of Texas and the A. & M. College is well known to every Texan. Only a few weeks before the Roundup, President H. Y. Benedict of the university had introduced me to the Austin Rotary Club as "The A. & M.-est of all A. & M. men." This undeserved, but to me most flattering, appellation did not dampen the enthusiasm with which I worked to make a success of the Roundup. Except for a few hours each Thanksgiving Day, I have always been a staunch supporter of Texas University.

213

At the University of Texas Annual Roundup in 1931. General W. W. Sterling on Zarco, Inez Sterling on Bootlegger and President H. Y. Benedict.

The committee gave me a free rein in the equestrian events. I felt that the most colorful spectacle we could put on would be a horseback quadrille. It would be the first time one of them had even been staged in Austin. The members of the Bit and Spur Club gave us their whole-hearted support. These charming young ladies quickly learned the intricate turns of the drill, and were soon going through them at a gallop.

Ranger Tom Heard of Company D was a typical Texan as well as an excellent horseman. He had ridden in the Falfurrias quadrille, knew all the figures and was a fine square dance caller. I assigned him to act as coach and instructor. Mounted on his spirited paint horse, Tom was a natural for this pleasant duty. By dint of constant practice, his pupils were soon doing the "grand right and left" in the manner of true Texas cowgirls.

Ranger Lockhart Hightower, scion of a pioneer East Texas family, furnished the music. He was billed as "The champion fiddler of the Big Thicket." The Ranger captivated the crowd with his rendition of the tune that has long been the favorite of old time square dancers. It is called "Hell Among the Yearlings."

The Austin newspapers carried glowing accounts of the rodeo, and everyone seemed to be particularly pleased with the quadrille. They were high in their praise of the part played by the Rangers. One correspondent stated that "General Sterling, riding his famous black paint horse, kept the show moving at a lively pace. He also led the mounted square dance. His little daughter, Inez, rode in the center of the ring with Governor Sterling."

During the four years he served as chairman of the Texas Highway Commission, R. S. Sterling made a careful on-the-ground study of the department. It disclosed the fact that numerous counties had voted bonds to finance the building of State highways. He felt that this practice was unjust, and advocated refunding to them all money hitherto expended on thoroughfares.

In his message to the Forty-second Legislature, Governor Sterling asked that a constitutional amendment be submitted to the people of Texas. The electorate would be given an opportunity to vote on a one hundred million dollar State bond issue. These were to be revenue bonds, secured solely by the gasoline tax. They would not place a levy on the lands, houses or personal property of any citizen. The users of the highways would pay for them. Many people who escaped every other form of taxation would be forced to bear a part of the load.

Funds raised by the State bond issue were to be used to reimburse the various counties for the amount they had spent on the State highway system. A very substantial part of the local tax burden would thereby be removed from lands and homes. The late Clay Grobe, eminent Texas newswriter and political observer, called Governor Sterling's brain child "The Unbonding Plan."

It was a sound and farsighted piece of legislation. The Ferguson bloc in the House conspired to defeat it, by fair means or foul. They employed the tactics with which they were most familiar. Their ringleader was a lawyer whose activities in commercialized clemency had been largely responsible for adding to the Texas vocabulary the infamous term "pardon broker." He was also author of the iniquitous law granting automatic continuances to clients of legislators while the legislature was in session.

When a final vote was to be taken on the submission of the bond issue, he induced a number of his cohorts to absent themselves. In shirking this duty, each one of them violated his oath of office. Speaker Fred Minor put the House "on call," thereby making any member who failed or refused to attend, subject to arrest.

The Sergeant-at-Arms of the House of Representatives was Joe White. He informed me that the missing legislators were in an apartment located on the premises of T. H. McGregor. They had ignored his summons and defied him to take them in. White made an official request for a Ranger to help carry out the mandate of the Speaker. He asked for Captain Frank Hamer. I knew that this veteran had small patience with any kind of violators. He would have even less with those who were supposed to make rather than break our State laws. In this particular case, he was liable to use more force than diplomacy. I decided that it would be prudent for me to accompany the Sergeant-at-Arms.

When we arrived at McGregor's place, the truant members were in an upstairs apartment. Several faces appeared at the windows. White called out that he had orders from the Speaker of the House to bring in all absent members. They went into conference. I recognized one of them and called him by name.

We started talking and I said, "You gentlemen know that you are doing wrong. Why don't you all come down and go with the Sergeant-at-Arms?" "All right," replied their spokesman, "we will go with him." Not a harsh word was uttered; no force was used, nor were there any threats made. Before arriving at the capitol, we stopped at a drug store and had coffee together.

After my acquaintance had resumed his seat in the House, and conferred with the Ferguson leader, he made what the newspapers

Ex-Ranger William A. Dial

described as an "impassioned speech." He is reported to have said that "the Adjutant General brought him in by force," and that he denounced the act. I later asked him why he had deliberately misrepresented the facts. He answered, "McGregor told me to cry."

News of the incident quickly spread over the city. It happened on the meeting day of my luncheon club, and several members asked me to relate the details. I told my fellow Rotarians: "The Rangers have earned a widespread reputation for bringing home the bacon. As far as I know, this is the first time we have ever been called on to bring in a ham."

On July 7, 1931, one of our best Rangers, Dan McDuffy, was killed in line of duty. The tragedy occurred in the East Texas oil town of Gladewater. His slayer was a man who had been constable of the precinct, and later served as city jailer. At the height of the boom, ex-Ranger W. A. Dial was appointed as chief of police. He had been forced to discharge the former officer, who then swore to wreak vengeance on the new chief. Armed with a 30-30 Winchester, the ex-constable appeared on the streets yelling and cursing. He defied anyone to arrest him, and threatened the lives of bystanders. Ranger McDuffy had befriended the man. He asked the other officers not to shoot the gunman and urged them to let him handle the matter in his own way. Dan McDuffy was the antithesis of a trigger happy officer. He gladly took a desperate chance to avoid bloodshed.

Chief Dial reluctantly agreed to this proposal, although it was against his better judgement. A frantic call came from a lady who had just seen and heard the berserk man shoot his rifle. The officers hurried to the scene in a police car. They were within approximately seventy-five feet of him when he opened fire, fatally wounding Ranger McDuffy. The assassin was instantly killed by Dial. The merciful but imprudent Ranger died in an ambulance en route to the hospital, unafraid to the last. He crossed the Great Divide with these words to his comrades, "Boys, I hope to see you all on the Other Side." A few months later W. A. Dial resigned as chief of police. He came to Austin, where we were glad to re-enlist him in the Ranger Service.

The annual encampment of the Fifty-sixth Cavalry Bridge was formerly held at Camp Wolters, near Mineral Wells, Texas. I arrived there on July 15, 1931. General Jacob F. Wolters, for whom the camp

218

To my General W.W. Sterling
With warmest regards.
Major Paul L. Wakefield

Major (later General) Paul L. Wakefield and Col. Selah (Tommy) Tompkins.

was named, gave me my first official salute. It consisted of eleven guns, the number rated by a brigadier general. We were assigned excellent quarters in the Baker Hotel and my family looked forward to an enjoyable time.

For several years the guest of honor at Camp Wolters had been Colonel Selah R. H. (Tommy) Tompkins, Retired. He was a hard riding cavalryman of the old school, and the most colorful character in the Army. Colonel Tommy once commanded the Seventh Cavalry, known since the Indian wars as "Custer's Regiment." His flowing mutton chop whiskers gave him an additional picturesqueness. He was a great favorite with men, women and children.

During intermission at the evening band concerts, the colonel entertained us with stories about his days on the frontier. He was a horseman par excellence, and it nearly broke his heart to think that some day his beloved Cavalry might be mechanized. He delivered an impassioned oration on the subject. With blazing eyes, Colonel Tompkins concluded his remarks by exclaiming, "My Comrades, could any of you picture yourself motoring up to a troop and giving the command, 'Present monkeywrenches'?"

Chapter 23
RED RIVER
BRIDGE DISPUTE

I SPENT one pleasant day with the brigade, and in the evening attended the officer's dance on the hotel roof garden. Shortly before midnight a bell boy approached, and said that he had an urgent call for me. I went to the telephone and ready on the line was Governor Sterling. He said, "Bill, Governor Murray of Oklahoma has opened the new Red River bridge at Denison. He did this without authority and in defiance of a Federal injunction. I want you to go up there as soon as possible and close it. Can you do this by daylight in the morning?" I replied, "Yes, sir."

Ranger Captain Tom R. Hickman of Company B happened to be in Mineral Wells. I notified him of the Governor's orders, and we immediately left for Denison. Two of his Rangers, J. P. Huddleston and W. H. Kirby, were in Fort Worth, and they joined us there. We arrived at the Red River just about daybreak.

A large signboard had been erected and placed on the south approach of the bridge. The word "Warning" was painted across the top in big letters. The balance of the sign stated: "This bridge closed by order of the United States District Court for the Eastern District of Texas." It was flanked by barriers. Alfalfa Bill Murray had caused these obstructions to be removed. We quickly replaced them and stopped all traffic. This time the bridge stayed closed.

Photograph taken immediately after the closing of the
Red River Bridge between Texas and Oklahoma.

Closing the bridge led to a wordy war between Oklahoma and
Texas. The telephone and telegraph companies proved that talk was
not cheap. Both of them reaped a rich harvest in long distance tolls.
Governor Murray announced that he was going to buckle on his horse
pistol and lead the troops. Those who were best acquainted with Alfalfa
Bill observed that a horse pistol would be the most appropriate weapon
for his personal use. He further declared that the bridge was going to
be opened if he had to use the entire Oklahoma National Guard.

The military phase had turned into a huge joke. All the fighting
was done in the newspapers. I yielded to temptation and applied the
old bromide "one riot, one Ranger" to the bridge situation. Adjutant
General Barrett, of Oklahoma, and I were good friends. Both of us

had recently attended a National Guard conference in Washington. I sent him word that the Texas end of the bridge was being held by four Rangers. If he was sending a brigade to open it, I would keep all four of them there. If only a regiment was to be used, I would let a couple of the boys go home.

Newspaper reporters flocked to the scene, and sensational dispatches were sent to all parts of the country. Photographers wanted a picture of the Texas Rangers. In a spirit of fun, I picked up my saddle carbine and struck a warlike pose. When the Governor summoned me from the dance at Mineral Wells, I was dressed in a white linen suit. There had been no time to change clothes, so I still had on the light trousers. They didn't go very well with my cowboy boots. I certainly would have worn a more compatible outfit, if I had known the ultimate destination of the picture.

Seven years later copies of it turned up in Germany. There, they were given wide circulation. *Life* Magazine reproduced the picture in 1938. The accompanying article stated that the Nazis were using it as propaganda to prove that we were a very loosely knit nation. Hitler claimed that the states of the Union were often engaged in civil war. I could scarcely believe that my joke could have such far reaching consequences.

I returned to Austin, leaving the Red River dispute in the hands of Captain Hickman. He kept the bridge closed in spite of all threats by Governor Murray. One of his men, Bob Goss, was an exceptionally fine shot with a pistol. His marksmanship was outstanding, even among those who earned their living by carrying six-shooters.

In this game of watchful waiting, the Rangers had a great deal of time on their hands. They spent a considerable part of it on the banks of the river in target practice. Goss gave several shooting exhibitions. In one of his stunts he placed a playing card sideways, and split the edge of it with a forty-five calibre bullet. Captain Hickman saw that this feat was having a good moral effect on residents on both sides of the Red River. He said to the spectators, "Bob is just a new man we are breaking in as a Ranger."

When I arrived at the capitol it was eleven o'clock. My secretary reminded me that I was scheduled to make a talk at noon. This appointment had slipped my mind due to the excitement in North Texas.

There was no time for preparation, so I decided that my best bet would be to make a few remarks about the feud between Texas and Oklahoma. To my mind, the whole affair was a sort of comic opera war. An Austin paper reported my effort, and headed it, "Bill Sterling has a laugh at the bridge."

After recovering somewhat from the case of rattle-hocks I always get when starting a speech, I compared the Red River controversy to a bridge party. Inasmuch as the trouble stemmed from a contract between the Texas Highway Department and the Toll Bridge Company, I added that "it might be fitting and proper to call it a contract bridge party." Switching from bridge to poker, I told the audience that "Alfalfa Bill thought he had openers. When his hand was called, however, it turned out he was only bluffing and Texas won the pot with a pair of sixes." From this brand of humor, I was probably in more danger of being shot by my listeners than I had been in the encounter with the Oklahomans.

On one occasion, the State senator from the twelfth district called on me in his official capacity. He stated that he wished to discuss a matter of considerable importance, and that it involved one of my Rangers. The senator further declared that the purpose of the conference was to avoid bloodshed. "General," he began, "I believe it would be wise for you to move Ranger Red Burton from Somerville County. If he stays there his old enemies will kill him as sure as the world." I replied, "I will investigate the matter thoroughly, and take whatever action the circumstances warrant." In getting to the bottom of the trouble, I found some interesting facts.

Somerville County, the third smallest county in the state, is in North Central Texas. It lies almost equidistant from Dallas, Fort Worth and Waco. The terrain is rough and wooded and numerous springs of fine water bubble out of a limestone formation. Glen Rose, the county seat, has long been noted as a health and recreational resort.

During the prohibition era, the county became a headquarters for moonshiners and bootleggers. These sinister characters took full advantage of the woods for cover and the pure water for distilling their illicit liquor. They operated on a wholesale scale, and the area became the principal source of supply for the large cities in North and Central Texas. Professional whiskey makers from Kentucky, Tennessee and

Oklahoma were brought in to operate the stills. These criminals were selected as much for their toughness as they were for their skill in making squirrel whiskey.

The huge profits in bootlegging caused otherwise respectable citizens to wink at this violation of the law. Some merchants chose to accept the money made indirectly from the traffic. They were able to sell large quantities of sugar, corn, and other ingredients to the bootleggers, who always paid in. cash. Several public officials also fell to the temptation of easy money and the situation became intolerable. The bootleggers waxed bold and defiant. Governor Pat M. Neff sent Rangers, headed by Red Burton, into the county, and they began a cleanup. The bootleggers raised a pot of ten thousand dollars, and prevailed on a local citizen to offer it for protection. The offer was spurned, and Ranger activities were redoubled.

One of the most flagrant violators announced that he would kill the first officer of any kind who tried to raid his still. His attempt to carry out this threat cost him his life. Burton, like all genuine fighting men, will never come out and say that he killed a man. He looks on it as an unpleasant duty and a task to be avoided as long as possible. "The bootlegger started shooting. I returned the fire and they took him to the Glen Rose funeral home," is the way he recounted the incident to me.

Marvin (Red) Burton was one of the greatest Rangers who served during the Sterling administration. Without a doubt he would have attained the rank of captain if the Service had not been broken down by Fergusonism. Tall, strong and intelligent, Burton was more than a match for the shrewdest or toughest lawbreaker. He has the blue-grey eyes and soft voice of the natural fighting man, yet there is no semblance of the bully in his makeup. His manner with inoffensive people is a model of gentility and courtesy, but when dealing with criminals, he becomes a one man riot squad. If a mission required four Rangers, the quartet could be completed by sending Red Burton and one companion.

During my administration, the good citizens of Somerville County petitioned for Burton to be returned there for some special work, and I complied with their request. After the senator's visit, I called Ranger Burton in for a conference. "Red," I said, "I don't want those scoundrels around Glen Rose to kill you, and I don't want you to have to kill any more of them. I am thinking of sending you somewhere else." He smiled and replied, "General, you are the boss. But if you move me out of Somerville now, I'll resign." "My only thought was to avoid trouble," I told him. "Don't you worry about that," he assured me. "You couldn't chop up one of those scrubs and throw him on me."

The peace seeking senator did not get his request, nor did the Somerville County bullies ever get around to making their wishful assault on Red Burton. Hale and hearty, and enjoying life at the age of seventy odd, he is one of the most respected taxpaying citizens of McLennan County.

Chapter 24
EAST TEXAS OIL FIELD

THE most serious problem that confronted Governor Sterling's administration was created by the opening of the gigantic East Texas oil fields. Almost with the speed of lightning, conditions in that explosive area became progressively worse. C. M. (Dad) Joiner drilled the first producer in September of 1930. Later the Bateman-Crim well was completed near Kilgore, nine miles north of the discovery. In January, 1931, and still farther north by twelve miles, wildcatters brought in the Lathrop well. These far flung extensions proved the existence of the world's largest oil field. A mad race of drilling ensued. By September of 1931, there were more than sixteen hundred producing wells in the area. In January of 1932, the number passed thirty-five hundred. This unprecedented boom, with all of its troubles, was abruptly laid in our laps.

On Sunday, March 8, 1931, the Dallas *News* carried a timely cartoon by Knott. It bore the caption, "In the Wake of the Gold Rush." The sketch depicted a great crowd of men headed for the new oil fields in East Texas. Close on their heels was a large wolf. His fangs were bared, and he was branded with the word "Lawlessness." The drawing made a deep impression on me, as it did on many other Texans. I cut it out of the *News* and put it in my scrapbook, where it has remained for more than twenty-five years. Cartoonist Knott, in my opinion, portrayed current events more vividly than any of his contemporaries. This masterpiece gave the public a better understanding of true conditions in East Texas than could have been told in many thousands of words.

In the Wake of the Gold Rush • • • • •   'By Knott

My extensive oil field experience was turned to good account in these critical times. Many of the Rangers were veterans of boom town cleanups, and they knew just what to do under all circumstances. We had learned that the best way to handle high-powered criminals was to wage a direct and aggressive war on them. Thugs and hijackers are unable to do a great deal of harm when they are not given time to get set, or establish a base of operations.

Pursuant to this policy, Captain Tom Hickman, Sergeant M. T. Gonzaulus, Rangers Stuart Stanley, Hardy Purvis, Hale Kirby and Bob Goss of Company B were ordered to Kilgore. Captain Frank Hamer, Sergeant J. B. Wheatley, Rangers B. M. Gault, Oscar Martin, George Allen, Jim McCoy and Earl McWilliams of Headquarters Company joined them there. They were accompanied by the Ranger Chaplain, Captain P. B. Hill. Out of this group, Wheatley, Gonzaulus, Gault and Purvis subsequently became captains.

Time Magazine for February, 1931, under the heading, "National Affairs," carried a full length picture. They titled it, "Chief Ranger Sterling. His men booked crooks from a pulpit." The article continued:

> Last week in Gregg County, the town of Kilgore and the nearby tent-town of "Little Juarez" had grown so rowdy, so full of wastrels and misconduct that the Texas Rangers had to take a hand. Five Rangers came up from the Rio Grande, five more converged on Kilgore from other parts of the State. Within two hours they had rounded up some 300 suspects and bad characters. The ten Rangers herded the lot of them into the Baptist Church, and booked them from the pulpit. They were a measley collection. Forty were cut out for detention, the rest were hustled out of town. Two of those detained were wanted for murder, three for bank robbery.

This was a sample of the early work done by the Rangers. On their editorial pages, several leading newspapers complimented us on the measures we had taken to head off a threatened crime wave.

The horde of underworld characters, who could readily be handled by the Rangers, did not constitute our worst threat to law and order in East Texas. Staring us in the face was a far greater hazard. While it did not come directly under the purview of the adjutant general, our department would be called upon for its enforcement.

The law of supply and demand had been grossly violated by the unrestricted flow of oil from hundreds of wells. Many of them, if allowed to run free, could produce five thousand barrels per day. The price went down to ten cents a barrel. Oil sands were being depleted, and the wells would soon go to salt water. Greed and ignorance caused some of the short sighted operators to "get theirs while the getting was good." If this suicidal practice was not halted, the entire field would be ruined. There was also a terrific waste of natural resources, both in oil and gas. Millions of dollars in taxes were being lost by the State.

There was only one answer to this problem. The production of oil had to be regulated by proration. Ordinarily, this was a function of the Texas Railroad Commission, but the magnitude of the East Texas field made it impossible for them to enforce their rules. Heedless operators ignored the commission's orders, and ran roughshod over the badly undermanned staff of supervisors.

For several months Governor Sterling had watched with growing concern the skyrocketing drilling race in East Texas. One day while we were discussing my Ranger cleanup drive he said, "It looks like I am going to be forced to take a hand in that mess over there. One of my responsibilities is to conserve the natural resources of the state. They must be saved for future generations. I am not going to allow a bunch of reckless operators to waste them. Landowners are being cheated out of their royalties, and are threatening to take the law in their own hands. If the commission is powerless to put a stop to that kind of abuse, I am going to do it with martial law."

On August 14, 1931, the following resolution was adopted by the East Texas Chamber of Commerce and sent to the Governor in Austin:

WHEREAS, the Legislature has enacted a new law looking to the conservation of the natural resources of this State and the prevention of the physical waste of oil and gas, and

WHEREAS, it will be impossible for the Railroad Commission under the terms of said law to prepare a proper order thereunder to effectuate the principle of said law and put the same in active operation in less than fifteen days, and

WHEREAS, there is now no effective order of the Railroad Commission or law of the State to prevent the actual physical waste of these important natural resources of the State by reason of injunction suits and other vexations and dilatory forms of litigation which have resulted in widespread violation of said present orders and existing law and that such chaotic condition will continue during the period necessary to pass and put into operation any new orders under the new law and that the present unequal and unfair withdrawal of oil from offset leases and the unfair taking of oil by various pipe line companies and purchasers will continue unabated and in all probability will increase, working undue and unreasonable hardships on that great majority who are complying with the present orders of the Railroad Commission under the existing law, and

WHEREAS such unequal production and taking which are now existent and which will continue until new and effective orders have been established and which is now causing great physical waste of the natural resources of oil and gas which are rightful property of the State of Texas and are causing great loss to the State of Texas not only of the natural resources itself, but in taxes, both gross production and ad valorem and depleted revenues rightfully belonging to the School and University Funds of the State, not alone in the revenues from producing properties but also the great loss which will result from the sale of mineral rights on the large areas of undeveloped lands belonging to the school fund and the University of Texas which are integral parts of the State government itself, and

WHEREAS, the present unequal production and taking has and will during the interim until the new law can be made effective by the Railroad Commission caused undue physical waste in the loss and depletion of gas pressure and energy necessary to produce the greatest ultimate recovery of these natural resources and loss caused by the rapid intrusion of salt water and in the coming and trapping off underground of great quantities of said minerals and the loss due to the burning of gas from the wells without extracting therefrom the large gasoline content, and

WHEREAS, the conditions have already resulted and caused threats of violence and the destruction of property and a further continuance may, in all probability result in actual destruction of property and a reign of lawlessness and as evidence thereof may be noted the tendency to a let down in the general enforcement of all conservation laws of the State and ruthless and unheeded violations of the same.

NOW, THEREFORE, be it resolved that in order to prevent this irreparable waste to the State of Texas and so that an equitable and unhampered basis of production may be fixed before the fact instead of after the fact and that unequal production and the consequent loss may be prevented during the time necessarily incident to determining, passing and putting into operation of a new and effective order of the Railroad Commission under the new law, we respectfully petition and urge His Excellency, the Honorable Ross S. Sterling, Governor of the State of Texas, that he forthwith and immediately declare Martial Law in the oil producing territory of Gregg, Smith, Rusk and Upshur Counties, Texas, to the end that the present enormous physical waste may be eliminated and huge loss to the State of Texas be prevented and that life and property may be safe during this hiatus of the conservation laws of the State and that said Martial Law be maintained and oil production completely shut down in said area for and during the reasonable period necessary to put into effect the new order under the new law.

This was followed by a petition to Governor Sterling from more than twelve hundred representative citizens of the East Texas oil field area.

Chapter 25
MARTIAL LAW

On the night of August 15, 1931, Governor Sterling called me to his office for a conference. I was accompanied by Assistant Adjutant General Horace H. Carmichael. We completed the last minute details of martial law. Out of this group, I am the sole survivor.

He asked me what branch of the National Guard should be used in the forthcoming expedition. I replied, "The Cavalry, by all means." Mounted men are best for any kind of semi-police duty, and patrolling the muddy oil fields could best be done on horseback. We would also need one hospital company and one ambulance unit.

I then requested Governor Sterling to let me command the troops in the field, for the duration of martial law. "I can't do that, Bill," he replied, "General Jacob F. Wolters is an authority on martial law and has written two books on the subject. I am going to place him in charge. It would break old Jake's heart to be left out of this campaign. Governor Murray of Oklahoma has put Cicero Murray in charge of the troops up there. Although we are not related, if Bill Sterling was in command during martial law, people will think it is a family affair."

The Governor made an excellent choice when he selected General Wolters.

On August 16, 1931, Governor Sterling issued the following proclamation:

To All to Whom These Presents Shall Come:

WHEREAS, Section 59-a Article 16 of the Constitution of the State of Texas declares that the preservation, conservation and development of all the natural resources of this State are each and all public rights and duties; and

WHEREAS, the Legislature in the Act effective August 12, 1931, declared the law of Texas to be: 'Neither natural gas nor crude petroleum shall be produced, transported, stored or used in such manner or under such conditions as to constitute waste'; and

WHEREAS crude petroleum oil and natural gas are natural resources of this State; and

WHEREAS, from facts presented to me by many responsible citizens including resolutions adopted at a meeting of producers and royalty owners of East Texas oil field on August 14, 1931, and representations made by a committee of citizens who called upon me and submitted facts as to the conditions that obtained in said East Texas oil field, it is evident that:

There exists an organized and entrenched group of crude petroleum oil and natural gas producers in said East Texas oil field, covering areas within the counties of Upshur, Rusk, Gregg and Smith who are in a state of insurrection against the conservation laws of the State relating to the prevention of waste of crude petroleum oil and natural gas, and are in open rebellion against the efforts of the constituted civil authorities in this State to enforce such laws; and that

By reason of the reckless, unlawful and criminal handling of producing wells in said district water is being rapidly drawn into oil sands, thereby creating enormous physical waste of crude petroleum oil, and more than 1,000,000,000 cubic feet of natural gas, rich in gasoline content, are being wasted, all of which causes a great loss of revenue to this State, and does, and will, affect the welfare of our educational institutions, including our common schools, eleemosynary institutions, and each and every State Department of the State Government, and will increase the burdens of taxation upon our people generally; and that

The existing condition has brought about a state of public feeling on the part of citizens, that if the State Government cannot or fails to protect the public interest and the interest of the land and royalty owners they will attempt to take the law into their own hands, and by force of arms shut down the producing oil wells in said defined district until the State can and will enforce the conservation laws; and that

In at least one instance, as reported to me, an oil company operating in said defined district has ordered representatives of the Oil and Gas Division of the

Railroad Commission of Texas who were performing their lawful and official duties from their leases; and

WHEREAS, this condition has caused threats of acts of violence on the part of indignant responsible citizens against those who openly, flagrantly and rebelliously violate the laws and defy the constitutional civic authorities of this State; and

WHEREAS, a state of insurrection, tumult, riot and breach of the peace does exist in the defined area; and

WHEREAS, in addition to the insurrection, tumult, riot and breach of the peace that does now exist in the said defined area, there is now imminent danger of said insurrection, tumult, riot and breach of the peace threatening serious danger to citizens and their property being extended not only in the territory heretofore described, but in other areas by operators who are obeying the laws relating to the conservation of crude petroleum oil and natural gas; and

WHEREAS, it is necessary for the preservation of the crude petroleum oil and natural gas in the defined district that the reckless and illegal exploitation of the same be stopped until such time as the said resources may be properly conserved and developed under the protection of the civil authorities; and

WHEREAS, Section 10 of Article 4 of the Constitution of the State of Texas makes it the duty of the Governor of the State to 'cause the laws to be faithfully executed'; and

WHEREAS, Section 7 of Article 4 of the Constitution of the State of Texas makes the Governor of this State the Commander-in-Chief of the military forces of this State; and gives him 'power to call forth the militia to execute the laws of this state';

NOW, THEREFORE, I, R. S. Sterling, Governor of the State of Texas, and Commander-in-Chief of the military forces of this State, do by virtue of the authority vested in me under the Constitution and laws of this State declare that the conditions above described do exist and are clearly violative of the Constitution and laws of this State, and that by reason of this the conditions contemplated in Article 5889 of the Revised Civil Statutes of Texas of 1925 exist in the following described territory, to-wit:

'The Counties of Gregg, Upshur, Rusk and Smith in the State of Texas.'

AND I do hereby declare Martial Law in said territory, effective at six A.M. the seventeenth day of August, A. D. 1931; and I hereby direct Brigadier General Jacob F. Wolters to assume supreme command of the situation in the territory affected and without delay shut down each and every producing crude oil well and-or producing well of natural gas, and to further take such steps as he may deem necessary to enforce and uphold the majesty of the law, subject to the orders of the Governor of Texas and Commander-in-Chief of the military forces of this State, as given through the Adjutant General.

IN TESTIMONY WHEREOF I have hereunto signed my name officially and caused the Seal of the State of Texas to be hereunto affixed at my office at Austin, Texas, this the 16th day of August, A. D. 1931, at twelve o'clock Noon.

s/ R. S. STERLING
Governor of Texas.

By the Governor:
WATT L. SAUNDERS,
Assistant Secretary of State.

When the proclamation was signed, I issued the orders necessary to put martial law in operation. The Cavalry was alerted and the rapidity of their mobilization was attributed to the efficiency and thoroughness of their training. They moved out on very short notice. The initial strength of the martial law force was ninety-seven officers, two warrant officers, and 1,104 enlisted men.

The effect of martial law was to immediately stop the flow of illegal oil in East Texas. While driving through this huge field in the fall of 1931 a stranger inquired, "What is the meaning of all these soldiers?" A native of Gregg County replied, "They mean dollar oil."

With the shutting down of the field in East Texas, a new term was added to the petroleum glossary. This innovation was "hot oil." It quickly became synonymous with illegal production, and was on the lips of practically everybody in the area. One speculator was reputed to have sold a huge quantity of oil on the Atlantic seaboard for two dollars per barrel. He planned to fill his contract with ten cent oil from East Texas, thereby making a profit of nearly half a billion dollars. This man was an old hand at sharp practice. He had figured in the Teapot Dome scandals. Rangers Tom Heard and J. L. (Chick) Rhem of Company D discovered a by-pass from a well that had been drilled on the grounds of the Negro school in Gladewater. It had sixteen outlets, and the school was only getting a fraction of the royalty due them. Countless tank trucks were hauling hot oil to refineries in Louisiana, Oklahoma and Texas.

Many waxed wealthy through overproduction. During a society pageant in one of the larger cities, a duchess from East Texas was being presented. When she was announced, one of the spectators recognized the name. Speaking in what might well be called a Texas size stage whisper, for it could be heard over half the auditorium, he said, "There goes a costume that was paid for with hot oil."

When Governor Sterling clamped down on the wasteful production with martial law, the hot oil boys began to howl about "rights." They had accumulated a huge war chest, and were able to employ a formidable array of attorneys. Claiming that their property was being confiscated, they secured an injunction against the Governor in Federal Court for the Eastern District of Texas. The case was appealed and set down for hearing before a three judge court in Houston. Circuit Judge J. C. Hutcheson presided, with Judge Randolph Bryant of the Eastern District of Texas, and Judge Barret of Alabama as associates.

During the trial Judge Hutcheson questioned the witnesses after the manner of Federal judges. He asked General Wolters: "Is it a fact that someone asked you, 'Don't you think martial law should be declared?' and you replied, 'Yes, where?' " "That is a lie," retorted General Wolters, his face livid with rage. He then said, "I withdraw the remark."

When I took the stand, Judge Hutcheson asked, "General, you were once a justice of the peace in a border county, weren't you?" "Yes, Your Honor," I replied, "and I know what you gentlemen on the bench have to contend with." The courtroom snickered. During the next recess, a bailiff said the judges wanted to see me in their chambers. When I entered, all three of them were laughing. Judge Randolph Bryant, who was one of my dearest friends said, "You son of a gun. Nobody else in the world would have said that." The Governor feared they had called me in to be reprimanded, and was relieved when I told him of our pleasant visit.

The three judge court, referred to by Governor Sterling as "the pre-judge court," decided that the Governor had exceeded his rights in declaring martial law. He appealed the case to the Supreme Court, which affirmed the ruling of the lower tribunal. They held that the action was taken to raise the price of oil, rather than to preserve the peace. The learned gentlemen did not believe that there existed any imminence of riot or bloodshed. They chose to disregard the oft-proven fact that men will shoot to kill in defense of their property. I made a personal survey of the situation, and will always believe that Governor Sterling was right in declaring martial law.

I was named as one of the defendants, and went to Washington for the final hearing of the case. The doorkeeper of the Supreme Court was a stately, austere Negro. Standing in the corridor one day somebody asked him, "This is a very high court, isn't it?" "Yes, sir, it's the highest," he replied with great dignity. "There is no appeal from this court, except to God."

Martial law accomplished a world of good for Texas, and put a stop to a large part of the crookedness in the oil field. Inasmuch as it was a brain child of Governor Sterling, it was violently opposed by the Fergusonites. It put many of them out of business. They started a scandal sheet in Austin, and had the temerity to call it a newspaper. In order to keep an eye on their deviltry, I took a subscription. One of their early editorials stated: "Oil Martial Law Wrecks State Finances." It was a typical example of the Fergusonite's reasoning. I sent them this letter, which they printed:

> Being a paid subscriber to your paper, I have just read your article and editorial stating that "Oil Martial Law Wrecks Finances." Both of these articles are very misleading. Martial Law in East Texas has cost the taxpayers $240,000 but has brought into general revenue $1,690,000 more than would have been received if Martial Law had not been declared. The natural resources have been conserved, and order maintained. If repaying the taxpayers seven and on-half for one is what you call wrecking finances, then it would be a fine thing to wreck the finances of every department of the government in the same way.

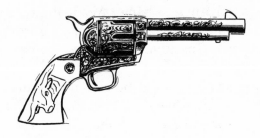

Chapter 26
SLOT MACHINES

Some wise man has said that there is a spark of the gambler in everyone. Whether it be a deacon sitting in the sacred precincts of the amen corner who gambles on the weather and crops, or a roistering blade who woos lady luck with spotted cards and galloping dominoes, each in his own way is a taker of chances.

I can see eye to eye and boot to boot with those cowboys who deal a few hands of saddle blanket poker. The same goes for the waddie who pounds leather all day long, and in the cool of the evening likes to buck a two card monte game. My inability to remain seated that long, rather than moral scruples, has kept me from extensive participation in these frontier pastimes. Be that as it may, both of them can be played on the level.

Western lore has it that old time gamblers adhered to a strict code, and that they prided themselves on running square games. In their fishy eyes, to be branded as a "tinhorn" was a fate worse than death. Frontier tradition also says that in defending their reputations for honesty, these faro dealers would not hesitate to kill. It was beside the point if a drunken cowboy happened to be cheated out of his life by a double barreled derringer concealed in the sleeve of a Prince Albert coat.

In all forms of gambling operated by human hands, the sucker gets at least some semblance of a run for his money. The play may properly be termed a "game of chance." By no stretch of the imagination can the same be said of slot machines. They are correctly and universally called one armed bandits. These mechanical highjackers are all too frequently allowed to infiltrate into counties, cities and clubs, under the guise of being harmless amusement devices. State officers are urged to overlook them, on the grounds that only petty cash is involved, and that they should be beneath the notice of Rangers.

The average citizen does not realize the tremendous impact made on the moral and economic life of the Nation by slot machines. He may think that the sum they divert from legitimate business is of small account. Such is not the case. One time I spent two weeks in Chicago judging a rodeo. It was freely stated that slot machines in that city constituted a fifty million dollar racket. Each year they exact a heavy toll from family finances. Many housewives squander their grocery budgets, and school children gamble away their lunch money in futile efforts to win. The kaleidoscopic whirl of the pictures seems to weave a hypnotic spell over the victim, just as snakes charm birds and rabbits.

Governor Sterling and I held a conference on slot machines, and we agreed that under his administration, they would not be allowed to operate in Texas. Pursuant to this policy, I sent copies of the law governing them to every sheriff in the state. Most county officers were glad to know that we were taking this vigorous action, and the others knew that failure to banish the illegal devices would bring in the Rangers.

The enormous profits enabled the manufacturers to spend a great deal of money on attorneys, and to lay up a rich war chest. This was used in attempts to corrupt public officials. They used every wile known to professional "fixers" in their effort to get me to relax our enforcement program. The racketeers could not find anybody bold enough to approach me directly. They sent out a great many feelers, however, coupled with adroitly veiled offers of large sums of money. I was invited to be the guest of a Chicago slot machine builder on his palatial yacht. When all else failed, they decided to try their luck in the courts.

They went into Federal Court in El Paso, and asked that all peace officers be enjoined from seizing or otherwise interfering with their machines. The claim was made that they were not gambling paraphernalia, but were merely amusement devices. Judge C. A. Boynton granted the temporary injunction. Final action on the case was to be taken two weeks later in Houston.

Among the defendants named in their petition was Ben D. Lee, sheriff of Nueces County. He was a native of Bell County, and my lifelong friend. Sheriff Lee brought his copy of the citation to Austin, and requested me to take the lead in the defense. He declared that if the State did not join with the counties, we would be flooded with slot machines. I fully agreed with him, and took immediate steps to meet the threat.

One of the duties of the Attorney General of Texas is to represent all State departments. The incumbent at that time was James V. Allred. I took Sheriff Lee's subpoena to him, and explained that dissolving this injunction would be of vast help to my law enforcement program. Thinking that he would be eager to rid the state of these illegal devices, I asked him to send an assistant to represent us in Houston. Allred replied, "General, I don't believe my department can do anything about this matter. Only some sheriffs have been cited." I reminded him of the seriousness of the slot machine racket, and stated that in my opinion it should be fought by all agencies of the State.

Hearing on the injunction was held before Federal Judge T. M. Kennerly, of the Southern District of Texas. Remembering his splendid work in Borger, I employed former Assistant Attorney General Galloway Calhoun, of Tyler, to represent us in this action. Ranger Chaplain P. B. Hill, Ranger Oscar Martin of Headquarters Company and I attended the trial in Houston. Judge Kennerly dissolved the injunction, which dealt a death blow to any semblance of legality in slot machines. I paid Mr. Calhoun's fee of $250, for the excellent service he rendered, out of the adjutant general's law enforcement fund. The cancelled warrant for this item can be found in the files of the State comptroller.

The old law governing the disposal of seized gambling paraphernalia was a good one. It stipulated that no suit could be maintained against any officer who destroyed slot machines, roulette wheels or similar layouts. During one administration, a squad of Rangers under a sergeant who was a hangover from the Ferguson regime raided a club in

Houston. They cut the draperies into ribbons, and destroyed other property that could not be classed as gambling paraphernalia. As a result of their vandalism, the legislature repealed the existing law, which had been of immense value to honest officers. It now requires a court order to dispose of this illegal property. Such a long drawn out process sometimes results in the gambler getting his machines back into circulation.

Chapter 27

MOB LAW

IN THE pleasant Central Texas town of Belton are to be found a large number of stately liveoaks. The most noted one of these grew only a short distance from my birthplace. From its sturdy, widespread limbs several men have been illegally hanged. As a child I used to ride my pony past this towering gallows tree. The story of one tragedy that was enacted under its branches left a profound impression on my youthful mind.

Bell County had been swept by a wave of horse stealing. The irate citizens were determined to put a stop to it, even if they had to take the law in their own hands. Several men charged with horse theft were in the county jail. Under cover of darkness a mob took all the prisoners out and strung them up to this convenient tree. One of the victims was a mere boy. He had only been charged with stealing a pair of socks, and the sheriff planned to release him the next day. Many years later a resident of the county lost his mind. Neighbors believed that it was caused by the remorse he felt over his part in the lynching. Early in life, the injustice suffered by this unfortunate lad taught me a lesson.

Mob Law

When I became a Ranger, and later adjutant general, I redoubled my efforts to stamp out lynch law in Texas.

On May 8, 1930, the Grayson County courthouse in Sherman was burned by a mob. Several thousand men participated in this infamous deed. A Negro was on trial for the offense that invariably causes deep indignation, and always results in mass hysteria. Four Rangers, under Captain F. A. Hamer, had been sent there to guard the prisoner. Out of this quartet, the only survivor is Jim McCoy. The Rangers repulsed several rushes by the crowd, but were forced to leave when the building was enveloped in flames. I asked Adjutant General Robertson why he had not sent more men, as these situations are always full of dynamite. He replied, "They only asked for four."

Mindful of the lack of foresight that resulted in the Sherman holocaust, I issued a directive calculated to prevent future occurrences of this kind. It read: "When a crime is committed anywhere in the State, the nature of which is liable to be followed by mob violence, every available Ranger is instructed to rush to the scene, without waiting for orders."

The success of our policy was reflected in an article that appeared in the Austin *American:*

> Completion of a year in office without a lynching to mar his record was made the occasion of a complimentary note Wednesday to Adj. Gen. Bill Sterling from his superior, Gov. Ross Sterling.
>
> It has been demonstrated conclusively, through the cooperation of local peace officers with the rangers, that mob violence can be prevented and that fairness and justice can be meted out by due process of the courts, the Governor wrote.
>
> The policy of this administration in such emergencies is based on the experience that a mob can be prevented more easily than it can be stopped. It is not the policy to supplant local authority but rather to strengthen and cooperate with local officers in emergencies.

My action was rewarded by the following telegram and several similar ones from kindred organizations:

> The Texas Council of Southern Women for Prevention of Lynching meeting today in Dallas express appreciation of your vigilance to prevent lynchings in Texas. We pledge cooperation in support of your efforts that this year be as successful as the year past.

Chapter 28
HIGHER EDUCATION

Iwas ordered to Washington, D. C. in the autumn of 1931, to take one of the courses at the Army War College. Each Regular, Reserve or National Guard officer cherishes the hope that some day he may be permitted to attend this post graduate military academy. Having heard its wonders discussed in awed tones at border Army posts, I was particularly gratified over my assignment.

Serving as commandant was Major General William D. Conner. When I reported for duty he gave me quite a start. "So you're the Adjutant General of Texas," he said. "Right now, I don't feel like graduating anybody from that state." The General then broke into a friendly smile, making it unnecessary to tell me that he was joking.

The depression had just begun to tighten its grip on the Nation, and the effects were felt in unexpected quarters. General Conner had invested a large part of his life's savings in the stock of a national bank in Texas. Not only had he lost the initial investment, but he had been assessed an amount equal to the value of his holdings. The letter notifying him of this fact reached him shortly before I arrived in Washington. Notwithstanding his first remark, he treated me with the utmost courtesy and consideration.

Shortly after the opening of the new term, Adjutant General Seth Howard of California called a meeting for the purpose of organizing

244

Yachting party on the Potomac River in 1931. Left to right, Mrs. George S. Patton, Adjutant General of Texas W. W. Sterling, Major (Later General) George Smith Patton, Jr., Mrs. Simon Bolivar Buckner, Miss Beatrice Patton and (back to camera) George S. Patton III.

our section. This group included officers of the Reserve and the National Guard. They were kind enough to select me as their president. My principal duty was to preside at the class dinner honoring the faculty of the War College. This traditional function was held at the Shoreham Hotel.

General Conner was most generous in his praise of the manner in which it was conducted. Among other kind remarks, he said, "Gentlemen, I must confess that to me these class dinners are usually a pain in the neck." Turning to me, he continued, "But this old Texas boy has made me feel so much at ease that I have thoroughly enjoyed this one." I considered this a tribute to the hospitality of our state, rather than a personal compliment.

245

Members of the Regular Army who were student officers at the War College included a colorful major named George S. Patton, Jr. He and I soon became good friends, as we both liked horses, guns and boats. Major Patton had served at many posts on the Texas border, and he was General Pershing's aide during the punitive expedition into Mexico.

Major and Mrs. Patton were very kind to me during my stay in Washington. On several occasions they took me sailing on their yacht, *Arcturus* which was the forerunner of the schooner *When and If*. I also enjoyed the hospitality of their home near Fort Myer. Georgie and I shared the belief that the best pistol ever made was the 45 calibre Colt Peacemaker. I showed him how to smooth up the action of this old gun, and still have the letter in my files that he wrote thanking me for this bit of Ranger instruction.

The heavy weapon requires a stout, well designed scabbard. Upon my return to Texas, I had one made to order for him. It was of the same model and type used by old time Rangers. The leather craftsman who fashioned this holster turned out a masterpiece. Little did he know that his handiwork would be seen all over the world, in pictures of General Patton.

During World War II he achieved undying fame. General Patton was the greatest exponent of offensive warfare in history. His name is further perpetuated by the Patton tank and the new song adopted by the Army. Soldiers called him "Old Blood and Guts," yet with everyone except the enemy he was gentle and kind.

Early in the war I was on extended active duty at Fort Sam Houston, under my reserve commission as a lieutenant colonel. I tried my best to get in his outfit, and asked him to help me cut some red tape. He recommended the transfer officially, and personally wrote me a letter from the Headquarters First Armored Corps, Fort Benning, Georgia. He signed it, "Devotedly, George S. Patton Jr., Major General, U. S. Army, Commanding." Shortly before her passing, his widow, Mrs. Beatrice Ayers Patton, presented me with a portrait of her distinguished husband. The splendid likeness, which shows his favorite six-shooter resting in the Ranger scabbard, will always occupy an honored place in my home.

Bascom Timmons, the author-journalist who befriends all Texans in Washington, was very kind to me during my tour at the War College.

On several occasions I went with him to visit the Speaker of the House of Representatives, John N. Garner. We would arrive late in the afternoon, and usually find the gentleman from Uvalde in a good humor. His rooms were in the Washington Hotel, just across the street from the Treasury Building. He told us that he wanted to be where he could keep an eye on "Uncle Andy," as he called Secretary of the Treasury Andrew J. Mellon. After "striking a few blows for liberty," he would relate the events of the day at the Capitol. I enjoyed these visits immensely, and Bascom got a great deal of first hand news for his papers in Texas.

On a previous trip to Washington, I had met the Secret Service chief, Colonel Edward Starling. He was a Kentuckian, and as natives of that state seem to have a great deal in common with Texans, we became good friends. On several occasions, when there were no classes at the War College, I went to see him at the White House. He showed me some of the methods used to protect the President, and took me to a sort of turret facing the front. From this vantage point, all visitors could be scrutinized before they entered the door.

Colonel Starling showed a deep interest in the Texas Rangers, and apparently liked to talk about them. One day he asked me, "What kind of pistols do the Rangers use?" "A few of them are changing to double actions or automatics," I answered, "but I still prefer the old 45 calibre single action Peacemaker." "I would like to see one of them," continued the Colonel. "All right," I said. "Mine is in my room at the Willard Hotel. The next time I come I'll bring it along." He replied, "I wish you would."

The student officers were taken to the Aberdeen Proving Ground to witness some tests, and more than a week elapsed before I went back to the White House. When leaving the hotel, I stuck my pistol in the waistband of my trousers, and walked on over to the main entrance. Colonel Starling was in his observation post and sent word for me to join him there. After we had conversed a few minutes, I said, "You wanted to see my Ranger pistol. Here it is." He took one look at the Texas size six-shooter, and called several of his aides. "You fellows are supposed to spot men who come in here armed," said the Colonel. "General Sterling walked right by the whole bunch of you. He was not carrying a pistol; he was carrying a cannon."

The Secret Service men were deeply chagrined. I hastened to explain that I could carry a horse pistol in evening clothes, without showing the slightest sign of having it on my person.

President Franklin D. Roosevelt made a trip to Dallas in 1936, where he joined in the celebration of the Texas Centennial. Colonel Starling came down ahead of him, to make the necessary security arrangements. He asked the Director of Public Safety where I could be found, and that former appointee of mine replied that he did not know.

When the presidential party arrived in Dallas, I was judging a World's Championship Rodeo at the Cotton Bowl. Naturally, the afternoon performance had been cancelled. The stadium was used to seat the crowd that came to see and hear Mr. Roosevelt. He was to speak from a temporary platform erected in front of the chutes. I stood around with the other rodeo cowboys who were waiting to hear the speech.

The motorcade came up with a roar, and it was hard to believe what I saw. Several highway patrolmen mounted on motorcycles rode on each side of the President. Strapped on each machine was a 30-30 Winchester carbine. They were the short barreled variety called saddle guns, and they were totally out of place in a city.

On reaching the platform, the riders parked their motorcycles against the corral, and rushed to surround the Chief Executive. They left their rifles on the machines, entirely unguarded. This injudicious act could have been a fatal error. It would have been simple for a crank or an assassin to grab one of the Winchesters, poke it through the heavy fence and kill the President before the officers could stop him. I recognized the danger, and called it to the attention of Ranger Captain Hardy Purvis, who was standing nearby. He and I watched the neglected weapons until their owners returned.

On December 22, 1931, my second child was born at Brackenridge Hospital, in Austin. By a coincidence, the local jewelers had launched an advertising campaign to promote the sale of silver. They adopted as their slogan, "Add to your Sterling for Christmas." When my luncheon club called on me to announce the new arrival, I responded with the following words: "You are all familiar with the signs appearing in the show windows of local jewelry stores. Highpowered advertising

W. W. Sterling in the Cotton Bowl at Texas Centennial Rodeo, wearing the shirt of an honorary member of the Hardin-Simmons University Cowboy Band.

sometimes exerts a vast influence on the public. We have been blessed by the addition of seven and a half pounds of pure Sterling. It's a girl."

We named her Sara Ross. The first name was for Mrs. Sara Kleberg Johnson, of Kingsville, and the second for Governor Sterling. Three months later we had her christened. Through the thoughtfulness of Governor and Mrs. Sterling, the ceremony took place in the Governor's Mansion. The rites were performed by the Reverend Dr. Pierre Bernard Hill, pastor of the First Presbyterian Church in San Antonio, and chaplain of the Rangers. The water used in the christening came from the River Jordan.

Of all the relations between two people, I believe the sweetest is that of father and daughter. Far from being disappointed because my children were not boys, I would not exchange my two daughters for the entire All-American Football Team.

One of the most attractive places in or around Austin is Camp Mabry. For many years, much of its beauty was marred by a narrow, unsightly entrance. Prior to the establishment of Camps Hulen and Wolters, the annual encampments of the National Guard were held there. The frontage property had been bought up by Austin merchants. They sought convenient locations from which to sell their wares, principally liquid, to the soldiers. Barely enough room was left for ingress and egress. During my term as adjutant general, I cherished the wish to acquire these vacant lots, in order that we could have a wide, landscaped entrance to Camp Mabry.

The adjutant general's department owned sixteen and two-thirds acres of land that was cut off from the main reservation by the Missouri Pacific Railroad. Gibb Gilchrist, chief engineer of the highway department, and I were members of a motorcade that drove to El Paso to attend the annual convention of the Texas and Southwestern Cattle Raisers Association. We had lunch with a group of friends at Marfa, then drove on to Mount Livermore, site of the McDonald Observatory.

From there to El Paso, Mr. Gilchrist and I rode in the same car. We got to talking about our respective departments. He said, "I am looking around for a place to build a set of shops, laboratories and things like that. We would like to have that small tract across the railroad." My reply was, "If you will take the money you have to purchase a site, and buy us a good entrance to Camp Mabry, I will do everything in my power to put the deal over. There will be no money passed; it will just be an intra-departmental trade for the good of the state."

For the final outcome of our negotiations, I quote Dr. Gilchrist's letter to me on that subject. He is now the retired chancellor of the A. & M. College System.

> . . . Since 1918 the Adjutant General's Office had possessed as a part of Camp Mabry a tract of 16⅔ acres separated from the main body by the Missouri Pacific Railroad. It was an ideal site for the development of a convenient center for shops, warehouses, laboratories and other facilities for the State Highway Department.
>
> I recall vividly my first conversation with you about the tract. I told you my plans and asked if you had any objections to our seeking the tract by Legislative action. You answered like this, "Not only do I approve your idea, but I'll help you get the land." You did just that. You saw Governor Sterling, gained his approval, and on February 29, 1932 the property passed into the posession of the State Highway Department. Later the Legislature formally passed actual title to the tract, and on it today will be found the most modern highway layout in the United States and one whose value to the people of Texas it would be difficult to estimate. Without your vision, statesmanship, and courage this would not have been possible . . .

Few people know or care how the present beautiful entrance to Camp Mabry was acquired. To me, however, the history of its consummation is a source of lasting pride.

Chapter 29

THE GREAT DEPRESSION

O N the first day of January, 1932, friends all over America exchanged greetings with a wishful "Happy New Year." There was little cause for optimism, however, as the outlook was far from encouraging. The 1929 stock market crash had made a terrific impact on the national economy, and its ill effects were felt throughout the land. Although more fortunate than many of the other states, Texas was squarely in the throes of the Great Depression.

The price of cotton went down to a fraction over five cents per pound, sinking to its lowest level in thirty-three years. In Texas, the cheapness of this principal money crop always spells hard times. Everybody cast about for a head on which to heap the blame for their misfortunes. They were eager to use someone for a scapegoat. Special objects of their wrath were the "ins." 1932 had all the earmarks of a "Ferguson year."

Jim Ferguson was highly elated over this calamity, for he and his doctrines thrived on ignorance and discontent. He placed his henchmen in pool rooms, domino halls and kindred hangouts. These heelers, as well as street corner loafers, were instructed to spread the propaganda that "Sterling was not making a good governor." The fact that they could not cite a single one of his acts that had not benefited the state meant nothing to these slanderers. They harped on the theme song,

"Texas needs the Fergusons." While driving through Bastrop County during the election I picked up a hitch-hiking farmer. "Who is going to get your vote for governor?" I asked. "Ferguson," he replied. "Why?" I inquired. "Because," the typical Fergusonite explained, "Ross Sterling put the three cent postage stamp on us."

The Fergusons opened their campaign in Waco. Jim used his customary tactics. He charged the opposition with the things of which he himself was most guilty. Being a native of Bell County, I had observed him since childhood. His methods always reminded me of a mischievous boy who shared my double desk in grade school. This rascal would throw spit balls while the teacher's back was turned. When she whirled around to look for the culprit, he would point his accusing finger at somebody else.

In 1924, many good people voted for Mrs. Ferguson, as a lesser evil than the Ku Klux. I was among that number. Ever since he was impeached, her husband had howled for "vindication." When the voters gave him another chance, he proved recreant to his trust. He inaugurated a colossal campaign of corruption. No State agency was immune from his graft, but the greatest sufferer was the highway department. It had the most money. Among other staggering blows, Jim Ferguson's pillage caused a threat to withdraw Federal aid from the highways of Texas. His malodorous connections with various phony road building companies are matters of record.

In view of these depredations, nobody but a man with the gall of Jim Ferguson would have the audacity to mention the principal victim of his looting. Yet he sought to cover his own record by shouting from the stump, "For the last five and a half years, there is a shortage of one hundred million dollars in the highway department." It is significant that the period he cited started from the date Attorney General Dan Moody, by exposing the road scandals, cut him off from the highway money. The State auditor's official report showed the highway funds to be in perfect order. This did not bother Ferguson, who had demonstrated throughout his political career that facts meant very little to him. He continued to make this mis-statement all over the state, and repeated it in his closing diatribe in Dallas.

Governor Sterling did not announce his decision to run for re-election until May. He was sorely beset by weighty problems, both in his private business and with State affairs. The fickleness of the public was discouraging, and he was becoming a disillusioned man. Instead of placing the stamp of approval on his faithful service, rendered under extremely trying conditions, he was being harassed on all sides. The enemies of honest government plotted his downfall. They were a vicious group of spoilers, not one of whom had ever done anything constructive.

While he was devoting most of his time to the State, his personal fortune, once rated among the largest in Texas, had been lost. When he declared in a speech, "I am broke," a horde of fair weather friends deserted him. Mercenary politicans, both male and female, scurried to the opposition. One of the women, who had been most vehement in her denunciation of the Fergusons, entertained Ma with a luncheon. Her about face was executed just as soon as she found that Governor Sterling was no longer wealthy.

The Governor opened his campaign in Waco. His candidacy was placed before the people of his native state in a forthright, dignified manner. He asked them the question: "Shall honest, responsible, businesslike government be continued in Texas?" In this speech, he painted a realistic picture of a Ferguson administration. He said, "A man is running for governor behind his wife's skirts. Mrs. Ferguson would take the oath of office. Jim would be the actual governor. He would have authority without accountability. It would be proxy government."

The accuracy of his statement was reflected by an editorial in the Dallas *News:*

> In effect the man who votes for the Fergusons votes to abolish the oath of the gubernatorial office. For, if successful, James E. Ferguson will be Governor of that office with none of its responsibilities. He will appoint a long list of holders of places under the Governor's patronage, with absolutely no obligation to anybody to choose good and reliable persons. He will have bills signed or vetoed, will force through appropriations, will distribute pardons, will dominate boards and committees, will hand out contracts for highways and public buildings, will dispose of millions of dollars with no more answerability in the courts or to any impeachment proceedings than if he were an alien non-resident.

The entire campaign was pitched on this and kindred issues. Governor Sterling made no pretense of being a gifted orator, but under pressure and with constant practice, he became a fine public speaker. His words carried the unmistakable ring of sincerity. Mrs. Sterling accompanied her husband most of the time and the newspapers referred to her as "The Governor's Best Campaigner." I also made many trips with the party. This was done for a two-fold purpose. First: It was a privilege to travel with them. Second: The election of Governor Sterling was of paramount importance to the Ranger Service.

I discussed the course they were to pursue in the forthcoming election with many of the Rangers. These conversations were strictly unofficial; just man to man talks between comrades who loved the Service. Everybody agreed that when two good men were running for governor, each Ranger should be free to vote for the candidate of his choice, and take no part in an election.

In the present case, however, the line of demarcation was clearly drawn. One candidate was a governor who had proved himself to be the best friend Rangers ever had in that office. He had given them better working conditions, more transportation, and had appointed one of their number adjutant general. The other was the wife of an impeached governor. She was simply a figurehead in the office and a rubber stamp for her husband. His leaning was always toward the criminal element, and he would repay their practically solid support by ruining the Rangers.

Every man in the Service realized that another Ferguson administration would bring nothing but shame and disgrace to our organization. They further knew that two more years under Governor Sterling would mean increased benefits, more respect from the public and a general improvement in morale. Jim McCoy, a seasoned veteran, came to my office a few days after the Governor announced. His voice trembled with emotion as he said, "General, I want to make a substantial contribution to the campaign fund. Since you took charge, everybody respects the Rangers. It has not always been like that. You have done a lot for us."

I was deeply touched at these words and said, "Jim, you don't have to give any money, but you can tell your friends what you have just told me." "This is not politics, General," he went on. "We are simply fighting for the life of our outfit." McCoy's sentiments were practically unanimous. Out of more than fifty men, there was only one Judas.

In the latter part of May, a pleasant interlude at College Station enabled me to enjoy a short respite from politics. Graduates of the Agricultural & Mechanical College who have completed their R.O.T.C. training are commissioned second lieutenants in the Officers Reserve Corps of the United States Army. It was my privilege to present their commissions to the class of 1932. Many of its members have gone far in the fields of business, education and statesmanship. Notable among these patriotic Aggies are Olin (Tiger) Teague and J. Earl Rudder. Both were wounded in World War II and both received multiple decorations for valor. Colonel Rudder's Rangers led the assault on the high cliff between Utah and Omaha beaches during the D-Day invasion, and he later served Texas as commissioner of the General Land Office. He is now president of the A. & M. College System, and is commanding officer of the Ninetieth Reserve Division, with the rank of major general. For many years Olin Teague has served the Sixth District in the Congress. He is presently chairman of the Veteran's Affairs Committee in the House of Representatives. I am immensely proud of having played a small part in launching these and the other 1932 men on their military careers. They have richly rewarded me by electing me an honorary member of their class.

Chapter 30
CAMPAIGN OF 1932

With the opening of the 1932 guber-
natorial race, a new figure appeared on the Texas political horizon in
the person of Tom Hunter. He was a wealthy oil man from Wichita
Falls, who aspired to round out his career by serving the state as
governor. In stature he was short, heavy set and stoop shouldered,
but his appearance was offset by a personality that appealed to voters.
Some of his ideas were sound, while others had all the earmarks of
demagoguery.

While serving as chairman of the highway commission, Governor
Sterling had demanded that all rights of way for roads destined to
become parts of the State system, be one hundred feet wide. This
action was based on vision, plus the best technical advice from a staff
of competent engineers headed by Gibb Gilchrist. The boundaries of
State owned property were marked with short concrete posts. Stamped
on them were the letters "ROW."

Hunter used these markers as a basis for his attack on the administration. In rabble rousing speeches he told his listeners that these letters
did not stand for "Right of Way." He climaxed his burst of pseudo-
oratory by shouting, "They stand for 'Rule of Waste.'" If Tom Hunter
had lived to the present day, he would have been forced to admit the

fallacy of his unwarranted, though vote getting, statement. By comparison with the modern four lane highways, Chairman Sterling's hundred foot rights of way became little wider than cow trails.

When the votes were tabulated after the first primary, Ferguson was first with 402,238, Sterling second with 296,383 and Hunter third with 220,391. Tom Hunter's surprisingly large vote showed that while many good people wanted a change, they could not stomach the Fergusons. The wife and husband team reaped a harvest of votes as a result of the national prohibition referendum appearing on the primary ballots.

The large vote for the Fergusons was a blot on the fair name of Texas. Many of Governor Sterling's supporters were discouraged, but he did not lose his optimism. He pointed out that they had also led in the 1930 first primary, and that he had emerged victorious.

On August 1, I drove the Governor to Fort Worth, where the Sterling supporters met to make plans for the second primary. More than a thousand leaders from all over Texas participated in the rally. Myron Blalock of Marshall served as chairman. Many stirring appeals were made for concerted action to save the state from Fergusonism. Sam McCorkle, from the oil town of Mexia, urged that the people be told the whole story of martial law. He stated, "The declaration of martial law was the greatest act of executive statesmanship ever performed by a governor of Texas." Publisher Amon G. Carter said that the eyes of the Nation were on Texas. He estimated that the election of the Fergusons would cost the Democratic National Ticket between three and five million votes. Other prominent Texans pledged their assistance. Among these were many former supporters of Tom Hunter.

In retrospect, it is difficult for an intelligent Texan to fathom the mental processes of the voters during the 1932 election. This does not take into account the natural born, snuff dipping Fergusonites, but the otherwise good people who, under some strange delusion, departed from their usual standards and principles. Many would "threaten" to vote for Ferguson just like they would threaten to commit suicide or take any other foolish step. During the heat of the election, a friend of mine told me, "If such and such a thing is not done, or if times do not get better quickly, I am going to vote for Ferguson."

A prominent West Texas cattleman was also a leader in one of the large protestant denominations. He had contributed heavily to their university, where Governor Sterling had served with him on the board of trustees. There was a State highway in his county that he wanted re-routed. This would involve moving a colossal amount of earth, as the proposed road would go through a pass in the mountains.

The ranchman asked his fellow churchman to order the road built on the site he favored. Governor Sterling informed him that he did not dominate the highway department. He stated, however, that he would gladly recommend that the request be granted, provided a survey by staff engineers found the route feasible. I went over the ground with Gibb Gilchrist, chief engineer of the highway department, and heard the remark he made about pressure deals. He said, "I am not interested in the political aspects of road building. I am an engineer. All I know is that a straight line is the shortest distance between two points." The project was totally impractical. The cowman was not accustomed to having his wishes thwarted. He had long been a foe of Ferguson and all his works. Yet he turned against Governor Sterling and supported proxy government with all his might. He was totally out of character in a group of Fergusonites. To his numerous friends and admirers, among whom I was numbered, his action was a sad disappointment.

Before he was elected governor, R. S. Sterling owned a tract of land on the Trinity River in Liberty County. It was leased by the Humble Oil and Refining Company. They did not elect to develop this land, so they paid him some advance royalty. The payment was made by check, as in the regular course of business. This was a deal made by a private citizen, and the details were recorded in the county courthouse, open to public inspection.

Jim Ferguson was serving as Governor of Texas. He had taken the oath of office which provided for the "faithful discharge of his duties." While liquor legislation was pending in the legislature, he received from the breweries $156,000 in currency, which was delivered to the Governor's office in a "little black bag." For accepting this bribe, as well as committing other crimes and misdemeanors, he was impeached.

The reasoning power of most Fergusonites was limited to ribald yells of "Hooraw fer Maw." They refused to make a distinction between a legitimate business deal and a bribe, and asked, "What's the difference? Jim took his from the breweries; Ross took his from the Humble."

259

Throughout my lifetime, I have held a high regard and deep esteem for Latin Americans. Some of my best friends are members of that important segment of our citizenship. I have lived among them for more than half a century. This close association has enabled me to make a careful study of their language and customs. Unfortunately, these good people often have been exploited. In many instances, false and self serving leaders have sold them down the river. Like sheep to the slaughter, they have been led to vote against their best interests.

When Governor Sterling visited Laredo, I took him to the home of Don Eusebio Garcia. On this occasion, he paid me a most gratifying compliment. Don Eusebio put his hand on my shoulder and spoke to the Governor in Spanish. A free translation of the words is "Governor, of all the Americans I have ever known, this gentleman has the best way of dealing with Mexicans."

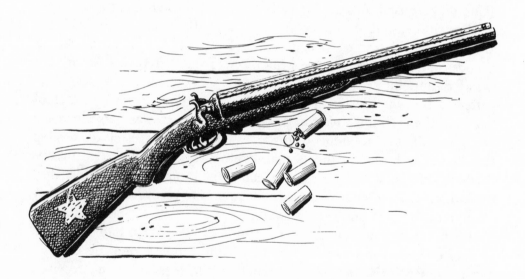

Each year the citizens of Laredo stage a magnificent celebration. These festivals do more toward fostering good relations between Mexico and the United States than a dozen official conferences. They are held on George Washington's birthday. Nuevo Laredo is situated on the opposite bank of the Rio Grande, and the two Laredos join in honoring the Father of Our Country. This spirit of cooperation and understanding widens the scope of the grand fiesta, and imparts an atmosphere that is decidedly international.

The festivities are climaxed by an official dinner. A galaxy of orators vie with each other in extolling the virtues of their neighbors. Many eloquent speeches are delivered in both Spanish and English. On one of these occasions, I was seated between two officers of the Mexican Army. At the conclusion of the ceremonies, the guests joined in singing the national anthems of the sister republics. When we began to sing the beautiful and stirring "Himno Nacional," my Mexican friends were amazed to hear me join in both the words and chorus. One of them caught me by the arm in a spirit of comaraderie, and continued to hold it until we resumed our seats. He asked in astonishment, "Where did you learn our song?" "I have known all the verses since boyhood," I replied. They were deeply touched by this episode. Both officers were quick to sense the sincere tribute to their nation. Small and apparently insignificant gestures of this kind do more to cement friendships with Latin American countries than a whole portfolio filled with propaganda. This is especially true when these stilted messages are delivered by one who does not speak their language.

Latin American residents of Texas received better treatment and more representation from the Sterling administration than they had ever before enjoyed. I gave one of the best positions in my department to Colonel Frank Chapa of San Antonio. Around Austin I became known as a sort of Mexican consul, and performed many services for the people on both sides of the border. We entertained the governors of several Mexican States, and always maintained the most cordial relations with our southern neighbors. Citizens of Mexican extraction knew that they could get a fair hearing on any of their problems. They did not have to employ attorneys, as I was always glad to help them.

These sentiments and ideas were not shared by the Fergusons. One of the impeached Governor's favorite wiles was the use of prejudice. He liked to array class against class for political expediency. The vast size of the state and the concentration of racial groups in certain sections enabled him to capitalize on this evil practice. When campaigning in the interior, he declared that Mexicans should not be allowed in first class coaches, but that they should be made to ride in segregated cars.

In the face of these insults and other abuses, some of the border politicos, notably in Webb County, turned their bloc of votes to the Fergusons. District Attorney John A. Valls wrote me under date of July 12, 1932:

> I want you to know the following facts concerning Webb County. There are several influential members of my party who are working hard for Mrs. Ferguson. The leader of this faction is a former member of the legislature, and he has several active followers. I am doing all I can in favor of Governor Sterling. I will continue to do my best but I can't help but feel somewhat discouraged. I find very little patriotism and very little loyalty.

He wrote the letter in longhand, and signed it "Sincerely Your Friend."

Colonel Sam Robertson of San Benito was a colorful character. He had built railroads and canals all over the country. During the Bandit War of 1915, he rode with us on many scouts. He later went to Mexico, where he was captured by revolutionists, but managed to make his escape. I saw him after he returned to Texas, and the rope burns on his neck were plainly visible. He had been dragged from a saddle horn by his captors. During World War I, he served as a colonel of Engineers in France. He laid a section of railroad under the cover of darkness that won him wide commendation from his superiors. Colonel Robertson also served as sheriff of Cameron County, and was never backward about expressing his opinion. He did not want to see the Fergusons in office, and he wired Governor Sterling urging him to withdraw in favor of Tom Hunter. The telegram read: "You are an 'in.' You cannot win in such a time as this. Thomas Jefferson, George Washington or Abe Lincoln, if in office today could not be re-elected. The voters of 1932 are as rational as the mob who crucified Christ."

One of Governor Sterling's least known but most important acts was one that resulted in the abolition of the iniquitous fee system. This practice not only wasted a large amount of public money, but it tended to corrupt many otherwise honest sheriffs. The Governor's extensive experience in business enabled him to detect this abuse. When the appropriation for "various fees" came up for his signature, he noted that it called for a round figure. He knew that if the bill for fees had been itemized, only by a miracle would it come out in even dollars. He ordered an investigation into the matter, and the auditors made some startling disclosures. I cite a few typical examples:

A sheriff in East Texas had loaned his railroad pass to a man who was a prospective witness in a felony case. The trial was to be held in the home county. He used this free transportation to ride to El Paso. The subpoena was sent to him there, and he rode the pass back home. Something like two thousand miles of mileage was collected. Another sheriff put in a bill for eight hundred miles north and a like amount south which he said he traveled in one small county. A Negro in jail was shown a list of purported witnesses in his case, and was told to sign a paper demanding that they be subpoenaed. He said that he did not even know the men whose names appeared on it. Fees were collected for serving these summonses. These abuses were the fault of the system rather than of the individual. Some good sheriffs justified the practice by claiming that the only way they could make a living wage out of their office was to pad mileage accounts. They further asserted that an officer who constantly risked his life to protect the people should be adequately paid, regardless of where the money came from.

When Governor Sterling put an end to this long established custom, he effected an enormous annual saving of the taxpayer's money. In bringing about the reform, however, he incurred the displeasure of the clique who at that time was in control of the Texas Sheriffs Association. Throughout his entire career, the Chief Executive had been a tried and true friend of honest officers. Two years before, he had appointed one of their members, W. W. Sterling, to a high State office. Nevertheless, in the 1932 gubernatorial race, the Sheriffs Association and its official publication supported the proven enemies of law enforcement.

Chapter 31

ELECTION FRAUDS
IN EAST TEXAS

SHORTLY before the second primary, I received reports of a steady influx of transients into East Texas. It was particularly noticeable in Gregg County. Several politicians who left unsavory reputations back home had reaped rich bonanzas in the oil fields of their adopted state. To show their gratitude for these bounties, they proposed to steal the forthcoming election. One of the principal steps in their nefarious plot was to import this horde of floaters. These "voters from other states" knew nothing of San Jacinto. They had never heard the battle cries "Remember the Alamo" and "Remember Goliad." During their brief sojourn in the Lone Star State they had only been coached to yell "Hooraw fer Maw." The criminal law practice enjoyed by the Ferguson leaders had been largely ruined by the Rangers, and their hot oil deals were ended when martial law was declared by Governor Sterling.

No group of men possess a keener insight into human nature than old time Texas sheriffs. They were also wise in the ways of politics and the tricks of politicians. The roster of our Rangers contained the names of many ex-sheriffs, including several who had served their association as presidents. In fighting a ruthless and unscrupulous enemy, I decided to avail myself of their sagacious counsel. The situation confronting us in East Texas was without precedent, and I determined to use original methods in preventing the contemplated theft of the election.

Pursuant to this idea, I called a solemn conference in my office. Those summoned were Captain Will Wright, Captain Albert Mace, Captain

J. B. Wheatley and Sergeant Earl McWilliams. Our Chaplain, Captain P. B. Hill, opened the meeting with prayer. He invoked Divine Guidance in the step we were about to take. I did not tell Governor Sterling anything about the proposed action. There was no thought of by-passing him, but throughout my service as adjutant general, I tried to take as much of the load from him as I could. It seemed to be particularly important at this time, for he was carrying a tremendous burden.

I said to the assembled group: "Gentlemen, a horde of floaters are lurking in the oil fields of East Texas. They are there for no good purpose, and their presence means that some form of wholesale crookedness is brewing. I am sure that they have been brought in to help steal the election. My plan is to send three companies of the Rangers over there next week. We will announce to the press that a drive is being made on the criminal element. I have made arrangements with the police departments of several cities to have representatives on hand. They can make identifications and take fingerprints. Honest citizens have nothing to fear. They will not be bothered in any way.

"Crooks always get itchy feet at the appearance of Rangers, and the wicked flee without waiting to be pursued. I believe that this move will do more to curb illegal voting than any amount of talk. It will also rid the state of many undesirables." The meeting was then thrown open for discussion. I said, "Boys, this is a fight for the life of the Service. Let's forget about rank. Speak freely and give your best thought to my proposal. If you see anything wrong with it, don't hesitate to tell me."

"General, it will work fine," said Sergeant McWilliams, who was immediate past president of the Sheriffs Association. "If those crooks are not stirred up, they will all vote. Not only once, but they will repeat." The others agreed without a single dissenting voice.

Our men were all set, and the zero hour was midnight. I was waiting in my quarters at Camp Mabry. Shortly after eleven o'clock I received a telephone call from Governor Sterling. He was spending the night at his home on Galveston Bay. He asked, "Do you have a bunch of Rangers in the East Texas oil fields?" "Yes, sir," I replied, "they are going to strike at twelve o'clock." "I am countermanding the order," he said. "A move like that would cost us the election." I was dumbfounded but managed to say, "On the contrary, it will win it. The place is flooded with illegal voters, and they are solidly against you." He repeated, "I still want to countermand the order." I got Captain Mace on the phone and transmitted the Governor's message.

This episode constituted the only semblance of a clash that ever occurred between the Governor and me. I learned my politics from such masters as James B. Wells and Marshall Hicks. The ex-sheriff Rangers had given me the best advice their combined experience could muster. More than once during his political career, Governor Sterling became the victim of unwise counsel. The countermanding of my order had always been a delicate subject, and we did not discuss it until his later years. When Ed Kilman started to write the Governor's biography, he asked me to furnish him with the details of this incident. I had always thought that the man responsible for it was General Jacob F. Wolters. When Kilman brought up the subject, the Governor said, "It was not Jake. The man who advised me to get the Rangers out was Amon Carter." Mr. Carter was on our side, and no doubt did what he believed to be in the best interest of the cause. The last conversation I ever had with Governor Sterling was held at his home in Houston. He said, "Bill, if I had let you go ahead and knock out those illegal votes in Gregg County, we probably would have won."

When the results of the second primary came in, the count showed: Ferguson 477,644, and Sterling 473,846.

My advance information that an election fraud was about to be perpetrated proved to be absolutely reliable. By no stretch of the imagination, however, could the audacity and method of accomplishing this theft be foretold. A large, synthetic Texan, who might well be called "Whale," and his accomplices had a bunch of "ballots" printed. No similar scheme had ever been concocted in Texas nor has one ever been attempted. There was no more authority for printing them than there would be for printing a ten dollar bill. They were marked "For Voters from Other States." I have a large number of them in my possession. Depicted here is a typical specimen.

Several years ago, an attorney general of Texas announced his intention to launch a vigorous crusade against all forms of election fraud. He was quoted as being eager to find evidence, either past or present, of ballot box corruption in the state. This would enable him to take the lead in drafting a bill aimed at stamping out such evil

FOR VOTERS FROM OTHER STATES

STATE OF TEXAS
COUNTY OF GREGG

Before me the undersigned authority, on this day personally appeared ....

.... known to me, and who being by me duly sworn on oath, deposes and says as follows:

"That on January 1st, 1931, I resided in the City of ..... *S America* ....,

County of ...., State of ....,

that I moved to the State of Texas on ..... *Jan. 30-31* ....

having resided in said state continuously since said date, making a period of ..... *12* ....

months continuous residence in the State; that I moved to the County of Gregg on ..... *Same* ....

............................, and have resided in said County continuously since said date, mak-

ing a period of ....months continuous residence in said County; that I

reside at ..... *Kilgore* ....

in said County of Gregg and am a qualified voter; that I resided in State of ..... *S.A.* ....

on January 1st, 1931."

Subscribed and sworn to before me this the ..... *27* ....day of August, 1932.

Notary Public, Gregg County, Texas.

FOR VOTERS FROM OTHER STATES

STATE OF TEXAS
COUNTY OF GREGG

Before me the undersigned authority, on this day personally appeared ....

.... known to me, and who being by me duly sworn on oath, deposes and says as follows:

"That on January 1st, 1931, I resided in the City of ..... *Seminole* ....,

County of ..... *Seminole* ...., State of ..... *Okla* ....,

that I moved to the State of Texas on ..... *Feb. 1931* ....

having resided in said state continuously since said date, making a period of ..... *Same 12* ....

months continuous residence in the State; that I moved to the County of Gregg on ..... *Same* ....

............................, and have resided in said County continuously since said date, mak-

ing a period of ....months continuous residence in said County; that I

reside at ..... *Kilgore* ....

in said County of Gregg and am a qualified voter; that I resided in State of ..... *Okla* ....

on January 1st, 1931."

Subscribed and sworn to before me this the ..... *27* ....day of August, 1932.

Notary Public, Gregg County, Texas.

Specimens of the psuedo-ballots used in Gregg County during the second Primary of 1932. Hundreds of them were printed and used by supporters of the Fergusons.

practices. His forthright declaration earned him a great deal of space in the newspapers.

On one occasion he came to Corpus Christi, where he delivered an address to the local Bar. I showed him a handful of the fraudulent Gregg County "ballots," vintage of 1932. Limitation had long since run on them, and I realized that no legal action could be taken. They were produced merely to aid him in his research. When he examined my exhibit, he struck his most official pose and stated, "I don't believe that these amount to anything."

I was astounded to hear these words from the lips of the man who so loudly proclaimed himself the champion of honest elections. It was hard to believe that he chose to ignore the most flagrant violation in the history of Texas. The answer came some time later. I mentioned the incident to one of my former comrades, who lived in this politician's home town. "No wonder," this gentleman explained, "one of Hasbeen's (that is not his name) not too distant relatives was very familiar with this deal."

The conspirators went to the hobo jungles and railroad yards, rounded up the riffraff, and brought them to the polls. Here they were handed one of the fishy "ballots" and permitted to vote. These tramps not only voted illegally, but they repeated. They were not even qualified voters in the states in which they claimed to reside on January 1, 1931. Honest voters had to be bona fide residents of Texas and pay a poll tax or take out an exemption, before they could vote. The ones who spawned this steal should be proud of their work. They not only stole the election from a good man but they used our state as a dumping ground.

One of the Rangers found a barrel of these "ballots" near the city hall in Kilgore, and brought them to me. The state of mind in Texas at that time is reflected in the way these false papers were received in Austin. I took one of them to the Senate Chamber and showed it to a State senator. He expressed no concern over the fact that a palpable election fraud had been committed. His only question was, "What business did the Rangers have to take those 'ballots'?"

When the Gregg County gang printed the counterfeits, they perpetrated an unparalleled election fraud. They were captioned "For Voters from Other States," and they served as invitations for criminals from other states to descend on Texas. Through the underworld grapevine we received reports that many gangsters had their eyes on our state. I made a number of talks during the campaign. They were charitably referred to as "speeches." In all of them I warned the voters that a Ferguson regime would unquestionably result in an influx of thugs.

Many otherwise intelligent people turned a deaf ear to my plea. Among numerous similar instances, this fact is reflected in a passage from a book titled *Crime's Paradise*. It deals with the kidnapping of a wealthy Oklahoma oil man. That dastardly crime took place in the year 1933. The kidnappers immediately brought their victim to Texas. There were several well prepared hideouts in that Ferguson governed state. The gangsters had no apprehension about the formerly dreaded Rangers. They knew there was a vast difference between a genuine Texas Ranger and a Ferguson Ranger. The author of *Crime's Paradise* laments the fact that the state at that time was overrun by criminals. He confesses his part of the travesty in these words: "I am a native and a resident of Texas. I voted for the Fergusons." He ignored the fact that his ballot was a contributing factor to the condition he decried.

In many parts of East Texas there were further evidences of fraudulent voting. The number of ballots cast in many boxes far exceeded the total of poll taxes and exemptions. Two typical examples were found in Panola County. The Logan box, with twenty-six poll taxes, came up with eighty-nine votes. The Dotson box, with eighteen poll taxes, turned in sixty-eight votes. An overwhelming majority for the Fergusons was revealed in every case of this kind. The Dallas *News* said, "Most impartial observers agree that fraudulent voting was widespread. In the counties under suspicion, the Fergusons received a majority of more than 75,000."

In the face of these facts, I could not believe that there was not some remedy for us in the courts. At a meeting of Governor Sterling's attorneys, everybody agreed that a wholesale fraud had been perpetrated. Former Governor Dan Moody warned, however, that an election contest was fraught with uncertainties.

Chapter 32
LUBBOCK CONVENTION

T HE LUBBOCK CONVENTION presented a sad spectacle. Hot oil men and other corrupt groups had put up money to pack it with the rag tag and bobtail of Texas. My boys were ready to get some justice in a practical way, but our attorneys warned that there must be no fights or bloodshed. Captain Frank Hamer used his sarcastic wit. "There will be no bloodshed, Judge. If we jump that bunch, the only thing that will be shed will be a lot of filth and corruption." At a caucus in Governor Sterling's room, it was decided to pass up the convention and try to get relief in the courts.

Ranger Oscar Martin and I made the trip in the adjutant general's car. On the way back to Austin we stopped at Sterling City, where we enjoyed a visit with Uncle Bill Kellis. This grand patriarch was one of my favorite persons, and a journalist of the old school. He had been to Lubbock, and was thoroughly disgusted with the farce they had made of the convention. Uncle Bill said that the gang he saw there must have been gathered from the pool halls of East Texas, and he wondered who had paid their transportation. I had long been a subscriber to The Sterling City *Record-News* and he told me to watch for the next issue.

When the motley state convention declared Mrs. Ferguson the winner, he wrote an allegory entitled, "And the Multitude cried, Give us Barabbas." Comparing the careers of Ross Sterling and Jim Ferguson, Uncle Bill wrote the following masterpiece:

When they brought Jesus before Pilate for trial on a charge that except for being honest with His God, Himself and His people He was guiltless, the following proceedings were had:

> Therefore when they were gathered together, Pilate said unto them, Whom will ye that I release unto you? Barabbas, or Jesus which is called Christ?
> For he knew that for envy they had delivered him.
> But the chief priests and elders persuaded the multitude that they should ask Barabbas and destroy Jesus.
> The governor answered and said unto them. Whether of the twain will ye that I release unto you? They said Barabbas.

Matt. 27: 17-18-20-21.

They crucified Jesus and glorified Barabbas.

Jesus had no fault except he stood up against hypocrisy, graft and general crookedness. He stood up for righteousness, truth and honesty. Even the savage old Pilate could find no fault in Him, and pleaded that he have their consent to let Him go. But they would not.

Barabbas was a convicted felon. He was a thief, a robber and a murderer, yet, they admired Barabbas and because of his iniquity, but they hated Jesus because he was opposite of all that was claimed for Barabbas.

That was nearly two thousand years ago, but in spite of the admonitions and preachments of the righteous and wise men since that time, that strong preference for the proven crook still exists in the minds and desires of a part of the people of all races. Why it is so, no psychologist has ever been able to explain. The Bible assigns envy as the cause, but that hardly expresses it in modern times when people have been brought up in the teachings of Jesus.

Not so many years ago, the time came to elect a new president of the United States. "Whom will you choose?" said the law of the land. "Give us Debs, the convicted felon in prison," said a part of the people. Debs was doing time in prison for treason to his country in time of war, and for which he would have been hung had he lived in the time of Washington. Yet, so great was the "give us Barabbas" sentiment, that thousands pleaded to elect Debs to preside over the country which he sought to destroy. They knew if he were elected, he would seek to destroy the greatest government that the sun ever shown on, but they wanted a proven traitor and criminal to rule over them.

We fail to understand these people's psychology. It is beyond our ken.

Take the case of jimferguson. In 1918 he was convicted of "high crimes and misdemeanors" by the Texas Senate, which is the highest court in the land. He was kicked out of the governor's office and forever barred from

271

holding an office of public trust or profit in Texas. Not only was he guilty thru the testimony of others, but by his own admission. Glorying in his crimes and boasting of his foxy cunning and hypocrisy, he brought his wife out as his proxy and the "Barabbas sentiment" elected her as governor of Texas for one term, and at the same time knowing that the poor woman was subservient to the will of her husband.

The orgy of crime, including indirect murder as well as unheard of waste that prevailed in that administration, stands without a rival in political history. This administration makes the patriots of Texas hang their heads in shame, altho they redeemed the good old state from the foul blot at their first opportunity, we are still made to suffer grief and shame as the Barabbas sentiment without a blush or qualm, tries to put the Fergusons back into power to do us further hurt.

Common honesty is penalized, while cunning hypocrisy is at a premium with those who love Barabbas and hate Jesus.

This is not written in the hope that anyone will be convinced of the enormity of the wrong in trying to foist jimferguson into power again, but it is written in wonder that Herod and those hooked nosed, bewiskered chief priests were able to transmit the Barabbas sentiment down to a part of the present generation. They hated Jesus and admired Barabbas for his cussedness. They hate Ross Sterling because he is wise and honest and admire jimferguson for his general and notorious cussedness, and had they been at the trial of Jesus before Pilate, they would have cried: give us Barabbas.

We wouldn't try for a moment to convince anyone that he is wrong in trying to put jimferguson in power again, because no argument of facts or fancy can change them, because the things we most detest in this creature, are the things which they most admire. But from a standpoint of logic and psychology, it is a strange question. We just cannot uderstand why some people admire a proven crook, but they do. If Barabbas found grace in the eyes of that mob to let him live, jimferguson has not only found grace, but he is admired and showered with honors for that which men should be ashamed.

Chapter 33
FERGUSONISM RAMPANT

I n the fall of 1932, it became apparent that through loopholes and weaknesses in our election laws, the Fergusons would be allowed to get away with their ill gotten gains. Announcement of this fact set off a chain of weird and unbelievable events. Jubilant Fergusonites began to hold "caucuses" in many counties of the state. Along with other campaign misstatements, the impeached Governor had shouted, "When we get in, there will be twenty-five thousand jobs for my friends." They lived to see him repudiate this statement. Taking him at his "word" these gullible followers were holding victory meetings to divide up the spoils. A frequent occurrence at these amazing gatherings would be the discovery that among those in attendance, several people had been promised the identical job. When one of their more intelligent neighbors pointed out this fact, each poor dupe would reply, "I know Jim won't let ME down."

A dozen or more had been promised the office of adjutant general. Hundreds were positive that they would be appointed Rangers. I asked one of my friends how the benighted Fergusonites thought the same job could be given to so many different men. He replied, "They don't think, period."

In the spring of 1932, Captain Frank Hamer, on behalf of the boys, presented me with a fine pistol. It was a Colt forty-five single action six-shooter, of the type long known on the frontier as the Peacemaker. They knew this grand old weapon to be my favorite. Although I rarely carried two pistols, it made a perfect match for the one I had used so long. Overlaid in gold on the backstrap of both of them is my name, plus the words "Texas Ranger." The lettering is identical except for the rank. One bears the title "Captain" and the other is marked "General." Engraved on the under side is a two word legend that to me makes the gift priceless. It is "From Rangers."

On Christmas day of 1932, the military section of my department presented me with a beautiful sabre. Engraved on it were my name, rank and native state. I was deeply grateful to the donors for this lasting memento of my service as adjutant general. It was not only a gift of great intrinsic value, but one that can be passed on to future generations. The moving spirits in this presentation were Colonel H. H. Carmichael and Colonel Taylor Nichols. Their thoughtfulness, coupled with that of Captain Hamer, enabled me to have permanent tokens of esteem from both branches of the state's armed forces.

On December 10, 1932, I went to the fall dinner of the Gridiron Club in Washington. My host for this occasion was the late Mark Goodwin of the Dallas *News*. I had long cherished a desire to attend one of these famous affairs, and to see the Capitol newspaper correspondents roast some of the country's most prominent men. When he selected me as his guest, my gratitude knew no bounds. In my letter of acceptance, I told Mark: "Throughout the length and breadth of Texas, you could not have picked a man who would be happier over the invitation." He remarked that I was rather profuse in my thanks and extravagant in the use of kind words, but both sentiments came from my heart.

The dinner itself and the entertainment that followed combined to present a grand spectacle. I sat between Senator Morris Sheppard and Chairman Jesse H. Jones of the Reconstruction Finance Corporation. The guests included a brilliant array of national figures. This list was augmented by the names of many foreign diplomats, whose presence added lustre to the scene.

I was introduced as Commander of the Texas Rangers and a constituent of Vice President-elect John Nance Garner. The principal address was delivered by President Herbert Hoover. Party lines were temporarily erased as both Republicans and Democrats joined in paying tribute to a great American. Remarks made at the Gridiron Dinner are privileged, but I am sure no breach of that rule will be committed by repeating one statement he made. Mr. Hoover said, "Gentlemen, this is the eighteenth Gridiron Dinner I have attended." Pointing to a corner of the banquet room he continued, "I have occupied every seat in this hall, from the most obscure one in the corner to that of the President of the United States, which I occupy tonight. I must say, gentlemen, that the most comfortable seat of them all was the obscure seat in the corner."

One morning as I stepped out of the elevator and started across the lobby of my hotel, I came face to face with Will Rogers. He had just arrived in Washington. I was in uniform, and wore the insignia of a brigadier general. Will had never seen me in this unfamiliar outfit, and he seemed to be especially puzzled by the Sam Browne belt. He grasped the part that goes over the shoulder and said, "I never expected to see this old Texas cowboy wearing a martingale."

On the night of the Gridiron Dinner, I was delighted to be seated at the same table with General Andrew Moses. He was commandant of cadets at Texas A. & M. during my sophomore year. His brother, Dayton Moses, served for many years as attorney for the Texas & Southwestern Cattle Raisers Association, and the general was a thorough Texan. He knew all about politics in his home state and was familiar with the ways of the National Guard. "Sterling, what about your military career after you go out as adjutant general?" he asked. "I don't know, General," I replied. He was then kind enough to say, "We don't want to lose you. The Army needs men of your background and experience. Before you go home, come around to my office. We can't commission you in your present rank, but I'll see that you get something decidedly worthwhile."

Senator Morris Sheppard was seated next to us. He joined in by saying, "General Moses, as you know I am chairman of the Military Affairs Committee. I will be happy to sponsor this gentleman." We later met Senator William Warren Barbour of New Jersey. We were named for the same man, and he had visited our ranch in Hidalgo County. He was also a member of the Military Affairs Committee, and said, "I want to add my endorsement to that of Senator Sheppard."

General Moses laughed and told these powerful gentlemen, "Giving Sterling a commission in the Organized Reserves was MY idea, and I need no help. However, I am glad that you Senators agree with me." Before leaving Washington I was commissioned a lieutenant colonel in the Specialist Reserve. It became effective on January 15, 1933, the day I relinquished the office of adjutant general.

The New Year of 1933 ushered in a sad day for Texas. The corridors of the capitol began to swarm with a strange conglomeration of humanity. Jim had promised them twenty-five thousand jobs. They were here to accept them. We who were about to surrender the reins of responsible government to this horde had to witness the disgraceful spectacle. Somebody in the office made up this descriptive verse of doggerel:

> Hark, Hark, the dogs do bark,
> The Fergusonites have come to town.
> Their looks are tough, their necks are rough,
> They love their Levi Garret snuff.

Many of them would look furtively at my office, each one expecting to be appointed adjutant general. Some of the Rangers joshed the poor fellows about the number who were on hand to receive the same job. Captain Hamer remarked, "There must be five thousand head of Fergusonites milling around the capitol." They stayed in Austin, eating dime chilis, and wherever possible, getting a dollar hot check cashed.

On January 16, I was deeply touched by an act of the commander of the Ex-Rangers Association, Major A. B. Coffee. He knew that the country was in the midst of the depression, and that at his age he could not hope to get another position. Nevertheless, he brought me his letter of resignation. It speaks for itself. Captains Brooks, Hughes and Gillett stated that under our administration the Rangers reached their greatest peak, and gratifying indeed was this added commendation from Major Coffee:

> Dear Sir: I herewith tender you my resignation both as Ranger and Clerk. I desire to go out at the same time you do, and under your administration, so that this, my last service, may, in no way, be connected with any other, for this has been, in the lines to which I was detailed, the most successful and satisfactory I have ever had.

In going out, I leave to you my most sincere personal friendship, regard and admiration, which, I hope, I have managed to show you heretofore in ways that could not be misunderstood, and wish to congratulate you, not only for the efficiency and diligence in which your own duties were handled, which all men know, but for having the most efficient, and congenial force I ever knew, and I have had more or less service or acquaintance with Ranger service since 1879, and do not remember ever seeing a force in which any one man, officer or private, could take a case, alone, from its inception to its conclusion; locate the offender, find the witnesses; sift the evidence; make the complaint; make the arrest or arrests; recover any stolen property involved in the matter; restore it to the owner, all with a promptness and efficiency seldom seen, and all on his own initiative and depending upon himself alone, which has been a constant occurrence during this administration. Looking at this from the outside and not involved; having no fear of falling down on the job myself, I may have noticed this more particularly than any of the participants who had to watch their own steps. Very respectfully, (signed) A. B. Coffee.

When there is a friendly succession in the office, the outgoing governor and his staff join in the ceremonies. In this case, however, we had concrete evidence of fraud, and wanted no part of the travesty. On the last day, I joined Governor Sterling in his office. The corridor was crowded with exultant Fergusonites. These included a number of shady characters who were to be used as Rangers. One of Governor Sterling's friends suggested that he go out the side door, to avoid any possibility of a clash. He brushed aside the idea by saying, "I came in the front door, and I am going out the same way." A number of my boys came to bid him farewell. They were in a dangerous mood for they realized that the Rangers were losing their best friend. One disrespectful remark from the Ferguson henchmen would have brought on a thinning of their ranks.

It is customary for the outgoing governor to mark a passage in the Bible for his successor. I suggested to Governor Sterling that he underscore the Eighth Commandment but he vetoed my plan. "The Lord will take care of old Jim," he said.

We entered the Governor's private automobile and drove to his home on Galveston Bay. Thus terminated the official careers of the two Sterlings. Throughout the administration of R. S. Sterling, both of us were deeply conscious of the meaning of our surnames.

PART TWO

Chapter 34

LAWRENCE SULLIVAN ROSS

Lawrence Sullivan Ross, eighteenth Governor of Texas, was born in the village of Benton's Post, Ohio, in 1838. A year later, his father, Captain Shapley P. Ross, brought the family to Texas. The elder Ross was a noted frontiersman, and always headed the forces engaged in protecting the settlers. Single handed, he killed Big Foot, a chief of the Comanches. Young Ross, who throughout his life was known as "Sul," grew up on the fringes of civilization, and as a boy had several narrow escapes from death at the hands of the Indians.

After attending such schools as the new country afforded, he was sent to Florence Wesleyan University in Alabama. At the age of twenty, he came home for a vacation, and was placed in command of a band of Caddo Indians. They welcomed any opportunity to fight their hereditary enemies, the Comanches. In a battle on the Wichita, Sul Ross received a severe wound. He was carried many miles on a litter borne by two pack mules. When the terrain was too rough to keep the burden level, the friendly Caddos carried him on their shoulders. Sul Ross' iron constitution, the fresh air and good Army surgeons combined to make his recovery complete. He was able to return to his studies, and to graduate from Florence Wesleyan University in 1859.

Statue of Ranger-Statesman-Educator Lawrence Sullivan Ross
on campus of Texas Agricultural & Mechanical College.

Students of Texas history are familiar with the story of Cynthia Ann Parker. In numerous books and articles, they have read how she was captured by the Comanches at a settlement called Fort Parker, near the present city of Weatherford. Her father and several relatives were killed, and she and her brother were carried away. Cynthia Ann grew up among the Indians, and became the wife of a great chief, Peta Nocona. The town of Nocona is named for him. One of their sons, Quanah Parker, became the most famous chief of the Comanches. He also has a town named for him. During the golden anniversary of the founding of Wichita Falls, I had a picture made with Baldwin Parker, son of the redoubtable Quanah. At the battle of Pease River in 1860, Peta Nocona was killed by Captain Sul Ross. Cynthia Ann, who had forgotten her mother tongue, was brought back to civilization. She was never happy in her new environment and died about ten years later.

Shortly after his graduation, Sul Ross was commissioned a captain in the Rangers by Governor Sam Houston. His service in the Comanche campaigns earned him the following commendation from Governor Houston: "Your success in protecting the frontier gives me great satisfaction. I am satisfied that with the same opportunities you would rival, if not excel, the greatest exploits of McCullough and Hays. Continue your good work, and the people of Texas will not withhold their praise."

With the opening of the Civil War, Sul Ross joined the Confederate Army. Some historians, with a flair for humble beginnings, state that he entered it as a private, but probably they were in error. It is not plausible to believe that the Confederacy would forego the talents and experience of a natural leader. He was also the son of a leader, the slayer of Peta Nocona and the deliverer of Cynthia Ann Parker. Ross had won fame as a Ranger captain, and doubtless went in with at least that rank. At any rate, he fully sustained his reputation as a fighter. Sul Ross participated in more than a hundred battles, and attained the rank of brigadier general.

At the close of the War Between the States, General Ross returned to McLennan County and took up farming. He was not permitted to pursue this peaceful occupation for long. Hundreds of lawless characters flocked into Texas, and a particularly vicious group of them landed in the new town of Waco. They became so firmly entrenched that they were able to run roughshod over the community. These desperados intimidated peaceful citizens and established a tyranny that was known as six-shooter rule. In 1873, the people induced General Ross to accept the office of sheriff. Using the tactics he had employed as a Ranger, he quickly put a stop to their outrages.

In 1886, James T. DeShields of Belton wrote a book titled *Cynthia Ann Parker, The Story of Her Capture,* and dedicated it, by permission, to General L. S. Ross. The author presented a copy of his work to my father, and it now belongs to me. General Ross' desire to live the life of a Brazos River planter is reflected in a letter to Mr. DeShields. In part it says:

> My father could give you reliable data to fill a volume, more than any living Texan, touching the Indian character, having been their agent and warm and trusted friend, in whom they had confidence. My early life was one of constant danger from their forays. I was twice in their hands and at their mercy. But I am just now too busy with my farm matters to give you such data as would subserve your purpose.

After serving in the State Senate, Lawrence Sullivan Ross was elected Governor of Texas. He took office in January of 1887, and gave the state one of its best administrations. During his four years in office, the citizens enjoyed an era of progress and good feeling. Taxes were low and adequate support was given to educational institutions. Ross became the first Texas Governor to declare a "Day" or "Week" for civic improvements. In order to encourage school children, as well as other Texans, to plant trees, he designated the third Friday in January as Arbor Day.

In 1889 he chose to make a personal reconnaissance of a strife-torn area rather than to sit in his office and receive reports from a subordinate. During the Jaybird-Woodpecker troubles in Fort Bend County, he went to Richmond and took personal charge. After a careful survey of the situation, he recommended that one of his Rangers, Sergeant Ira Aten, be appointed sheriff, and the commissioners court acceeded to his request. Placing this outstanding, impartial man in the office was a wise move, and it went a long way toward restoring order. The Governor also acted as mediator between the warring factions. In this capacity, he used the prestige of his office as well as his experience as a Ranger.

At the expiration of his second term as governor, Lawrence Sullivan Ross became president of the Agricultural & Mechanical College of Texas. Established in 1876, this land grant college was in the throes of what might well have been a struggle for its existence. Torn by strife among the members of the faculty and lacking competent leadership, it had fallen into disrepute in the eyes of many Texans. The board of directors of A. & M. realized that if steps were not taken to correct these evils, the institution would suffer irreparable damage. They decided to place at the helm the strongest man they could find.

David Brooks Cofer, college archivist, in his *Second Five Administrations of Texas A. & M. College,* states:

> In June of 1890, the Board of Directors abolished the office of Chairman of the Faculty and re-instated that of President. At the same time they called to occupy this position of president of the oldest State college in Texas the foremost citizen of the State,. Governor Lawrence Sullivan Ross.

The office was held open for him until he finished his tenure of office.

> On February 1, 1891, the distinguished Confederate soldier, Indian fighter, eminent statesman and successful ruler of men, came to head this struggling college near Bryan. Immediately, he applied his talents in controlling and judging men to strengthen and develop in many ways the institution. From the very beginning, he had the confidence and support of the parents who sent their sons to the College, and his great knowledge of men and affairs maintained that support throughout his successful administration.

Governor Ross succeeded an eminent scholar who had been educated abroad, and who was the first doctor of philosophy to become a member of the faculty at A. & M. This learned gentleman had married a daughter of Sam Houston. However, he lacked the firmness, experience and tact required to make an administrator. While he was acting president, affairs at the college became steadily worse. Ranger-Soldier-Statesman Ross was a university graduate who in each of the stations had shown outstanding ability as an executive. The Galveston *News,* at that time the foremost newspaper in Texas, expressed the approval of the new president in a strong editorial.

Governor Ross, as he was still called, strengthened his faculty and increased the student enrolment. He added men to the faculty who were outstanding in their fields. Notable among these was the professor of veterinary medicine, Dr. Mark Francis. He subsequently made a contribution to the cattle industry that in dollars and cents, has more than paid the taxpayers for all the money they have spent on the animal husbandry department since its inception. He identified the tick as the transmitter of the so-called Texas fever.

President Ross also brought about a strengthening of relationships between cadets and faculty. In dealing with the young men who made up the corps of cadets, he constantly employed those talents he had used and developed in his service on the frontier. His colleagues marvelled at his insight into human nature. He did not arrive at a youth's fitness for admission by means of a questionnaire. A short interview and a few glances from his soul searching eyes were all he needed to form an almost infallible opinion. This faculty is a prime requisite for a Ranger captain, and was possessed by all the truly great leaders in the annals of the Service.

He also had a great deal of patience with boys who had gotten off on the wrong foot, and would go to almost any length to save a cadet from the stigma of expulsion. He realized that in saving a man from disgrace, he was creating an asset instead of a liability to society and his state.

The cadets quickly responded to this treatment. They began to make better grades, their parents were happy and a general aura of good feeling prevailed on the campus. A crack drill company was organized and named the Ross Volunteers. It still flourishes, and is used as the guard of honor at the leading state functions. The newest dormitory was named Ross Hall. My days at College were spent there, and when it was demolished I brought a brick from the historic old place and use it as a doorstop in my home. Altogether, President Ross brought a new era of prosperity to Texas A. & M. College.

Again quoting Archivist Cofer:

When Governor Ross was about to accept, at least many people thought his acceptance was near, the appointment to the Railroad Commission, the citizens of Bryan and Brazos County met, formulated and signed this petition, urging the President to remain at the head of College, where his work had been so effective.

We the undersigned citizens of Bryan and Brazos County, have heard with deep concern and sincere regret that you contemplate accepting the position of Railroad Commissioner, whereby the State will lose your services as President of the Agricultural & Mechanical College of Texas.

The prosperity that has attended your administration of this institution for nearly four years: the harmony that has existed during his time between the faculty, the Corps of Cadets and yourself, the beneficent influence of your past life, with your daily example upon the students; your popularity and extensive acquaintance in the State and with all parties, lead us to assert that there is no other person in Texas that can so efficiently fill the position as president of the college.

We hold furthermore, that the educational interests of any state are paramount to all others, and that these appeal to you in the strongest terms to remain where you are. Should you leave the College at this most inopportune time we have many reasons to feel the deepest anxiety for its future. We firmly believe therefore, that duty calls on you to remain in this most important position.

Governor Ross continued as president and guiding spirit of A. & M. until his death on January 3, 1898. Under his administration, the college had changed from a maligned institution to one that commanded the respect of all Texans. For his success as an educator, many honors were bestowed on Lawrence Sullivan Ross. Sculptor Pompeo Coppini was commissioned to make a statue of him, which is placed in the most prominent spot on the campus. One of the traditional duties of the freshmen is to keep it properly policed. The legislature also named the school they established in 1920 at Alpine the Sul Ross State College.

Today the Agricultural & Mechanical College of Texas is the largest military school in the world. More than twenty thousand A. & M. men served creditably in the armed forces of their country during World War II. Of this number, some fourteen thousand were commissioned, and twenty-seven of them were general officers. Six sons of A. & M. were awarded the Congressional Medal of Honor, four of them posthumously. The record in World War I was equally impressive.

A large part of this spirit of militant patriotism was engendered by Lawrence Sullivan Ross. The greatest man ever to be connected with the A. & M. College was a Captain in the Texas Rangers.

Chapter 35
ROSS S. STERLING

DURING the administration of Governor R. S. Sterling, we enjoyed a heart warming custom. When official business did not call him away from Austin, I made regular Sunday morning visits to the mansion. Seated in the historic living room, we would talk over our problems and discuss the topics of the day. He was glad to have me bring along members of my staff, or any other interesting friends. The Chief Executive welcomed the opinions of his guests on any subject that concerned the welfare of the state. While not always agreeing with the views expressed, he never failed to give the speaker an attentive hearing. These casual visitors were soon converted into staunch friends. They invariably left the presence of the big, kindly gentleman feeling that the affairs of Texas were in capable, honest hands.

On one of these occasions, I was accompanied by Colonel Taylor Nichols. He had made an enviable record in World War I, and was a member of a pioneer Texas family. One of his brothers, R. H. Nichols, had just served as president of the Texas Press Association. Colonel Nichols was presently my United States Property and Disbursing Officer. He and the Governor engaged in a conversation dealing with the Texas National Guard. It lasted nearly an hour, and when they had finished, we took our departure.

Colonel Nichols and I drove to our quarters at Camp Mabry. He was in a thoughtful mood, and did not say a word for several minutes. Finally, he turned to me and said, "General, isn't it a pity that the people of Texas can't really know that man? If they could talk to him, like I have just done, and could see what is in his heart, very few votes would be cast against him." These words, spoken by a patriotic Texan, furnish the answer to R. S. Sterling's single term as governor.

Ross Shaw Sterling was born in Double Bayou, Chambers County, Texas, February 11, 1875. His parents were Benjamin Franklin Sterling, who had served in the Confederate Army with the rank of captain, and the former Mary Jane Bryan, member of a family of early Texas patriots.

Governor Sterling's life and achievements proved that there is a vast amount of difference between schooling and education. He was not able to receive a great deal of the former due to the unsettled conditions that existed in East Texas for several decades following the Civil War. His native ability, keen intellect and thirst for knowledge, however, made it possible for him to become a man well versed in business, political and cultural subjects. By dint of copious reading, he compensated for the lack of what is known as formal education.

Texas history was his principal literary interest. Books dealing with the founders of the Republic and State were treasured by the future Governor. They made welcome additions to his extensive collection of Texas works. Judging from his comments on early Texans, I would say that Sam Houston was his favorite among those pioneers. Governor Sterling studied Governor Houston's inaugural addresses and other speeches with great care. He was profoundly moved by the persecutions heaped on the head of the old hero in his latter days. These were particularly galling to the Governor's sense of fairness, for they were perpetrated by fickle and ungrateful people who were enjoying the fruits of old Sam's victory at San Jacinto.

A large portion of Chambers County is taken up by bays and bayous. Absence of railroads or highways caused early day residents of the area to depend entirely on water transportation for passengers, freight and mail. In common with other lads born in the coastal region, the future Governor spent a great deal of time on boats, and naturally became a good sailor. Captain Benjamin Franklin Sterling and his sons

Schooner "Sterling" moored at landing on Double Bayou in Chambers County. Fourth from left is Captain Benjamin Franklin Sterling.

built a schooner for their own use, and she attracted wide attention on the bays. This vessel was unusual in that she had a shovel nosed, or spoon, bow of the type originated by Francis Herreshoff. From the board of this premier yacht designer came many of the majestic sloops that were successful defenders of the America's Cup. This craft, fittingly named the *Sterling* was constructed from the best materials obtainable, and built to endure time and tide. I saw her a few years ago in Port Lavaca where she was still going strong as an oyster boat.

In 1931, the German cruiser *Karlsruhe* made a voyage to the Texas coast on what was ostensibly a good will visit. In the full uniform of my rank, complete with sabre and aide, I accompanied Governor Sterling to Galveston, where we attended an official dinner aboard the man-of-war. After the ceremonies were concluded, farewells exchanged and our party had gone ashore, the Governor decided to drive by the slip in which the small craft were moored. With a touch of nostalgia he viewed once more the collection of shoal draught boats known as the Mosquito Fleet. The sight of this flotilla brought back many pleasant memories of his youth. Today, as Governor of Texas, he had officially welcomed a foreign battleship to his native shores. This auspicious event took place on the same waterfront where he had unloaded watermelons from the family schooner.

Governor Sterling walking down the gangplank of the German Cruiser "Karlsruhe" in Galveston. In uniform is W. W. Sterling.

Sailing was not the only art mastered early in life by Ross Sterling. Large droves of cattle and horses grazed on the level prairies of Chambers County, and every boy learned to ride soon after he was able to walk. From this early start, the young horseman acquired an easy, natural seat in the saddle that can never be attained by one who has not ridden since childhood. In 1931, young Allan Shivers, chairman of the committee in charge of the Annual Roundup at the University of Texas, asked me to help with the celebration. The Rangers staged a quadrille on horseback. Our partners in the figure were members of the university riding club. The Governor, mounted on his five gaited saddler, Black Gold, was placed in the center of the galloping dancers, where he presented a magnificent equestrian figure. The spectators were delighted by his skillful riding, and the newspapers reported that "Governor Sterling proved to the crowd at the Roundup that he was a great horseman in his own right."

From early youth Ross Sterling evinced a marked aptitude for business which at the age of twenty enabled him to establish a general store of his own in Double Bayou. Certain sections of Chambers County were adapted to growing rice, and around the turn of the century a number of farmers and developers from the north moved into the area. They purchased large tracts of raw land, made the required improvements and began to raise the new crop on an extensive scale. After a few successful years, encroachment of salt water in the canals rendered their rice fields unfit for futher farming. Notwithstanding this setback, few of these families returned to the rigorous climate of their former homes. Most of them chose to remain in Texas, where they have made valuable contributions to the progress and welfare of their adopted state.

Three years after he had embarked on his mercantile career, the future Governor found his bride among these good people and married Miss Maude Abbie Gage. She has been an inspiration to those who can appreciate true worth in a wife, mother and friend. I deem the friendship of this noble woman one of the richest blessings of my life. When reading the thirty-first chapter of Proverbs, beginning at the tenth verse, Mrs. R. S. Sterling always comes to my mind as symbolizing the wife depicted in that beautiful portion of the Holy Writ. She did not faint in the day of adversity but stood steadfastly at her husband's side when his fortune was ruthlessly wrested from him. After

Holland Stokely Reavis, founder of the Oil Investor's Journal.

the Governor was deserted by ingrates, and they had joined the rabble in crucifying their benefactor, she did not falter. I talked to her in the Governor's Mansion soon after she had received the news of their property losses. Not a word of reproach did she utter, but took her misfortunes with a magnificent exhibition of Christian fortitude.

On January 10, 1901, a well being drilled under the direction of Captain Anthony F. Lucas blew in with a tremendous roar.

The solid column of oil that shot high in the air led the Hamill Brothers and other members of the drilling crew to estimate the flow at close to one hundred thousands barrels per day. The spectacle presented by this petroleum geyser prompted the onlookers to augment the American vocabulary by the coined-on-the-spot word "gusher" This appellation for a flowing well, while capturing the fancy of the public, is never used by practical oil men. The site of this epoch-making producer was five miles from Beaumont, on a king sized knoll rising out of the Coastal Plain. From its somewhat rounded shape, it bears the name Spindletop. The rush that followed the Lucas discovery filled the streets and sidewalks of the nearby town with a seething mass of humanity. Beaumont became the first oil boom town in history.

As a boy I lived for several years in the Lucas house. It was situated on the east side of the Shell Road, about a mile from Spindletop. The large, two story dwelling was bought from Captain Lucas by Galey and Guffey's superintendent, Cap Forney, who rented it to my father. A wide gallery on two sides provided grandstand seats from which we watched the parade of early oil field characters. These people, both male and female, kept the Shell Road hot between Beaumont and the "Hill." They traveled on horseback or in buggies and hacks, often going at breakneck speed. I rode my pony to South Park School. At that time it was a one room frame building on the Port Arthur road. Janitor service was undreamed of, and on cold days the larger boys had to cut wood for the stove. In 1903, at our house, which was still pointed out as the former home of Captain Lucas, James A. Elkins, a young attorney from Huntsville, and Miss Isabel Mitchell of Galveston were married. The Mitchell family were long time friends of my parents, and the charming bride had frequently visited in our home. Since that happy event, Judge Elkins has rendered me numerous kindnesses. This friendship is carried into another generation through his sons, William S. and James A. Elkins, Junior.

A noted figure in oil circles who spent a great deal of time at our Shell Road home was the late Holland Stokley Reavis. He founded the first petroleum trade publication in Texas and named it the *Oil Investor's Journal*. His sparkling wit kept everybody around him in laughter, and he was popular with men, women and children. Each issue of his magazine carried a humorous section called the "Tank

Strapper's Column." In it he poked good natured fun at the early oil operators. Holly Reavis was a feature writer on one of the St. Louis newspapers who came down to report the Spindletop discovery. While in Beaumont he saw the potentialities of the oil industry and decided to remain in Texas. Several years later he moved the publication to Houston.

In 1907, I was elected athletic editor of the *Battalion* at Texas A. & M. College. As a result of this literary achievement, Holly gave me a summer job as general flunky in the office. Even in this lowly capacity, working for the great man was an inspiration. He prudently saw to it that my duties did not include any campus calibre writing. By wise investments in oil stocks, Reavis made a fortune. He then moved to New York, where he continued his feature writing. We remained close friends until his death, which occurred at San Angelo, an estate he had purchased in Virginia.

The second coastal field was opened in 1902 when wildcatters found oil in commercial quantities at Sour Lake. In locating their well, they were guided by the small, muddy pond which gave the town its name. This bubbling pool was partially surrounded by springs, seeps and wells, each of which produced a different kind of mineral water. Most noted of these were the "polecat well" deriving this name from the vile taste of its water, and the "tar well" from which an oily substance had oozed since the Civil War. Mud from this sour lake was believed to possess medicinal properties. The owners claimed that skin diseases could be cured by applying it on the sufferer's body. After other remedies had failed, many health seekers came to this shady spot on the edge of the Big Thicket. Presiding over the men's bath house was a tall, stately Negro. His Prince Albert coat and stovepipe hat lent additional dignity to his courtly bearing. He ruled his domain with an iron hand, and plastered the male patients with the wonder working slush. With great pompousness, he would announce to each new patient that his name was "Dr. Mud." I was well acquainted with him, as my father made me take a course of his treatments for a summer rash. Like all charlatans, both white and colored, he was addicted to the use of big words. These irritated the victim more than the actual daubing of the mud.

Oil was discovered at Saratoga a short time after the Sour Lake

294

strike, and the third Hardin County field was opened in 1903 at Batson's Prairie. Men from all parts of the world flocked to these boom towns in search of fortunes. Many Texans availed themselves of the opportunities offered by the new industry that had sprung up in their state. Among them was Ross Sterling, less than thirty years old and with a good merchandising background from his store in Chambers County.

A large number of horses and mules were required to carry on early oil field operations. The only means of hauling machinery, timber and pipe was by wagon and team. Huge earthen reservoirs had to be built hurriedly to save the countless barrels of oil flowing from uncontrolled wells. Levees and dams were required for the same purpose on creeks and sloughs draining the area. Every yard of the prodigious amount of dirt used in this work was moved by mule drawn scrapers. Oil men of all stations, whether owner or roughneck, rode in buggies or on horseback. The future Governor realized that these animals had to be fed every day. With characteristic business discernment, he opened a feed store in Sour Lake.

It prospered from the beginning. The owner was soon able to open branches in Saratoga and Batson. He divided his time between the three stores and rode to them on horseback. In order to arrive by opening time, the young merchant was obliged to get a very early start. Governor Sterling told me of an incident that happened on one of these pre-dawn rides which made a lasting impression on his mind. He said, "The route of my trips, which I made on a regular schedule, led me by a large country home. I always passed this house before daylight, and one morning the owner was standing in the road waiting for me. After introducing himself, he said, 'Young man, I don't know what you are striving for in life, but I'll bet you succeed for you are up and going while most people are still in bed'."

In 1904 the future Governor met Ranger Captain John A. Brooks. Despite the twenty year's difference in their ages, the two men had similar ideas about law and order. This meeting of minds resulted in a friendship that lasted throughout their lives. The presence of Captain Brooks and Sergeant Winfred Bates in Batson was an epoch making event. It marked the first time that Texas Rangers ever were used to protect life and property in an oil field. Although they resided in distant parts of the state, and there was a wide diversity in their vocations, I was befriended many times by both Governor Sterling and Captain Brooks.

The firm of R. S. Sterling & Company continued to expand. The reputation for integrity and square dealing established by Ross Sterling prompted oil operators, contractors and other businessmen to use him as their local banker. This custom led to the opening of a private banking business in connection with the stores, and was the forerunner of his connection with many financial institutions.

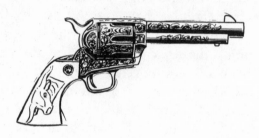

In 1905 the first oil field in Harris County was opened at Humble. As a result of this discovery, only seventeen miles away, numerous residents of Houston became interested in the petroleum industry. R. S. Sterling & Company kept pace with this development and moved their headquarters to the new field. In 1910 they purchased two small wells, thereby making their initial entry into the oil business. From this modest beginning was formed, a year later, the Humble Oil Company.

While carrying on his business in the several fields, Merchant-Banker Sterling had dealt with numerous early day oil men. Close contact with them had given him an opportunity to evaluate their characters and abilities. He had observed that some were content with the crude methods then in use, while others were more resourceful and constantly strived to improve drilling equipment. The future Governor surrounded himself with a group of the best operators. They organized the company that today is the largest producer of crude oil in the United States. It would be a misnomer to say that the Humble was formed by outstanding "men" for one of the incorporators was Miss Florence Sterling. This capable lady, sister of R. S. and F. P. Sterling, contributed a great deal to the early success of the company.

296

The epic story of the Humble Oil & Refining Company, which was organized in 1917, has been written by various eminent authors. No attempt will be made here to deal with the history of that petroleum empire. As a measure of his stature, it is only necessary to state that the first president of the company was R. S. Sterling.

I was personally acquainted with several founders of the Humble Oil & Refining Company, but outside of the Sterlings, who were not related to me, the one I knew best was the late Walter W. Fondren. In 1905 my father, Edward A. Sterling, bought a home in the Westmoreland addition to Houston, and our house was in the next block from the Fondren residence. One night a bunch of the neighborhood schoolboys were engaged in the 1905 version of juvenile delinquency, known as "tick tacking" a nearby house. Included in this nocturnal prank were the late Percy Booth, J. Weston Meek and several other lads whose names have escaped my memory. From an open window the outraged householder fired a small pistol in the air to scare away the marauders. In this gesture of righteous indignation, he succeeded beyond his fondest expectations. His shot, which was heard all over Westmoreland, was the starting gun for some record breaking running. Mr. Fondren heard the report and hurried outside to learn the cause of the commotion. At this moment I was passing his house in full flight. When he tried to ask me about the shooting, I was unable to stop. After I had been appointed a captain of the Texas Rangers. Mr. Fondren enjoyed telling about my baptism of fire, to which he was a witness.

In 1920 I went to the Breckenridge oil field with the late T. H. (Tumps) Bass whose holdings were later merged with the Kirby Petroleum Company. They contemplated buying some production held by two of the largest land owners in Stephens County. Honorable John Henry Kirby wanted to make a personal inspection of the properties. Breckenridge was overrun with thugs and hijackers at that time, making it unsafe for a citizen to walk around without armed protection. Mr. Bass, who was a Spindletop pioneer and a former business associate of my father, asked me to act as bodyguard and companion for Mr. Kirby. I enjoyed this assignment very much as it enabled me to become well acquainted with the great man. The friendship formed during the Breckenridge trip lasted until his passing. Mr. Bass and the other gentlemen connected with the company always addressed Mr.

297

Kirby as "Governor." From their conversations I learned that he had hoped to round out his career by serving as governor of Texas. Unquestionably, he would have made a splendid chief executive.

Some of the wells in the Breckenridge field produced over ten thousand barrels per day. Great quantities of waste oil had accumulated in Gonzales Creek. While riding horseback across one of the leases Mr. Kirby had inspected, I saw some roustabouts burning trash on the banks of this oil stream. I recognized the danger and told the Mexicans in their own language that they had better put out the fires at once. The gang pusher was a Californian wearing lace boots and a sheep herder's hat. He informed me that he knew his business and that no hazard existed. Naturally, the creek caught on fire and burned up an immense quantity of oil that could have been salvaged. The blaze also imperiled many producing wells.

The Humble pipe line crossed the creek at a point near the origin of the fire, and the lease owners attempted to place the blame on the pipe line. I went to the Humble superintendent for that district and told him the circumstances. Through this evidence, the responsibility was placed where it belonged. Although I owned no stock in the Humble Oil & Refining Company, I had always admired R. S. Sterling, and was glad to be in position to make him a witness.

In 1925, the president and co-founder of the Humble Oil & Refining Company sold his interest in that corporation for a fabulous sum. While he had heretofore taken an active part in public affairs, this sale enabled him to devote even more of his time and resources to civic matters. The talents he had used to attain eminence in business were now turned to community building and to serving his fellow man. The aid and counsel of Mr. Sterling were in constant demand. The citizens of Houston realized that his participation in any project insured its success. Colleagues and co-workers recognized his capacity for leadership by placing him at the head of virtually every group with which he was identified.

He was a member of the original Houston Port Commission, and for many years served as its chairman. Through the efforts of this Commission, Buffalo Bayou was transformed from an insignificant watercourse into the present ship channel. Houston was raised from its former status of a barge terminal to high rank among the ports of the

United States. The magnitude of this undertaking and the value of the commission's services in completing the work can scarcely be over estimated. From her location on the Gulf, Galveston had long enjoyed the position of Texas' premier seaport, and citizens of that city derisively predicted that no ocean going vessel would ever dock at Houston.

The future Governor's civic activities also included service as chairman of the board of trustees of Hermann Hospital. Funds for its construction and maintenance were bequeathed to the people of Houston by a German immigrant, the late George Hermann. This philanthropist practiced the utmost frugality in both his dress and living habits. As a boy I saw him many times when he came to my father's office in the Binz Building, Houston's first "skyscraper." His ill fitting suits were the cheapest that could be bought, and he wore coarse brogan shoes. His scant imperial beard with moustache and goatee was like those worn by Buffalo Bill and the German Kaisers. Despite the whiskers, however, there was no semblance of the haughty Prussian in the bearing of the kindly, slightly stooped man. George Hermann's life and actions proved that the worth of a man cannot be judged from his outward apearance. Some called him a miser but at his death he left the fruits of self-sacrifice and thrift to the alleviation of human suffering. The wisdom exercised by the trustees in carrying out the provisions of the will is reflected by the present plant of the Hermann Hospital. Walter Gage Sterling, son of the late Chairman, is now a member of the board over which his father presided.

Mr. Sterling was a staunch friend and supporter of the Houston Y.M.C.A. He served this organization first as a director and later as its president. In 1924 tragedy struck in the Sterling family with the untimely passing of their younger son. In his memory, the parents gave a beautiful tract of wooded land on Galveston Bay for a Y.M.C.A. summer camp. Through this donation countless boys from the Houston area have been able to enjoy seashore outings. The delightful spot is named Camp Ross Sterling, Junior.

The future Governor was a proven friend of Texas Christian University, and was a member of its board of trustees. In 1923 he entered the publishing field by launching a daily newspaper, the Houston *Dispatch*. It was later consolidated with the long established *Post,* which had been purchased by the Sterling interests. The result of this merger was the Houston *Post-Dispatch*. One of his favorite properties was the Chupadero ranch, which lies along the Rio Grande in Webb and Dimmit Counties. Here Governor Sterling enjoyed many outings, and invited friends to share the fine deer hunting in his chaparral covered pastures.

From offices on the twenty-second floor of the Post-Dispatch building, he guided the affairs of many firms, establishments and industries. No attempt is made here to enumerate all of R. S. Sterling's activities and interests prior to his appointment as chairman of the Texas Highway Commission. Only enough of these will be mentioned to reflect his calibre. The wealth of experience gained by directing these multiple enterprises he proposed to give without stint to his native state.

The number and extent of Ross Sterling's benevolences will never be known. Unlike some of the so-called philanthropists, he believed in doing good by stealth. Each instance cited was related to me by the recipients or their friends, with never a word of them coming from the donor. He showed profound consideratioin for those who had once held high station in life, but whose later years were clouded by struggles with adversity. Several of these genteel unfortunates occupied offices in the Sterling owned buildings, where they remained indefinitely as non-paying tenants. One of them had formerly been a national figure, and was several years behind in his rent when he passed away. The Governor would never allow his building manager to bother the threadbare gentleman.

After he became wealthy, Mr. Sterling supplied the financial backing that made it possible for a number of men to achieve success in their respective fields. In many instances this aid was proffered without solicitation on their part. He drew a clear line of demarcation between an act of charity and lending the prestige of his name to a worthy man. The capitalist believed that the best way to help a man was to make it possible for him to help himself.

A case in point was recounted to me by a Gulf Coast rice farmer, whose business had been saved by one of these acts. Due to adverse seasons and low prices, this man, along with a majority of his contemporary agriculturists, was in dire financial straits. He and the future Governor were boys together in Chambers County, but had not seen each other for many years. They met by chance on a Houston street. Mr. Sterling greeted his old friend cordially, and asked how the world was treating him. "Not so good, Ross. Nice to have seen you. So long." "Hold on a minute; maybe I can help you," said the financier. "No," was the reply, "I am in too deep and don't want to take advantage of friendship. You can do nothing to help me." "How do you know I can't?" was the rejoinder. "Come to my office at two o'clock this afternoon. I want to talk to you." The farmer still believed that the visit would be futile, but he appeared at the appointed hour. Mr. Sterling's first question was, "How much money will it take to make you captain of your ship?" The astonished planter replied that it would take $60,-000. "All right," he said, "I will arrange for you to get that amount." It was typical of the future Governor that he did not ask the distressed one if he could not "get by" on a lesser amount, but wanted him to be "captain of his ship." As a result of this assistance, the farmer made the grade and remained a solvent citizen instead of sinking into bankruptcy.

Another instance of this generosity happened in the course of his ranching operations in Southwest Texas. Through the future Governor's backing, an ambitious young man was able to rise from a filling station owner to high rank in livestock circles.

The 1928 Democratic National Convention was held in Houston, and Will Rogers covered it for a large newspaper syndicate. I divided the time between serving as an assistant sergeant-at-arms at the convention and acting as a judge of the World's Championship Rodeo on the football field at Rice Institute. Will attended as many of the cowboy performances as his schedule would permit, and we were able to hear first hand many of his comments on the topics of the day. On one trip back to town, I shared a taxicab with him and several other nationally known correspondents who had been guests at the rodeo. Rogers said, "I have just been on a swing through the North and East, and have talked to some of the leading financiers of the country. All the wealth of the United States has gotten into the hands of about five thousand families and their connections. You know, if something is not done pretty soon to get this money out of cold storage, we're going to have the doggondest panic this country ever saw."

After selling his holdings in the Humble Oil & Refining Company,

Mr. Sterling could have invested his fortune in bonds, annuities and other securities that would involve no risk. He had no intention of becoming an idle coupon clipper, however, and announced that his wealth was going into the channels of commerce and trade. In this way, he said, the money would be kept in circulation and many people, from mechanic to manufacturer, could get a share of every dollar. If all capitalists in the United States had adopted this plan, the depression of the thirties could have been avoided. The man who had made a success of his own business and yet was deeply concerned with the welfare of others decided to run for governor in 1930.

The Texas A. & M. Association of Former Students honored me with the presidency of that organization in 1929 and the term lapped over into 1930. I was also captain of Company D, Texas Rangers, and my duties required attendance at many courts. I appeared both as a witness and to prevent mob violence in trials of capital cases. Mixing business with pleasure, I went to numerous conventions, barbecues, rodeos, ball games and other public gatherings. These assignments, plus the fact that I have always liked people, enabled me to form an acquaintance that was one of the largest in Texas.

The nature of my vocation required me to make a close study of human nature. I had learned the hard way that voters were very fickle. They could be swayed easily by rabble rousing politicians. I warned my friend about the pitfalls of State politics. "Why," I asked him, "in your secure position would you put yourself up as a target for the poisoned arrows of the demagogues?" In reply to my question, R. S. Sterling said, "Bill, Texas has been good to me. I would like to do something for Texas."

He was elected governor in 1930, and took office in 1931. Two years later, by reason of the depression and wholesale election frauds, he was defeated.

History repeated itself in the depression year of 1932. Men and women who drove their automobiles over superb highways and crossed streams on magnificent bridges voted against the man largely responsible for these benefits. They ignored the fact that the present highway department, which built these roads, had been salvaged from the corruption ridden administration of the Fergusons. Many chose to forget that R. S. Sterling was the man selected to serve as chairman of

Last photograph of Governor R. S. Sterling taken at his home in Houston.

the fumigated highway department by Governor Dan Moody, original exposer of the highway scandals. Under the administrations of these two gentlemen, all money allotted for road work reached its legitimate destination and not the pockets of political henchmen. Many oil operators in other fields, whose business had been saved by Governor Sterling's declaration of martial law in East Texas, voted against their benefactor. An inexcusable number of ranchmen, who would benefit most from the statewide bond issue designed to take highway taxes off their lands, also supported the impeached Governor's wife.

Apropos of the way Texas voters often reward faithful public servants is an incident I witnessed several years ago. The Houston Fat Stock Show was then in its infancy, and I accompanied a motorcade of businessmen on a good will trip to advertise the new exposition. I had appeared in many big time rodeos and President J. W. Sartwelle believed that my wide acquaintance among stockmen might be of value in the publicity. Our itinerary included a noonday stop in Seguin, and the chamber of commerce entertained the visitors with a luncheon. The manager of the organization acted as master of ceremonies and did a fine job of welcoming the guests. In the course of his remarks, that gentleman said, "Guadalupe County has many advantages but we take the greatest pride in our splendid system of highways and the orderly withdrawal of oil from our fields." The electorate of that county voted against the man largely responsible for those bounties and gave a majority to enemies of both programs.

The East Texas oil fields offered countless opportunities for high State officials to wink at violations and thereby receive large rewards. If there was ever a case wherein this could be justified, it was in that particular situation. Many claimed that the Governor had no right to declare martial law. Three Federal judges had ruled against it. Their decision had been upheld by the Supreme Court. By rescinding his order, Governor Sterling could have won the financial support of many oil operators. With all these temptations and semi-justifications, not even a hint of graft appeared in his administration. By comparison, the sums proffered in the East Texas oil fields made the money involved in the recent State scandals look like petty cash.

Governor Sterling's effort to render unselfish service to his native state had left him shorn of his wealth. It also taught him a bitter lesson. He learned about man's ingratitude, and could fully appreciate the statement made by Sam Houston: "An ingrate has all the qualities of a dog except fidelity."

Ross Shaw Sterling's farewell to public office can best be expressed by paraphrasing the epitaph of Phillip Nolan in Edward Everett Hale's "Man Without a Country:"

"Never did a man deserve more at the hands of his fellow Texans. Never did a man receives less."

Chapter 36
J. A. BROOKS

I N WRITING about Captain Brooks, I find it very difficult to avoid the boyhood hero worshiper's tendency to use superlatives. It is hard for me to keep my expressions of admiration within the bounds of propriety. My friendship with him over a period of more than forty years never waned. He deserved to have a whole book written about his life.

Captain Brooks exemplified the ideals and principles of a real Texas Ranger. In addition to being a valiant warrior, he was a statesman, builder and faithful public official. The multiple wounds on his body bore graphic witness to his devotion to duty, and were mementos of the dangers he had faced while protecting the people of Texas. On Captain Brooks' countenance were sculptured the marks of character, fearlessness and determination. Yet his soft voice and kindly manner revealed a gentleness that made him, in the estimation of those of us who knew him, "the noblest Roman of them all."

John Abijah Brooks was born in Bourbon County, Kentucky, November 20, 1862. The love of adventure that attracted so many young men to the frontier after the Civil War prompted him to come to Texas. In 1882 he arrived at Laredo, where he secured employment at the nearby coal mines. His love for horses and the outdoor life soon impelled him to take up the occupation of a cowboy. It was easy for

Company "F," Frontier Battalion, Texas Rangers. From left, standing: Frank Carmichael; Bob Bell; Kid Rogers; Gene Bell; Jim Harry. Sitting: Tupper Harris; Sgt. J. H. Rogers; Capt. J. A. Brooks; Charley Rogers; Bob Crowder. Photo made 1888. (November 20, 1940 Captain Brooks will be 85, the only one of this group living.)

the young Kentuckian to become an expert in this line, and he went up the Big Trail with a herd from Southwest Texas. Like most natives of the Blue Grass State, he was an excellent rider and a fine marksman. In 1883, at the age of 21, young Brooks joined the Texas Rangers.

Adjutant General W. H. King assigned him to Company F, which was commanded by Lieutenant Josephus Shely, and stationed in Frio County. A short time later, Shely was promoted to captain and his command moved to Cotulla, in LaSalle County. Recruit Ranger Brooks began his service in the toughest town in Texas or anywhere else in the West. At that time, there was no danger of the claim taking in too much territory.

El Paso, Tombstone, Tascosa and the other widely publicized frontier towns could not equal the deadliness of this cattle center on the Nueces River. In most of the rough places, a noted officer could make his play stand up on the strength of his reputation. This was not the case in Cotulla. Ranger or not, anybody was liable to have his hand called. He had to prove that he covered the ground he stood on. John Brooks' steely blue eyes, square jaw and panther quick movements were the marks of a good man to let alone. After sizing him up, the array of local gunmen decided to take him at his face value. He quickly became a veteran.

The conflict between the pasture men and the fence cutters had become serious enough to be called a "war." In 1884 a law was enacted that made fence cutting a felony. Later on in the year, Lieutenant Bill Scott and a detachment from Company F which included Ranger Brooks were ordered to the scene of an outbreak in Brown County. The fence cutters openly defied the local officers, and announced their intention of shooting it out with anybody who sought to restrain their activities. When the Rangers went out to look at a destroyed fence, the vandals opened up on them. Scott and his men returned the fire. Two men, named Roberts and Lovell, were killed. This slowed up the fence cutting in Brown County, and the center of the "war" moved to Coleman County. The Adjutant General arrived at the front and made a personal survey of the situation. General King announced that he would keep as many Rangers in the area as were needed to prevent the destruction of fences or any other property. For some years, this continud to be one of the major problems faced by the Rangers.

Adjutant General King's report to Governor John Ireland announced the following promotions in Company F, and the reasons therefor:

> The difficult and intricate character of the new duties imposed on the rangers by the fence cutting lawlessness, made a relative increase of commissioned officers necessary to the force. On May 1st of this year First Lieutenant Joe Shely was promoted to Captain and Sergeant William Scott was promoted to First Lieutenant, both officers being members of Company F.

In 1885, Captain Shely, one of the five famous brothers serving as Rangers, resigned from the company and was succeeded by Lieutenant Scott, who immediately promoted John A. Brooks to the grade of sergeant.

The year of 1886 was a busy one for Company F, and the newly elevated Sergeant Brooks had many opportunities to smell gunpowder. On April 3, Lieutenant Knight of the Indian Territory police asked the Rangers for help in capturing a badly wanted desperado who dodged back and forth to Texas. Sergeant Brooks, with two men, was ordered to comply with the request. In carrying out this assignment, they killed Albert St. John when he resisted arrest. This encounter took place on the banks of the Red River.

In the spring of 1887, a call for Rangers came from the eastern edge of the state. It was made by citizens of Sabine County, where the cypress fringed river of that name forms the boundary between Texas and Louisiana. Sabine is one of the original Texas counties, having been organized in 1837, eight years before annexation to the United States. The western landing of historic Gaines Ferry, where so many hopeful settlers crossed the river into Texas, was in this county. It is a heavily timbered area where tall virgin pines and thick undergrowth provided a shadowy cover. One prominent native son of Sabine County described his homeland as a region "where the pine trees pine and the paw paws paw."

Included among the number of fine pioneers who crossed the ferry into Texas was a sizable percentage of criminals. Some of them did not choose to continue their flight toward the setting sun. They felt that the mere fact of being on the west bank of the Sabine was ample assurance of safety from pursuit. These transplanted villains resumed their evil ways and the piney woods were soon infested with bands of outlaws.

Adjutant General King states in his report of 1887:

> Peculiar circumstances have led to the employment of members, detachments and in one instance a company of rangers in some of the extreme eastern counties of our State, though their ordinary field of duty is and has been the Western and Northern parts of our territory. For several years past a gang of outlaws of desperate and dangerous character and conduct, have been troubling the good people of Eastern Texas—particularly in Sabine and adjoining counties. Various efforts have been made by this department to aid in the capture, dispersal or destruction of this band. Detectives have been sent into that section and from time to time small detachments of Rangers have gone, but the densely wooded character of many parts of the country, and the immense swamps; the grouping of population at particular points and its scarcity in others, the bold and cunning character of these desperados with their

wild natures and skill in woodcraft, seemed likely to render all efforts futile for their capture. Continued appeals from the good people of that region caused another effort to be made in this direction.

The favorite weapon of these piney woods warriors was the shotgun, generally of the double barreled variety. They were made in both twelve and ten gauges, with an occasional eight gauge goose gun, but the ten bores predominated. They loaded their own brass shells, which could be decapped and used again and again. For deer, varmints or feuding, these cartridges were charged with three and a half drachms of black powder and an ounce of buckshot. In order to add a personal touch, hot wax was often poured on the shot, which when cooled would hold the pellets together. These deadly missiles would compare favorably or unfavorably, depending on whether one was dishing it out or was on the receiving end, with the war head on a modern torpedo. When stalking an enemy, the point of aim was just where a man's suspenders cross.

The most audacious band of desperados in deep East Texas was led by an old outlaw named Conner. He was the father of several stalwart sons whom he had trained in the ways of violence and bloodshed. This family lived like savages in the dense thickets. They trapped, stole livestock and defied the local authorities. When the depredations of the Conners could no longer be tolerated, a petition for Rangers was dispatched to the governor. Pursuant to this appeal, Company F was sent to Sabine County in the latter part of March, 1887, with orders to round up the outlaw gang. Captain William Scott, Sergeant John A. Brooks with Rangers Rogers, Moore, Carmichael and Treadwell made up the personnel of this picked group. Two members of Captain Scott's company, John A. Brooks and John H. Rogers, both of whom received severe wounds in the forthcoming fight, subsequently became captains.

Experienced man hunters have found that the early morning hours are best suited for capturing desperados. They know that criminals are drowsy in the gray dawn following a restless night, and their senses somewhat dulled. Therefore, Captain Scott made plans to strike the outlaws at daylight on April 1. The Rangers experienced great difficulty in finding a trustworthy man to guide them in the heavily wooded habitat of the Conners. They shifted camp almost daily, transporting their meager outfit on a pack horse. This animal was belled at night. A suitable guide, who had fire hunted with the outlaws, was finally found. He depended on the tinkling of the bell to lead him to the present camp. The crafty woodsmen, however, suspected that the Rangers were hunting them, and removed the bell from the pack horse. Without his principal sign, the guide was soon lost. The absence of any sound added to his confusion. There was no such thing as taking the Conners by surprise. They possessed the wariness of wolves, and their senses of sight and hearing were as keen as those of any four legged forest dweller.

As the poorly guided Rangers came within a few steps of their camp, the Conners loosed four vicious dogs on the officers. They also opened fire with rifles and shotguns from behind huge pine trees. The ferocity of the outlaws was evidenced by the fact that they did not wait for the Rangers to demand their surrender, but carefully planned an ambush calculated to wipe them out. At the first volley, Jim Moore fell dead with a bullet in his heart; Captain Scott was shot through the lungs; Sergeant Brooks in both hands, and Rogers received wounds in the arm and side, which completely disabled him. When the Rangers got into action, one of the Conners was killed and another wounded and captured. The four dogs and pack horse were also killed in the melee. The fight took place before daylight and in the dense woods the visibility was poor. The Rangers were at a great disadvantage as they were on unfamiliar ground. Bright blazes from the black powder cartridges lit up the battlefield, where the range was never more than twenty or thirty feet. The short distance which separated the combatants accounts for the fact that four of the six Rangers engaged were either killed or wounded.

The Conner episode was one of the bloodiest chapters in Ranger history.

I had known Captain Brooks since my early boyhood and his wounded left hand, from which the two middle fingers were missing, could not go unnoticed. He had told me about losing them in East Texas when the Rangers fought the Conners. Captain Rogers was also seriously wounded in the same battle, and I had been his friend nearly all my life. We served as contemporary Ranger captains under Governor Dan Moody.

A. Y. Baker once told me about being sent to East Texas while serving as sergeant in Captain Brooks' company. He liked good food as well as anybody I ever knew and had visions of fried chicken, backbone and other tasty changes from the *frijole* and goat meat fare of most border Ranger camps. Upon receipt of the orders from Austin, A. Y. began dancing a jig while gleefully saying, "We're going on a picnic, we're headed for East Texas." Captain Brooks held up his wounded left hand where all could see the missing fingers and said, "It may not be a picnic boys, this is what I got over there." He further warned his adventure craving men that death lurked behind the long leaf yellow pine trees on the banks of the Sabine as well as in the chaparral along the Rio Grande.

Every time Captain Brooks recounted the facts of the Conner fight to me, he heaped high praise on the valor of his comrade, Jim Carmichael. The captain said that if it had not been for his bravery and marksmanship, all the wounded Rangers would have been finished off by the outlaws with the aid of their man killing dogs. In 1939, I received a letter from Jim Carmichael, who was then seventy-five years old. He had been out of the state since 1888, and on his return to Texas had heard of my efforts to get pensions for old time Rangers. When I told him in my answer that Captain Brooks had given his courage in the Conner fight full credit, the gratitude of the veteran over his comrade's praise was unbounded. Ex-Ranger Carmichael stated in his letter that Jim Moore was shot squarely in the heart, and killed so dead by the bullet that there was not enough contraction of his muscles to pull the trigger of his cocked Winchester. His last word, which was spoken to Carmichael, was a joke, and Moore died with a smile on his face. The gallant young Ranger went out like a man, dead game and facing the enemy. This kind of finish was the expressed wish of many a good boy in the Service, when the time came for him to ride out on his last scout.

Miss Corrinne Brooks of Falfurrias in Brooks County, daughter of Captain John A. Brooks, told me of a merciful deed performed by Captain Scott's sister, Miss Vernon Scott, after the battle. She had gone to Sabine County to be with the captain, and was in Hemphill anxiously awaiting news of her brother, and the outcome of the desperate fight she knew to be inevitable. When word reached her that several Rangers had been killed or wounded, Miss Scott procured a wagon and team and drove furiously to the scene. She did everything that could be done for the wounded men on the spot, then carefully brought them to town where they received medical attention. Captain Scott, who received a bullet through his lungs, was carried on a litter by relays of men afoot all the way to San Augustine. Brooks and Rogers made the tortuous thirty-mile journey in a wagon. Captain Brooks told me many years afterward that this trip was the most painful experience of his entire life. Miss Scott looked after the Rangers so well that all three made complete recoveries and died peaceably in bed after reaching a ripe old age.

Captain Scott resigned from the service in 1888 and went to Mexico where he became a large scale railroad contractor. Brooks and Rogers stayed in the Rangers where they made enviable records and both of them have chapters in my book. Jim Carmichael left the state July 1, 1888, and did not return until October 1, 1935, when he moved to Abilene. I corresponded with him until 1939. After Billy Treadwell left the Rangers, he went to work for the eminent Buck Pettus on his vast ranch in Goliad and adjoining counties. Treadwell was a native of Tennessee, and when a mere youth killed two men who had murdered his brother. After avenging the death, Billy came to Texas and joined the Rangers. He was a fine guitar player, graceful dancer and a great favorite of the Pettus family as long as he rode for the Cross P. Treadwell killed another man while engaging in the hazardous pastime of attending a Saturday night dance on the Sarco. In that unique and bellicose region, a visitor could become involved in a personal combat at the drop of a hat.

In this fight Billy was shot through both legs, but managed to get on his horse. Badly wounded and bleeding profusely, he rode to the Pettus Ranch. Uncle Buck put a bed in a light spring wagon, and sent his cowboy to a secluded spot in a mesquite thicket on the San Antonio River. He then dispatched a rider to Goliad for Dr. Joseph Getzweller, a pioneer medico about whom a book should be written. He began his rough and ready treatment by running a silk handkerchief through the bullet holes. The good doctor made tri-weekly trips to the brush arbor hospital, and through his ministrations, Treadwell fully recovered. He was brought to trial in Goliad, and the jury found him not guilty.

Some of the old timers say that a fast horse, ready saddled and with a Winchester in the scabbard, had been tied in a convenient spot by Billy's friends. If the verdict had gone against him, he intended to burn the wind for Mexico.

T. Wheeler Pettus, a surviving member of that pioneer family, supplied me with the data on Billy Treadwell. The Pettus Ranch was called Ranger Heaven by those who were fortunate enough to enjoy its hospitality. As a lad Wheeler Pettus spent so much time with Captain Lee (Red) Hall's Ranger company that his friends in Goliad nicknamed him "Red." He also gave me a summary of Treadwell's life. It enumerates more virtues than vices, and would fit a sizable percentage of the Rangers in the seventies and eighties. Mr. Pettus said, "Billy Treadwell was a lovable vagabond, loyal, trustworthy and a fightin' fool."

Fighting dogs of the type used by the Conners were fully as dangerous as their owners. They feared neither man nor beast. Their undying loyalty was often misused by cutthroats who took them on lawless missions, where they would die in the defense of their masters. Many years after the Sabine County affair, Graves Peeler had a battle with some ferocious dogs and their master. Peeler was as good a Ranger and brand inspector as was ever born in the state. While trailing a cattle thief in East Texas, he caught up with him in a small clearing. The outlaw sicked four bloodthirsty dogs on the Ranger, and at the same time shot a nick in his ear with a Winchester. Peeler possesses nerves of steel, which he had never abused by the use of liquor or tobacco. He did not even drink coffee, which is the standby of most outdoor men and of all camp cooks. Peeler was one of the best shots I ever saw, and was at his best under fire. He used a Savage hammerless rifle, and when he got his old muley gun in circulation, which he could do with amazing speed, the vicious canines quickly joined their cow stealing owner in the great beyond.

I was ordered to Sabine County in 1929, which was the first time a Ranger captain had been sent there for many years. This official visit afforded me the long desired opportunity to go over the scene of the noted Conner fight. The Sabine County attorney, Honorable James Gordon Barker, who was well versed in East Texas history, took me to the battle site. Here we painstakingly went over the details of the fight.

On this heavily wooded spot, both Captains Brooks and Rogers, as young Rangers, had received serious wounds, the story of which had been related to me many times. Being on the ground and having discussed it with actual participants as well as reading all adjutant general's reports on the subject, I was able to visualize each phase of the bloody conflict.

Sergeant Brooks was soon promoted to lieutenant, and in 1889, only six years after he enlisted, former Ranger Sul Ross, then serving as Governor of Texas, appointed him captain. He was placed in command of Company F and sent back to Cotulla. The young recruit who had reported for duty there in 1883 was now a seasoned, battle scarred veteran, well qualified to take charge of his old outfit. The work consisted mainly of rounding up the heavy brush pastures of suspected cow thieves, and trying to maintain order among the numerous fighting men who harbored there. They were not entirely successful in this endeavor, but they did their best to lighten the burden of the overworked justice of the peace, who acts as coroner.

In October of 1889, Sheriff S. A. Brito of Cameron County, appealed for Rangers "to suppress cattle thieving from Mexico, and Mexican bandits, outlaws and marauders. They cannot be taken care of by the county authorities." Company F, under Captain Brooks, was sent to that border county. On February 21, 1890, in response to a request from the county judge of Hidalgo County, the company moved up the Rio Grande to old Edinburg. Rumblings of another Mexican revolution caused great unrest and renewed outbreaks of lawlessness on the American side of the river. The instigator of this short lived insurrection was Catarino Garza.

The Rangers were ordered to cooperate with the United States Army in preserving the neutrality of Texas soil. Company E was organized, and placed under the command of Captain J. S. McNeel. It was ordered to the troubled area as a reinforcement for Brooks. The Federal and State forces worked in harmony, and gave the *insurrectos* no rest. They had several running fights, and kept them on the move. These skirmishes were so numerous that Captain Brooks did not bother to report them in detail. The nearest thing to a pitched battle took place about twenty-five miles northeast of Carrizo (later Zapata and now inundated by Falcon Lake). The rebels fled, leaving behind some

Adjutant General W. H. Mabry and Captain Brook's Company on the Rio Grande during the Catarino Garza War. War correspondent Richard Harding Davis visited this camp and described it in his book "The West From a Car Window."

twenty horses and saddles. In all these clashes, the Rangers turned over both prisoners and horses to the Army.

The eminent war correspondent, Richard Harding Davis, came to the border in 1891 to report the Catarino Garza revolution. In his book, *The West from a Car Window,* he tells of a visit to the Ranger camp of Captain Brooks. His host on this trip was Adjutant General W. H. Mabry. Davis commented, "These men are the special pride and joy of General Mabry." The lack of chaparral in the country at that time is attested in his statement, "They were eating their breakfast of bacon and coffee under the shade of the only tree in ten miles."

His story continues:

General Mabry told me some very thrilling tales of their deeds and personal meetings with the desperados and "bad" men of the border; but when he tried to lead Captain Brooks into relating a few of his own adventures, the result was a significant and complete failure. Significant, because big men do not tell of big things they do as well as other people can—they are handicapped by having to leave out the best part; and because Captain Brooks' version of the same story the General had told me, with all the necessary details would be: "Well, we got word they were hiding on a ranch down in Zapata County, and we went down there and took 'em—which they were afterwards hung." The fact that he had had three fingers shot off as he "took 'em" was a detail he scorned to remember, especially as he could shoot better without these members than the rest of his men, who had lost only one or two.

Richard Harding Davis, like many others, was mixed up on his geography of Texas. Captain Brooks lost his fingers in a fight on the Sabine River instead of the Rio Grande.

Boots above the knee and leather leggings, a belt three inches wide with two rows of brass-bound cartridges, and a slanting sombrero make a man appear larger than he really is; but the Rangers were the largest men I saw in Texas, the State of big men. And some of them were remarkably handsome in a sun-burned, broad-shouldered, easy, manly way. They were also somewhat shy with the strangers, listening very intently, but speaking little, and then in a slow, gentle voice; and as they spoke so seldom, they seemed to think what they had to say was too valuable to spoil by profanity.

General Mabry had Captain Brooks demonstrate his marksmanship with both rifle and six-shooter. Their visitor was amazed at the accuracy and rapidity of his fire. Some Western historians deny that the old single action Peacemakers were ever fired by "fanning the hammer." Captain Brooks used this method repeatedly, and it especially suited his game left hand. He gave me a personal demonstration of how it was done, and the spur on the hammer of my pistol is filed smooth to facilitate this practice. It is only effective at close range.

I recently spent some enjoyable days with William J. McBride, foreman of the Encino division of the King Ranch. His grandfather was my friend as is his father. After graduating from Texas A. & M. College, he served with distinction in the Second World War. Billy grew up in Brooks County, and knew Captain Brooks all his life. Speaking of shooting, he said, "When Captain Brooks was well past sixty years old, I saw him shoot five shots at a knot on an oak tree. He fanned the hammer of an old forty-five so fast that it sounded like an automatic and hit the target four times. It made him mad when the fifth shot was a little wide of the mark. The distance was about ten steps."

The Ranger accouterments described by Mr. Davis as "a belt three inches wide with two rows of brass-bound cartridges," is known as a scout belt. This staple item in every Ranger's outfit was fashioned from a strip of good, light leather six inches wide. It was doubled in order that the hollow part could be used for a money belt. Extending part of the way around were two rows of loops for pistol cartridges. The balance of the belt was fitted for rifle shells, so there was small danger of running out of ammunition. Tucked away in a slot was a small L shaped screwdriver, made of very fine steel. The Colt pistol factory put out this handy tool, and it was used to keep the screws tight, both in six-shooter and rifle. The loosening effect of horseback motion and recoil on the weapons made it necessary to tighten them up at regular intervals. Some of the old timers soaked the screws of their pistols in salt water. They called this crude but effective process "rusting them in." Every Ranger owned two kinds of scabbards, one for his scout belt, and the other for town or "Sunday" wear. The one he used for horseback work was equipped with a thong to hook over the hammer of his pistol. This was to keep from losing the gun when he was running through the brush or riding on steep trails. The boys called these devices "retreating straps." They explained, "If you forget to loosen them before a fight, you had better retreat or get high behind."

Richard Harding Davis had a nose for war news. In 1914 he returned to the border to cover the various revolutions in Mexico. It appeared that the United States would be forced to intervene in order to restore peace below the Rio Grande. When the distinguished war correspondent went to Houston, he visited the old armory of the Houston Light Guards. It was situated on the site of the present Sterling Building. The general factotum of the club was a dignified, ante-bellum type colored man. The visitor walked in and said, "I'm Mr. Davis." "Have a chair, Mr. Davis," said Uncle Tom. "I'm Richard Harding Davis," stated the great man. "Oh," was the reply. "Have two chairs, Mr. Davis."

In 1892 Brooks' station was moved to Realitos, Duval County. Thefts of livestock, fights and killings kept his company busy. The railroad strike of 1894 threatened to tie up all lines in Texas. Violence broke out in several of the junction points. Governor Hogg lost no time in using the Rangers. Captain Brooks was ordered to Temple, and his company stayed there until the strike was settled. Captain Brooks told the union men, "We're here to protect life and property. We are not taking sides in the dispute." His tact and firmness kept down violence in that railroad center.

The first concentration of all four companies of the Rangers took place in 1896, at El Paso. It was occasioned by an attempt to hold the Bob Fitzsimmons-Peter Maher prize fight in Texas. Governor Charles

A. Culbertson declared that he would use every means at his command to prevent what he called "a public display of barbarism." He ordered Adjutant General Mabry to assemble the Rangers at the border city. An unusually large number of men was employed on this mission. The sponsors had announced that they were bringing a gang of gunmen to guarantee that nobody interfered with the staging of the bout. These pistolians were headed by the former buffalo hunter and marshal of Dodge City, Bat Masterson.

The promoters finally gave up the idea of holding the fight in Texas, and transported their ring, boxers and spectators down the Rio Grande. Near the office of Roy Bean, they crossed over into Mexico, and held the fight. Masterson had roughed up many drunken Texas cowboys in his capacity as marshal, and had wounded the brother of one of the biggest ranchmen in the state. He was employed on account of his reputation but the circumstances now were different. The redoubtable Bat was not in his own backyard and the men facing him were not amateurs. Captain McDonald called his hand. Brooks, Rogers and Hughes were there to "keep the flies off." The number of Bat's backers was reported to be a hundred, but he did not choose to ante. At the El Paso County courthouse, the Rangers were assembled for a picture. General Mabry with Captains Hughes, Brooks, McDonald and Rogers are in the foreground. The most tangible result of the Fitzsimmons-Maher fiasco is this excellent and widely used photograph.

In 1898, the United States declared war on Spain. This brief conflict lasted only about one hundred days, and did not cause any extra work for the border Rangers. The inhabitants of Captain Brooks' territory had no love for the *Gachupines* as they called the Spaniards. Most of them sympathized with the Cubans, and quite a few enlisted in

the American Army, Juan B. Vela, of Cameron County and one
of the Hinojosa brothers of Hidalgo County joined the Rough Riders.

In September of 1899, Captain Brooks and several of his men attended court in Colorado County, at Columbus. They were ordered
there at the request of the district judge, who feared a new outbreak
of the Townsend-Reece feud. Order was maintained and both parties
were disarmed. Adjutant General Scurry reported, "If it had not been
for the continual searching by Captain Brooks' Rangers, it is certain that
trouble would have occurred."

General Scurry continued:

> Since the spring of 1899, detachments of Rangers have been frequently
> called for by the officials of Colorado and Bastrop Counties and once by the
> officials of Wharton County, for the purpose of preventing a fight between
> the Townsend and Reece factions, in Colorado and Lavaca Counties, re-
> spectively. Whenever one of the Reece party had trouble with one of the
> Townsend party, the former would make a call for their friends and kins-
> men to assemble at Columbus. Before they could gather, as a rule, the
> Rangers, by request of the civil authorities, would reach there in time to
> prevent trouble between the two parties. . . .

In the latest fight between the clans, Jim Townsend killed Dick
Reece. He was indicted for this homicide, and on a change of venue,
his case was sent to Bastrop County. When the principals, witnesses
and kinsmen of the defendant and the deceased arrived there, another
fatal clash occurred. Walter Reece and his party killed Arthur Burford
and wounded Will Clemens, both members of the Townsend faction.
The Rangers present were not sufficient in number to keep both parties
disarmed.

However, within twenty minutes after the killing, Captain Brooks
and his men arrested and put in jail seventeen of the Reece faction.
Lieutenant William F. Bates was stationed at the door of the courthouse to prevent the entry of the Townsends. When they started up the
steps, the Ranger said, "That's far enough, boys. This is the end of the
line."

Attorneys for the Reece faction sued out a writ of habeas corpus for
their four members who were charged with the killing of Burford, and
the wounding of Clemens. The hearing was to be held in Bastrop,

where local officials made an urgent appeal for Rangers. During this proceeding, Captain Brooks was reinforced until he had, including himself, sixteen men. Their entire time was occupied in keeping the feudists separated and disarmed. Both sides resorted to ruses in order to get weapons into their hands. One trunk of arms was shipped to the Townsends, and several similar boxes were sent by express to the Reeces. The Rangers were kept busy preventing shipment of arms by baggage, freight or express. They inspected all suspicious incoming packages and intercepted a number containing weapons.

As a consequence of the Townsend-Reece feud, local authorities made probably a dozen calls for Rangers. There was only one point on which the belligerents were in accord. Both factions had confidence in the Rangers, and both agreed that the treatment they received at their hands was fair, even if it was sometimes a trifle rough.

It was five years after the Fitzsimmons-Maher brawl on the Rio Grande before another attempt was made to stage a prize fight in Texas. Then, as now, the island formerly inhabited by Jean LaFitte aspired to be a law unto itself. Many splendid physical specimens were to be found among the longshoremen and stevedores who loaded ships in Galveston. One robust colored youth could toy with a five hundred pound bale of cotton. He was also as lithe as a black panther. A combination promoter and third rate pugilist taught him the rudiments of boxing and matched him with a leading heavyweight of that day named Joe Choyinski. The cotton-jammer's mentor brought him along too fast, and Choyinski won by a knockout in three rounds. The loser fared considerably better in his later bouts. After winning the world's heavyweight championship, he wired the good news to his mother in Galveston, and coined a phrase that has been added to the vocabulary of many Americans. "I'm bringing home the bacon," the telegram stated, and it was signed Jack Johnson.

Numerous citizens were outraged over the forthcoming prize fight, and they appealed to Governor Sayers to stop what they termed "a blot on the fair name of Texas." In this case, the officials pursued a different course from the one they followed in El Paso. They made no attempt to prevent the fight, but decided to let it go long enough to demonstrate that the law was being violated, and then make the arrests. Captain Brooks, with Rangers Baker, Bates and Sanders, was sent to

Galveston. They were ordered to report to Judge John Lovejoy, and to act under his orders. The border Rangers played the unfamiliar role of working in disguise. By this ruse, they were able to mingle unnoticed with the spectators. Neither Judge Lovejoy nor Captain Brooks was a competent referee. They were hard put to decide just when the bout could properly be called a pugilistic contest. They were spared the necessity of making a decision by Choyinski's knockout punch. When the fight was over, the Rangers entered the ring and arrested the principals. Bond was set at $5,000 which they could not furnish. An obliging justice of the peace reduced the amount, and they were released. Three grand juries in Galveston County refused to return indictments. This kind of duty was very distasteful to Captain Brooks.

One of the most unique episodes in the history of Western gunfighting took place on May 16, 1902. It had its setting in Southwest Texas, near the Urracas well on El Sauz Ranch, which was then in Cameron County. Here, a sharpshooting cow thief and an ace Ranger fought an offhand duel to the death. Through the alertness and sagacity of his horse, the Ranger emerged unscathed in the exchange of fire.

The ranch on which this combat occurred was extremely vulnerable to wholesale cattle stealing. It is covered by some of the thickest brush to be found in the United States. Most of the undergrowth consists of heavy mesquite, with huisache, coma, granjeno, chapote and kindred varieties of chaparral. Giant nopal, tazajilla, jacobo, biznaga and numerous other members of the cactus family interlaced their spiny fingers to complete the prickly maze.

Captain Brooks' official report to Adjutant General Scurry recites that: "Sergeant A. Y. Baker rode up on Ramon Cerda while he was branding a stolen calf. Baker shot and killed Cerda after the latter had fired on the Ranger, the bandit's bullet killing Baker's horse under him."

I knew A. Y. Baker intimately and was one of his deputies during his early years as sheriff of Hidalgo County. From this association with the surviving principal, my information on the Cerda episode came first hand. I also scouted on El Sauz ranch, and had the opportunity to make a study of the battle site.

The vital role played by Baker's horse vindicated the opinion of all true Rangers and cowmen. We maintain that among animals, the horse is man's best friend. The greatest thrill any Ranger can experience

is to feel and observe the performance of an intelligent mount while on an outlaw trail through a brushy country. The horse becomes closely attuned to his rider and puts his whole heart into the chase.

In the Baker-Cerda fight at El Sauz, the Ranger's horse, sensing the presence of an enemy, raised his head just as Ramon fired. This move saved his master's life. The bullet struck the gallant animal squarely between the eyes, killing him instantly. Baker, whose speed with guns was described by his comrades as "chain lightning," was also one of the best shots in Texas. He killed the ambusher as the horse hit the ground. Some writers who know nothing of such things personally state that Baker's horse shied. A Ranger's mount does not shy under those circumstances, but always keeps his head and ears pointed toward the enemy, just as a top cow horse will never turn his tail to a cow. The horse that saved Ranger Baker's life had been presented to him by E. B. Raymond, for whom the town of Raymondville is named. Stamped on the noble animal's left hind leg was the Pitcher. This noted brand is still used by E. C. Raymond, son of the original owner. He grew up at El Sauz, and many facts were furnished me by this pioneer ranchman. A former McNelly Ranger, George (Josh) Durham also lived on the ranch. One of his comrades, N. A.

Jennings wrote a book titled *A Texas Ranger,* in which he referred to Durham as "the wit of the company." *Tio* Josh described the Baker-Cerda fight in these words: "Cerda killed Baker's horse by shooting him in the left eye. A. Y. killed Ramon by shooting him in the right eye." The inquest over Ramon Cerda's body was held by Justice of the Peace Esteban Garcia Osuña.

A virtual state of war between the Rangers and the border bravos was precipitated by the killing of Ramon Cerda. His family had wealthy friends in Brownsville whose cattle interests conflicted with those of the ones who backed the Rangers. They furnished legal and financial assistance to the outlaws. Although only four years had elapsed since the Spanish-American War, the leader of the anti-Ranger faction was a Spaniard. When the Rangers searched his warehouse and found Ramon Cerda's brother, Alfredo, hiding there, he reported the incident to the Spanish consul. This official filed a protest with the State Department in Washington. The Secretary of State requested the Governor of Texas to take adequate steps to protect the Spanish subject. When this order was transmitted to Captain Brooks, he offered to camp his entire company in the front yard of the complainant.

On the night of September 9, 1902, the trouble was further aggravated. The Ranger camp was about a mile from Brownsville, on a small ranch owned by Judge James B. Wells. As Rangers A. Y. Baker, Emmett Roebuck and Jesse Miller were riding home, they were fired on from ambush. The bushwhackers numbered five or more, and they used shotguns loaded with buckshot. Roebuck was killed instantly; Baker was wounded; and Miller's horse was killed. The two Rangers, in a boyish caper, had swapped horses for the trip back to camp. Baker and Miller returned the fire with their pistols. The dense undergrowth favored the assassins, however, and if any of them were killed, they were never found. The belief that A. Y. Baker bore a charmed life had its inception in this incident.

Captain Brooks and City Marshal Lawrence Bates, who was Baker's cousin, rushed to the scene. Six men were arrested for the murder of Roebuck, and placed in the Cameron County jail. Public indignation over the killing reached a high pitch, and a mob formed to lynch the prisoners. Despite the fact that they had assassinated one of their comrades, the Rangers dispersed the crowd.

Company "A" in 1903. Front row, left to right: Jesse Miller, Sergeant Winfred Bates, Captain J. A. Brooks, Lonnie Livingston. Back row, left to right: Tom Franks, A. Y. Baker, John Puckett and George Wallis. Captain Brooks and Sergeant Bates were the first two Rangers to serve in an oil field.

Since the killing of Ramon Cerda at El Sauz, Alfredo Cerda had made repeated threats on the life of A. Y. Baker. There is no question but that he instigated the September ambush of the Rangers and he probably was an actual participant. His family had also offered a heavy reward to anyone who would kill Baker.

On October 3, less than a month after the midnight ambuscade, Alfredo Cerda was shot and killed by A. Y. Baker. They met on Elizabeth Street, the main thoroughfare of Brownsville, near the corner of Thirteenth. The Ranger used a 30-40 Krag Winchester. Ex-Ranger Sergeant Winfred Bates, who is also a cousin of the late A. Y. Baker, is the sole survivor of the men who served under Captain Brooks. He was a witness to this shooting. Brooks and Bates accompanied Baker

324

to Fort Brown, which was only two blocks away. The Rangers remained in the post until bond could be arranged for Baker. This procedure may seem strange to those who are unfamiliar with early conditions on the border, but it was often employed. The overwhelming preponderance of Latins in the counties along the Rio Grande at that time made it advisable. The step was taken by the Rangers to keep from being forced to kill more of the excited friends and relatives of the dead man, rather than the fear of losing a battle with them. When asked by the adjutant general if he needed help, Captain Brooks answered, "My men are all crack shots. I am not afraid of them getting the worst of anything."

In September of 1903, Sergeant Baker was acquitted in Brownsville for the killing of Ramon Cerda. In September of the same year, also at Brownsville, he was acquitted of killing Alfredo Cerda. The Ranger was defended by Judge James B. Wells, and in each case the jury found that he had acted in self defense.

The next grand jury commended the Rangers for their good service, and especially commended Captain Brooks. In protest against the removal of Captain Brooks' company, District Judge Stanley Welch wrote, "All the ills of the Cerda killings have settled themselves, and I believe that with the aid of the Rangers under Captain Brooks, crime can be eliminated from Cameron County. The local officers cannot reach the outlaws." Judge Welch recommended an increase in the number of Rangers.

When Captain Brooks was stationed in Alice, it was the largest cattle shipping point in the United States. Livestock from as far south as Cameron and Hidalgo Counties were brought there to be loaded on the railroad. During the busy season, as many as a dozen herds would have to wait their turn. At these times, the streets and wooden sidewalks would be crowded with saddle weary stockmen. The saloons did a thriving business. When cowboys come to town and get a few drinks under their belts, they like to yell. Many of them want the world to know how bad they are. This tendency is found from Texas to Montana.

Captain Brooks and his men came to town every night, mainly to watch the fun. They were sympathetic and patient with the revelers, not bothering them unless it became an absolute necessity. One night a particularly loudmouthed waddy made his appearance. He whooped and hollered, announcing that he was a badman from the salt fork of Bitter Creek, with many other declarations of being double tough. The man eater finally got out of hand, and Captain Brooks told Lonnie Livingston to lock him up. Just as the Ranger started to carry out this order, the cowboy bellowed: "Whoopeeee! I'm the worst pill in the box." "All right podner," said Lonnie as he headed him for the calaboose. "You may be the worst pill in the box, but the doctor says take you."

One December day in 1903 my father and I were passengers on a Southern Pacific train en route from Beaumont to Houston. Occupying the two seats facing us were Former Governor James Stephen Hogg and his business associate, James Swayne, of Fort Worth. These gentlemen owned the fabulous Hogg-Swayne tract on Spindletop. My father was well acquainted with both of them. He had been interested in several oil deals with Mr. Swayne. The adults carried on a general conversation and discussed topics of the day, while I listened in respectful silence. The awe inspiring presence of the distinguished ex-Governor, who was a giant in stature as well as in intellect, had a quieting influence on me.

Around the turn of the century, virtually every Texas school child had heard that Governor Hogg had a daughter named Ura and another named Ima. I was tempted to seize the present opportunity and boldly inquire about the truth of the legend. I did not learn until many years later that the story was only half true.

As our train passed Sour Lake Station, which is now called Nome, the gentlemen's conversation centered on the lawless conditions that had arisen in Hardin County since the discovery of oil. Sour Lake had simmered down somewhat but Saratoga and Batson's Prairie were running hog wild. Batson held a thin edge over the others for sheer deviltry in the rough. Human life was cheap. Shootings and cutting scrapes were common occurrences while thieves stole any property that was not guarded day and night. It was claimed that a boiler with steam up had recently been hauled off from a drilling rig without the owner's knowledge or consent.

My father, who had been in all three fields, stated that the local officers were both unwilling and unable to cope with the situation.

I have never forgotten Governor Hogg's next statement and can clearly recall his words spoken on that occasion. Pointing his finger toward the new oil fields, he said in emphatic tones, "There is only one way to stop that lawlessness. If I were still governor, I would have Rangers in Batson before sundown tomorrow. When I get to Houston, I am going to wire Sam Lanham and urge him to send them there."

Governor S. W. T. Lanham followed the former Chief Executive's suggestion by ordering Captain Brooks to make a hurried reconnaissance of the oil district and report his findings to the adjutant general. A few hours in Batson convinced the advance guard that a general cleanup was imperative and long overdue.

Upon receipt of the report, Adjutant General Hulen instructed Captain Brooks to take three other members of Company A and proceed immediately to Batson's Prairie. This proved to be an epoch making order, for it was the first time in the annals of Texas that Rangers were used in an oil field. The Rangers named for this historic assignment were Captain John A. Brooks, Sergeant Winfred Bates with Privates Lott Tumlinson and Clyde McDowell. The only surviving member of this pioneering quartet is Sergeant Bates. This vigorous gentleman is a splendid example of the Ranger type I seek to portray. He and his wife have been of vast help in my endeavor to chronicle authentic though little known events in Ranger history.

Captain Brooks and his men proceeded by train to Liberty, which was the railroad point nearest to Batson, and made the rest of the trip in a hack. Upon arrival at their destination, the Rangers put up at the local hotel, which was a typical example of the rooming houses found in the early oil fields. It was a long, barn-like structure made out of cheap, unseasoned pine lumber with resin still oozing out of the unpainted boards. A narrow hall ran lengthwise through the middle of the building. It was divided into small rooms having a single window for light and ventilation.

It would be extremely difficult for oil workers of the present generation to visualize the crude mode of life in an early Texas boom town. The comfortable, well kept company camps of today, where a man can take a bath any time he needs one, were undreamed of by the oil field pioneers. Mud, filth and squalor were the by-products of every new discovery. False-fronted pine shacks served as places of business, legitimate or otherwise, along the unpaved streets. These crowded thoroughfares were soon turned into quagmires by the heavy rains which seem to go hand in hand with petroleum production. Pipe and boiler wagons, drawn by multiple hitch teams, floundered their way through deep mud holes, with one or more outfits usually bogged down. A seething mass of humanity moved restlessly on the rough board sidewalks, with frequent fights breaking out among these rowdy men. Any fancied act of hostility such as a slight jostling was ample provocation for a pair to square off and go to it. Sometimes these spontaneous skirmishes were fought fist and skull, but all too often, deadly weapons were drawn by the combatants, with fatal results.

After spending one miserable day in the so-called hotel, the Rangers procured a tent, borrowed some cooking utensils and pitched camp in a grove on the edge of town. In the absence of any sort of calaboose, prisoners were chained to a nearby tree until they could be transferred to the county jail. On a busy day, more than a dozen men were held at one time in this crude but effective manner.

The coming of Brooks, Bates and company was hailed with relief and delight by the substantial citizens of Batson but viewed with alarm by denizens of the underworld. The crooked officers particularly resented the Rangers. These badge wearing grafters could see an early end of their corrupt practices, as well as the termination of the reign of terror they had imposed on inoffensive working men. Hardin County had voted local option, but beer was openly sold in the oil fields. The beverage was priced at ten cents per bottle above the market. It was freely charged that the extra dime went to a county official.

The chief law man in Batson was a huge deputy who obtained his commission by being a relative of the county sheriff. He was a typical example of the overbearing peace officer whose brutality breeds contempt for all law enforcement agencies. This fellow had previously killed a drunken man and laughingly remarked that he "liked to shoot 'em to see 'em kick." True to form, he felt that this wanton deed should entitle him to a big reputation, and he fancied himself a dreaded gunman. It was common knowledge that the deputy was taking bribes by the wholesale. The only respect he could command was the fear of his six-shooter. This giant was on hand when the Rangers arrived. He boasted that the State officers' sojourn in Batson would be of very

Winfred F. Bates, who was a member of the first detachment of Rangers ordered to an oil field. In 1904 they cleaned up Batson's Prairie. Hale, hearty and happy, he is still going strong in 1959.

short duration if they dared to interfere with his business. The towering deputy's confidence was bolstered when he noted the size of Sergeant Bates, who was a small man and weighed around one hundred and twenty-five pounds. He figured that his immense advantage in size plus his local reputation would have a quieting effect on the Ranger sergeant. This error came very close to costing the counterfeit badman his life. Captain Brooks, guided by the reports he had' received about the hulking deputy, was rather inclined to take him at face and bulk value. The captain remarked that one of the company would probably be forced to kill him but Sergeant Bates believed he could be tamed without any shooting.

On the following day the local bully decided to give a public demonstration of his prowess, and at the same time make an example out of a Ranger. He started to beat up a dance hall girl, and the proprietor shouted for the Rangers. Sergeant Bates heard the call and rushed to the place where he found the deputy in a murderous mood. When the latter reached for his pistol, he was treated to a private exhibition of lightning gunplay, for Sergeant Bates "bent" his six-shooter over the big man's head, the blow knocking him cold. The Beaumont and Houston newspapers reported "120 Pound Ranger Whips 220 Pound Deputy." The Ranger chained the addled fellow to a convenient tree. After he came to and partially recovered from his astonishment at the rapidity of the Ranger's draw, he threatened to wreak vengeance when he got loose, if only he could get his gun back. When Sergeant Bates assured him that he was welcome to his pistol, he reconsidered and stated that he did not want it. He further declared that the Rangers were simply doing their duty. With sound logic he reasoned that if the one hundred and twenty-five pounds of dynamite could get his gun out that fast, then a shooting match with Bates was not for the likes of him. In the old Texas custom of comparing men to pistols, the deputy was a 22 on a 45 frame, while Sergeant Bates was a 45 on a 22 frame.

The local constable had volunteered to aid and abet the gigantic deputy in his plan to rid their joint bailiwick of the obnoxious Rangers. But when this precinct pistol toter attempted to rescue one of his pets, who had been arrested by Lott Tumlinson, the Ranger gave him an old fashioned Texas booting. The justice of the peace joined the fray and received similar treatment.

When the Batson businessmen saw the large number of prisoners the Rangers were forced to chain up, they got together and built a small jail. It was made out of two by fours, wide side down. The first occupant of the new bastile was not, as might be supposed, an Irishman, but a Scotsman. He was the only member of his clan in town. This thrifty gentleman was one of the best men in the community, a fine physical specimen and quite a skilled boxer. A few drinks of whiskey, however, would cause him to go berserk and fight everybody he could lay his hands on. The Rangers had to lock him up during one of these battling sprees, although they liked him personally. The next inmate of the new jail happened to be one of those unspeakable creatures who live on the earnings of unfortunate women. He had unmercifully beaten one of his harem because she was not making enough money to keep him in the style he desired. The Rangers knew very little about this type of vulture and they believed that the punishment should fit the crime. They decided to handle his case in their own way, instead of taking him before a judge where he would get off with a light fine. The Scotch pugilist was just sobering up and had a magnificent hangover when the procurer was thrown in with him. Sergeant Bates made a fair proposition to the Scot. If "MacDuff" would work over prisoner number two in a manner befitting his means of livelihood, the Rangers would release him from custody. The Scotch are a very thoroughgoing race.

The pattern set by Captain Brooks and Sergeant Bates at Batson has been closely followed in all subsequent oil field cleanups. Their plan has never been improved upon. Rangers first go in and handle any corrupt officers found preying on the working men. The next step is to round up the other criminals. Most of these usually depart on the heels of the deposed officials. In the early Western gold rushes, vigilance committees and miner's courts dealt with the spoilers. Texas oil booms were fully as wild as the mining camps, and they were held in check by the Rangers.

On November 17, 1906, Captain Brooks resigned from the Rangers. In accepting his resignation, General Hulen wrote:

> The Governor as well as myself deeply regret that it becomes necessary for you to leave the Service. You have been a Ranger since 1883, during which time you have served from private to Captain; having served as Captain since 1889. You have made an enviable record, and the loss of your experience to the State cannot be estimated. You have always most faithfully and excellently performed your duties and you can, and doubtless will, look back upon your long service as an officer of the State with pride and satisfaction.

General Hulen's observation, "the loss of your experience to the State cannot be estimated," is a sad commentary on governors whose only criterion for fitness was "how many votes can you pull for me?"

Captain Brooks owned a tract of land south of Falfurrias. He intended to improve it and live the life of a ranchman. Powerful land owners in the vicinity would not let him retire from public life, however, and he was elected to the legislature. Falfurrias was in the extreme north end of Starr County, and almost a hundred miles from the county seat. If a citizen wanted to reach Rio Grande City by rail, he would have to take a most circuitous route. First, via the San Antonio and Aransas Pass Railway northward to Alice. Thence eastward via the Tex-Mex to Robstown. Thence southward via the St. Louis, Brownsville and Mexico Railroad to Brownsville. There he would cross over to Mexico and take the Mexican National Lines to Camargo. Then he could recross into the United States and Starr County at Rio Grande City. The alternate and most used routes were by rail to Sam Fordyce. From there to the county seat, twenty-three miles by hack, or a ninety mile journey overland. Obviously, another county was badly needed, and the citizens of Falfurrias worked toward that end. Ed C. Lasater, one of the largest land owners in Texas, initiated the movement, and Captain Brooks pushed it through the legislature. The new county was created in 1911 and organized in 1912. It was named for Captain John Abijah Brooks.

At a hotly contested school election before the organization of Brooks County was completed, the citizens of Falfurrias named Captain Brooks "officer of the day." A former Ranger who lived in Alice came down to watch the excitement. He did too much drinking, and was always dangerous when in that condition. The ex-Ranger, who was afterward killed by another ex-Ranger, was rated as one of the fastest men in the country with a pistol. Captain Brooks went to him and said, "Jim, you used to be in the Service, and I have always liked you, but you are heading for trouble. You can't vote in this county, and I wish you would get on the train that is leaving in a few minutes and go home." The man was just drunk enough to be reckless. He had told many men to get out of town, but he didn't like to be on the receiving end himself. He asked, "Cap, what are you going to do if I don't leave?" "I'll have to take your gun away from you," was the reply. The visitor exclaimed, "No man in the world can take my gun." Captain Brooks' eyes blazed, and with one lightning movement, he disarmed the recalcitrant ex-Ranger. "Now get on that train. When you come to your senses, I'll send you your gun." Liquor had made the younger man forget with whom he was dealing. Captain Brooks used to tell me, "I've still got one more good fight left in me."

Captain Brooks became engrossed in his judicial duties and for a long time took no interest in law enforcement. He told me once that he did not even own a six-shooter, as he had loaned them all out. One of McNelly's men, Charlie McKinney, was killed while serving as sheriff of La Salle County. Charlie McKinney, Jr., son of the slain sheriff, gave me a good Peacemaker pistol and I presented it to Captain Brooks.

There is a unique and unparalleled circumstance in the history of Brooks County. It was named for Captain Brooks, and when it was organized in 1912, he became its first county judge. He held this office continuously until his passing in 1944. His successor was his son, Honorable John Morgan Brooks, the present incumbent. In the forty-five years of its existence, Brooks County has had only two county judges. Both have been named Brooks.

On his eightieth birthday, Captain Brooks sent us a reproduction of a picture taken in Alice about 1900. His eighty-eighth birthday came during World War II, and I was in the Army. He wrote me a fine letter on that day, and said, "My dear old friend and comrade, my eyes are dim, but my prayers are always with you." Two months later he died peacefully.

With his passing, Texas lost one of its best citizens and I lost the man who inspired me to be a Texas Ranger.

Chapter 37
CAPTAIN W. J. McDONALD

THE most spectacular Ranger commander of his era was Captain William Jesse McDonald. He possessed more showmanship, was given wider publicity, and received better newspaper coverage than either Brooks, Rogers or Hughes. The locale of his activities required him to do a great deal of traveling on the railroads. During these journeys he usually attracted and held the undivided attention of his fellow passengers. Reporters and feature writers, then as now, were constantly on the alert for good copy. When the gentlemen of the press needed an interesting story, it could always be obtained by interviewing Captain Bill.

My acquaintance with Captain McDonald was not as extensive as it was with his three contemporaries. However, it was close enough to give me an insight into his life and character. His strong personality, picturesque speech and originality of thought made him popular with many prominent people. These included both state and national figures. He was most fortunate in having for his friend and sponsor Colonel Edward M. House. This eminent Texan always saw to it that Captain McDonald was in the right place, at the right time and with the right people. In this profitable endeavor, the doughty Ranger cooperated to the fullest extent with his mentor. He invariably furnished the proper amount of color to any occasion.

Captain William J. McDonald

Colonel House, the confidante and adviser of Woodrow Wilson, had Captain Bill named as the presidential candidate's bodyguard. Upon his election, President Wilson appointed him United States marshal for the Northern District of Texas. Captain McDonald's gratitude to his benefactor was expressed when he dedicated his book in these words: "To Edward M. House, without whose enduring friendship, wise counsel and active interest this book would never have been written."

Captain McDonald was censured by quite a few Texans, including several Rangers, for the way his biography was handled by Albert Bigelow Paine. They seemed to construe Paine's work as a history of the Rangers. Critics charged that the sole personal pronoun in Captain Bill's vocabulary was "I." They further believed that he had deliberately enhanced his own reputation at the expense of his men. This was not the case, nor was McDonald to blame for the featuring of his name.

Albert Bigelow Paine was the foremost biographer of his day. Colonel House, with characteristic astuteness, would not permit any second rater to write the life story of his protege. Paine simply carried out his mission in Texas. It was to write the biography of William Jesse McDonald. He was not here for any other purpose. This is probably the first time anybody, particularly a Ranger, has defended Captain Bill's attitude in the book by Paine. He was not personally at fault over the apparent slighting of his men. Having been both a Ranger and a captain myself, I can understand how this could have been done by a biographer. Several books and hundreds of articles have been written about the exploits of Captain McDonald. My sketch will be confined to incidents in his career that were related to me by him or his Rangers.

Shortly before the turn of the century, Captain McDonald was ordered to San Saba County. He took Sergeant W. J. L. Sullivan, Rangers Barker and McCauley from his own company, together with Rangers Edgar Neal and Allen Maddox from Company C. Their mission was to break up the worst murder syndicate that ever existed in Texas.

For many years the county had been terrorized and practically ruled by an organized mob. They had started out as a vigilance committee with the high purpose of maintaining law and order. Soon, their original good intentions were lost in the lust for power that invariably

Members Company "B," Texas Rangers, camped on San Saba River, Sept. 1896. Left to right: Edgar T. Neal; Allen R. Maddox; Tom Johnson (cook); Dudley S. Barker; John L. Sullivan.

goes with mob rule. The guiding motives behind every act became greed, spite and personal vengeance. Under cover of darkness, they held regular meetings at a sinister spot aptly called Buzzard's Hole.

At these nocturnal conclaves, they marked for slaughter any unfortunate who had incurred their displeasure, or who owned property coveted by a favored member. When the victims of the mob totaled more than two score, a group of citizens petitioned Governor Culbertson to send Rangers.

Out of the men who were ordered to San Saba in response to this appeal, I knew Captain McDonald, Ranger Edgar T. Neal and Ranger Dudley S. Barker. First hand details of the episode were supplied me by Rangers Neal and Barker.

When Rangers are ordered in to handle a case of this kind, the tactics employed by the assassins and mobsters generally follow a fixed pattern. The most valiant of the local badmen endeavors to show his fellow townsmen that he is not afraid of the Rangers. He indulges in a great deal of war talk. This bolsters his courage and makes his cronies think he is the king of gunfighters. True to form, this happened in San Saba. One of the mob's ambitious gunmen took his Winchester and came to town with the avowed purpose of killing a Ranger. He picked the youngest man in the company, Dudley Barker, and threw down on him with the rifle. This hostile act was like hitting a grizzly bear over the head with a panama hat. Dud got his six-shooter in circulation and gave the natives a magnificent exhibition of fast gunplay.

337

He hit the rifleman five times before he could get off a shot. All the bullet holes could be covered with a silver dollar. The closely grouped 45 calibre slugs served to discourage all further attempts on the lives of Rangers. The work of McDonald and his men broke up the murderous Buzzard's Hole mob and the leader was sentenced to a life term in the penitentiary.

Dud Barker established his reputation as a just though firm man with honest citizens, but quick and fatal when dealing with desperados. After retiring from the Rangers, he served for many years as sheriff of Pecos County. By practicing thrift and sound business principles, he was able to accumulate a comfortable fortune while making one of the best sheriffs in Texas. Ex-Ranger Barker was so outstanding that I offered him a captaincy in the Service. When a criminal was killed while resisting arrest in Pecos County, the local newspaper reported that he had been "Barkerized." Dud Barker expressed his high regard for Captain McDonald in these forceful words, "I would crawl on my hands and knees clear across Texas to get any man who killed Bill McDonald."

Ranger Edgar T. Neal went to San Saba with McDonald. He also rendered outstanding service in the suppression of the mob. After that mission was accomplished, Mr. Neal resigned from the Rangers and was elected sheriff. He served in this office for many years and kept San Saba County free from mob activities. In 1931 he returned to his first love, the Texas Rangers. We were delighted to have this veteran with his mature judgment back with us. I had looked forward to making him a captain but when the Fergusons ruined the Rangers, he was one of the casualties. Texas thereby lost a wealth of experience and ability.

One incident in the service of Captain McDonald that I talked to him about personally was the slaying of Ranger T. L. Fuller. It took place in the Sabine River town of Orange. Rangers had been sent there on several occasions to handle race troubles and family feuds. The county and city peace officers were not only out of harmony, but were gunning for each other. Citizens of Orange had appealed to the Governor for Rangers. The home town officers not only failed and refused to cooperate with the outsiders, but threw every obstacle in their way. As a culmination of this official friction, Ranger T. L. Fuller was forced to shoot and kill one of the deputies. After Fuller was cleared and exonerated, relatives of the dead man worked out a plan of revenge. On a charge of "false arrest," Fuller was summoned to Orange, where the assassins had him in their own back yard.

While seated in a barber chair preparing to get a shave, Ranger Fuller was killed by a bullet from a Winchester. It was in the hands of a brother of the man he had slain. The rule and custom of Rangers when working in a town filled with enemies was for one man to stand guard while his companion got his barber work. Hot towels usually covered the face and eyes of the man in the chair, rendering him temporarily defenseless. Captain McDonald fired the Ranger, whose name is best left unmentioned, for his fatal carelessness in failing to protect the back of his comrade. On hearing the shot, Captain McDonald, who was a few doors away, ran to the scene. Fuller was dead, and the killer had already given himself up to a local officer. He was therefore a prisoner. By the Rangers' code, a man in custody must be protected at all costs. The quick surrender was fast thinking on the killer's part, and prevented McDonald from dealing out summary punishment. In counties of corrupt officials and jurors, a criminal can flaunt justice in the face of conscientious officers. Under these circumstances, the Rangers have been known to term the killing of a notorious criminal, "getting a conviction." Captain McDonald told me it was the regret of his life that he did not get there in time to kill the murderer of his Ranger. Captain McDonald keenly felt the loss of young Fuller, and particularly resented the manner in which he was assassinated. Carl T. Ryan was enlisted to fill the vacancy caused by the death of Fuller.

Through a technicality in the wording of the law creating the Frontier Battalion, only officers were empowered to make arrests. The inconsistency of this restriction lay in the fact that privates in the organization could ASSIST in making arrests, but could not make them alone. The criminal lawyers soon discovered this flaw, and when a Ranger took a man into custody, he was liable to be charged with false arrest. This was what happened in the case of Fuller and a good man had to be sacrificed to get the law changed. The tragedy resulted in the passage of a new statute, clothing every Ranger, regardless of rank, with the powers of a peace officer in any Texas county. This new law went into effect July 8, 1901.

State Militiamen and Rangers guarding the Jackson County jail at Edna, Texas in 1905 to prevent the lynching of Monk Gibson. Shown in civilian clothes are Rangers Herff Carnes, C. T. Ryan and Milam Wright.

Captain McDonald's record in the Rangers was not confined to successful passages at arms. He paraphrased Davy Crockett's injunction, "Be sure you're right, then go ahead," into the Ranger motto, "No man in the wrong can stand up against a fellow that's in the right and keeps on a'comin'." There never was a body of men who so highly regarded the word "right" and all that it implies, as do the true Texas Rangers. Captain Bill also claimed to be a pretty good single handed talker. His originality in speech and choice of picturesque words was only approached in Ranger history by Ira Aten, formerly a sergeant in Company D, and later a foreman on the vast XIT Ranch in the Panhandle.

Five years after the turn of the century, the attention of all Texas was focused on Jackson County. In that normally pleasant community, one or more fiends in human form had committed a wholesale murder.

340

There were neither radios nor television in those days but the case received full coverage in the press. Special correspondents were dispatched to the scene by many of the leading newspapers. Details of the massacre were headlined in both their regular editions and in numerous extras.

This furor was caused by the brutal slaying of a mother and four children, members of a family named Conditt. The first suspect to be arrested was a sixteen year old Negro. From his name, which was on the lips of practically everybody in the state, the shocking crime became known as the Monk Gibson Case.

The tragic story began when J. F. Conditt moved to a small place about two miles from the town of Edna. It was near a settlement inhabited entirely by Negroes. The advent of a white family in that neighborhood caused open resentment, and Felix Powell, colored, had reportedly made an insulting remark to Mildred Conditt. Before the Conditts came, a windmill on their premises had furnished drinking water for the community. This practice was stopped by the new occupants.

On September 28, 1905, Conditt was working with a rice threshing crew about seven miles from his home. Some time during that morning Mrs. Conditt and four of her children were bludgeoned to death. The youngest child was a boy of three and the oldest was a girl aged twelve. She had been violated. The instrument used in this mass butchery was a two handed chopping tool called an adz.

Monk Gibson was plowing a field near the Conditt house. In the early afternoon he ran to the home of John Gibson, a white man, and reported that he had seen two men chasing the Conditt family. The neighbor hurried to the scene and found that the yard had been turned into shambles. Five bodies lay where the killers had left them, and the only child spared, a baby, was crying piteously. Gibson sent Monk after the father, while he went to Edna and notified the sheriff.

Shortly after the officers arrived at the death farm, Monk Gibson came back with J. F. Conditt. It was noticed that the boy had blood on his hands, and he could give no satisfactory account of his movements during the morning. He was arrested and taken to jail at Edna. The news spread like wildfire, and the entire countryside was aroused. Crowds of angry, armed men converged on the town.

They were determined to take the law into their own hands and make short work of the case by lynching the prisoner. It was reported that a special train from a nearby town was bringing two hundred men to Edna to aid the local mob. The infuriated crowd was temporarily appeased by the explanation that Monk was needed to give evidence against others. Under questioning and persuasion, which was not always the gentlest variety, Monk's answers were contradictory and unsatisfactory.

Authorities decided that it would be wise to take him to the adjoining county where he would be safer. Fresh, grain-fed saddle horses were hidden behind the jail, and Gibson was taken out through a rear window. Under cover of darkness, Sheriff Egg, Deputy Sheriff Jim Powers and Tom Hayes, a citizen, rode toward Halletsville with their prisoner. He was not handcuffed, for they wanted him to be able to ride unhampered in case they had to make a run for it. The officers reasoned that he would stay with them for protection. After they had

Veteran Albert Egg in 1958. As the young Sheriff of Jackson County he handled the celebrated Monk Gibson Case.

342

traveled several miles, the lane made a bend. Gibson suddenly jumped his horse through the fence and got away into the night. His guards followed as quickly as possible. They found the horse where Monk had quit him, but the prisoner had made his escape on foot.

When the sheriff and his party returned to Edna, the news leaked out that Monk Gibson was at large. Feeling ran high and soon reached a fever pitch. Stockmen of the county brought in entire *remudas,* and placed their best horses at the disposal of possemen. Other mounts were shipped in by rail from the more distant ranches. The greatest manhunt Texas had seen since the pursuit of Gregorio Cortez in 1901, was in full hue and cry.

During this crisis, Jackson County was most fortunate in having as its sheriff a man of the calibre of Albert Egg. He was barely twenty-six years old, and the terrific responsibility suddenly thrust on his young shoulders would have baffled a less capable man. Not only was it his duty to solve the crime and apprehend the murderers, but he had to cope with the ever present menace of mob violence. His stature was further proved when he realized that in a situation of this gravity, all available assistance should be utilized, and he did not hesitate to call for Rangers.

Adjutant General John A. Hulen, in his report to Governor S. W. T. Lanham for the period ending December 31, 1906, stated:

> On October 2, 1905, Your Excellency ordered myself, in command of Company A, 1st Infantry of Houston; Co. L, 1st Infantry of Austin; Troop A, 1st Cavalry of Houston; Troop C, 1st Cavalry of Austin; and the following officers: Lieutenant Colonel Albert E. Devine, Assistant Quartermaster General; Major C. Towles, 1st Cavalry; Major J. L. Short, Surgeon; Captain James L. Loving, Assistant Surgeon; and Lieutenant Theo. Bering Jr., Battalion Quartermaster, 1st Infantry, to Edna, Texas, for the purpose of protecting the lives of certain persons there threatened with lynching and burning, which grew out of the murder of the Conditt family.
>
> Troop A. of the 1st Cavalry and Co. A, 1st Infantry of Houston, were ordered to Edna by special train. Troop C, 1st Cavalry and Co. L, 1st Infantry from Austin, with Quartermaster's supplies, also went to Edna, by special train. These trains reached Edna about four o'clock in the morning of the 3rd of October, and the troops immediately proceeded to the county jail, where the command was encamped. In addition to the military ordered there, I also ordered Captains McDonald and Hughes with several of their rangers.

General Hulen knew Bill McDonald to be the Ranger captain best suited for the present duty. Born in Mississippi, he had grown up in deep East Texas. The ways of Negroes, both good and bad, were to him an open book. Brooks, Rogers and Hughes, his contemporary captains, could not be surpassed for service on the Mexican border. They were experts in dealing with criminals of both sides of the Rio Grande, but colored residents of their territories were few and far between. Captain Hughes only stayed a short time in Edna.

When the State forces arrived, everything was in a turmoil. Hundreds of men on foot and on horseback were searching for the escaped Monk Gibson. Whole packs of well trained bloodhounds vainly tried to pick up his scent. Wild rumors were flying, and everybody seemed to be running in circles. Captain McDonald was a good organizer, and had a commanding personality. He went to work with all his might. If there could ever be any justification for the cliche "bring order out of chaos," it could be applied to Captain Bill's work on this occasion. That is exactly what he did.

In the recapture of Monk Gibson, which was really a surrender, there occurred one of those phenomena that is hard to explain. Hunted by hundreds of outdoor men, including sheriffs, deputies and Rangers, he was able to remain hidden for several days in his father's barn. Burrowed under a pile of oat straw, he lay undetected while the place was searched innumerable times. Even the bloodhounds failed to find him. He was finally driven by hunger to come out and tell Warren Powell that he wanted to give up. Warren was a brother of Felix Powell. He tied up the hunted youth, then ran to town and notified the officers that Monk had been found. General Hulen, Captain McDonald, Sheriff Egg and his deputies, together with several Rangers hurried out to the farm. They placed Monk in a buggy and brought him back to jail. This was no simple task, as the angry crowd shouted their determination to take the prisoner.

The National Guardsmen came from the best families in Texas. Most of them were young men still in their teens. They had plenty of courage. Many of them gave their lives to their country in the First World War. However, they were not trained for the grim work of repelling mobs. When the crowd was working up their courage, Dutch and otherwise, to storm the jail, somebody said it would be easy to overpower the militiamen.

Those pioneer brothers, Joe and Ed Pickering, of Victoria, were living in Jackson County during that period. They recently supplied us with many facts about the Gibson case. One of them recalled a man saying, "Those soldiers are nothing but kids." "That may be true," replied a grizzled old timer, "but you better go slow. They are backed by six Rangers."

After a careful study of the case, Captain McDonald became convinced that sixteen year old Monk Gibson could not have been the sole perpetrator of the crime. The physical facts showed that older and stronger men were implicated, and that they must have taken the lead. The grand jury, however, gave no credence to his theory, and refused to indict anybody but Monk. That august body apparently felt that one man already in jail was worth several suspects that they believed existed only in the mind of the Ranger captain.

Monk Gibson's case was moved to San Antonio on a change of venue. The Rangers assisted Sheriff Egg in transferring him to the Bexar County jail. When his case came to trial, both Felix Powell and Henry Howard appeared as witnesses for the State. The jurors could not agree, as many of them felt, like Captain McDonald, that others were involved. The trial resulted in a hung jury, and the case was again moved, this time to DeWitt County. Here Monk Gibson was assessed the death penalty. He was hanged in Cuero in June, 1908.

After the first feeling of horror and indignation had simmered down, some of the people in Edna began to wonder if Captain McDonald might not be right. Chief among these was Sheriff Egg. When several local stockmen attended the annual convention of the Texas Cattle Raisers Association in Fort Worth the following March, they discussed the case at length with the captain. As a result of these conversations, he was ordered back to Jackson County and given a free rein in his investigations.

Captain McDonald and Sheriff Egg found a colored witness who had seen Felix Powell riding down the road carrying a bundle of bloody clothes. He was looking for someone to wash them. The first woman he asked refused to touch the stained garments, but he found another one who reluctantly consented to perform this gruesome service.

The most valuable piece of evidence found on the scene was a board from the wall of the death house. One of the murderers had touched it with his bloody hand, and had left a clear print. The piece containing this picture had been sawed out and taken to town for study. It was plainly too big to be the hand of Monk Gibson. The officers were eager to try it for size on Felix Powell. The print did not fit Felix's open hand, but when it was closed as if clutching a weapon, it matched perfectly.

Captain McDonald was a master psychologist when dealing with mobs, and could get his meaning over to excited men by turning a timely phrase. When the mobsters at Edna declared that they were going to storm the jail and hang Monk Gibson, McDonald replied, "If you all try it, there will be crepe on many a door in Jackson County."

General John A. Hulen, who, as adjutant general, came to Edna and took personal charge of the State forces, now lives at Camp Hulen. Among his other distinctions, he is the only living man who has a World War II camp named for him.

I recently had a nostalgic visit in Austin with former Adjutant General Dallas J. Matthews. He is now a member of the State Armory board. This grand veteran was General Hulen's right bower, and had more to do than any other man in making the Thirty-sixth Division the pride of Texas. When Adjutant General Mark McGee resigned from Mrs. Ferguson's first administration, General Matthews agreed to fill out the term. He did this at the behest of General Hulen and many other National Guardsmen, for the express purpose of "saving the Guard from Fergusonism."

General Matthews was serving as captain of the Houston Light Guards during the Monk Gibson campaign, and told me of an incident that occurred at that time. "I was standing on the depot platform in Edna, when the morning train came in from Victoria. A fine looking cowman got off, and I noticed that he had a .45 calibre pistol in his waistband. He announced to the bystanders that he had come to organize a bunch to hang Monk Gibson. I returned to camp, and told Captain McDonald that I believed the man should be taken into custody. The Ranger commander left, and was back in less than half an hour. 'Captain Matthews,' he said, 'your man is in jail and here is his six-shooter'."

Sheriff Albert Egg still lives peacefully in Edna, cherished by his family and friends. He is hale and hearty, and furnished me with a great deal of first hand information. To illustrate his youth at the time of the celebrated event, Mr. Egg told this story: "The next year after the Gibson case, I went to the convention of the Texas Sheriffs Association. Upon being introduced as 'Albert Egg, of Jackson County,' one member said, 'Oh, yes. You're the son of the sheriff who handled the Monk Gibson case'."

Felix Powell was tried for his part of the murder in Victoria County. The jury found him guilty and sentenced him to death. He was hanged in Victoria on the second day of April, 1907. The case of Henry Howard, an early suspect, was dismissed.

After the execution of Felix Powell, his brother Warren swore vengeance on Sheriff Egg. If he did not actually participate in the murder of the Conditts, there is no question but that Warren Powell had guilty knowledge of the crime. Armed with a double barreled shotgun, he came to town one day with the expressed purpose of killing the sheriff. A faithful Negro friend, who had been a childhood coon hunting companion of Mr. Egg, warned him of the impending danger. Sheriff Egg took one of the semi-automatic Winchesters that had only recently been placed on the market, and met the would-be killer half way. He found him in a store, and when the shooting stopped, Warren, with five bullets in his body, had joined his brother Felix.

A significant fact about the case was the attitude of the Rangers toward the prisoner. He was a member of a minority race and was guilty of a heinous crime. Nevertheless, they would protect him at all costs. Members of the mob shouted, "Would you fellows kill good citizens just to save a murdering scoundrel?" "Regardless of what he was before, he is now our prisoner," replied Captain McDonald. "We don't like him any better than you do but he is going to have a court trial." Many Texas Rangers have given the same answer to mobs.

In the summer of 1906 at Brownsville another dramatic chapter was written into the saga of Captain McDonald. It was the old sordid story so familiar to residents of Army post towns on the border. The War Department continued to send colored troops to these stations in spite of the fact that trouble was the inevitable result. The movement to Fort Brown was no exception. Almost immediately on arrival of the Twenty-fifth Infantry, a series of "incidents" began to take place. A soldier jostled a lady as she was crossing a street, and Fred Tate, an ace customs inspector, promptly "bent" a .45 Colt pistol over the offender's head. Mr. Tate, one of my staunchest friends, was afterward killed in line of duty by a smuggler. Another black enlisted man made the usually fatal mistake of trying some funny business with the redoubtable A. Y. Baker, who had resigned his sergeant's rank in the Rangers to enter the United States Customs service. The sable soldier's rabbit foot must have been working overtime, or maybe one of his African ancestors had him under a voodoo charm, for all A. Y. did was knock him in the mud along the river bank.

A Negro ex-soldier owned a gin mill just outside the military reservation. In this hell hole, alcoholic fuel was constantly added to the flame of strife. The personnel of the Twenty-fifth Infantry was made up of the most ignorant class of Negroes from the old Southern states, most of them signing their enlistment papers with an "X." These illiterates were easily agitated into violence, and when plied with busthead whiskey, they could be led into any sort of deviltry. One of my good friends, Louis Kowalski, was born and reared in Brownsville. In talking to me about the Brownsville riot, he said, "The night before the outbreak I was standing in my father's yard, in the shadow of a palm. A party was in progress at my home, and music and laughter were coming from the parlor. Two Negro soldiers came by on the sidewalk and I heard them say, 'They are having a good time now, but tomorrow night they won't be laughing'." This incident, among others, proves that the entire affair had been carefully planned, and that many, if not all, of the soldiers had guilty knowledge of it.

The Brownsville riot is history. On the night of August 13, 1906, a bunch of Negro soldiers left the Army post and shot up the town. They killed a bartender, wounded the night chief of police and killed his horse. The rioters shot into residences with army rifles, and blasted the Miller Hotel, which is only two blocks from the main gate of Fort Brown. The fusillade lasted ten minutes and left the town terrified.

The citizens of Brownsville spent the balance of the night in a state of frenzy, but no new outbreaks occurred. The following morning Western Union did a land office business. The Governor, both United States Senators, the Adjutant General and even the President of the United States received messages begging for relief and protection. Numerous committees convened and many resolutions were passed. In spite of these measures, eight days elapsed before McDonald or any other State official was ordered to Brownsville. The overworked alibi, so familiar to real friends of worthy Latin Americans on the border, was tried by both officers and enlisted men of the command. They attempted to shift the guilt from themselves by blaming the riot on "Mexicans from both sides of the river." The officers at Fort Brown, of whom Major Penrose was senior, seemed inclined to shield the colored soldiers. They took this attitude despite the fact that their men had wantonly violated laws, both military and civil. Major Blocksom was ordered by the War Department to proceed to Brownsville and conduct a thorough investigation of the entire affair. His attitude was reassuring to the citizens, and he gave some promise of achieving success in punishing the culprits.

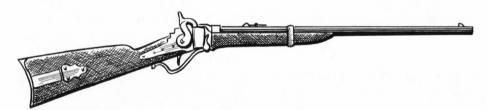

Captain McDonald could see but one point in the whole matter. A breach of the peace, which included murder, had been committed on Texas soil. By his line of reasoning, the fact that the guilty parties were soldiers of the United States and were quartered on a Federal reservation did not render them immune from arrest. He deemed it a Ranger's duty to question, investigate and apprehend all criminals, if they were within the boundaries of his state. Neither Army post, sentry, sergeant of the guard, officer of the day, nor orders were going to prevent his pursuit of offenders against the peace and dignity of Texas.

Before McDonald's arrival in Brownsville, Sam McKenzie and Blaze Delling, who were stationed in the Valley, had done some shrewd investigating. They had clearly established the fact that the rioters were members of the Twenty-fifth Infantry from Fort Brown. Captain McDonald determined to go into the post and question the suspects named by his Rangers. When advised that the sentries were under orders to allow no one to pass, the captain replied that he had business on the inside.

Accompanied by Sergeant Billy McCauley, Captain McDonald walked to the main gate of Fort Brown. The Rangers were challenged by the sentries. In describing the next move, Ranger Carl T. Ryan said, "Captain McDonald had a voice that withered the guilty. When he approached those guards, his eagle face and gimlet eyes bored into their souls. When he commanded, 'Put up them guns,' they forgot all about their orders and lowered their rifles."

Mr. Ryan also told me that he had been with McDonald and heard him talk that way to mobs, desperados and other hard cases. There was something about the man and the methods he used that made his talk stand up.

With one possible exception, this was the only time in American military annals that two men forced their way past sentries at gunpoint. In the other case also, the crashers of the gate were Texas Rangers. Back in 1881 at Fort Concho, Captain Bryan Marsh stormed into the post commander's office and gave him a severe tongue lashing. The tactics used by both Rangers had a decided similarity. The one-armed Marsh stationed several men at strategic points to cover the rear, and kept at his side the youngest Ranger, nineteen year old Jeff Davis Milton. There is no record of their having been challenged by sentries. They proceeded straight to Colonel Grierson's headquarters. While Marsh delivered his blistering lecture, Milton backed the Captain's play with his Winchester. At Fort Brown, Captain McDonald and Sergeant McCauley twice overran the sentries. The second time was in direct defiance of repeated orders to keep them out.

As long as the Twenty-fifth Infantry remained at Fort Brown, the citizens kept their weapons ready day and night. Among the varied types carried by the men assembled at the Miller Hotel was an unusual shotgun owned by Lon C. Hill. The exploits and achievements of this grand developer would fill a book. His old spattergun was an eight gauge goose gun, a young cannon long since outlawed by game conservationists. Within its range and when loaded with double 0 buckshot, it was the equal of half a dozen rifles.

Lon C. Hill, Jr., is now a distinguished industrialist who will never lose his interest in the real Rangers. He told me recently that he remembered the old gun distinctly. Mr. Hill related that they loaded their own shells, which had brass cases. He said, "The big charge of black powder would not only kick a boy down, but also would stomp on him." Ex-Ranger Ryan recalled the goose gun with a great deal of interest, and wondered what would have been the result if it had been turned loose on the rioting soldiers.

The net results of the Brownsville raid were as follows: There were no more outbreaks or bloodshed. Major C. W. Penrose, after witnessing the two routs of his sentries, declared that, "Bill McDonald would charge hell with a bucket of water." Senator Foraker of Ohio championed the cause of the downtrodden colored soldiers and according to reports, advised them to stick by their original falsehood. He was dubbed "Senator Firecracker" by Captain McDonald. I heard Captain Bill use the appellation several times. The soldiers were shipped out of Fort Brown. Captain McDonald was ordered by the governor to act under and through the district judge and sheriff. Judge Stanley Welch, for whom a midnight assassin's bullet was waiting farther up the Rio Grande, signed the order forbidding McDonald to hold the train on which they were leaving. The rioters were tried in a military court, and a board of officers found them "not guilty."

The final chapter was written by President Theodore Roosevelt. The Rough Rider, who had served with many Texans in '98, reviewed the findings of the court martial, and using his prerogative as Commander in Chief of the Armed Forces, dismissed without honor the three companies of the Twenty-fifth Infantry involved in the Brownsville raid. Teddy obviously held his presidential nose at the findings of the prejudiced board.

On the night of November 7, 1906, a noted Ranger drama was staged by Captain McDonald and his men. It took place in Starr County, about eighty miles above the mouth of the Rio Grande at Casitas. This rancho is one of the clusters of *jacales,* or thatched roofed huts, that sprawl along the Military Road. The trouble was an aftermath of an unusually violent eruption of the political pot. It boiled continuously in that dry, thirsty land where the Latin American residents take their politics very seriously.

The two parties carried on a never ending struggle. They were nominally Democrats and Republicans but were locally designated as *Colorados y Azules* (Reds and Blues). In these contests for political and therefore financial supremacy, they often resorted to bloodshed. After a political rival was eliminated, the survivor only had to step across the river until the adjournment of the next grand jury. If his party was in power, he returned and received a hero's welcome.

This time the machete men had used a gun instead of the keen edged blade of their ancestors, and they had gone too far. One or more of them murdered District Judge Stanley Welch as he slept in a small brick building near the Starr County courthouse. His quarters were shared with District Attorney John I. Kleiber. This distardly assassination had brought down on them their most dreaded scourge, *Los Rinches,* as they called the Rangers.

The death of Judge Welch was reported to Governor S. W. T. Lanham by a telegram dispatched from Sam Fordyce. This was the nearest railroad point, twenty-three miles from the scene of the murder in Rio Grande City. The message also contained an urgent request for Rangers. The pitch of excitement in Starr County cannot be visualized by one who does not understand the people and conditions as they then existed. The custom and practice was for each party to round up as many potential voters as they could a week or more before election day. These ignorant *hombres,* ninety-five per cent of whom could neither read nor write and fully half of them not even knowing their age, were plied with mescal until they were beastly drunk. They were then herded into enclosures surrounded by high rock walls, in the tops of which were imbedded broken bottles.

Here they were stabled until voting time. They would then be given a red or blue rag to denote their party, and marched drunkenly to the polls where they were counted by the head. At that time, mescal was the standard border beverage, tequila not becoming the staff of life there until prohibition. It was transported in bladders and goat or pig skins. The potency of pre-tequila mescal and its effect on all creatures who drank the fiery liquid, could hardly be exaggerated. This can be illustrated by an old border yarn. Once when a group of Mexican farmers were waiting to have their cotton ginned, one of them spilled some mescal on the ground. A tumblebug drank a drop of it, backed up against a five hundred pound bale of cotton and said, "Let's go, Big Boy." Captain McDonald and his boys were not going to a pink tea when the Governor sent them to Rio Grande City, or, as the county seat was still called by old timers, Rancho Davis. An election, the murder of a prominent public official, plus an unlimited supply of liquor in the raw, had fired the addled brains of the populace into frenzy.

When the Governor called, Captain Bill was in Alice, the traditional Ranger station for Southwest Texas. The camp was within a hundred yards of where I now sit, hard at work on my book. I have experienced the same routine and it was always thrilling. The governor or adjutant general calling with an order to proceed on some mission, the outcome of which no one could foretell. In camp with Captain McDonald was his nephew and sergeant, the intrepid Billy McCauley. In stature, he was one of the smallest Rangers, but he had the heart of a lion. His .45 Colt six-shooter, which he handled with the speed of lightning, was just as big as the one used by the two hundred pound six footers. Governor Lanham ordered McDonald to hurry to Rio Grande City and to take all available men. Pursuant to these instructions, he immediately started out, accompanied only by Sergeant McCauley. The two Rangers rode the Tex-Mex to Robstown, where they could catch the newly constructed St. Louis, Brownsville and Mexico railroad to Harlingen. Here they took the branch of the same system to Sam Fordyce, the western terminus of the railroad. On the way, the captain had the good fortune to pick up some valuable reinforcements. When Sam McKenzie, Blaze Delling and Crosby Marsden joined the hell bent for election pair of Rangers, they added a trio whose gameness, marksmanship and all around ability could not be surpassed. Even if their mission had not been along the Rio Grande, they were men who would "do to ride the river with." Each one spoke Spanish, and was wise in the ways of the border denizens. Crosby Marsden was a member of a fine old Bee County family; Blaze Delling was a graduate of Southwestern University and Sam McKenzie was one of the best border Rangers who ever wore a scout belt. When biographer Paine said that "Captain McDonald gathered up a young fellow named Marsden, who had Ranger ambitions," the talented author gave a sample of the writing that was so distasteful to the boys. Marsden did his share and more in the Casitas fight, always showing to best advantage when the chips were down.

Captain McDonald, Sergeant Billy McCauley, Rangers Sam McKenzie, Crosby Marsden and ex-Ranger Blaze Delling, now a United States Customs Inspector, made up the party. They were bound for Rio Grande City to carry out the Governor's orders. At Sam Fordyce, they hired an open hack drawn by a tough pair of those little Spanish mules that ranchmen call "rats." Just before sundown, they started out on the Military Road. A description of this historic trail may help the reader appreciate the sinister conditions it presented for a perfect ambuscade.

The Military Road was hewed out of the dense semi-tropical vegetation along the lower Rio Grande. It was built by United States Army engineers, to open a route between Fort Brown and Ringgold Barracks. The *camino* roughly followed the river's course, marking as nearly a straight line as the meandering of the stream would permit. The Signal Corps constructed a telegraph line on the edge of the clearing. Some of the slender poles used to hold up the wire were still standing a few years ago. These time and rust defying posts made good targets for travelers, practically all of whom went fully armed. The metallic ping of a six-shooter bullet richocheting off one of these wrought iron pipes made a far more musical sound than the dull thud of a practice shot striking a mesquite. Granjero, jarachina and numerous other varieties of chaparral made an almost solid wall on both sides of the road. The spiny leaves of the giant cactus, which is the largest found in Texas, pinned this undergrowth to the bigger trees. These were principally mesquites, ebonies and willows. One of my Rangers in Company D declared that he had seen a rattlesnake backing out of a thicket on the Military Road. O. Henry said, in one of his Ranger stories, "To be lost in a prickly pear flat is almost to die the death of the thief on the Cross," and he wrote of the cactus growing in the Nueces River bottom. He had no way of knowing that the ones mentioned in his tales were a dwarf variety compared with those on the Rio Grande. Here, as was so extensively advertised by real estate developers, "the soil is richer than the Valley of the Nile." The size of the cactus added prickly testimony to the fertility of the land.

The inhabitants of the numerous *pueblitos* lived mainly by smuggling. The men ran contraband cattle and horses. The women planted small patches of corn for *tortillas* and stock feed. These wives also served as lookouts. They had a system of signals that would be a model for any major league baseball manager. At the approach of Rangers or river guards, as the Mounted Inspectors of United States Customs are locally called, the housewife would hang the family wash on the clothesline. Different colored garments flashed the warning message to the smuggler on the other side of the river. I questioned a female member of this *contrabandista* signal corps one day and she said, in her most saintly manner, "But surely senor, you cannot object to a woman hanging out the clothes?" When I pointed out that the garment was not even wet, *la senora* shrugged her shoulders, rolled her eyes toward heaven and said, "But of course, *Mi Capitan,* the climate she is very dry, no?"

The countless rattlesnakes in the Rio Grande bottom are much larger than those found anywhere else in the United States. They are of the diamond back variety, several shades darker than the ones living in the sandy country. These monsters are more sluggish than the smaller snakes. Their laziness is the only good thing that can be said about them.

I investigated a killing at La Grulla, one of the Military Road settlements near the scene of McDonald's Casitas fight. One of the leading citizens had slain another prominent resident of that river community. Under inquiry, it developed that the deceased had ridden to the middle of the town and announced that HE was the most bravo inhabitant of La Grulla. "No, you're not, but I am," contradicted the leading citizen, and shot his challenger dead.

When Captain McDonald and his Rangers made their nocturnal trip to Rio Grande City, they were not exactly traveling through Peaceful Valley.

The word had gotten to Rio Grande City that two Rangers were on the way. Farther up in Texas, the rumor route is known as the "grapevine." On the border it is called the "cactus telegraph." By this thorny system, the news had reached Rancho Davis. A bunch of *valientes* decided, after copiously fortifying themselves with mescal, that they could avenge the deaths of many ancestors by waylaying the pair of hated *Rinches*. Any place along the Military Road would be ideal for this deadly business. There were countless brush fences, goat pens, big mesquites and other kinds of cover from which a bushwhacker could shoot, with minimum danger to his own hide. These Ranger hunters procured a hack and set out down the river, fatally bent on michief. Five bravos constituted the reception committee and on reaching Casitas they were reinforced by several local patriots. These were eager to join the Ranger exterminators. Their aid was especially valuable, as they knew all the nearby points of vantage.

As the Rangers approached Casitas from the opposite direction, all conversation ceased. On the slow mule paced journey from the rail head, they had discussed in low tones the business at hand. They commented briefly on the pitch blackness of the night (which I always believed to be darkest along the Military Road) and the plainly outlined target they made when skylined. As the Ranger hack neared the wide place in the road that indicated a settlement, another conveyance approached from up river. McDonald's driver pulled out to let it pass. The Rio Grande City avengers had figured the distances and timing to a fine point. They knew that their intended victims were the occupants of the other hack. An outburst of cursing, yelling and shooting came from the passengers of the east bound vehicle. Amid the usual epithets, the leader ordered his companions, *"Tiran los. Tiran los."* (Shoot them.). The words were readily comprehended by the Spanish speaking Rangers. They were ready, able and almost eager to meet the challenge. The cry of a border bravo merits a full description. To one who has never heard the "mescal yell," it is impossible to describe the ferocity of that ribald *grito*. The war whoop of the Comanche, or even our heralded Rebel yell fail to equal the mescal variety by several

356

decibels. McDonald shouted in his commanding voice, "Hold up there, we are Rangers." Tyler Mason in his *Riding for Texas* states that Billy McCauley repeated this order in Spanish, but he is in error. Sam McKenzie was absolutely bi-lingual, frequently acting as interpreter in courts, both State and Federal. He translated the captain's words. McCauley was one of the best Rangers Texas ever produced, but most of his service had been in the Panhandle. He had neither the reason nor the opportunity to learn Spanish.

In speaking of the Casitas affair, McKenzie told me that not much time was wasted in conversation. When the Rio Grande City contingent declared their intentions and started firing, they invoked the old Ranger rule of shooting first and talking later. There was no danger of killing an innocent man at that time and place. At the strange sound of words spoken in English, the ambushers opened fire, and the battle was on.

The hated *Rinches* did not play fair. They had let it be known that only two would make the trip, and had failed to publish the news about reinforcements. When the firing ceased and the results were tabulated, it was found that there were four dead, one wounded and two captured. The casualties were all on the side of the committee for the extermination of *Los Rinches*. The only near injury on the Ranger side was a scratch wound received by the hack driver, Joe Inman, who was scorched by a bullet that narrowly missed his ribs. The Rangers' fire was deadly, and proved the military adage that the best defense is a vigorous offense.

The affair at Casitas was the first *rinchada* that had taken place since the early nineties, when the companies of Brooks and McNeel conducted a mop-up of the revolutionaires headed by Catarino Garza. McNelly's famous Red Ride of the seventies had also been forgotten. The country was again overrun by bad *hombres*. On the Mexican border, Spanish speaking inhabitants referred to any clash with Rangers that resulted in the death of bandits as a *rinchada*.

In the Casitas fight, Captain McDonald carried a semi-automatic rifle. It was the first weapon of that action put out by the Winchester Repeating Arms Company. His companions were armed with the favorite rifle of most old timers, which was the kind I always cherished. It was taken to the hearts and hands of the Rangers soon after the 44-40 became too short ranged for modern use. This grand old Winchester was the Model 1895 box magazine carbine, shooting the 30-40 Krag-Jorgensen cartridge. The Rangers called them Krags, or as some of the boys from East Texas pronounced it, "Craigs." Along the Rio Bravo del Norte, from El Paso to Brownsville, more justice has been dealt out with this trusty arm, than with all other rifles combined. Most Rangers of that time would have no other, and they are still hard to beat.

The captain could not be blamed, however, for constantly seeking new and improved guns. It was his duty to set the example, especially in the matter of procuring better weapons. These were the tools of their trade. The border Rangers were slower and more reluctant to place their stamp of approval on the new automatics which they jokingly dubbed "systematics." These seasoned riflemen preferred to stay with the proven arm and the one that had sustained them in many tight places. They feared that the automatics would fail to function in an emergency. This is exactly what happened in the Casitas fight. Captain McDonald's automatic Winchester jammed after the first shot. It went wild when the mules lunged as the shooting commenced. The boys using the slower but more reliable Krags accounted for all the enemy casualties.

In discussing the battle on the Rio Grande with his biographer, Captain McDonald did not utter an untruth. He said to Albert Bigelow Paine, "From where I was standing in the hack (The boys, being more agile and wiser in the ways of brush fighting, had already jumped to the ground.) I felt as if I could pick the buttons off their coats." Upon being pressed to give the number of the enemy falling to his automatic, the doughty captain would evasively answer in his most pleasing drawl, "Well, I don't guess I MISSED any of them." This statement was literally true. It is impossible to miss if your gun won't shoot.

A border character, Manuel Cabrero, was arrested for the murder of Judge Stanley Welch, and subsequently was indicted by the Starr County grand jury. On a change of venue, the case was transferred to De Witt County. When the Rio Grande contingent arrived in the pretty oak shaded town of Cuero, the number of fighting men on the streets brought back memories of the Taylor-Sutton feud. While the trial was in progress, a rumor reached the courthouse that Don Manuel Guerra had been killed in Starr County. Court was recessed and the

"Shot all to pieces. Everything quiet." This message was sent by Jim Dunaway (left). Pictured here with Captain Tom Ross and Ranger Milam Wright.

district judge, with biting sarcasm, remarked, "That would be impossible. All the killers are here at this trial. There is nobody left down
there to commit a murder."

When I was appointed a Ranger captain, the late Marshall Hicks
was the law partner of my chief endorser, Robert Lee Bobbitt. Mr.
Hicks had served in the State Senate and as mayor of San Antonio.
He was one of the "Immortal Forty" who swung the presidential nom-
ination to Woodrow Wilson at the Democratic National Convention in
Baltimore. One day in their Laredo office, the conversation turned to
Ranger captains. Senator Hicks said, "One of the best stories about Bill
McDonald is little known. It happened in Washington." My friend
continued, "An unworthy applicant for a high Federal position had
secured strong endorsements, hurdled every obstacle and appeared certain to get the job. Mr. Wilson's real friends had exhausted every means
in their power to block the obnoxious candidate. After everything else
had failed, I suggested that they take the matter up with Captain
McDonald, who was in high favor with the President. When informed that the objectionable aspirant was about to get the place,
Captain Bill snorted and said, 'Is he fixing to appoint that scoundrel?

I'll give the Old Man hell about that'." President Wilson showed his high regard for his Ranger friend and protector in many ways. One of these gestures was to invite him and his nephew, Colonel S. Jerry Houghton, to the wedding of his daughter at the White House.

The deadly manner in which buckshot has been used in East Texas is illustrated in the case of Ranger Jim Dunaway, one of Captain Bill McDonald's Rangers. In 1907, he was on duty at Groveton, in Trinity County. Dunaway and the local county attorney were walking to the courthouse when they were fired on from an office window. Their assailant used a shotgun loaded with buckshot. The lawyer was fatally wounded by the blast, and the Ranger received a number of the "blue whistlers" in his back.

Adjutant General J. O. Newton had instructed Jim to report by wire any happening of importance. Although badly wounded, Dunaway's first thought was obedience to orders rather than his own need of medical attention. Calling for pencil and paper, he dispatched a telegram to Austin that read something like this: "I am shot all to pieces. Everything quiet." Jim's classic message, with variations usually occurring at each retelling, has become famous in Ranger annals. It has been widely quoted in camps from the Red River to the Rio Grande.

Ranger Dunaway was summoned as a State's witness when the case of the Groveton assassin was called for trial in Houston, where it had been moved on a change of venue. He met the man who had shot him, face to face in a Main Street drug store. Dunaway knocked him down. The ambusher started yelling at the top of his voice, "Murder! Murder!" The Ranger scathingly remarked, "The boot is on the other foot now. You didn't holler murder when you were pouring those buckshot into my back in Groveton."

In later years I served on the border with Jim Dunaway and knew him well. He had one of his thumbs shot off in a night battle with a band of smugglers on the banks of the Rio Grande. Captain Frank Hamer, who at that time was a special officer in Houston, was present when Dunaway booted his attacker, and gave me an eyewitness account of the affair. The owner of the pharmacy changed its name to the Ranger Drug Store, and it went by that title for many years.

Sam McKenzie was deeply steeped in the ways of the border and its people. His Spanish was as good as his English. With rifle and pistol he was one of the fastest men in the Service. As an orphan child in Live Oak County, he was adopted by a kindly lady, and had taken her name. This phase of his life was used by Rex Beach in his novel *The Heart of the Sunset*. It dealt with ranch life in Southwest Texas, and one of the principal characters was a Ranger. Sam never married, and was very thrifty. He saved most of his wages even when the Rangers were paid thirty dollars per month. This money was loaned out at interest and wisely invested. At the time of his death he had accumulated a comfortable stake. His reluctance to unbelt was famous all along the Rio Grande. One of his comrades remarked, "If Sam was as slow on the draw as he was in picking up a dinner check, he would have been killed long ago."

In common with most old time Rangers, his language was pointed and picturesque. When a pistol was cocked, he said that it was "roostered back" and he called a Winchester a "gunchester." When one of the border bravos appeared on the plaza with his sombrero tipped at a rakish angle, the veteran remarked, "When one of those *hombres* wears his hat 'ace-duece' like that, it's a sign that he's up to no good."

Sam was wounded in 1915 by a man suspected of smuggling. The fight took place in Mission, and a bullet passed through his chest, barely missing his heart. It was fired from a Colt single action .45 frame pistol, that used 32-20 Winchester cartridges. The range was so close that the soft point did not expand, and he soon recovered. Sam had the bullet made into a watch charm, which he wore for the rest of his life.

The only person immune from McKenzie's stinginess was his foster mother. In her old age he delighted in trying to repay her for the kindness she bestowed on him as a boy. They are buried side by side. To his dying day, Sam honored the name of his old captain, Bill McDonald.

Blaze Delling resigned from the Rangers to become a United States immigration inspector. Like many other excellent men, the better pay offered by the Federal Government lured him away from the Service. Most of his time was spent in and around Laredo, where he died several years ago. Mr. Delling told me many stories about Captain McDonald, and always held him in the highest esteem.

Shortly before his passing, I enjoyed a pleasant visit with the late Carl T. Ryan at Orange Grove in Jim Wells County. He was a native of Fort Bend County, and enlisted in Captain McDonald's company in

1900. After retiring from the Rangers, he became sheriff of Cameron County. His mind and memory were perfectly clear. He supplied me with many valuable details about the Rangers.

Ex-Ranger Ryan was a participant in the episodes at Edna and at Brownsville, and his account of them was first hand. Just as Captain Marsh had provided a rear guard when he entered the post at Fort Concho, Captain McDonald deployed Rangers Ryan, McKenzie and Delling for the same purpose when he entered Fort Brown.

Mr. Ryan was most sympathetic with my determination to write a book about the Rangers. His eyes lit up at all mention of Captain Mc-Donald. "I used to tell him," said the veteran, "Cap, you're going to get all of us killed, the way you cuss out strikers and mobs." " 'Don't worry, Ryan,' " he would say. " 'Just remember my motto.' "

My conversation with the venerable Texan confirmed the impression I always had about the old boys who served under McDonald. After riding the river, quelling riots, mobs and feuds at his side, as well as burning a considerable amount of powder at his orders, all of them cherished his memory. Chief among these admirers was Carl T. Ryan, last man of Company C, Texas Rangers, when it was commanded by Captain William Jesse McDonald.

Old Rangers everywhere trust that Saint Peter and his Aides who ramrod that glorified Range beyond the Pearly Gates, will keep in mind the main gate at Fort Brown. In case any rioting demons get to raising the devil in Hades, all they have to do is order a charge by Captain Bill. He will soon quell them, and the only weapon he will need is a bucket of water.

Chapter 38
JOHN H. ROGERS

Rogers, Brooks, Hughes and McDonald, by virtue of their long, outstanding, and unhampered service, aptly have been called the "Four Great Captains." In this quartet of contemporary commanders, only John Harris Rogers could claim Texas as his birthplace. There were sound reasons for this minority of native Texans holding top rank in the Rangers. It was due to the sparse population of the state, and to the turmoil found in many of its counties as an aftermath of the Civil War.

For several decades following that fratricidal struggle, Texas was plagued by a series of deadly feuds. They involved many local families and their clannish kinsmen. The suppression of these conflicts was a major objective of the Rangers. Each adjutant general felt that the companies engaged in this task should be composed of men who were total strangers to all factions. Although he was a native Texan, Captain L. H. McNelly showed marked preference for daring youths who were born in other states. He went so far as to enlist three bold lads from the British Isles.

The incomparable McNelly, even at the risk of offending life-long friends and neighbors, determined to take every precaution. He did not want any of his Rangers to be entangled in alliances of kin or friendship. McNelly's hand picked company, in the captain's illness commanded by Lieutenant Lee (Red) Hall, broke up the widespread Taylor-Sutton feud in DeWitt and adjoining counties.

Company "C" Texas Rangers taken at Colorado City early in the present century. Seated left to right: Capt. John H. Rogers, Ranger Will Burwell and unidentified City Marshal. Standing: Rangers A. Y. (Augie) Old, John Hinnant and Gene McMeans.

Major John B. Jones, commander of the Frontier Battalion, likewise was confronted with the problem of native versus imported personnel. With special interest, I have studied the life and service of this eminent gentleman. He and I are the only Rangers in the history of our state who have been appointed Adjutant General of Texas. This officer, up until 1935, was in sole charge of the Rangers, and responsible for their administration only to the governor.

In the fall of 1875, a feud between German settlers and native born Americans broke out in Mason County. It soon reached such proportions as to be called a war. Several murders had been committed by each faction, and a general outbreak appeared to be imminent. The anti-German party was led by a former member of the Frontier Battalion named Scott Cooley. It came to the notice of Major Jones that some of his Rangers were in sympathy with their erstwhile comrade. There was also reason to believe that they acted as spies and kept the former Ranger informed about the movements of the company. This accounted for the fact that he had not been captured.

Absence of telegraphic communication on the frontier at that time made it impossible to wire headquarters for instructions or advice. No courier could make the ride to Austin and get back in time to be of help. Major Jones saw that the emergency called for immediate and drastic action. He also realized that full responsibility for any decisions made would rest solely on his shoulders.

Jones ordered the company to form in a single line, so that he could look each man squarely in the face. Striding up and down the column, he addressed them in forceful and eloquent language. His choice of words showed why he had won statewide fame as an orator in addition to renown as a fighting man. His admonition was a masterpiece of understanding, justice and firmness. From long experience on the fringes of civilization and in the Confederate Army, Major Jones understood the adventurous natures of his men. These intrepid riders had originally been picked for their proven courage, horsemanship and skill with firearms. If each one had not been, in the language of their kind, "game to the core," he would never have joined the Frontier Battalion.

Major Jones showed due consideration for those Rangers who were bound by ties of blood to the feudists, or felt a sense of loyalty, however mistaken it might be, to their former comrade. He was reluctant to place the stigma of a dishonorable discharge on the names of those otherwise good men, which summary dismissal from the Service would entail. Nevertheless, the Major held with his former commander, General Robert E. Lee, that "Duty is the most sublime word in the English language." Nothing could shake him from this belief. In his speech, the Major reminded them of the oath taken by each man. It was "to defend the State of Texas against all enemies whomsoever," and he warned them that he would brook no dereliction of duty from those who elected to remain.

Their commander then offered them a proposition never made before or since to a company of Rangers. He said, "If every man who for any reason whatsoever is not willing to pursue Scott Cooley to the bitter end will step out of ranks, I will give him an honorable discharge and he can quit the Service clean." Fifteen Rangers out of the forty took one pace forward. As a result of Major Jones' words and action, the men who stayed renewed their determination to halt the feud, regardless of whom they might be called upon to arrest.

The personnel problems encountered in the seventies by Major Jones and Captain McNelly furnish the background and reason for an amazing situation in the Service. At the turn of the century, the sole native Texan in command of a Ranger company was Captain John H. Rogers. Since that date, however, some good men have grown up in the Lone Star State; feuds have subsided and it is no longer necessary nor the part of wisdom to import our Rangers.

Captain Rogers was one of the two Ranger leaders whose precepts and examples filled me with an ambition to join their organization. When he and the members of Company C rode through the streets of Cotulla or out to my father's ranch on Espio Creek in La Salle County, they made a profound impression on my youthful mind.

They always seemed to have the best mounts that could be raised in a country noted for its good horses. Their riding outfits were splendid examples of the saddle makers' art, with neat flower designs carved by craftsmen who learned their trade in Mexico. This hand tooling of the Ranger's trappings was not altogether a matter of vanity. They had learned that only the best leather will take a good stamp job. Furthermore, the men knew that fast pistol holsters, on which their lives might depend at any time, could not be made from inferior material. Forty-five calibre six-shooters hung from cartridge filled scout belts and Winchesters in scabbards nestled under one stirrup leather completed the picture of frontier manhood.

It made these horsemen the idols of every Texas ranch boy. When dismounted, the suntanned Rangers stood straight as ramrods in their high topped boots and looked everyone squarely in the face. Captain Rogers' level gaze was especially penetrating. It bored into a man's soul and caused criminals who came under his scrutiny to claim that he was "gimlet eyed." They were almost without exception men of pleasing personalities, good manners, and they showed deep consideration for women and children.

The Ranger's easy, natural seat in the saddle was a fine example of equestrian balance and relaxation. It was not the sloppy slouch of the moving picture cowboy nor the heavy horse-killing squat of the rodeo rider. Without the least bit of stiffness, they sat straight on their mounts, leaning slightly forward. In this position the rider can help, or lift, his horse instead of sitting like dead weight on the animal's back. Riding in this fashion will not cause saddle galls or kidney sores, and it enables a horse to go a long way after a poorly ridden one has played out. Cavalry officers believed that the acme of perfection in equitation was the West Point seat. The genuine Ranger seat combines the erectness of this style with the modes of Pony Express and "long" riders of the West, Mexican *vaqueros,* range cowboys and jockeys, utilizing the best features of each method.

Captain Rogers possessed one trait which set him apart from his contemporary commanders in that he was a deeply religious man. Captain Brooks once told me that the memory of his dear old Presbyterian mother had sustained him in many battles. Captain Hughes sometimes taught a Sunday school class, and Captain McDonald, in characteristic language, claimed to be a brother-in-law of the Church. Writers of wild West fiction would be amazed if they could have heard Captain Rogers scold a miscreant or seen him in a deadly gunfight. Instead of bellowing a string of profanity in keeping with the dime novel concept of a he-man, Captain Rogers was wont to say in a soft voice, "My, my, you ought not to act like that." The man receiving this mild reproof would likely be getting on his feet after having been knocked down, or, as they used to say in Cotulla, "having a horn slipped" by a six-shooter in the deft hand of the ministerial appearing captain. He and his methods of dealing with bullies always reminded me of the philosophy of Theodore Roosevelt. The Rough Rider's motto, "speak softly and carry a big stick," with the Texas version of the cudgel being a .45 Colt pistol, was the creed of Captain Rogers many years before Teddy charged up San Juan Hill.

Among pioneer officers on the frontier, "bending" a gun over a man's head was standard procedure. Various writers of Western stories relate in their thrillers that "Obnoxious Oscar knocked Caseknife Charlie in the head with the butt of his heavy revolver." In real life the blow was never struck in this fashion. No one but the rankest tenderfoot would change ends with a pistol or relinquish his hold on the stock.

The six-shooter favored by most Rangers and Western sheriffs was the Colt .45 single action, with a five and one-half inch barrel which extended three-quarters of an inch beyond the shell ejector. When this overhang struck a man's head as a result of the "bend," he would fall like a poll axed steer. Widely publicized marshals in the terminal towns

on the Chisholm Trail applied this inhospitable treatment to celebrating cowboys and called it "buffaloing."

Like other drastic tactics, the practice had its good and bad features.
Judicious use of his pistol as a club would sometimes enable an officer
to subdue a desperado without shooting him, but at the hands of an overbearing man, it could quickly become an act of wanton brutality. Captain Rogers gave his men strict orders not to hit a man with a gun unless it was the only alternative to killing him.

During the trial of a Negro, who was charged with the murder of a
white man in Nacogdoches County, a mob formed and attempted
to take the prisoner. A former sheriff led the would-be lynchers.
He announced that he was going to rush past the prohibited line.
Captain Rogers told him in a quiet voice to stop. When the ex-
sheriff tried to push by, Rogers "bent" his six-shooter over the man's
head. Two of the Rangers who were there are still living, J. C. (Doc)
White and John L. Dibrell. On a recent visit with these veterans I was
privileged to hear again a participant's account of the affair. "Captain
Rogers always cautioned us to use just enough force to carry out our
duties, but no more," said ex-Ranger White. "He said he only intended
to 'tap' the ex-sheriff on the head with his six-shooter. The blood flew
from his scalp. I said, 'Cap if that's what you call tapping a man I
would hate to see one who was really hit'."

During one of the low periods in Ranger history, a newly appointed
captain explained the "technique" of "pistol whipping" to a newspaper
writer, who gave the travesty wide publicity. This fellow, who was an
imported product, used a double action pistol with which the real
"bend" cannot be executed. Furthermore, he used very poor taste and
no judgment at all in airing an unpleasant and seldom used measure.

Captain Rogers was born in Guadalupe County, Texas, October 19,
1863. On the 5th day of September, 1882, he enlisted in Company B
of the Rangers, which was commanded by Captain S. A. McMurray.
He served for something over a year, then resigned and returned to his
home near Kingsbury. Several months later young Rogers re-joined the
Rangers, this time in Company F under Captain Joe Shely. Lieutenant Will Scott was second in command. W. T. (Brack) Morris, who
subsequently became sheriff of Karnes County and was killed there by
Gregorio Cortez, served as sergeant. In 1889, Rogers was advanced to

sergeant, and on October 19, 1892, he was promoted to the rank of Captain by Governor James Stephen Hogg.

When young Rogers reported to Captain Shely for duty, Company F was stationed at Cotulla, in La Salle County, where violence fully justified the constant presence of Rangers. This town was used as a testing ground for new Rangers, and with civic pride numerous men who lived in the region did their utmost to sustain its reputation for truculence. When a recruit proved to the killers, cow thieves and other outlaws who harbored there, that to him they "looked like thirty cents in Mexican money," he had won his spurs. After a tour of duty in this rough and rowdy pueblo, all other service, regardless of how rugged it might be, had the earmarks of a vacation.

The veteran Ed Dubose, who served under Captain Rogers in Cotulla, now lives in San Patricio County and has been my friend for more than forty years. His keen mind and retentive memory have enabled me to clear up several points in Ranger history. *Tio Eduardo* was one of the best pistol shots I ever saw, and he participated in numerous border battles, both as a Ranger and mounted customs inspector. He recently told me a story that illustrates the cheapness of human life in the early days of Cotulla. The ex-Ranger said, "A homemade coffin had just been built at the lumber yard for the latest victim of a shooting scrape. The carpenter had completed his job and nailed down the lid when a boy rode up on his pony and said he was sorry he arrived too late to view the remains. The lumberman replied, "Just wait a few days, sonny, there will be another killing by that time."

On one occasion when Captain Rogers was absent from Cotulla, Ranger Dubose and another good friend of mine, the late Woodlief Thomas, went into Capp's Saloon for a few drinks. They had gotten pretty well organized when County Judge Knaggs, who wore the only stovepipe hat between San Antonio and Laredo, walked in front of the saloon. The target offered by his two-story headpiece proved irresistible. The roistering pair ventilated it with .45 calibre bullet holes, against the peace of the state and the dignity of the judge.

Captain Rogers was in San Diego attending district court, and Ranger Dubose knew him to be an exponent of the axiom, "Liquor and six-shooters won't mix." He resigned from the Service by wire, packed his outfit and rode back to Alice where he had lived for several years. Mr.

Dubose relates that a few days after his arrival, Captain John R. Hughes enlisted him in the renowned Company D. Captain Hughes did not permit drinking among his men, but recognized that Dubose's knowledge of the country, command of the Spanish language, and fine marksmanship more than made up for any indiscretions he might have committed.

The maltreatment of Judge Knagg's high hat figures in O. Henry's story entitled "The Marquis and Miss Sally." Will Porter (O. Henry) spent considerable time on the Dull ranch near Cotulla which was managed by his fellow North Carolinian, Captain Lee (Red) Hall. This ex-Ranger supplied background for several of O. Henry's ranch and Ranger stories.

Brigadier General Pleas Blair Rogers of the United States Army was born in Alice, Texas, at the Rogers home, which also served as Ranger headquarters. At that time, Alice was in Nueces County. After serving with distinction in both world wars, he retired and now lives in Virginia. He and his sister, Mrs. Lucile Rogers Reeves of San Antonio, have been most helpful to me. In response to my request, they sent me a memorandum which they called "The Combined Recollections of Lucile and Pleas." I gratefully reproduce their letter with a few minor changes:

We will not try to outline the official accomplishments of Captain Rogers for they are matters of record. You and one or two other surviving ex-Rangers know more than we do. The following things come to mind. They are indications of our father's character. He was born and reared in very modest circumstances, and his formal education was limited. At the age of nineteen he joined the Texas Rangers and served intermittently from 1883 to 1930. He resigned his captaincy in the Rangers when Oscar B. Colquitt was elected on the anti-prohibition platform. Father was firmly convinced that whiskey was to blame for the majority of all crimes, and he wanted no part of an administration that was friendly to the liquor traffic. It would have been particularly distasteful for him to serve under a Governor whose middle initial was jocularly said to stand for "Budweiser." In 1913 President Woodrow Wilson appointed him United States Marshal for the Western District of Texas, and he held this position for eight years. Father was once more placed in command of his cherished Company C of the Rangers by Governor Dan Moody, who became Chief Executive in 1927. He served in this capacity until 1930, when he passed away at the Scott & White hospital in Temple.

He saved a part of his salary each month and made sound investments in upper Rio Grande Valley lands near El Paso. When my father died he left an estate that was sufficient to provide a modest living for my mother the balance of her life. He gave ten percent of his income to the Church on a scheduled plan, made contributions to special appeals and helped at least one niece, besides his own children, to get a college education.

His principal interest outside of the Ranger Service was his religion. He joined the Presbyterian Church after he met my mother, the former Harriet Randolph Burwell of Cotulla, Texas, and lived his faith from that day forward. He was an elder in every church of which he became a member for as far back as I can remember. He was a total abstainer from liquor and I never heard him utter an oath of any kind. When traveling on his own time, father would get off the train at the first stop on Sunday morning, attend Sunday school, morning and evening worship and then continue on his journey. He was very fond of smoking cigars, but when his first son was born he gave up the habit in order not to set him a bad example. When he caught his son smoking at the age of sixteen, the reason for his abstinence was removed.

. . . Next to his faith, modesty was probably father's outstanding characteristic. When not actually on a scout, he wore simple business suits with his pistol under his coat. He had a soft spoken voice and was modest in his demeanor. He almost never spoke of his experiences and when he did they sounded very simple and unexciting, although on two occasions, my mother was notified that he had been killed. She did not learn until the next day that he had only been wounded. During the smallpox epidemic of 1899 in Laredo, when he was shot through the shoulder, the newspaper headlines stated that "Captain Rogers fell to the ground full of lead, bleeding and unconscious."

During the last of the nineteenth century the Texas Rangers had established a reputation for hard riding, straight shooting, two fisted and efficient peace officers. They made this reputation dealing with the murderers and fugitives from justice who gathered in that neutral strip of land between the Nueces River and the Rio Grande. These outlaws were godless men and had little respect for law enforcement officers in general, and even less for a Sunday school teaching Ranger captain. That was the situation in Cotulla when Captain John H. Rogers received orders to move his company there and restore order. The usual shooting started in the corner saloon the first Saturday night after his arrival. When the smoke cleared away, the ruffians were in jail and the keys to the calaboose were in the pocket of the Sunday school teacher. By this shrewd move, the culprits were assured of spending a long overdue night in the bastile, instead of the customary release through a writ of habeas corpus. The Ranger captain who had been the butt of countless saloon jokes prior to his arrival was now in supreme command.

In 1884, Lieutenant Scott and a detachment of Company F were ordered to Brown County, where the conflict between land owners and fence cutters had grown into a shooting war. Young Rogers received his baptism of fire when two of the vandals were killed in a fight with the Rangers. He saw further service of this kind in Coleman County, where the opposition to barbed wire was so well organized that Adjutant General King made a personal inspection of the situation. In 1887, Ranger Rogers was severely wounded in the sanguinary Conner fight which took place in Sabine County on the Louisiana state line. An account of this battle appears in the chapter on Captain Brooks, who was also wounded on that occasion. When I asked Captain Rogers for some details, he replied with characteristic truthfulness and reticence, "Sterling, I was shot down early in the fight and can tell very little about it."

During the Mexican revolution fomented by Catarino Garza, the Texas Rangers worked in close cooperation with the Army. State and Federal forces combined their efforts in the enforcement of our neutrality laws. Garza was a pseudo-editor who published an inflammatory Spanish language paper in Palito Blanco, Texas. This Mexican settlement was at that time in the southwestern part of Nueces County, just on the line of Duval. Through a reorganization in 1912, it is now located in Jim Wells County. Palito Blanco was used by Garza as his headquarters and base of operations.

The *pronunciados,* as he called his followers, were recruited among the idlers and malcontents from both sides of the Rio Grande. Duval, Starr and Zapata Counties were used as their rendezvous and training ground. In this region, fully ninety-eight per cent of the inhabitants were of Mexican extraction. This fact made it comparatively easy for Garza to assemble his band without detection.

Garza made his first move on November 15, 1890. His force crossed the Rio Grande and laid waste to the Mexican town of San Ygnacio, killing many of its inhabitants. The *insurrectos* then recrossed the border into Texas, where they were safe from pursuit by the army of President Diaz.

The Mexican Government dispatched a sharp protest to Washington. Secretary of State James G. Blaine called on the Governor of Texas to use every means at his command to apprehend the revolutionists. Governor Lawrence Sullivan Ross, himself a former Ranger, immediately complied with this request.

He ordered Company E, commanded by Captain J. S. McNeel, and Company F, under Captain J. A. Brooks, to proceed without delay to the troubled area. They were instructed to render every possible assistance to the Army. This plan proved to be of mutual benefit. The Rangers rounded up many border characters, who in addition to breaching neutrality laws, had violated numerous State statutes. The region was a fertile field for this operation, for it harbored many killers and livestock rustlers, as well as countless smugglers. John H. Rogers was the sergeant of Company F.

The Third United States Cavalry, stationed at Fort McIntosh in Laredo, was commanded by Colonel Albert Payson Morrow. He dispatched Company C under Captain Harding down the Rio Grande to Carrizo, which is now Zapata. They were ordered to preserve the neutrality of American soil. The revolutionists ambushed a patrol from this company, killing Corporal Charles H. Edstrom.

Captain Allen Walker, with whom I served as deputy sheriff in Hidalgo County, was a private in Company C of the Third Cavalry. He later commanded a company of Philippine Scouts. For gallantry displayed in a battle with Garza's men near El Randado, he was awarded the Congressional Medal of Honor. Captain Walker spent many years in Laredo, where he was a deputy United States marshal. He would not talk to anybody he did not like, but we were good friends. He gave me a detailed account of the engagement, and related the circumstances under which he won the most coveted of all military decorations.

When the Army and the Rangers were conducting their campaign against Garza in the early nineties, the terrain was more open than it is today. However, many areas were overgrown by dense chaparral. These thickets provided ideal cover for ambuscades, and were well suited to the tactics favored by guerillas. The threat of night assaults on their camps was constantly faced by the American soldiers. In an effort to lessen this danger, some of the cavalrymen were allowed to carry shotguns.

Under the rules of civilized warfare, which were sadly out of place in this campaign, the War Department could not arm soldiers with these lethal weapons. Therefore, the enlisted men of Company C, from their mess fund, bought several ten gauge, double barreled shotguns. Officially, they were supposed to be used as fowling pieces. Unofficially, however, when they were used to exterminate midnight marauders, the commanding officer gratefully winked at the infraction. The country was teeming with deer, and all cartridges brought along by the soldiers were loaded with buckshot. One of the men entrusted with a shotgun was Private Allen Walker.

On the night of December 30, 1891, a bunch of the Garza rebels made a sneak attack on the bivouac of a detachment which included Walker. He used his shotgun with such deadly effect that most of the raiders were killed and the others put to flight. His comrades were saved, and his heroism was suitably rewarded by Congress.

Don Porfirio Diaz succeeded in suppressing Catarino's attempt to overthrow his government, but sporadic fighting continued on both sides of the Rio Grande. Garza was never captured. He boarded a ship and escaped to Honduras. Soon after arriving there, he became involved in a revolution, and was killed in a battle at Boca del Toro. The seeds of revolt Garza had sown on the lower border yielded a bitter harvest. After the lazy and exciting life of an *insurrecto,* most of his followers looked with disdain on any form of honest toil.

The rebels integrated with the inhabitants on the American side of the river, where they gave considerable trouble for several years. Governor James Stephen Hogg succeeded Governor Ross in 1891. He carried on his predecessor's plan to wipe out banditry in the counties along the Rio Grande. The Rangers did a thorough mopping up job on the remaining revolutionists.

Two bravo brothers, Juan and Pancho Ramirez, while loafing in an outlying *cantina,* boasted that they were the ones who had killed Corporal Edstrom. Sergeant John H. Rogers and a detachment from Company F made several scouts after them. On May 30, 1892, the Rangers finally ran onto the soldier slayers. In the ensuing fight, Juan was killed and Pancho escaped in the dense chaparral.

In December, 1892, Rangers "Kid" Rogers, brother of the sergeant, and George Bigford killed Juan and Gabriel Longoria. These brothers were notorious border characters. They divided their time between stealing livestock in Texas, and fighting for Catarino Garza in Mexico.

Captain Brooks and McNeel, in rendering accounts of their activities, made this statement:

> A large number of alleged revolutionists were arrested and turned over to United States officers, but are not reported here. Company E encountered a force of thirty rebels on January 4, 1892. They immediately fled, leaving twenty horses and saddles behind.

I was well acquainted with several Rangers who participated in the scouts against Garza. These included Captain Brooks, Captain Rogers, Sam Lane and Charles Premont. From them I learned many details of the campaign. I have on numerous occasions ridden horseback over practically every foot of ground they covered. The history of the Third Cavalry is very familiar to me. I own copies of most adjutant general's reports for that period, and have access to the others. They show that Sergeant John H. Rogers, soon to be promoted to captain, had a leading part in putting down the Garza revolution.

He was again wounded in Laredo during the smallpox epidemic of 1899, while assisting State Health Officer Blount in the enforcement of quarantine regulations. Some of the Latin population opposed compulsory vaccination, and offered armed resistance to it. While dispersing a group of these people, the Rangers were fired on, and Captain Rogers was disabled by a rifle bullet. The man who shot the captain was immediately killed by Ranger A. Y. Old, and another rioter was killed by the youngest Ranger in the company, Creed Taylor. Captain W. L. Wright often said, "Creed Taylor saved the day in Laredo."

Augie Old was one of the best men in the Service. Like his captain, he was deeply religious. He was as staunch a Methodist as Rogers was a Presbyterian. These Christian Rangers were absolutely without fear. Their matchless devotion to duty was inspired by implicit faith in the Almighty. Woe be unto the misguided ruffian who mistook their piety for weakness. He was in for a rude awakening, if he awoke at all. Rogers and Old heeded the Biblical admonition to "turn the other cheek" but between changes they would either shoot or knock the devil out of their adversaries.

A. Y. Old entered the Methodist ministry after his service with the Rangers. I would travel a long way to hear him preach. Captain Rogers never fully recovered from the wound he received in Laredo, and his arm was shortened by the removal of a piece of bone. This seriously interfered with his rifle shooting, and he was forced to use a specially constructed Winchester. It was one with an off-set stock, as he was no longer able to align the sights of a standard weapon. He asked no odds, however, and to the end of his career carried out every assignment in spite of his handicap.

About the turn of the century, the Townsend-Reece feud in Colorado County made a fair bid to rival the Taylor-Sutton vendetta of the seventies. Rangers had been ordered to Columbus at various times and their efforts to keep down trouble were successful. However, the danger of renewed outbreaks posed a constant threat to the peace of the community. Captain Rogers and Ranger A. Y. Old had been sent to the troubled spot by the governor, who felt that their presence would have a quieting effect on the feudists.

Light Townsend, nephew and namesake of the family leader, served under me in the Rangers for nearly six years. When I was captain of Company D, he was sergeant, and after my appointment as adjutant general, I promoted him to the rank of captain. This sketch is interpolated to show that he and I were well acquainted. Captain Townsend always enjoyed telling the circumstances under which, as a youth, he met Captain Rogers.

During one of the lulls in the feud, he rode in to Columbus. Naturally, he had on a pistol, which was concealed by his coat. Experience had taught the Rangers that the best way to keep peace was to disarm both factions. They carried out this policy with strict impartiality. The future captain had just tied his horse to one of the beautiful liveoaks that grow on the square when a man of benevolent mien approached him. This kindly gentleman, whom Light took to be a preacher, spoke to him in one of the mildest voices he had ever heard. He said, "My friend, I believe you are young Light Townsend?" "Yes, sir," replied the youth. Captain Townsend's story, as he related it to me was as follows: "And before I knew what was happening, he had my gun and I was in jail." This youthful encounter with Captain Rogers did not embitter Light Townsend against the Rangers. On the contrary, he determined to join the organization headed by men who could handle a bad situation in such a calm, tactful manner.

One of the worst all-around desperados who ever shot and stole his way into Texas was Hill Loftis, alias Tom Ross. He was a natural born outlaw, but it may not have been his fault. His elongated skull probably caused some pressure on the brain, and might account for his vicious tendencies. The Fugitive List, known to Rangers as the "Black Book," the "Preferred List" and the "Ranger's Bible," carried the following in its 1900 edition:

> Wanted for highway robbery, Hill Loftis. Age about 32. height 5 feet 9 inches, weight 160 pounds. Has a very peculiarly shaped head, being very long behind with a high forehead. Occupation, cowboy. Probably in New Mexico. Indicted in 1896. Reward by sheriff of Wilbarger County.

The size of his mis-shapen head with its shaggy hair, and the loose skin of his throat, which resembled the dewlap of a cow brute, caused some to call him "Buffalo Head."

An early companion of Loftis was the bloodthirsty Red Buck Waightman of Indian Territory infamy, who was so wantonly murderous that neither the Dalton nor Doolin gangs would let him ride with them. On a freezing day in 1896, Hill Loftis, Red Buck, Elmore Lewis and Joe Beckham were barricaded in a dugout north of the Red River. A detachment of Captain Bill McDonald's company under Sergeant W. J. L. Sullivan charged this crude fortification at a gallop. The desperados responded with rifle fire that killed all of the Ranger's horses. It was so cold that Sullivan's men could scarcely work the levers of their Winchesters, but they gave the criminals a thorough shelling, then walked to a Waggoner line camp about twenty miles away. Here the Rangers secured horses and went back to the scene of the fight. They found Beckham dead and the others gone. Beckham had once been sheriff of a Panhandle county. Lewis was later hanged by a mob in Wichita Falls.

Red Buck returned to his old haunts in the Territory, where he was soon killed in another dugout near Arapaho, by a posse under Deputy United States Marshal Chris Madsen. This officer was a Danish soldier of fortune who reached a ripe old age and died peacefully in spite of many battles with Indians and outlaws. He served under United States Marshal Emory D. Nix, and with ex-Texas Ranger Heck Thomas and Bill Tilghman made up a famous trio known in the Territories as the "Three Guardsmen." During the Spanish-American War, Madsen was regimental quartermaster sergeant of Roosevelt's Rough Riders. In their latter years, I was acquainted with all of these gentlemen except Captain Thomas.

Hill Loftis went back on the dodge, which might well be called his natural state. He had spent the greater part of his adult life running from the law. His favorite range was along the Texas-New Mexico border where he could skip from one side of the state line to the other as the occasion demanded.

In June, 1904, Sheriff Charles Tom of Terry County learned that Loftis was working on a ranch in the sand hills, near the New Mexico line. He requested Captain Rogers to help him arrest the badly wanted man. Rangers have always realized that pistols are of no value in a long range fight. They seldom leave town, and never go on a scout, without taking their rifles. Captain Rogers knew this as well as any man in the world, and for many years I was unable to understand why he had gone out after an outlaw of Loftis' stripe without his Winchester. The explanation was furnished by my pioneer cowman friend, the late Billy Connell, who witnessed the incident. He told me that the sheriff persuaded Captain Rogers to leave his carbine. Tom hoped to make Loftis think the approaching horsemen were cattle buyers coming to the ranch on business. By this ruse, they expected to get up close to the desperado before he discovered their identity.

The wary cow thief had been jumped by officers many times before, however, and at a single glance he saw through the trick. He got his own Winchester, ran around a sand hill and laid in ambush for the captain. When he rode by, Loftis shot his bridle reins in two, the bullet grazing the horse's jaw. The terrified animal reared up and threw Captain Rogers off in the sand. The outlaw ran up and covered the half-stunned officer. He then took his pistol and declared that he was going to kill him. Captain Rogers knew that he was dealing with a depraved criminal who would kill without the slightest hesitation, and one who held a special grudge against Rangers. Speaking in a calm voice he told his captor that he would only bring more trouble on himself by killing a Ranger, as the deed would be quickly avenged. The captain also told Loftis that the pistol meant a great deal to him, as it was a present from the men of his company. He asked the desperado to give it back. Loftis finally acceded to this request, and after taking all the cartridges out of the cylinder, he threw the gun in a sand hill. He then rode off toward New Mexico.

Captain Rogers' official account of this affair as contained in his report to Adjutant General John A. Hulen is as follows:

> In June, 1904, while scouting in the plains country near the line of New Mexico, I made an unsuccessful attempt to arrest Hill Loftis, alias Tom Ross; he ran out of shooting distance from me, thereby avoiding arrest. Later in the day he lay in wait and waylaid me, shooting my horse in the jaw, getting the drop on me with a big Winchester, while I had only a pistol. I was completely in his power; and it looked as if he would kill me in spite of all I could do or say. This party is an old time robber of a hard gang.

After his crimes were barred by limitation or all adverse witnesses had died, Loftis returned to Texas under the name of Tom Ross. He began to traffic and trade in livestock, but continued his old habit of ignoring such trifles as titles, bills of sale or brands. H. L. Roberson and Dave Allison, two field inspectors of the Texas and Southwestern Cattle Raisers Association, were hot on his trail. They had secured enough evidence against him and an accomplice to have both of them indicted for cattle theft. The association officers, both of whom held Texas Ranger commissions, were in Seminole for the purpose of presenting their findings to the Gaines County grand jury.

On the night before that inquisitorial body was to convene, Roberson and Allison were seated in the lobby of the local hotel. Mrs. Martha

Plummer Roberson, who had accompanied her husband to Seminole, was upstairs in their room. Suddenly, the door was pushed open by a third man; Loftis and the other cow thief opened fire on the inspectors with a shotgun and six-shooters. Allison was instantly killed and a bullet hit Roberson's pistol stock, putting the weapon out of commission. Dave Allison was a veteran brand man but was not the equal of his companion as a gunfighter. Hod Roberson was more than a match for the rustlers in anything like an even break. With any chance whatsoever he would have killed at least one, and probably both of them. Mrs. Roberson heard the shooting and rushed downstairs. The gallant lady shot at the assassins with a small automatic pistol and hit them both. The accomplice was wounded, but Ross' belt buckle deflected the light bullet, thereby saving his worthless life.

Tom Ross was brought to trial in Lubbock for the double murder. Captain Rogers was subpoenaed as a witness for the state. On this occasion the veteran Ranger proved that he possessed great moral as well as physical courage. He refused to say a word against the defendant, stating that Loftis, now called Ross, once had him at his mercy and that he owed his life to the outlaw. Gratitude was one of the greatest virtues in the code and creed of Captain Rogers. Ross was sentenced to serve thirty years in the penitentiary, but soon escaped from the walls in Huntsville. Rumor has it that he received financial and political aid from powerful people Hill Loftis had served in bygone days. He fled to Canada, but later came down into Montana, where his experience soon earned him a job as a ranch foreman. After working a few months, his quarrelsome nature and hard drinking caused the owner to discharge him. The ranchman prudently refrained from doing this in person. He employed his new foreman in town, and sent a letter by him advising Ross that he was fired. Upon reading the note, Tom flew into a rage, jerked out his pistol and killed the bearer on the spot. The crime-weary old outlaw then went to the bunkhouse, pulled off his boots, crawled into one of the beds and turned his six-shooter on himself.

For the information about Tom Ross' last days and demise, I am indebted to the veteran Marcus Snyder, whose family and mine have been friends for three generations. He is a native of Williamson County, Texas, but has spent a great deal of time in Montana. Mr. Snyder also knew the outlaw in West Texas and New Mexico. Here Tom Ross divided his time between working on various ranches and dodging the law. Mr. Snyder is a cowman of the old school and has handled as many cattle all over the West as any living man.

Many Rangers who became noted in the Service received their early training under Captain Rogers. Best known of these was the late Captain Frank A. Hamer. He never missed an opportunity to express the highest regard for his first commander. John L. Dibrell served for many years in Rogers' company and finished his official career as a United States Customs Inspector. Although he is now totally blind, this courageous gentleman enjoys good health and still has the cheerful disposition which made him popular among his comrades. He is an authority on Ranger history, and owns one of the most complete collections of frontier pictures in Texas. Ex-Ranger Dibrell furnished me with several rare items from his scrapbook. The late T. H. (Chub) Poole of La Salle County, was one of Captain Rogers' former Rangers. Under his long tenure as sheriff, Cotulla changed from the wildest town in Texas to a community of good schools, splendid churches and fine citizens. John Hinnant, member of a pioneer Southwest Texas family, also served under Captain Rogers. He lived in Falfurrias while Company D was stationed there and I frequently sought his advice on matters pertaining to the good of the Service.

Charlie Burwell, nephew of Captain Rogers' wife, is in charge of the Laureles division of the King Ranch. He is a native of Cotulla and his father served as sheriff of La Salle County. He joined the Rangers in 1917 and rode horseback over most of the danger spots on the lower Rio Grande. His training in the Service, plus the fact that he is a natural born cowman, earned him the high position he now holds. The Burwell family have been of great help to me in writing this book, for they supplied information and encouragement when both were needed.

In the deadly Conner fight on the Louisiana border early in Captain Rogers' career, he received a severe wound. The shot would have killed him if the bullet had not been deflected by a small book he carried in his breast pocket. Because of the captain's well known religious leaning, some accounts of the incident have it that his life was saved by a Bible. This would have been entirely in character, but it is not true. The life saver was a notebook in which the Ranger kept his personal and official accounts.

When Governor Dan Moody announced the appointment of the Ranger captains selected to serve in his administration and my name appeared on the list, it was one of the proudest moments of my life. The boy who had longingly watched the Rangers in Cotulla was now a comrade of one of his childhood heroes, Captain John H. Rogers. I saw him for the last time in Del Rio and he appeared to be in good health.

In concluding the chapter on Captain Rogers, I return to the last paragraph of the letter from Brigadier General Pleas Blair Rogers. It reads:

> I am now a retired soldier who served over thirty years in the United States Army and fought in two wars. I have seen many good men die, but my father was the best man I ever saw live.

Chapter 39

JOHN R. HUGHES

JOHN Reynolds Hughes, peerless captain of my old Company D, was, next to McDonald, the most publicized Ranger leader of his time. The reason for this wide acclaim was that in addition to his ability and color, he operated in the section of Texas traversed by the Southern Pacific, and the Texas & Pacific Railroads. Captain Hughes also spent a goodly portion of his time in and around El Paso, where many newspaper men were clamoring for stories about the Rangers. These action-packed tales were profusely printed in the local press, as well as being dispatched to distant newspapers.

Captain Hughes is the subject of numerous articles and several books. Authors and feature writers have vied with each other in praising his service as a Ranger. I have never seen a derogatory word in print, nor have I ever heard one spoken against him. My brief chapter will touch only a fraction of his exploits, plus a few incidents of which I have personal knowledge.

I have carefully studied the combined service of the "Four Captains," and have endeavored to ascertain the reasons for their greatness. It is not difficult to find the answer. Each one of them was endowed with all the essentials of a Ranger commander. An equally important factor,

A widely used photograph of Company "D." Seated, left to right, Prisoner, George Tucker, Wood Sanders, Carl Kirchner, Captain Hughes. Standing, left to right, Frank McMahon, Billy Schmidt, J. V. Latham, Joe Sitters, Ed Palmer, Thalis T. Cook. Captain Hughes discharged Ranger Tucker for leaving his pistol within reach of prisoner.

however, was that they enjoyed freedom from political interference longer than any four captains who served under an adjutant general. The downward trend began with Ferguson. The governor who ruthlessly terminated Captain Hughes' long and honorable career was subsequently impeached. Texans often decried the lack of Rangers who could compare with the old timers. The reason can be found in the legend of King Canute and his courtiers. One day he sorrowfully said to them, "Alas, gentlemen, isn't it a pity that there are no longer knights like those who lived in the days of King Arthur?" To which one of the bolder ones replied, "Alas, Sire, isn't it a pity that we no longer have rulers like King Arthur?" Several captains after the days of the Big Four might have equaled their records if they had been given the opportunity.

Distinguishing traits of the Four Captains were their reserved bearing and marked dignity. Three of them bore the given name of John.

Neither their associates nor the gentlemen of the press ever referred to one of them as "Jack." They would spurn the use of any awe-inspiring sobriquet, and nobody even thought of giving them any dime novel nickname.

The territory patrolled by Captain Hughes and his men was larger in area than the combined New England states. It contained several hundred miles of Mexican border, the outlaw infested Big Bend and a king size portion of that rowdy region known as "West of the Pecos."

Any reference to railroads does not mean that he saw much of his service from the ease and plush of a passenger car. Captain Hughes always said, and proved, that he was a horseback Ranger. When the occasion demanded, he did not hesitate to requisition either freight or express cars to transport his saddle stock. He shipped them to the point nearest the scene of action where they were unloaded and the trail followed on horseback. This coordination of effort by the railroads and Rangers resulted in the capture of many criminals who otherwise would have escaped.

As soon as the fresh, grain fed horses, selected for their stamina, were on the ground, the manhunt was on. Joe Sitters, one of the best white trailers in Ranger history, and later killed in action, started looking for sign. The bandits, usually mounted on grass fed animals, were sure to be tracked down if they stayed in Texas.

After Sitters had maneuvered his comrades into shooting range, Thalis Cook, church-going Ranger and crack shot among expert marksmen, was the one most likely to side Captain Hughes. Carl Kirchner, Wood Sanders, Ed Palmer and others were held in high esteem by their captain. However, when speaking about his old Company D boys, and in expressing his opinion of their all-round ability as Rangers, it seemed to me that he leaned a little toward Cook. There was a saying in the western part of the state that "When Thalis Cook comes to the east side of the Pecos, the outlaws go to the west side. When he crosses that salty stream, they reverse their direction." A Ranger captain is like the father of eight or ten sons. He loves them all and has a deep knowledge of their strong points and their weaknesses. While he endeavors to show no partiality, it is humanly impossible not to have one son or one Ranger that he would just a little rather have along when he goes to ride the river, be that stream the Rio Grande or the River Jordan.

John R. Hughes had every requisite of a great captain: initiative, courage, intelligence and judgement. He loved the Service. One of the axioms that he used in enlisting his men, and one that I emulated, was "Nerve without judgment is dangerous, and has no place in the Ranger Service." He was the only dark eyed member of the Big Four, Brooks, McDonald and Rogers having the traditional blue-gray eyes of the gun fighting man. His pleasing personality, kindly eyes and soft voice were not to be mistaken as evidences of weakness or timidity. More than one blustering badman discovered this error too late for his own longevity. The captain's courtly bearing won him the appellation of "The Chevalier Bayard of the Southwest." Some writers also referred to him as the "Border Boss." In his early youth, Captain Hughes' right arm was partially disabled as a result of a fight in the Indian Territory. This injury forced him to use his left hand for pistol shooting, but he could raise his right arm high enough to support a rifle, which he shot from his left shoulder. He asked no odds on account of this handicap, and could more than hold his own in any kind of gun fighting, regardless of how fast the company might be.

He practiced frugality from the start, even saving money while drawing the meager pay of a Ranger private. The mines at Shafter were running full blast, and the company supplemented his State pittance with a substantial honorarium. They could well afford to do this, as a reward for protecting life and property at the diggings. The manager knew that it would be bad business to run the risk of having a man of Hughes' ability lured away by the higher salaries paid by others. Frequently appearing in a Ranger captain's report to the adjutant general was the complaint that "there was increasing difficulty in keeping good men. As soon as the Ranger proved to be outstanding, he was offered a job with much better pay." The United States Customs, express companies, and railroads particularly needed men with Ranger backgrounds to fill positions requiring nerve and experience.

Young Hughes invested his earnings wisely, using the same intelligence in business as he did in Rangering. Unfortunately, these talents do not often exist in the same man, as is witnessed by the sad spectacle of many a fine officer spending his old age in poverty, probably serving as night watchman in some small town. None of that for Hughes. He reaped a rich harvest from a lifetime of thrift and at the age of seventy, was president of a bank.

In these words, Captain Hughes related to me the termination of his long and honorable career in the Rangers: "Jim Ferguson turned me out to starve. But," he added with a chuckle, "I didn't starve." Ferguson repaid this outstanding public official for his faithful service by displacing him in a manner best described as "swapping a Kentucky thoroughbred for a Mexican burro." The good people of Texas were shocked at this act of ingratitude; the criminal element delighted. They knew that the way of the transgressor would be easier with Hughes out of their crooked road.

The gallant captain never married. Many stories have been told about the reason for his bachelorhood, but it certainly was not for a lack of personal charm. He was handsome, and a good conversationalist. Men, women and children enjoyed being in his company. Maybe he was wedded to the Service. His devotion to duty certainly would be grounds for this speculation. One time in the adjutant general's office, the day the picture of Captains Dan W. Roberts, John R. Hughes, John A. Brooks, Frank A. Hamer and me, was taken, Captains Hughes and Brooks spent the afternoon talking over old times. It was a rare privilege to listen to them and I realized that two veterans of their stature in Ranger history might never get together again. I listened to their reminiscences, drinking in every word. There was no boasting, no profanity, nor any tall tales. Just memories of their old comrades and of early days on the frontiers of Texas. Most of the conversation was about some exploit of the Rangers. Everything said about their old time friends was complimentary. They would recall that in a certain fight one of the boys took a long chance, and in another instance, somebody made a great shot. Their entire talk was a contrast to some of the present day discussions, and I was fascinated.

Late in the afternoon, just before time to close the office, Captain Hughes looked at Captain Brooks and said, "John, do you remember the letter I gave you to mail to that young lady, about forty years ago?" Captain Brooks replied, "Yes, John, it was when I was leaving camp for a month's furlough. I rode home, about two hundred miles, and when I got there I hung up my coat, with your letter in the pocket.

Ira Aten, ex-Texas Ranger, while Sheriff
of Fort Bend County, Texas, 1889.

I forgot all about the letter and didn't mail it until I put the coat on
again, and started back to camp, a month later." That was all that
was said. A lifetime of association with the breed had taught me not
to intrude on the privacy of these tight lipped, battle scarred old war
horses or disturb their past memories, so I can give no further information. Did the tardiness in mailing a *billet doux* have anything to do
with Captain Hughes' bachelorhood? The answer is borrowed from
my Mexican *amigos; "Quien Sabe?"*

On one of his visits to my office, I asked Captain Hughes to identify
the men in the most widely used picture of Company D. It was taken
while Hughes was in his prime. We were looking at Captain James B.
Gillett's splendid book, *Six Years With the Texas Rangers.* Captain
Hughes demonstrated by his story of the picture the intelligence and

constant vigilance used by the really great Ranger leaders. After identifying the men for me, the captain said with a twinkle in his eyes, "Bill, I fired a man over that picture." "You did. Why?" I inquired. He was in a jocular mood and asked me, "Don't you see the reason?" I had always prided myself on being fairly observant, but was forced to admit that I couldn't see anything wrong, especially not enough to warrant the discharge of a man from the Service. He then pointed to the prisoner in the lower left corner of the picture. Next to the captive sat a member of Company D. This young man, like many Rangers past and present, was eager to show his white handled pistol, and to be sure it was not left out of the picture. Photographers were slower in those days, and they took longer to do the job. Everybody had to hold very still and give their undivided attention to the little birdie. Captain Hughes then explained, "The prisoner could have grabbed that pistol and killed several of my boys." A close examination of the picture shows that the end Ranger's six-shooter was in easy reach of the captive's hand, and in a tempting position. Fortunately, for all concerned, the *bandido* was just as deeply engrossed in *mirando al pajarito* as was the candidate for summary discharge from the Rangers. While Captain Hughes was a strict disciplinarian, especially where the safety of his men was involved, I would bet a good horse that after letting the lesson soak in, he re-instated the Ranger.

His visits were always an inspiration, and his counsel and advice of great worth. He was much gratified to know that the Sterling administration was trying to carry out his ideas and those of other leaders who had made the Ranger Service a source of pride to all good Texans.

Captain Hughes' alertness, even in his old age, was demonstrated by an incident that happened just outside Austin, Texas, at Camp Mabry. There are several large two story brick buildings at the post, that were formerly used as barracks by the Texas National Guard. They have wide galleries on the front, and Captain Hughes loved to bring his camping outfit and sleep on one of them. Fresh air was one of the secrets of his long life and vigorous old age. Although he could afford the best, he scorned hotels when there was a good camping spot available. One of his favorite jokes was that he once lost a job as cowboy, because the boss wanted him to sleep under the chuck wagon, but he couldn't stand it; it was too confining.

We were always delighted to have him, and to know that he felt at home with us. He had spent a number of winters in California with his old comrade, Ira Aten, and while sojourning in that state of unusual weather, had learned to recognize an earthquake when he felt one. In 1931 or 1932, a slight tremor occurred in Austin, coming very early in the morning. I was sleeping in the next building, and thought it was only the vibration of a passing train, as the railroad runs very close to Camp Mabry. Captain Hughes instantly recognized that the disturbance was an earthquake shock. He remembered the brick construction of the building and the possibility of being buried under the debris. The captain climbed up a gallery post so that if it fell, he would be on top of the pile.

Speaking of earthquakes, while visiting Will Rogers at his ranch near Santa Monica in 1934, I asked him to tell me something about them. He replied, "There has been only one slight quake since I've been here, but it nearly cost me my life. I was about half way between the house and the stable when it started, and I ran to the barn to get the horses out. My wife teased me nearly to death for thinking of the horses first instead of the children." How the veteran Rangers miss old Will. We always issued him a Special Ranger's commission, although he never cared for or used a gun. Ropes and horses were his favorites. He could never bear to hurt anybody, even if it became a stern duty, such as the Rangers are sometimes called upon to perform.

Captain Hughes' favorite side partner was Ira Aten. A book and many articles have been written about this great Ranger. Texans like to claim "firsts" and to Aten belongs the dubious honor of bringing out the first booby trap. These infernal machines were widely used by our enemies in World War II. In the barbed wire troubles during Governor Ireland's administration, Ranger Sergeant Aten proposed to rig up some dynamite caps on the fence posts. These were set so they would explode if the wire was pulled, cut or otherwise molested. He claimed to have his bomb perfected to the point that livestock rubbing or leaning against the fence would not set it off. Aten had no intention of really using the devices, but he wanted to throw a scare into the anti-barb-wire group. By this stratagem he could be relieved from the disagreeable duty of working under cover. His assignment also involved some hard work on farms and in hay fields. The most distasteful part to Aten was that it had to be performed on foot. In any event, his forerunner of the modern booby trap gives one an insight into his original mind. He became a wealthy citizen of the Imperial Valley of California, a bank director and large land owner. He exemplifies the point I am stressing, namely, that the really great Rangers were producers, as well as shooters. In addition to being one of Texas' best Rangers, he was a first class cowman. Aten worked on the vast XIT Ranch for many years, where his fighting background had a salutary effect on the rollicky cowboys, as well as on potential rustlers.

While guarding this three million acre ranch, he incurred the mortal enmity of the cattle thieves and other outlaws. His method of dealing with the boys who swung the wide loop and made free use of the running iron reflected his early training in the Rangers. Another ex-Ranger of the same mold who resided in the Panhandle was Captain George W. Arrington. The rustlers made many threats and hatched numerous plots against the lives of this formidable pair. They were extremely careful, however, to do their scheming at long range, none of them choosing to face either of the old war horses. The two comrades adopted a unique and effective plan to discourage ambushers and assassins. Each announced that he would "get" the man or men who killed the other party to the pact. Both died peaceably in bed. Many years later a somewhat similar deal was made in Duval County. Ranger Captain Alfred Y. Allee, one of my old boys, used the same deterrent on a once powerful but now deposed political dictator.

For several decades following the Civil War, an unusual situation existed in Fort Bend County. The inhabitants were divided into two factions who carried their party affiliations into political, business and social life. They did not take the names of Democrats or Republicans, but called themselves "Jaybirds" and "Woodpeckers." Both sides sought to overthrow carpetbagger rule, and both had some strange political bed-fellows. A noted member of the Woodpeckers was Kyle Terry, son of the Confederate general who organized and commanded Terry's Texas Rangers.

These hot headed people maintained a sort of armed truce, but everybody knew that they were on top of a smoldering volcano. Early in 1889, citizens asked for Rangers. Captain Frank Jones, Sergeant Ira Aten and six men were sent in response to this appeal. The trouble subsided to some extent, and the great demand for Rangers in other parts of the state led the adjutant general to move the captain and three men out of Richmond. This left four rangers: F. H. Schmidt, the Robinson Brothers and Sergeant Ira Aten. On August 16, 1889, the long expected battle took place. Four persons were killed and several wounded. The dead included the sheriff and a colored girl who was hit by a stray bullet. Among the wounded was Ranger F. H. Schmidt.

Just as a student of military science makes critiques of famous battles, I have made, from a Ranger's standpoint, a study of the melee in Richmond, Texas. In it the Rangers played the unfamiliar role of by-standers. It is true that Sergeant Aten implored both sides to listen to reason, but no effort was made to disarm them. The reason for this seeming neglect is at once apparent. The sheriff was the leader of one party, and he could arm his side by giving them deputyships. It would have been suicidal to deprive the others of their weapons. Another factor was the shortage of manpower among the Rangers. Four men were not enough to handle a situation of that gravity. The adjutant general must have been lulled into false security by the calm before the storm. There can be no other explanation for reducing his force in the face of an emergency, when it should have been increased.

Ranger F. H. Schmidt was wounded by a stray bullet. He was given medical attention by two Houston doctors. They sent their bill to the State, but Adjutant General King refused payment, as he deemed it excessive. There was never any provision made for the care of wounded Rangers, and Schmidt was kept on the rolls of Company D. In many pictures taken on the border, he may be seen on his crutches. The controversy over medical services was settled by the eminent Dr. Ferdinand Herff, of San Antonio. He treated the wounded Ranger until he completely recovered, and did not bother to render a bill.

On the recommendation of the governor and other prominent citizens, Aten was appointed to fill the unexpired term of the deceased sheriff, and he held the office for four years. His judgment and fairness, together with a sense of humor that he could apply to any situation, contributed to his success in keeping down further killings. There was never any doubt about what he meant. If Sergeant Aten had chosen to stay in the Rangers long enough to get his captaincy, he would have equaled or surpassed McDonald in the choice of caustic words. Aten also had a large fund of jokes, generally dealing with one of his cases, and the people involved. His classic on the Jaybirds and Woodpeckers was about a farmer who had just moved to Fort Bend County. This inoffensive newcomer had no desire to take sides. He simply wanted to till the fertile Brazos bottom soil, and have a reasonable chance to reach a ripe old age in peace. He was plowing his field one day and on reaching the end of a row, ten men armed with Winchesters and six-shooters, rode out of the woods. The leader asked, "Are you a Jaybird or a Woodpecker?" The terrified granger was between a rock and a hard place. Scholars would say he was in a quandary. He did not know whether his formidable and unwelcome visitors were Jaybirds or Woodpeckers. From their looks, he might well believe that a wrong answer could be fatal. After thinking it over carefully he replied, "Well, gentlemen, I guess that I'm a Jaypecker."

Among those present at the Jaybird-Woodpecker battle were three gentlemen who later became good friends of mine. Judge J. V. Meek, and his son, Weston, who was born many years later, bestowed many kindnesses on me in my youth. Walter Williams, a cowman of the old school, was driving a herd of cattle through Richmond when the shooting took place. Both he and his gracious wife, Miss Rosa, were my warm friends. Albert George was a small boy at the time, but remembered all details of the incident. He was a typical Texas ranchman, and an authority on the history of Fort Bend County.

Captain Hughes read a great deal and his favorite book was reputed to be the Fugitive List. The Rangers variously referred to it as the "Black Book," "Bible Number Two," or the "Preferred List." The compiling of this roll of fugitives from justice was inaugurated by Adjutant General William Steele in 1876. Major Jones, and the members of the Frontier Battalion did not particularly relish the idea of giving up Indian and border fighting for the more prosaic (to them) duty of rounding up this bunch of feudists, livestock thieves and killers.

It was my privilege to know Mrs. Anna J. Hardwicke Pennybacker and to study her Texas history in grade school. In the chapter covering Governor Hubbard's administration, she gives as one of his principal achievements, "Frontier Protected and Crime Punished." The text states:

> Governor Hubbard was vigorous in his defense of the frontier, and the results are encouraging. For years bands of robbers and other lawless characters had held portions of the state in terror. The Governor offered heavy rewards for the capture of such persons. As a result, criminals who had long laughed at the laws were brought to justice. A battalion of Rangers was detailed for frontier duty in order to protect the settlers from Indian and Mexican raids.

The gentle lady historian probably did not know that an order had already been issued by the adjutant general, directing Major Jones to pay less attention to Indians, and to spend more time and effort in handling the white criminals. Some idea of their number may be drawn from the fact that the first Fugitive List contained over three thousand names, with more coming in daily. Texas was sparsely settled in 1876. The high percentage of outlaws, particularly on the frontier, was not conducive to the safety of life and property, especially if the latter had hoofs or horns.

The Fugitive Lists contained the names and descriptions of all criminals who were known to be wanted, or had been reported by sheriffs or other officers. General Steele's office acted as a clearing house in this work, his clerks cataloging and indexing the miscreants by county and by name. The descriptions were of more aid than the names that were easily shed like the skin of a snake, and changed with every nocturnal flight from justice. The list was warmly received by the Rangers in the field, as it enabled them to hold many suspects who otherwise would have lied themselves out of custody. So numerous were the outlaws, and the efforts of the civil authorities so feeble, that the desperados were literally running wild in the state. Hence, the order changing the prime objective of the Rangers, and the publishing of the Fugitive List.

That Captain Hughes used and studied these "Black Books" is evidenced by the many thumbings and pencil marks on his copies. Among my most prized possessions are his collection of the Fugitive Lists that he presented to me, together with his latest photograph, which was used in Walter Prescott Webb's *Texas Rangers.*

One adjutant general's report states: "On December 25, 1889, Private J. R. Hughes and two men with a deputy sheriff and posse, attempting arrest of Will and Alvin O'Dell, for murder in Edwards County, were fired upon. Fire was returned, and both the O'Dells killed." On my copy of this booklet, Captain Hughes took a pencil and corrected the spelling of the names of the deceased. He changed it from "O'Dell" to "Odle."

The last survivor of those stalwart riders who served under Captain Hughes in Company D is J. C. (Doc) White. He comes from an outstanding family of Rangers. One of his brothers, John Dudley, was killed in line of duty while rounding up slackers in the piney woods of East Texas, during the First World War. In this fight, Ranger Walter I. Rowe was severely wounded. Another brother, Tom White, also received his training in the Rangers. Both he and Doc entered the Federal Bureau of Investigation. Tom later became warden of the two different Federal penal institutions. Dudley White, Jr., is upholding the family tradition by serving in the present day Rangers. Doc was born in a log cabin near Austin around 1885. He still lives on a tract of land that was owned by his father, who served Travis County as sheriff, and later as county judge. Vigorous in mind and body, he does not live in the past. His vast knowledge of Ranger history, his retentive memory and his eagerness to help a friend, have contributed a great deal to the authenticity of this book. While serving with the Federal Bureau of Investigation, ex-Ranger White took a prominent part in the celebrated Urschel kidnapping case. One of the gangsters, with the awe-inspiring nickname of "Machine Gun" Kelly, attacked him in the Federal courthouse in Oklahoma City. Doc "bent" his gun over the public enemy's head after the fashion of old time Rangers. This hair combing by a Colt forty-five in the hand of an experienced Texan took all the bravado out of the machine gunner.

My life was enriched by the friendship of John Reynolds Hughes. The Texas Ranger name and fame have gained added luster by his having been one of its captains. I heard him recite this verse several times and trust he is still unfenced, in the Valhalla reserved for great Rangers.

The last part of it goes like this:

When my old soul hunts range and rest
Beyond the Last Divide
Just plant me in some strip of West
That's sunny, lone and wide.

Let cattle rub my headstone round,
And coyotes wail their kin,
Let hosses come and paw the mound,
But DON'T you fence it in.

Chapter 40

WM. L. WRIGHT

CAPTAIN William Lee Wright was born in Caldwell County, Texas, February 19, 1868. While he was still a baby, his parents moved to DeWitt County, and he was reared near Yorktown. Soon after reaching his majority, Wright moved to Wilson County, where he served several terms as sheriff. He made an enviable record in this office and was considered one of the best in the state. His ability was recognized by his brother officers, who elected him president of the Texas Sheriffs Association. If he had been free of political interference and changes in administration, Captain Wright could have equaled the record of any leader in the annals of the Rangers. He possessed all the requisites of a great captain: judgment, initiative, and high moral courage. This virtue is sometimes lacking in men who have a surplus of the physical variety.

Captain Wright unquestionably knew more Southwest Texas lore than any man of his day. This was particularly true when it dealt with the Rangers. He was a natural raconteur, and his inexhaustible supply of stories fascinated listeners of all ages. There was neither counterfeit tall tales nor dime novel fiction in the captain's collection. His narratives were never boring, and he told them in an inimitable manner. The amazing memory he possessed enabled him to recall every detail

Company "D" at the Indian Crossing on the Rio Grande. Left to right: Captain W. L. Wright, Rangers Dan Coleman, W. A. Dial, Tom Brady and Warren Smith. Both Dial and Smith have served as presidents of the Ex-Rangers Association.

of his experiences. He never pictured himself as the hero, nor did he overwork the personal pronoun, "I." Captain Wright always preferred to give his men credit for the success of a campaign, rather than to take it all unto himself. Like Aten, McDonald and Hamer, he had a quaint vocabulary. He used several unique expressions in describing a favorite Ranger. When he said of one of his boys, "He is a GOOD 'un, he'll do to ride the river with," or, "He is one of the old blue hen's chickens," it meant you could stake your life on the man's gameness. He called all men who carried six-shooters "pistolians." The usual concept of a fighting man is the quiet, silent type. Captain Wright refuted this belief. He was extremely loquacious, but nobody ever questioned his ability as a fighter.

When this grand old warrior passed on without having his vast store of frontier history recorded, it was a distinct loss. One South Texas newspaper columnist contemplated writing a book on the life of Captain Wright. I urged him to do this, and told him that he had picked the richest living source of Ranger material. The newsman delayed too long, however, and with Captain Wright's passing, a gold mine of first hand information was buried with him. An author fortunate enough to collaborate with this history minded veteran could have written a great book on the Rangers.

Young Wright grew up in the locale and atmosphere of the Taylor-Sutton feud. It was the most deadly vendetta in the annals of our state. The bad blood between the two families originated in the red hills of Georgia, and followed their migration into Texas. Soon after the settlers reached their new homes, the smouldering embers of the conflict burst into flame. No attempt will be made here to write another history of the celebrated case. Many pages of fact and fiction have been printed about it. Only enough will be related to explain the presence of the Rangers in DeWitt County, the impact they made on the citizens in general, and on Will L. (Bud) Wright in particular.

After the feud had held several counties in its grip for more than ten years, it became apparent that the civil authorities were both unwilling and unable to stop the bloodshed. Elected peace officers were either connected with one of the factions by family ties, or had been intimidated by the bands of armed men who rode defiantly around the countryside. Conditions grew steadily worse. Midnight assassins committed dastardly crimes with seeming impunity and the threat of sudden death lurked in the shadows. Inoffensive citizens and their families lived in dread, as no one could foretell who would be the next victim. Everybody in that section of the state realized that their only hope lay in asking the governor for Rangers.

Those who sought to restore law and order in DeWitt County were led by their fearless district judge, Henry Clay Pleasants. He wrote to Governor Richard Coke, and gave him the facts of the feud. Through many anonymous letters, the judge was warned that any appeal for State assistance would cost him his life. Nevertheless, he went to Austin and made an official request for Rangers, and urged the Governor to lose no time in sending them to his bailiwick.

Shortly before Judge Pleasant's visit to the capitol, Governor Coke had held a momentous conference with Adjutant General Steele. They perfected plans to wage a vigorous war on lawlessness that ran rampant in the state. A study of the newly published Fugitive List convinced them that it would be wise to shift the activities of the Frontier Battalion. By this change in the nature of their duties, the Rangers would give less attention to Indians, whose numbers were decreasing, and concentrate their efforts on "civilized" desperadoes, whose ranks were increasing at an alarming rate. The names appearing in the "Black Book," which at its peak contained over five thousand, did not include five hundred or more feudists. The state officials also decided to recall McNelly from his work on the border and use him in the suppression of feuds.

McNelly's company was not a part of the Frontier Battalion. In some records it appears as a "Special Troop" and in others as "Company A, Volunteer Militia." Regardless of military nomenclature, to the public and to the men in the Service, they were Rangers. This particular unit of the state's armed forces needed nothing but the captain's name to give it identity and distinction. It was McNelly's company. Their theatre of operations was Southwest Texas. Wealthy stockmen south of the Nueces River as well as those of Goliad and Victoria counties were glad to finance these cow thief repellers. While Major Jones and the Frontier Battalion worked on the Mason County "war," the Horrell-Higgins feud in Lampasas County and other assignments on the upper line, McNelly, Hall and company were dispatched to DeWitt County.

The Constitution of 1876 had been adopted during the administration of Richard Coke. Among other duties of the governor, Article 4, Section 10, provides: "He shall cause the laws to be faithfully executed." Pursuant to this mandate, McNelly was ordered to DeWitt County. Thus Governor Coke became the first chief executive to use the Rangers in their prime function. This was, and always should be, to act as the strong right arm of the governor.

Captain McNelly was a sick man. Exposure, hardships endured on long scouts and a tendency to tuberculosis had brought on this condition. By receiving the proper care, he would be able to continue his service for a long time. In dealing with this peerless leader, Adjutant

General Steele set a pattern that has sometimes been followed by those in authority over the Rangers. He knew prices but not values. Captain McNelly was dropped from the rolls. Steele sought to justify his ungrateful act by stating, "McNelly's medical bill constituted one-third of the bill for the entire company." In terms of services rendered and leadership provided, the State could have afforded to pay Captain McNelly's medical bill many times over. He died on September 4, 1877, at the age of thirty-three years and seven months and was buried at Burton, Texas.

When the time came to name a successor to McNelly, two men stood out among the other members of the company. One was Lee (Red) Hall, a native of North Carolina and the other was John B. Armstrong, a native of Kentucky. Hall was a good mixer and wrote numerous elaborate reports. He spent a good deal of time around Austin, and had ingratiated himself with the Adjutant General. During the latter part of McNelly's captaincy, Steele had instructed Hall, a lieutenant, to make his reports directly to him. This order was not only unfair to McNelly, but showed a lack of executive ability on the part of the Adjutant General. Hall was given command of the company.

Many old timers who knew all the facts, stoutly maintained that Sergeant Armstrong should have been named to succeed McNelly. He had been with him in the Rio Grande campaigns, and was an intelligent, educated man. The late Walter Billingsley, who was president of the Old Trail Drivers Association, told me that Armstrong was by far the better Ranger. The later lives of the two men bore out Mr. Billingsley's opinion. John B. Armstrong entered the adjutant general's department in Austin and attained the rank of lieutenant-colonel. Friends continued to call him by his, former title of Major. He established the Armstrong Ranch in what is now Kenedy County, and his descendants are among the state's most prominent stockmen.

When Lieutenant Lee (Red) Hall succeeded to the command, no officer could hope to inherit a gamer company of fighting men. These McNelly selected and trained veterans had invaded Mexico, killed numerous bandits on the Red Ride and performed other similar exploits. To these daredevils, the scout against a crowd of nightriders was just another lark that would break the monotony of camp life. They sprang to obey the Adjutant General's order with eagerness and gusto.

When Lieutenant Hall and his company rode into Clinton and pitched camp near the courthouse, consternation spread through the ranks of the feudists. News of the feats in arms accomplished by these fast shooting warriors in the Rio Grande campaigns had already reached DeWitt County. The bushwhackers knew that dead or alive, the Rangers would bring them to book. Hall's presence with his men in DeWitt County was a source of relief to the sorely distressed citizens. For the first time in many years, the law abiding element felt that justice was literally in the saddle. They now had good reason to hope that at long last the blood feud would be ended. A close scrutiny of the Rangers convinced friend and foe alike that these iron nerved boys would stand no foolishness. In the parlance of the old time gunfighters, they would "play for keeps." Determination and fearlessness were written on their weather beaten countenances, and each one firmly believed that he had RIGHT on his side and the State of Texas at his back. This is an unbeatable combination, particularly when it is augmented by deadly skill with both six-shooter and rifle.

Judge Pleasants now had officers at his command who were both willing and able to serve all criminal processes issued by his court. The Rangers would also arrest any man named in the vast accumulation of murder indictments. Most of the accused were still at large through failure of the local authorities to perform their duty. The one hundred and fifty odd true bills returned by DeWitt County grand juries bore vivid witness to the appalling conditions in Judge Pleasant's turbulent district.

The first batch of warrants turned over to Lieutenant Hall for execution numbered over thirty. They included the names of seven men who had been indicted for the murder of Doctor Brazzel and his son. Hall had information that their ringleader was to be married on a certain night in the near future, and that the other six would doubtless be present at the ceremony. The bride's family planned to see that the affair was a great success, as befitting a groom who was not only the leader of the assassins, but was a deputy sheriff to boot. A sumptious supper was to be served after the exchange of marriage vows, which would be followed by dancing. Most members of the Sutton party were expected to attend.

It was on a rainy December night that Lee Hall and sixteen other Rangers rode out to attend the feudist's wedding. They would take an active part in the festivities, though not exactly as invited guests. A short distance from their destination, the lieutenant called a halt. The men dismounted, tied their horses to convenient trees, and quietly walked the rest of the way. Hall ordered twelve of his Rangers, who were armed with Winchesters, to surround the house. He then placed four men who carried double barreled shotguns at the corners. From this position, they could rake the gallery with their fire. The Ranger leader had carefully planned his strategy and tactics. He had previously requisitioned the 10 gauge shotguns from Adjutant General Steele especially for the campaign in DeWitt County. The lieutenant realized the value of these spatterguns loaded with buckshot, particularly in night fighting. He also had a full appreciation of the moral effect they had on people who understood their deadliness. Very few pistol men wanted any part of a battle in broad daylight, much less in the dark, with a cool headed man using one of them. Lieutenant Hall had weighed all these factors when he stationed the four shotgun Rangers close at hand, well within the sound of his voice. He made a final check of positions and satisfied himself that each man knew his assignment. The guests were dancing when Hall, with a Winchester in his hands, entered the house. It would be difficult to describe the consternation caused by the unheralded appearance of the Ranger. Women screamed, excited men gasped in astonishment and confusion overwhelmed the entire gathering. The bridegroom was the first to recover a part of his composure. He demanded the reason for this invasion of his wedding party, and asked if anybody present was wanted. Hall calmly replied that he held warrants for the groom and six other men in the room. He called out each name in a loud voice, so that the entire company could hear. Some of the feudists yelled that they would resist the arrest, and that the Rangers could not take them without a fight to the finish. Hall replied that this would suit him fine, as his boys were spoiling for a scrap. He added that he couldn't hold them off much longer. "Get your women and children out of harm's way and we'll fly to it," he said. One of those indicted, who was also a town marshal, asked Hall how many men he had. The lieutenant did not try to make them think that he had a large force. He truthfully answered that his entire company numbered seventeen, including himself. The marshal-wedding-guest then tried to intimidate Hall. He stated that there were over seventy in their crowd and warned that they did not want to kill all the Rangers. This attempted bluff did not daunt Red Hall. He replied that the odds of seventy to seventeen suited him exactly, and he ordered his shotgun boys to move in closer.

At this fearsome command, the feudists wilted and surrendered. The cool confidence of the lieutenant, backed by buckshot and sixteen McNelly trained Rangers, completely cowed them. Hall and his men collected all weapons, and in a few minutes the male guests were disarmed. At this point, the groom made a most unusual request, although he was now a prisoner. He asked, with a logic that appealed to the romantic Rangers, that inasmuch as it was his wedding night, the food already prepared and a good dance going, that they be allowed to continue the festivities until morning. Hall agreed to this request. The Rangers entered the house in pairs to partake of the wedding supper. They also joined in the dancing. With this unorthodox arrest, there was enacted one of the most celebrated and amazing episodes in the history of the Rangers. It literally proved that they were always ready for a fight or a frolic.

After the grand ball was over, daylight saw the prisoners on their way to the county seat, where they were safely landed in jail. Hall bluntly warned the crowd of sympathizers that he would order the captives killed first if a rescue were attempted, so the feudists kept their distance. A new day was also dawning for the peaceful citizens of DeWitt County as the power of the bushwhackers was broken.

Of the actual participants in the wedding festival arrest, I knew personally Corporal, later Lieutenant, W. L. Rudd, George W. Talley and George (Josh) Durham. In 1911, while shipping some Ed C. Lasater cattle from Katherine (now Armstrong), I saw Major John B. Armstrong. His descendants are among my best friends.

The jailing of the seven principal terrorists, plus the manner in which they had been plucked from the midst of a large assembly of their own cohorts, set the county agog. The name of Lee Hall was on every tongue and the fame of his unprecedented exploit spread over the entire state. He gave most of the credit for his success to his men, and to Captain McNelly who had selected and trained them.

Having fared so badly in their encounters with the Rangers, the feudists, after many clandestine meetings, decided to renew their threats on the indomitable Judge Pleasants. On his aging, but resolute, shoulders rested the responsibility of ruling on the defendants' application for bail. Every conceivable means, legal or illegal, was used by the culprits and their attorneys to influence or frighten him. His friends feared that he would be killed in the courtroom if the prisoners were remanded to jail. They also knew that he would never swerve from his duty. The excitement had reached a fever pitch. Additional Rangers reinforced the sixteen, until the augmented company now contained thirty men.

On the day set for the final decision, the courtroom was crowded with feudists of both parties. It would be impossible to exaggerate the tenseness of the situation. The judge took his seat on the bench, with a dignity and calmness that showed his utter contempt for the bushwhackers. Six Rangers were stationed around the rostrum, three on each side. Their new Winchester repeating rifles were cocked, and triggers fingered. Judge Pleasants was ready to announce his momentous decision.

I have always been interested in N. A. Jennings' account of the Rangers' movements at the trial of the feudists. He states in part:

> Just before Judge Pleasants rose to give his decision, six of the Rangers stepped up to the bench and stood beside him. I was one of the three on his right and was next to his side. Like the other five men, I had my carbine in my hand, and like the others, I threw a cartridge in the breech and cocked the gun in plain sight of all in the courtroom.

To Rangers of a later date, this would be a strange proceeding. When any immediate shooting was in prospect, we always kept a shell in the barrel. The purpose of this practice was twofold. First the gun could be fired by merely cocking it and pulling the trigger. No time was lost in working the lever. Second, it left room for one more cartridge in the magazine.

It is possible however, that the Ranger-author from Philadelphia was correct. The Model 1873 Winchesters were innovations. They were as far ahead of the 50 calibre Sharp's carbines furnished by the state, as the single shot, sawed off buffalo guns were ahead of muzzle loaders. Captain Richard King had furnished the modern gun to the Rangers under Captain McNelly. It was and still is safer to carry a rifle on horseback with the barrel empty. To avoid accidents, the captain could have ordered his men to do this. It is also easy to believe that when the Rangers jacked the shells into the barrels, it had a good effect on the crowd. They doubtless had a wholesome respect for the fire power of the new fangled repeaters.

The sharp tongued jurist did not mince words. He excoriated the assembled crowd of feudists, and denounced their dastardly deeds in what was unquestionably the most scathing language ever to fall from the lips of a Texas judge. In his castigation, he called them midnight assassins, cowards, and ambushers, adding that many men within the sound of his voice should long ago have been hanged. Every real Texas Ranger or ex-Ranger now living will derive great pride from one statement made by Judge Pleasants on this historic occasion. It was made out of the fullness of his heart, and should be an inspiration to every man in the Service. I quote the words of the eminent judge, "When you deal with the Texas Rangers, you deal with men who are fearless in the discharge of their duty and will surely conquer you." To hit the mark set by Judge Pleasants should be the aim of every Ranger. Captain Will Wright, who had heard these words repeated numberless times in his boyhood, never forgot his obligation to vindicate the good judge's high opinion. Judge Pleasants followed his blistering remarks by announcing that the prisoners would be denied bail.

This decision, with its far reaching consequences, broke the back of the feud and the spirit of the feudists. When Rangers cleared the court-room, the only resistance offered by the bushwhackers was in the form of murderous glares levelled at them. If looks could kill, both the judge and his guard would have died instantly. The local gunmen wanted no part of a shooting match with the Rangers, even though they outnumbered Hall's men many times, and were in their own back yard.

The descendants of both warring factions have long since realized the futility of bloodshed, buried the hatchet and smoked the pipe of peace. At one time many years later a Sutton and a Taylor served in the same Ranger company where as comrades in arms they fought side by side to uphold the peace and dignity of their native state. I have scouted with these men who bore the names of the blood feudists in DeWitt County. There was nothing in their demeanor reminiscent of the fact that two generations ago their ancestors were gunning for each other.

Judge Pleasants, in his history-making stand against the feudists, demonstrated that the courts, backed up by Rangers, could bring law and order to any county in Texas regardless of how grave the situation might be. By the same token, the Rangers, when properly backed up by the courts, can accomplish untold good, provided that the governor will do his part, as is required by the Constitution of 1876.

Latent embers of the Taylor-Sutton conflict continued to smoulder for several years, and Rangers had to be kept in DeWitt County to prevent further outbreaks. They also served as bodyguards for Judge Pleasants, whose life was still in danger. Four men generally accompanied him at all times until the trouble was over.

Bud Wright spent a great deal of his time at the Ranger camp, which was near his father's home. His boyhood idols were members of the company. To them he confided his determination to join their organization as soon as he was old enough. Many other Texas boys shared this ambition.

Captain McNelly would not enlist a man who did not come from a good family. From combat experience he had found that a gentleman would stand fire where a scrub or a bully might show the white feather. A majority of his Rangers were dashing young men from the old South, with England, Ireland and Scotland each furnishing a member. Most of them had joined purely for the love of adventure. These hard riding cavaliers cut romantic figures that won the hearts of several local belles. Five of them found brides in DeWitt County.

In describing these weddings, editors of the weekly papers in that part of the state held a literary field day. Following the custom of the times, they vied with each other in using their most flowery language and romantic phraseology. One of them wrote: "While serving in DeWitt County not a single Ranger lost his life from bullets. However, several single ones lost their hearts from cupid's darts."

Young Wright practically grew up on horseback, and used to say that he cut his teeth on a six-shooter. He worked cattle all over Southwest Texas and soon became an expert rider and roper. Uppermost in his thoughts was the determination to be a Ranger. With this idea constantly in mind, he acquired more skill with guns than with any other tool of a cowboy's craft. He first worked on the Eckhardt Ranch in DeWitt County, and then went to the Rutledge Ranch in Karnes County.

One of his best friends was the owner's nephew, Will J. Rutledge. Besides being a large cattle owner and a top steer roper, he was an ace brand inspector for the Texas Cattle Raisers Association. In this capacity, he held a commission as a Texas Ranger. The inspector possessed a keen eye and a phenomenal memory, together with a true cowman's instinct. Ranchmen who knew him best would bet a horse that he never forgot an animal. They believed that if he had ever seen a calf one time, he could recognize it anywhere. The brute could have grown to maturity, and been in a herd of a thousand cattle, or in a shipment at one of the terminal stockyards, Will Rutledge would pick it out and tell you where he saw it last.

Once in a generation a detective will be born with this talent. They call it a "photographic mind." The range land version is invaluable to those who have the responsibility of deciding the ownership of livestock by reading their brands. Through years of association with this remarkable man, I learned many valuable lessons.

After several years on the Rutledge ranch, Wright moved to Wilson County. He served for a short time as justice of the peace. This humble office is an unequaled school of experience. It is very close to the people, and it teaches a man all about the weaknesses and frailties of human nature. Everybody liked the young judge with his pleasing personality, friendly smile and fondness for telling interesting stories. He soon became a deputy under Sheriff John Craighead. When a vacancy occurred in John H. Rogers' Ranger company, the sheriff was glad to recommend Will L. Wright. He was accepted and ordered to report to the captain at their station in Cotulla, La Salle County.

Service in that unhobbled cow town quickly separated the men from the boys, wood from timber and the game cocks from the Dominickers. In some tough Texas communities, Rangers could control the situation merely by a look of determination and fearlessness on their countenances, but not so in Cotulla. Valor had to be proved and demonstrated to her pistol wielding citizens. When pulling a six-shooter, it had better be smoking when it cleared the scabbard, if the Ranger craved to have his name included among the list of survivors.

Will Wright's introduction to Cotulla followed the well established pattern. An old renegade who was a past master in the art of preventing a Ranger's life from growing monotonous was in personal charge of the welcoming ceremonies. He was aided and abetted by the local newspaper man, who aspired to be a tough.

The following excerpt from Captain Roger's annual report to Adjutant General Thomas Scurry gives an official account of the meeting of Ranger Will L. Wright and Jim Davenport. Because of a defect in the act creating the Frontier Battalion, which provided that only officers were empowered to make arrests, Rangers were given the rank of lieutenant.

> On the evening of October 24, 1900, Lieutenant W. L. Wright of Company E attempted to arrest James R. Davenport for being drunk and firing his pistol in the town of Cotulla when the latter resisted, drew his pistol and fired at Wright, the ball passing through the latter's coat. Lieutenant Wright immediately shot and killed him. Davenport had been wounded by rangers once before when arrested for murder, on which charge he was convicted and served a sentence for five years. While in Cotulla, he had frequently been arrested for drunkenness and for firing his pistol and for carrying concealed weapons.

This concise report gives no hint of the deep human interest story that involved the Ranger's loved ones, when in line of duty he killed Jim Davenport. I now live only a few blocks from the widow of Captain W. L. Wright, and from her lips I recently heard the wife's version of the affair. She was in Cotulla on that momentous night, and heard the shots fired in the duel. It closed the stormy career of an outlaw and firmly established the reputation of Will Wright as a man among men. Anxiety and apprehension are the lot of a Ranger's womenfolk. Those unsung and unheralded heroines have to wait in dread uncertainty for their warrior's return from dangerous missions. Lieutenant Wright's mother was visiting her son and daughter-in-law at the family home, which was near the center of the small town. A lady ran to the front door and reported to Wright that Davenport was flourishing his pistol and creating a disturbance in a nearby store. The Ranger left his mother and wife to go make the arrest.

Naturally, the Mesdames Wright were greatly concerned about their loved one, but they did not give way to tears nor become panic stricken. The hopes and prayers of wonderful women have sustained many a Ranger in times of stress, and steadied his hand when a split second was the difference between the quick and the dead. Lieutenant Wright's womenfolks knew that he could take care of himself in any kind of gunplay, and they trusted that justice would prevail. Several shots rang out in the clear night air, coming in rapid succession, and the anxious listeners' hearts stood still. In Cotulla at that time, gun reports meant sudden death, and they had no way of knowing who had been killed. In about a minute, which seemed like hours to the watchers, old Dr. Livingston, who acted as a sort of town crier, galloped up on a gray horse. He called out these welcome words, "It's all right ladies; Will killed old Davenport." All mothers and wives can well imagine the relief of these two good ladies upon hearing the vociferous old doctor's soul healing message.

Wright's trial by fire proved to the hard cases around Cotulla that he was more than a match for any of them, and he had no further trouble there. The Wright-Davenport duel followed the pattern of many blazing dramas enacted in Texas. Some fast shooting took place. The outlaw missed; the Ranger didn't.

It would be impossible to overestimate the desperate character of Jim Davenport. On one occasion while two Rangers were hunting for him in the brush, he shot into their camp, and wounded Rangers Bass Outlaw and J. Mize. Davenport was wanted for the murder of a man named Hereford. He delighted in defying sheriffs and particularly disliked Rangers. The late Ed Dubose, who was in both Rogers' and

Hughes' companies told me that Wright, being the youngest Ranger, was left in town while the company was on a scout. Davenport told his saloon cronies that he was going to take advantage of this rare opportunity, and run this kid Ranger out of town.

After several months of routine service, Lieutenant Wright and another Ranger were ordered to Bandera County. Former sheriff William E. Jones had been assassinated some time before, and although there were several witnesses, they would not testify. They had been threatened, and were living in fear of their lives. In this case, Will Wright showed the all around ability that made him a great Ranger. He succeeded in convincing the reluctant witnesses that the Rangers could and would protect them. People are often afraid that the culprit or his relatives will wreak vengeance on them after the Rangers are gone. Lieutenant Wright's manner of reassuring the state's witnesses won them over, and they came forward and gave the necessary testimony. His work in this case resulted in the conviction of the guilty party, who was sentenced to serve ten years in the penitentiary.

After the impeachment of Jim Ferguson in 1917, he was succeeded as governor by William Pettus Hobby. The new Chief Executive appointed Will L. Wright Captain of the Rangers. The boy who had told Captain Hall's men back in DeWitt County that he would some day be a Ranger, had been given the top rank in the Service. Ranchmen in Southwest Texas and all honest residents along the lower border were gratified at his selection. We realized that he was the man for the place. Captain Wright took over his company in Laredo.

He found himself confronted by a grave problem. It called for a momentous decision. For its background, it is necessary to go back to the days of the Frontier Battalion. At that time, couriers and mail hauled by stage coaches were the principal means of communication. There were only a few telegraph lines on the frontier, and oxcarts were still used in freighting. The Ranger companies in the field were largely on their own, and maintained only a loose contact with Austin. The method of handling Ranger accounts used in those days had never been changed. The subsistence and forage allowances for the company were drawn by the captain. He in turn disbursed it to the men. Practically every cowman in the country was eager to have

411

a Ranger stationed on his ranch. They were glad to furnish board for the men and feed for his horse. When this was done, the amount of these two items was profit for the captain. The practice could be justified in the early days, but was now outmoded.

Many fine and scrupulously honest captains followed this custom. None wanted to be the first to make the change. Like many other governmental matters, the fault lay in the system rather than with the individual. One of the older captains went to Laredo to show the new company commander how to make out his accounts. After it was carefully explained to him, Captain Wright said, "Hold on a minute. I don't like the looks of this deal." "It's all right," the other hastened to assure him. "It's only a form. All the captains sign it." "That may be so," replied Captain Wright, "but none of that for me." His action broke up an abuse of long standing. As a former Ranger captain, and an ex-Adjutant General of Texas, I am of the opinion that Captain Wright's stand in braving the wrath of those who had followed the old system was the greatest exhibition of moral courage that has happened in the history of the Rangers.

Captain Wright had many fine men in his company. Some of those I remember best are W. A. Dial, Marvin Butler, Bryan Butler, E. Holleman, Jack Webb, Lake Webb, Hubert Brady, Bill Miller, Tom Brady, Chell Baker and Hays Wallace. In 1919 or 1920, they made a scout down the river, and arrived at our ranch in Hidalgo County on Thanksgiving Day. My sister had invited a number of guests from Mission, and had prepared a fine Thanksgiving dinner. The road to the ranch was unpaved, and a big rain fell in the early morning. No car could pull through the mud, so the crowd did not get there. Captain Wright and his company were returning from a scout, and rode up to the ranch about eleven o'clock. They had been eating bacon and *frijoles* for several weeks. All of them declared that the turkey and trimmings made the best meal they had ever eaten.

Shortly after World War I, Captain Wright was standing in front of the building that serves as a combination post office and custom-house in Brownsville. He was reading his mail and smoking a cigar. A man who had apparently been using marihuana started throwing bottles at people on the sidewalk. In keeping with the Ranger custom, Captain Wright carefully avoided playing policeman or taking any part in local affairs, so he looked around for a city officer. When none was in hailing distance, he told the weedy *hombre* to quiet down and behave himself. Instead of complying with this order, he attacked the captain with a dagger. A can of pipe tobacco in the breast pocket of his coat kept the blade from reaching his heart. The berserk man was instantly killed by the Ranger. An eyewitness said that he never stopped smoking his cigar. Captain Wright later remarked to me, "I wonder why that crazy scoundrel jumped on me? I never saw him before."

From this episode came a gem that was often quoted by Rangers. One adjutant general had issued an order requiring Rangers to make written reports of all their activities down to the smallest detail. Old timers believed that Rangering and bookkeeping were not compatible. Captain Wright particularly abhorred all clerical work. The current adjutant general had ordered elaborate report forms, which were supposed to cover every phase of a Ranger's duties. The last question to be answered was: "Disposition of Prisoner?" In this space, Captain Wright wrote, "Mean as hell. I had to kill him."

In 1922 the railroads of Texas were crippled by a general strike. Outbreaks of violence were daily occurrences. The railway companies had employed a large number of guards to protect their yards and other property. They were commissioned as deputy United States marshals. This inexperienced, untrained force was totally incapable of handling the situation, and the strikers laughed at their amateurish efforts. The railroads finally appealed for Rangers.

Captain Wright and his company were sent to Cleburne, a division point on the Santa Fe. For sleeping quarters, the railroad furnished them a Pullman car, which was sidetracked near the center of the town. The Rangers basked in its luxury. Captain Wright remarked that there was a lot of difference between his present plush bed, and having to sleep in his saddle blanket along the Rio Grande.

The tactics used by the marshals had been to post guards all over the railroad yards. They made good targets for the strikers, who showered them with rocks and other missiles. On the Rangers first night in Cleburne, the superintendent asked Captain Wright where he was going to station his men, who were only eight in number. In his inimitable manner, the captain replied, "I have never had it so easy in my life. The boys and I dearly love to sleep in this fine Pullman. We are going to stay right here, and not lose a minute of it." The railroad man was flabbergasted. "How on earth are you going to protect us?" he asked. "The first man who interferes with a train, or who bothers a working man, just come and tell me," replied Captain Wright. The superintendent went away shaking his head. He thought that the strikers would surely take over unless guards patrolled the yards.

The Rangers took their meals at a boarding house some distance from the Pullman. The superintendent warned Captain Wright to take a roundabout way, for if they went in a straight line they would pass the hangout of the most militant strikers. These included the "beef squad" who were especially hostile toward officers. "My boys are all horsebackers," said the Captain. "They don't want to do any extra walking. We'll go the shortest way."

Captain Wright and Sergeant Jack Webb were the first pair who started to dinner. When they got to the forbidden corner, the crowd of strikers started to jeer them, as they had done the marshals. Sergeant Webb was as good a Ranger as the Service ever produced. He and A. Y. Baker were the only two men I ever knew who had the genuine "graveyard grin." They laughed when they fought, which is the infallible mark of a man to be dreaded. Jack singled out the loudest mouthed agitator and "bent" his gun over his head before the striker knew what struck him. He rolled like a top into the arms of his cohorts. The sergeant quickly returned his pistol to the holster and flashed his smile on the group. With no profanity, he inquired in a mild, pleasant voice: "Any of you other gentlemen want your hair combed?" That ended the violence and no patrolling was necessary. The strikers did not know at what moment they might run afoul of the man who grinned while he wielded a forty-five.

Captain Wright and his Rangers rendered valuable service to the United States Government during the First World War. Mexico was infested with German and Japanese agents. Constant vigilance had to be maintained on the border, and a great deal of this service was performed by the Rangers under Captain Wright.

In 1925, when the Fergusons went in, Captain Wright was replaced by an ex-bartender. This man made a farce out of the company. An old

Ranger Jack Webb. The smiling warrior.

time Ranger, S. V. (Pete) Edwards, boxed his jaws on the streets of
Laredo. The Rangers sank to the level of the administration.

With the election of Governor Dan Moody, Captain Wright applied
for an appointment as Ranger captain. A new chief executive is
confronted with the problem of giving representation to all parts of
the state. This is the only fair way to distribute the positions, provided

that the applicants are of equal merit. I also applied for one of the captaincies, and we were both from Southwest Texas. For a time it looked as if one of us would have to give way to geography. Honorable Robert Lee Bobbitt, Speaker of the Texas House of Representatives, endorsed both of us. I told him that if only one could be appointed from our section of the state, to give it to Captain Wright. He was older and I could wait. We were both appointed.

Captain Wright served with distinction during the four years of the Moody administration, and two under Governor Sterling. He said that he enjoyed this more than any other of his career, for he had as the adjutant general an old Ranger comrade and lifelong friend.

It would give me great satisfaction to be able to relate that my native state had permitted Captain Wright to close his Ranger career in a manner befitting a veteran of his stature and background. I would like to write that this gallant warrior and faithful public servant had been suitably honored by a grateful citizenry. However, the facts do not warrant any expressions of this nature. While counterfeit Rangers who were not worthy of blacking his boots were basking in the favors of those in charge, Captain William Lee Wright terminated his service patrolling the docks in Corpus Christi. His vast experience as a leader was lost to the state. The poor judges of ability in Austin had him serving as a Ranger private. A politically motivated administration forced this outstanding gentleman to suffer this ignominy, and to end his long service in this shameful manner.

Chapter 41
FRANK A. HAMER

Ex-Ranger Dudley Snyder Barker, during his long tenure of office in the king sized county of Pecos, was generally regarded as the best sheriff in Texas. Several years before he passed away I made a trip to Alpine for the sole purpose of talking at length with him. No conversation with Dud Barker could be dull, and this one was particularly interesting to me, for in it we discussed the various Rangers he had known throughout his career. He sized up a number of good men, and recalled that many of his former comrades had made enviable records. I finally asked him point blank who, in his informed opinion, was the best all around Ranger. The veteran replied, "Well, I've never seen a better one than Frank Hamer."

Sheriff Barker was the man who first recommended young Hamer for enlistment in the Rangers. Throughout his life, he was deeply interested in the career of his protege. While writing *The Texas Rangers,* Dr. Walter Prescott Webb asked me if I agreed with him that Captain Hamer was the best living example of a modern Ranger. My reply was in the affirmative with the further statement that in any era he would have been great.

Captain Hamer was a remarkable man in many ways. His knowledge of nature, wild life and the outdoors could only be equaled by the

Indians. During the first cleanup of the Borger oil fields he and I were driving through the 6666 Ranch in the Panhandle, when a covey of quail ran across the road ahead of us. Captain Hamer stopped the car and said that he was going to call them. I was skeptical, but he proceeded to do this by making a chirping sound that is best described as a sort of cross between whistling and hissing. The partridges turned and came up to the automobile, some of them even getting under it. Of course we did not shoot the little fellows, and I was amazed and delighted to see and hear the plainsman talk to his feathered friends. Mrs. Hamer told me that her husband could work this magic on many kinds of birds. She said that it was particularly interesting to see him call owls. When driving through the woods in the daytime, Captain Hamer often stopped his car and gave what must have been their distress cry. All sleeping owls within the sound of his voice would wake up and fly to the spot, with ruffled feathers. They were completely puzzled at the familiar calls coming from such a strange place as an automobile, and their antics were very amusing.

With either rifle or pistol he was unquestionably the best practical shot in Texas. There may have been better exhibition marksmen among the arms company professionals like Winchester's Ad Toepperwein, but under fire Hamer topped them all. He had exceptionally good eyesight and was a fine billiard player. The coordination of eye and hand in that precision game seems to be the same gift or talent that is required to make a good shot with firearms. He always showed a preference for Remington rifles. While most of the other Rangers used the larger calibre Winchesters, Captain Hamer stayed with his little .25 automatic, which he later exchanged for a .30 of his favorite make.

Frank Augustus Hamer was born in Wilson County, Texas, on March 17, 1884. Six years later his father took the family to San Saba County. In his youth Frank worked on various ranches and soon became an expert cowboy, although guns were his principal interest. Years later when Tom Hickman and I, as his contemporary Ranger captains, judged rodeos, Captain Hamer declined to take any part in them. He explained his reason for this attitude to me in these words, "For many years I had a rodeo every morning by myself on the Pecos, and do not care to see another one." He never lost his love for horses, however, and was one of those good riders who, while weighing over two hundred pounds, could cover long distances without tiring his mount. Young Hamer enlisted in the Texas Rangers on April 21, 1906, joining Company C which was commanded by Captain John H. Rogers.

Captain Hamer and I were close friends for more than forty years. We scouted together on the Mexican border, beginning with the Bandit War of 1915, when I was a ranchman commissioned as a Ranger. We both served as captains under Governor Dan Moody for four years and I was adjutant general for two years while he commanded the headquarters company. By virtue of my office, I was in charge of all the Rangers, but our cordial relationship remained the same throughout these changes in official status.

Frank Hamer and his brother, Harrison, spent the Christmas week of 1918 at our ranch in the western part of Hidalgo County. During this visit the elder brother gave several exhibitions of his skill with rifle and pistol, in which he used moving targets. Captain Frank walked out into heavy brush to get a fat young deer for camp meat, and saw a spike buck jump over a clump of prickly pear more than a hundred yards away. At the crack of the .25 Remington, the animal fell dead, with the bullet hitting him squarely in the head. The Captain jokingly remarked that he was going to give the gun away on account of defective sights, for he had missed the deer's eye almost half an inch.

His pistol demonstrations were given at the home ranch, where they delighted the family, guests and *vaqueros*. The one who enjoyed Hamer's marksmanship most was our foreman, Edgar Magee, who had seen a great deal of rugged service on the border as a member of both the Arizona and Texas Rangers. He was one of those gunfighters sometimes found on the frontier who couldn't hit a barn door in target practice but never failed to get his man in actual combat. A single blackbird was perched near the top of a tall willow that grew on the edge of a nearby earthen tank. Although the wind was blowing and the tree swaying, Captain Hamer killed it with the first shot. After witnessing this feat, Magee announced that never again would he doubt any story told about the marksmanship of Frank Hamer.

The gun used for this shot was my Colt .45 single action six-shooter with a five and one-half inch barrel. Hamer had never fired it before. Fitted on this old pistol were an unusual pair of stocks. They were carved from guayacan, a variety of lignum vitae found in the semi-arid regions of Southwest Texas and Mexico. This wood is extremely hard and difficult to work but once properly shaped, its greenish serpentine grain takes on a beautiful finish. These handles were made for me by a retired carpenter named Robinson, who had taken up some school sections in Starr County. In common with all homesteaders, he had more time on his hands than anything else. He utilized his skill with tools to fashion many useful articles from the native bushes that grew in profusion on his land. A few years ago I found that Captain Hamer had wanted this pistol for a long time and I gladly presented it to him. The trigger guard has been filed off, and it is now in the collection of Charles Schreiner III.

He could hit targets with a pistol at greater distances than any man I ever saw. A Panhandle sheriff, who was the best marksman in that part of the country, came to Borger one day for a friendly shooting contest with Captain Hamer. We drove out to the edge of town, and before targets were set up, Hamer saw a small white rock glistening in the sun over a hundred yards away. He fired and hit the pebble, much to the sheriff's disgust. That gentleman refused to take his gun out of the holster, declaring that he came to shoot at pistol distances, and that anything beyond forty yards was a range for rifles. The boys used to ask Captain Hamer if he were not afraid that one of those long shots was liable to strain the barrel of his six-shooter.

Captain Hamer had thought out every detail of his profession. He said that there was a definite reason for perfecting his long range pistol shooting. During his lifetime, he had known of several cases where men using shotguns had run amuck in towns. The city or county officers, armed only with their pistols, had been killed. If he were ever caught in this predicament, the farsighted Hamer wanted to be sure that this six-shooter could outrange a shotgun.

Captain Hamer in his prime was one of the finest physical specimens in Texas. He stood six feet three inches in height, weighed two hundred and thirty pounds and did not have an ounce of fat on his body. He handled this great bulk easily and moved with the agility of a dancing master. His usual method of subduing a tough in oil fields or other trouble spots was to slap him on the ear with his open hand. The Captain's forearms were extremely well developed. When he boxed a man alongside the head, it reminded me of a grizzly bear cuffing a steer. If he ever used his pistol as a club, I never heard of it. Captain Hamer's open palm always took the fight out of the hardiest ruffian. For many years I had marvelled at the strength of his arms, but its background and source were not disclosed to me until 1930.

In that year Sheriff Murray of Mason County was murdered by a rumrunner. On a change of venue, his case had been transferred to Llano County. Feeling against the defendant reached such a high pitch that mob violence was feared and local authorities appealed for Rangers. Adjutant General Robert L. Robertson ordered Captains Hamer and Sterling to attend the trial and assist the sheriff in preventing an outbreak. We left Austin by automobile early in the morning, drove to Llano and escorted the prisoner from the jail to the courtroom, where he was given the death penalty. Our route took us through San Saba County and Captain Hamer stopped the car in front of an old roadside blacksmith shop. He said that it had once belonged to his father. As a youth he had put in many hours of toil at the anvil, swinging a sledge hammer and working with other heavy tools. This was where Frank Hamer got his brawny arms.

In World War II, a group of picked soldiers known as Commandos were given special training in jungle warfare. They were taught barroom, fist and skull, judo, or any other kind of hand fighting calculated to disable the enemy. Captain Hamer would have made an excellent instructor for these troops. He believed like the Army that an adversary should be defeated as quickly as possible, without regard to the tactics employed. The Captain used his feet with great skill, and few antagonists could stand up under his mule-like kicks. I once asked him if he ever had received instructions in *Savate,* the science of foot fighting practiced by the French. From the way he performed, I thought perhaps some adventure seeking Frenchman had drifted into the Pecos country and shown him how it was done in France. His answer was that he had never taken any lessons other than those given by the school of experience. In youthful fights when older boys ganged up on him, he discovered that his feet could be turned into high-powered weapons, Hamer continued to use them in later battles, for as he said, "they were always loaded."

When Captain Hamer was well past sixty years of age, he handled

421

a strike of milk workers in Houston. The parent union sent one of their most experienced strong-arm men from Chicago to head up a group they called the "beef squad." Their job was to beat up or maim any man who dared to cross the picket line. This imported thug was particularly hostile toward any officer who tried to protect the non-strikers. He boasted that he could tear any Texas Ranger, past or present, apart with his bare hands, and that he was going to make an example of the first one who bothered a striker. When Captain Hamer arrived at the milk plant gate, the plugugly started toward him, and was met more than half way. Hamer lashed out with several well placed kicks that sent his attacker to the hospital for extensive repairs, and to reflect on the indiscretion of assaulting an ex-Ranger who was more than twice his age.

In all its eleven hundred miles of meanderings that make the boundary between Texas and Mexico, the Rio Grande's most blood-stained spot is probably Tomate Bend. This sinister curve near Brownsville is one of the southernmost points in continental United States and a frequently used blind crossing. Here numerous *contrabandistas* plied their nocturnal trade and did not hesitate to shoot when anybody attempted to stop them. The fertile ground is covered with granjeno, jaraschinas and other varieties of semi-tropical undergrowth, interwoven by tazajilla and kindred cacti. The shadows provided by this river bottom jungle have made it a favorite rendezvous for smugglers since the Treaty of Guadalupe Hildalgo was signed in 1848.

At Tomate Bend on a dark night in 1918, Frank Hamer again proved that he functioned best when under fire and pressure. Ranger Captain W. W. Taylor, Sergeant Delbert Timberlake, Frank Hamer, Sheriff W. T. Vann of Cameron County and Ben Tumlinson, Sr., were scouting in that vicinity. Vann had been advised by an informant that a bunch of smugglers would cross the river with a load of contraband, and that several men wanted on this side were in the gang. The marauders always sent a *guia,* or guide, ahead of the main party. His job was to give them the signal when the coast was clear. If challenged, he could usually escape by diving headlong into the underbrush, with the odds of a bullet hitting him a hundred to one in his favor. The *hombre* who served as *guia* literally had to walk into the mouth of the gun, and his courage was bolstered by mescal or marihuana. A man does not become a smuggler nor prowl the Rio Grande at night if he expects to reach a tranquil old age.

Shortly after the officers had taken their stations, the guide stealthily crossed the river and reached the American side. He carried a cocked 45 calibre six-shooter in one hand and a dozen extra cartridges in the other. At the command, *"Alto"* (Halt), he fired his pistol toward the sound of the voice and started to duck in the brush. The bullet ricocheted off a tree, turned sideways and struck Sergeant Timberlake in the abdomen, inflicting a fatal wound. The sheriff was armed with a big bore shotgun, and he fired both barrels without effect. I went over the details of this fight carefully with both Captain Taylor and Ben Tumlinson. The latter came from a family of gunfighters and was rated as a top man in any shooting match. He frankly told me that the action was so sudden and the night so dark that he did not get off a shot. All the survivors agreed that if it had not been for the coolness and marksmanship of Frank Hamer, the slayer of Sergeant Timberlake would have made good his escape. In describing the way Hamer's 25 Remington automatic spewed a solid stream of fire, Captain Taylor said, "Bill, it looked like Frank was burning him up with a pear burner." This device works under pressure and throws a sheet of flame to which the ranch-raised Taylor likened Hamer's rapid shooting in the inky blackness.

Sergeant Delbert Timberlake, whom we always called Tim, was one of the best Rangers who ever died for his native state. He was a wonderful shot and carried out his duties in a manner that commanded the respect of all good citizens. Before that fatal night at Tomate Bend, I had heard and read of men who felt a premonition of coming death, but Tim's case is the only one of which I have any actual knowledge. He freely discussed this foreboding with his comrades and said he knew that his number was up. It was characteristic of Delbert Timberlake that he made no effort to avoid the assignment even though he felt that certain death awaited him that night. The coat he wore may have been one of the reasons the sergeant was struck by the smuggler's bullet. Like all Southwest Texas ranchmen and horseback Rangers, he used a short brush jacket made out of heavy duck. This was for protection against thorns. It had been laundered many times by native washerwomen, and the homemade lye soap they used had bleached it out. In contrast to the darkness of the river bank, this white garment made a plain target for the cat-eyed *guia*. Timberlake was the only casualty on the American side, as Hamer's burst of fire caused the dead smuggler's companions to beat a hasty retreat across the river without doing any shooting. The wounded Ranger was taken to the hospital in Brownsville and given the best possible medical attention, but he died the next day.

Less than six hours before Sergeant Timberlake was shot, he drove me to the railroad station in Brownsville, where I took the train for Del Rio. On my arrival there, I went to the headquarters of my boyhood friend, Ranger Captain Lon L. Willis, and spent the night. The next morning we received the news of Timberlake's death, and were advised that he would be buried in Uvalde. Captain Willis, Red

424

Hawkins, who subsequently became a Ranger captain, and I attended the funeral. The service was conducted by that grand pioneer preacher and friend of the Rangers, Brother Bruce Roberts.

Captain Hamer, who had temporarily severed his connection with the Rangers, was wounded in Sweetwater, Texas, by a neighboring sheriff. This was a personal matter having no connection with law enforcement, although both men had formerly been members of Captain Rogers' company. In the surprise attack on Hamer, which cost the sheriff his life, the latter was aided by an accomplice armed with a shotgun. While Hamer was defending himself with his pistol, a 44 calibre Smith & Wesson, this second man fired on him at close range. The charge of buckshot went over his head but the concussion knocked Captain Hamer down. Harrison Hamer ran up and leveled his gun at the would-be assassin, who had taken to his heels when he saw he had missed. Although wounded by the sheriff's bullet and dazed by the shotgun blast, Frank Hamer told his brother not to shoot the fleeing man in the back.

The Sweetwater duel is mentioned here mainly for the purpose of bringing out a remark made to Captain Hamer in my presence by a veteran Ranger, the late Captain J. A. Brooks. He had some years previously resigned from the Service and spent the balance of his life as judge of the county named for him. The three of us were chatting one day in the adjutant general's office when Captain Brooks said, "Hamer, that fellow you had the trouble with in Sweetwater was the only man I ever dreaded." From over forty years acquaintance with the speaker, I emphatically state that anybody he dreaded must have been the toughest man in the world.

In the pioneer days of silent motion pictures, the greatest Western star of them all was the late Tom Mix. He had many friends in Texas, and I gave him a Special Ranger commission as a reward for his help to Colonel Lee Simmons at the first prison rodeo. On his last trip through the state, Mix was pretty badly shaken up in an automobile wreck near Houston. He decided to stay over for a few days' rest. Captain Hamer and I happened to be in the city at the same time. We went to his suite in the Rice Hotel and announced we had come to "tail him up." The movie cowboy was delighted to see us and with a whoop, declared that this reunion called for a celebration topped off with champagne. Although he knew that I did not drink, he ordered a bucket of ice and several bottles of his favorite vintage. After the cork was popped, the wine poured and my customary "windmill high-ball" drawn from the ice water tap, Captain Hamer paid me one of the most genuine tributes of esteem and respect that I have ever received. He said, "Tom, General Sterling has never seen me take a drink, and I am not going to let him start now." He then stepped into the bathroom, drained his glass and returned to his chair. We had been out of the Ranger Service for several years and there was no official restraint involved. It was simply a thoughtful gesture to an old comrade.

Captain Hamer proved his love for the Service when Quartermaster R. W. Aldrich was permitted to usurp the authority which was by statute delegated to the senior captain. He assumed command of the Rangers, and the fault for allowing this unwarranted action lay with the adjutant general. Complete details of the Aldrich matter will be found in another chapter of this book. In a personal encounter or a gun fight, he would have stood no more chance with Hamer than a ten year old boy with the heavyweight boxing champion. Captain Hamer showed great forbearance in putting up with the interloper, for he remembered an episode in 1919 when a captain killed another Ranger in a brawl on the outskirts of Austin. He was not present and had no connection with the incident, but it almost caused the Rangers to be abolished. One of my first official acts was to discharge Aldrich because he was a detriment to the Service. Some people chose to believe that this summary action was taken at the instance of Captain Hamer. To keep the record straight, I make the statement that he knew nothing about it until my decision had been made.

On May 23, 1934, the careers of Clyde Barrow and his cigar smoking consort, Bonnie Parker, ended in a hail of bullets. The fatal shots came from guns in the hands of Texas and Louisiana officers headed by ex-Ranger Frank Hamer. Justice overtook this elusive pair on a country road in the piney woods of Louisiana, a little over three months after he had taken their trail. They were killed in an isolated place where the only lives jeopardized were those of the hunted and the hunters. The first newsman who reported the killing referred to it as an "ambush" and nearly all subsequent accounts have followed suit in copying this misnomer.

It is true that a trap was set for Barrow and Parker, but they were given a chance to surrender. Barrow was a mad dog killer who realized that he could not escape the electric chair if caught, and therefore determined to die fighting. Captain Hamer told me, as one old comrade to another, that he had hoped to take them alive, for among other reasons he did not want to be forced to kill a woman. When the outlaws drove up, he ordered them to "stick 'em up" and when no hands were raised, the officers opened fire. Sob sisters and others filled with maudlin sympathy for criminals make the claim that Barrow and Parker were ruthlessly shot down. They seem to forget that Barrow was charged with fifteen killings, and that his car contained fifteen guns, which ranged from Browning automatics to sawed off shotguns. Three thousand rounds of ammunition completed the arsenal, which proved that Captain Hamer was right when he concluded that the couple were not a pair of Sunday school students out for a peaceable automobile ride.

Some law enforcement agencies, while making arrests of public enemies, keep one idea uppermost in their minds, and that is to get their men. If innocent bystanders are by chance killed in the process, it is regrettable but purely incidental to the over-all success of the mission. Gangsters of Barrow's ilk showed in the Kansas City Union Station massacre that they would not hesitate to turn sub-machine guns loose in a crowd. Captain Hamer had his own code and ideas in handling matters of this kind. He believed that the first duty of an officer was the protection of women, children and other inoffensive citizens. I discussed this phase of law enforcement with him on a number of occasions, and he held very decided views on the danger of promiscuous shooting. On the Rio Grande, in oil field dives or any other outlaw dens, he was always willing to match wits and shots with the worst of them. The state and society invariably benefited from his acumen and marksmanship. Barrow and Parker were not ambushed, and the public should be everlastingly grateful to Captain Hamer and other prudent officers who do their shooting in places which bring no danger to non-combatants.

The aid of Captain Hamer was first enlisted by the superintendent of the Texas Prison System, Colonel Lee Simmons. In 1955, he and I performed our last service to the captain by acting as pall bearers at his funeral. In a break at the Eastham penal farm, four convicts escaped through the aid of Clyde Barrow. He killed one guard and held the others at bay with a hot fire from his machine gun. When a situation of this kind arises in Texas, the natural procedure is to call the Rangers. This could not be done in 1933, as the state was in the throes of a Ferguson administration. A large majority of their Rangers could not be depended upon for any service, much less to apprehend Barrow. Lee Simmons, himself a former sheriff, knew that having these fellows on the case would be the same as putting chicken hawks to guard hen roosts. He received one of their number a short time afterward as a convict. Therefore, Colonel Simmons turned to a man who had long served in the real Texas Rangers as senior captain, but who had resigned because his principles did not fit the pattern set by the Fergusons.

In April of 1934, two highway patrolmen were killed on a side road near Grapevine by Clyde Barrow and Bonnie Parker. L. G. Phares, who might well be called the father of the highway patrol, also realized that it would be futile to expect help from the Ferguson Rangers. Chief Phares, who invited me to make a talk at the first class at the highway patrol school, joined the prison system superintendent in his effort to capture Clyde Barrow. He authorized Captain Hamer to select another man as a companion, and B. M. Gault, who subsequently became a Ranger captain, was the one chosen. They made a good pair, as they had served together for six years in the headquarters company.

This chapter touches only a fraction of Frank Hamer's life and exploits. It contains a few of the lesser known facts about his career. I trust that some day an entire book will be written about him, and for that reason this sketch is very brief. He passed away peacefully in Austin in June of 1955. The leading Texas newspapers noted his death with fitting editorials; "We shall not see his like again" and "There were Giants in those days" were the themes of these tributes.

Chapter 42

JAMES B. GILLETT

J AMES B. Gillett represented the ideal type of Texas Ranger. His life story depicts the standard of the Service that I strive to portray. Courageous as a lion, kind and gentle as a good woman, he might well have been the inspiration of Bayard Taylor's quotation: "The bravest are the tenderest; The loving are the daring." After retiring from the Rangers and kindred activities, he became a successful cattleman, author, historian and one of the most highly respected citizens of his native state. He referred to his achievements in later life as "fruits of the Ranger Service." Much of his success was attributed to the experience he received in that rugged organization which afforded him a keen insight into human nature.

Upon resigning from the Rangers on December 26, 1881, James B. Gillett had completed six years and seven months' service, but with characteristic honesty, he titled his subsequently written book *Six Years with the Texas Rangers*. Among my most treasured possessions are copies of all three editions of this splendid work, each suitably inscribed by the author. At the time Captain George W. Baylor signed his honorable discharge with commendations, Gillett held the grade of sergeant.

It would be impossible to pick a combination of geography, times and circumstances that could produce a tougher town than El Paso,

Captain James B. Gillett, Captain W. W. Sterling and Captain J. A. Brooks taken in Falfurrias at the Brooks County Courthouse. The county was named for Captain Brooks.

Texas, in the early days of its turbulent existence. Situated on the Mexican border, it was just the right distance from Arizona, New Mexico and the Trans-Pecos region to attract wild and restless characters from each of those badman producing districts. The "front" of new railroads with their construction crews and hangers-on brought additional parasites and adventurers, none of whom would hesitate to cheat or kill in order to get what they considered their share of easy money. The El Paso crop of gunmen included some of the worst that the West ever produced, saloon keepers and gamblers generally considering killing a necessary adjunct to their profession.

James B. Gillett became the fourth marshal in the city of El Paso. The first and second holders of that office were killed by the third incumbent. Only the most modest accounts of his work in handling the El Paso badmen appear in ex-Ranger Gillett's book. Other Western writers, notably Eugene Cunningham, have related the marshal's service in an entertaining and truthful manner. Further accounts of his exploits on these pages would be superfluous and mere repetition. I simply hope to touch on some angles of Captain Gillett's widely publicized El Paso and Alpine episodes that appealed to me. My ideas and conclusions were formed from conversations with him and several of his contemporaries, plus my own experience with a later edition of similar characters.

There was an old saying on the frontier that certain gunfighters, when seeking to widen their reputations, used great care in picking the time, location and especially the crowd for their demonstrations of prowess. This stigma could not be coupled with the name of James B. Gillett. He was never backed down and would fight in any company, any place and under any circumstances that a call to duty demanded. He chased, captured and killed outlaws in the brake of the Llanos, helped stop the Mason County "war," guarded John Wesley Hardin, and was present at the death of Sam Bass. He fought Indians on both sides of the Rio Grande and invaded Mexico to bring out a man wanted in New Mexico for a foul murder. There never existed a tougher school of fire than the one in which Captain Gillett's mettle was proven with a post graduate course in the university of gun smoke.

Early Western pistol artists were tacitly rated according to the reputations they had gained in past duels. They might be compared to a top polo player who is handicapped a given number of goals denoting his skill in that hard riding game. John Wesley Hardin might be comparable to a ten goal polo expert with less formidable pistolians being scaled down to the bottom of the list. The vital difference was that the loser in the powder burning contests was playing for keeps and could be allotted only one chance to prove his proficiency with weapons. The penalty for awkward gun handling was permanent occupancy of a small and unhallowed plot in Boot Hill.

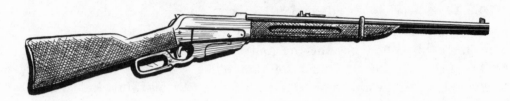

Dallas Stoudenmire was a ten goal gunman by every Western yardstick. He was a giant in stature, courage and marksmanship. His fighting background included service as an ex-Confederate soldier, ex-Texas Ranger, and ex-city marshal of early El Paso. In the acquisition of these exes, his actions had hardly been those of a pacifist. His saga does not record the score while he battled the Yankees, nor how many outlaws fell to his six-shooter when he was in the Rangers, but he had accidently and by design killed four men since coming to El Paso. Two of the local dead men were ex-city marshals. One of them had ambushed Stoudenmire, using a shotgun loaded with buckshot. Several accomplices helped the bushwhackers. The big man not only killed his assailant but charged the others. In spite of a wounded foot, he put them to flight. When Bill Johnson refused to turn over the jail keys, the redoubtable Stoudenmire obtained them by the direct and violent means of shaking him as a bulldog would handle a rat. The fact that Johnson carried in his pistol pocket what was supposed to be the equalizer between large and small men did not deter Dallas Stoudenmire.

The foregoing incomplete account of Dallas Stoudenmire's exploits in El Paso is given, not only to describe briefly one of that border town's most noted figures, but to give an idea of the type with whom

Marshal Gillett had to deal. He fell heir to the ticklish and potentially fatal chore of taking over the marshalship from this extremely dangerous man who felt that he had been unjustly deposed. Stoudenmire had neither the inclination nor the ability to treat his successor as he did his predecessor. While he had shaken Bill Johnson until his teeth rattled, he shook Jim Gillett's hand, congratulated him on his appointment and wished the new marshal well. Stoudenmire's extensive experience with fighting men had taught him the difference between wood and timber, between a game man and a Dominicker. Marshal Gillett later had occasion to arrest Stoudenmire and another well known gunman who were in the process of shooting it out when the marshal arrived. They were drinking, fighting mad and in about as dangerous a mood as men of their type can get. The words Gillett used in subduing this desperate pair were totally devoid of profanity and blustering, and have always remained classic. He threw down on the belligerents with a sawed off shotgun and in his quiet, even voice said, "Gentlemen, stop it or I will have to blow you in two." It was not necessary for the ex-Ranger to bellow his command in order to make it stand up. Both hardened gunfighters realized that Captain McNelly's statement made on the lower Rio Grande would hold true in this case. This peerless Ranger said, "A fighting gentleman is far more dangerous than any loudmouthed bully, when the going is rough and there is gunpowder to be burned."

Another episode in Captain Gillett's career which always intrigued me was his encounter in Alpine with a non-producing wastrel bearing the name of Bass Outlaw. He was a perfect specimen of those hard cases who brought no credit to the organization, but caused the Service to bear forever the stigma of their being classed as ex-Rangers. There have been far too many of these sorry examples running loose in later years, those foisted on our beloved state by the last Ferguson regime being the worst illustrations. The Alpine affair reflected an old and vicious pattern, all too familiar in Texas. Many times a worthless scoundrel would make a nuisance of himself, and either murder a useful citizen or force some good man to kill him.

After leaving the marshal's office in El Paso, Captain Gillett moved to Brewster County, where he had cattle interests. As a public service, and to supplement his income, he was serving as sheriff. The pioneer ranchmen of that new country were much too astute to allow the ability and experience of a veteran like Gillett to be wasted. His fellow citizens drafted him, realizing that a man of his calibre in the sheriff's office would go a long way toward maintaining the safety of their lives and property.

Company D was stationed in Alpine at this time. It was commanded by one of the finest Rangers in history, Captain Frank Jones. He was later killed in action near El Paso. In those days, the sound practice of allowing each captain to name his sergeant was in vogue. In some unexplained manner, Bass Outlaw had been given this grade. I was in the same position in Company D at a much later date and can appreciate Captain Jones' problem. Outlaw possessed all the physical requisites for a good Ranger, being a fine shot and very fast with a gun. When these abilities were used in the right direction, he could be of great value to the state. Doubtless, he promised Captain Jones that he would not drink. As sergeant, Outlaw was in charge of the Ranger company during his superior's absence. This made him doubly guilty in the events which led to his discharge. Getting drunk was not only a flagrant violation of a rule, but also a betrayal of Captain Jones' confidence.

Upon Captain Jones' return to the Ranger station, a citizen of Alpine informed him that Outlaw had gone on a spree. The commander lost no time in taking disciplinary action against his erring sergeant. Outlaw was considered double tough, chain lightning with a gun, and to cross him was generally regarded as a fatal mistake. But he had disgraced the Service, so Captain Jones called his hand and fired him as though he were a common sheep herder. His formidable reputation did not mean a thing to the commander of Company D, whose level and piercing gaze were too much for Outlaw's bleary eyes and whiskey jaded nerves. In discharging the man-eater, Captain Jones was not forced to use any gunplay; as they say on the border, the Captain simply "looked him down."

After his summary dismissal from the Rangers, Outlaw concentrated on heavy drinking. He blamed everybody but himself for his downfall. While cashing his State warrant, he told the owner of the store, ex-Ranger J. D. Jackson, that Jim Gillett was responsible for Captain Jones kicking him out of the Service. Jackson knew this to be untrue, and when Outlaw added threats against his friend's life, he determined to bring the sheriff face to face with his accuser. J. B. Gillett's answer to Outlaw's message could well be a model for all sheriffs. With a gesture of contempt, Gillet replied, "Wouldn't I be a fine sheriff to let a fellow like Outlaw run loose in my county? Let's go see him."

Now comes the part that has always been most interesting to me because it concerns the main point of fast gunplay. Bass Outlaw was known in all the border towns from Cotulla to El Paso as one of the speediest gunmen of his time. He was in the right frame of mind to commit a desperate act. He had blood in his eye, murder in his heart, whiskey in his stomach and a pistol in his well worn scabbard. When Sheriff Gillett braced him, he would have gone for his gun if he had had the faintest idea he could have won. I know his breed all too well. How fast was Gillett? He was just as fast as the occasion demanded. Just as fast as he had to be. Captain Gillett exemplified my ideas and practice on that score. Dudley Snyder Barker was that way. Ex-Ranger Jeff Milton and Sheriff John Slaughter of Arizona, both former Texans, were out of the same mold. Many good men of their type did not court a reputation for lightning pistol pulling, but had killed several gunmen who were supposed to be unbeatable. Outlaw quailed under Gillett's scathing remarks and ate all his hostile words. Various Western writers have speculated on what would have been the outcome if Outlaw had elected to shoot it out with Gillett. They figured that both would probably have been killed. Having been something more than a bystander when a deal or two of this kind was going on, I unhesitatingly state that Gillett would have downed Outlaw without receiving a scratch. Captain Bill McDonald's creed would have held good in a duel between this clean living ex-Ranger and a non-producing booze hound.

Jim Gillett had called Bass Outlaw's bluff many years before Bill McDonald's day, but Rangers of all times have believed firmly in the power of RIGHT, and have relied on this sustaining ally in many a tight place. Gillett, with his iron nerves unmarred by either liquor or tobacco, would simply have demonstrated the truth of McDonald's motto one more time.

In frontier annals, there have been countless instances of pistol fights between a man needing whiskey to bolster his nerves, and an adversary who was cold sober. Where their respective gun skills were anywhere near equal, the one carrying his load of Dutch courage invariably lost. The outcome of these fatal affairs was generally considered to be poetic justice, as the drinking combatant was always hunting for trouble when he met his match and demise. With safety engineers' efforts to curb traffic deaths on the highways, their researches have definitely proven that there was a scientific reason for the drinker's downfall. Even one drink of whiskey will slow a man's coordination enough to spell the difference between winning and losing, the odds increasing with the added alcoholic intake.

Ex-Ranger J. D. Jackson demonstrated on more than one occasion that the worth of a Ranger is not to be measured alone by his personal prowess. While he was president of the Texas and Southwestern Cattle Raisers Association, a stag breakfast was given in his honor at a Fort Worth club. On this occasion, there occurred the most magnificent display of moral courage I have ever been privileged to witness. A local publisher was preparing to tell a dirty joke at the head table. He knew of the honor guest's religious background and paused half apologetically, saying, "If Mr. Jackson will excuse me, I will tell one I heard the other day in Washington," thinking of course, that the president would say, "Go ahead, don't mind me." Under similar circumstances even some ministers will give their permission for these low anecdotes in their eagerness to be classed as good sports. The clean minded ex-Ranger, who by any rugged Texas yardstick or standard, was a man among men, replied with quiet but withering dignity, "Mr. Blank, I thank you for showing me that respect." The hitherto irrepressible newspaper man, for one of the rare times in his turbulent career, was subdued and did not attempt to complete the sordid story.

This brief sketch of Captain Gillett does not cover even a fraction of his full and useful life of service. In my chapters on Sam Bass and Frank Jackson, he is the principal source of information. In fact, a large part of my knowledge about those two outlaws was gained from conversation and correspondence with him.

My life was enriched by the close friendship of this great man. He maintained a keen interest in the welfare of the Rangers until his passing, stating to me that one of the saddest moments of his life was their descent into the mire at the hands of Ferguson in 1933.

436

Chapter 43
GUS T. JONES

A NUMBER of Rangers who subsequently made splendid records in similar fields did not get to be captains. There is no doubt but that most of them would have attained the top rank if they had continued in their first love. They were of the same mold and calibre of the great commanders. Almost without exception, these men preferred to stay in their old organization, but they could not afford to forego the better salaries paid by others. The Service was a rugged training school whose graduates were in constant demand, especially by agencies of the Federal Government. They were always glad to enlist men with good backgrounds in the Rangers.

The most outstanding product of this situation is Gus T. Jones. His Ranger comrades call him "Buster." He likes to hear the nickname of his youth, for the use of it denotes early and enduring friendships. Mr. Jones is a true Texan and a genuine frontiersman, having been born at old Fort Concho in Tom Green County. His father, W. W. Jones, was a lieutenant in Company A, Frontier Force of Rangers.

Gus T. Jones is the subject of several books, as well as countless newspaper and magazine articles. This brief chapter can relate only a small portion of his accomplishments and exploits. His long and distinguished career proves that there are few worthwhile things that

Gus T. (Buster) Jones of Company "A" Texas Rangers in 1907

cannot be done by a real Ranger. It further demonstrates that the experience he gained in that hard riding outfit fitted him for the responsible positions he held afterward and the important services he performed.

Abraham Lincoln judged men by their faces. The life and character of Gus T. Jones is revealed by a study of his visage. The broad forehead marks him as a man of high intelligence, while his square jaw and tight lipped mouth denote great determination. In ordinary conversation his words are spoken in a soft, refined voice, but when dealing with hard cases, his tones leave no doubt that he means business. The level gaze from his wide set eyes can penetrate the deepest mask, and his silvering crown of reddish hair completes the picture of a fearless though kindly gentleman.

The first phase of Mr. Jones' career began in 1898, when he volunteered for service in the Spanish-American War. Not quite sixteen years old, he may have resorted to the ruse sometimes used by boys who were the antitheses of slackers. They would write the word "eighteen" on a piece of paper and place it in one of their shoes. When the recruiting officer asked, "Are you over eighteen?" the patriotic youth could answer, "Yes, sir."

Early in life, Gus Jones demonstrated that he was endowed with the talents that are found only in the makeup of great officers. Although an excellent marksman with pistol, rifle and sub-machine gun, his greatest weapon was his intelligence. He used his head, and out-thought every criminal with whom he dealt. These ran the gamut from a frontier bully he handled during his tenure as night marshal of San Angelo, to the current public enemy number one whom he captured while serving as an agent-in-charge of the Federal Bureau of Investigation. Throughout his official career, Jones planned his campaigns with care, and prepared in advance for any contingency that might arise. Backed up by unlimited nerve and the knowledge that right was on his side, this strategy caused the downfall of countless lawbreakers. At the age of twenty-one, Gus T. Jones became night marshal of San Angelo, Texas. No man ever had a rougher assignment saddled onto his youthful shoulders. His bailiwick was the terminus of the Santa Fe branch line that extended westward from Temple. It was the railhead of a territory larger in area than several eastern states, and one of the leading livestock shipping points in the world. This fact brought countless cowboys in from distant ranches, and made it a mecca for all those who wanted to celebrate. A trip to town often meant a ride of over a hundred miles, and many of the waddies hailed from the "slick slopes of the salty Pecos."

They craved entertainment in the raw, and resented any interference with their rowdy pastimes such as shooting up the town. Restraint from a marshal who looked like a mere youth was particularly obnoxious to the guardians of the flocks and herds. After a few snorts of busthead whiskey, they turned into badmen from the headwaters of Bitter Creek. They liked to split the air with bloodcurdling yells, and to announce that, "The click of a six-shooter is music to my ears." The duties of a night marshal were particularly arduous as the prowling and howling did not start until after sunset.

San Angelo was the outfitting and supply center of Western Texas. Numerous freighting outfits with huge wagons drawn by multiple hitch teams picked up the vast quantities of merchandise brought in on the railroad. They hauled it overland to the surrounding ranches and inland towns. Between trips, the long distance mule skinners employed in this trade laid over in San Angelo. Very little of this time was spent in peaceful pursuits, and they liked to paint the town red. On paydays and Saturday nights, many of them became candidates for the hoosegow. Along with the cowhands, they soon learned that they could not run any sandies over Buster Jones.

While most of the railroad men were hard workers, many of the boomers were as tough as any of the other groups. Being the end of the line, San Angelo became their gathering place. The night marshal gave those who rode the iron horses the same fair but firm treatment that he meted out to the other riders and drivers.

The fourth bunch that Jones had to deal with was the gamblers, saloon bums and would-be badmen. These tallow faced parasites are always a problem for an officer, but the night marshal took them in stride. By applying the toe of his boot where it would do the most good, or "cutting biscuits" in their middle with the barrel of his 45, he soon had them eating out of his hand.

The first one who learned that Night Marshal Jones was smart as well as game was a noted badman who did his celebrating in San

Angelo. He had disarmed and "hoorawed" several town marshals, and was eager to add another name to his list of victims. Soon after young Jones took up his duties, this ruffian appeared at a popular saloon and announced that he had come to town for the express purpose of staging a repeat performance. He was about twice the size of the marshal, and was built like a gorilla. After taking a few drinks, he started the ruckus that he knew would be reported by the bartender. He awaited the arrival of Buster Jones with great glee, blood curdling yells and dire threats. The marshal was not hard to find, and he approached the disturber in a businesslike manner. Jones' pistol was stuck in the waistband of his trousers. The ring tailed tooter could scarcely believe what he saw. Disarming this youth would be easy. He grabbed the six-shooter and started to clamp down. A split second later, a shot rang out, he dropped the seized gun, squalled like a panther and began to count his fingers. The benighted bully was too dumb to reason out that Jones had purposely placed the pistol in an inviting position, and that the play was backed up by a second gun. The marshal took his prisoner on a personally conducted tour of his old haunts. At each one of them, he made the voluntary statement that he was not the curly wolf he had fancied himself to be, but was merely a mangy coyote. Buster did not have to run him out of town. He was so thoroughly cowed and his ego so deflated that he sneaked away in the night.

After serving in this capacity for a year, Jones accepted a commission as deputy sheriff of Tom Green County. His duties took him out into the ranch country, where he handled many cases involving the theft of livestock. The Rangers were selected mainly from men who had made good records as deputy sheriffs or other officers. Captains were looking for men of Jones' calibre, and at the age of twenty-four, he entered the Service.

The lower Rio Grande Valley was just beginning to develop, and his company was stationed at Harlingen. The St. Louis, Brownsville and Mexico Railroad extended their branch westward from this point, and it made a fair bid to become another "Six-shooter Junction." A large mesquite tree near the saloon of Domingo Roach, to which sometimes a dozen prisoners were chained, served as the jail.

The land was rapidly being cleared and put into cultivation. It was covered with heavy semi-tropical brush that had to be grubbed out by hand. This operation furnished employment for hundreds of laborers from Mexico. Many gamblers and other parasites of their own race followed them to the United States, where they joined forces with the native sports. They reaped a rich harvest from the toil of the ignorant workers. Among them were numbered some of the most desperate characters on the border, who were emboldened by the ease with which they could commit a murder and flee across the Rio Grande.

Grubbing contractors kept their men in large camps. On Saturday nights each one of them staged a dance, or *baile*. The dancing was done either on a platform, or on a smooth spot of clay. These were gala occasions for the gamblers. By the light of a kerosene lantern or by a mesquite wood fire they ran their games. Some of the fleeced Mexicans had complained to their employers, and the Rangers arrested a bunch of the crooks and chained them up. They swore vengeance.

One Saturday night Jones was alone in the Ranger camp. The other members of Company A had gone on a scout. He heard shooting at one of the camps, and went to investigate. A *sendero,* or straight trail, had been hewed out through the heavy brush, and it was the only road leading to the place. Three of the gambler-gunmen laid a trap for the Ranger as he came along this narrow path. They fired several shots to bring him out, and stepped back in the brush for the ambush. Jones was prepared for this move, and approached them with due caution. He heard one of them say, "Shoot again; he'll be along in a minute."

An axiom of old time Rangers when they found themselves outnumbered was, "Get in the middle and shoot your way out." On this occasion, it was closely followed by Buster Jones. When the melee was over, two of the bravos stayed on the ground, and the other one escaped in the darkness. The young Ranger was partially deafened in his right ear from the concussion of a pistol shot fired at close range by one of his assailants. The adjutant general commended him, and his comrades who are usually very sparing in their praise were particularly pleased with the way he handled the ambuscade.

For three years Jones served with the Rangers, where his outstanding work attracted the attention of the United States Customs. He became a mounted inspector of that agency, and guarded the border against smugglers for two years. At the age of thirty, he transferred to the Immigration Service, and became a member of the border patrol. Much of his service was on the Pacific Coast. During this time he was twice cited for meritorious conduct.

In 1916, Jones joined the Criminal Investigation Section of the Department of Justice, forerunner of the present Federal Bureau of Investigation. After one year's service, he was made special agent-in-charge of the El Paso district, which included all of West Texas, New Mexico and Arizona. When the United States entered the First World War in 1917, numerous German agents and spies were active in Mexico. One of the most dangerous of these was Lothar Witcke, who used the alias of Pablo Werbiski. There was no doubt about his guilt, but the German was beyond their reach. Agent-in-Charge Jones formulated a plan to get him on the American side of the international boundary, and it succeeded. The details of this coup are still a military secret. Witcke-Werbiski was tried as a spy at Fort Sam Houston, and sentenced to be hanged. The verdict was reduced to life imprisonment by President Wilson. This was the only spy captured in continental United States during the First World War.

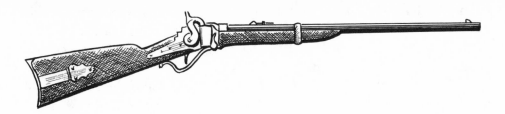

In 1921 he was made division superintendent of the Federal Bureau of Investigation in the territory covering Western Louisiana, Texas, New Mexico and Arizona. When the division system was abolished in 1922, Jones was designated as special agent-in-charge at San Antonio, Texas.

No wiser choice could have been made. The Federal Bureau of Investigation gave preference to men who were lawyers or accountants. Gus T. Jones belonged in neither category. However, he possessed a natural talent that is more valuable than any number of college degrees. He had horse sense. Will Rogers described this faculty as "something a jackass can't have." Horse sense plus experience made the ex-Ranger the ideal man to take charge of any operation in the Southwest.

Under his administration a number of public enemies were captured. He always took the lead and never left the rough work to his subordinates. Jones went to Houston and captured two of the most wanted men on the list, Dewey Hunt and Hugh Gant.

His most publicized case was the capture and conviction of the kidnappers of Oklahoma oil man Charles F. Urschel. It is a source of pride to all ex-Rangers that the man who was most responsible for bringing these criminals to justice received his early training in their organization. Mr. Urschel is a very intelligent man, and his observations during his captivity were largely responsible for locating the outlaws' hideout. However, without the cooperation and prompting of the equally intelligent Jones, it would have never been discovered. The two went over the minutest details of the evidence collected by the victim, and through their combined efforts, succeeded in pinpointing the place. Mr. Urschel did not choose to sit back and let the officers do all the dangerous work. He was game to the core. Shotgun in hand, he went with them to capture Bailey and Shannon.

At some point during his service, every real Ranger has experienced moments that can be understood only by those who have been in similar situations. Their thoughts and feelings at these times cannot be explained in an interview. Gus T. Jones gave me a man to man account of the capture of Harvey Bailey. It was carried out in the manner used by old time Rangers. No fan-fare, no loudspeakers and the like; he just walked into his lair and "gathered" him. At that time, Bailey was unquestionably the most dangerous criminal at large. He was sleeping on a bed laid on top of two sawhorses in the yard of the kidnappers' hideout in Wise County, when Jones awakened him with the muzzle of a Thompson sub-machine gun. The outlaw was a big man in stature. Like all hunted creatures, he awoke in full possession of his faculties. There was no more drowsiness in Bailey than there would be in a panther.

"Get your hands up, Harvey," ordered Jones. "If there's a shot fired from the barn or house, I'll cut you half in two." Bailey's pistol was lying at his side only a few inches from his hand. The ex-Ranger read in the outlaw's eyes what was going on in his mind. He was figuring his chances on being able to get his gun. Jones warned, "I'm getting tired of waiting, Harvey. Last call." Bailey knew that a single false move meant death. He surrendered. The ex-Ranger had learned to shoot

444

with the old reliable Colt forty-five single action six-shooter, but he kept abreast of the times and learned to handle the semi-automatic weapons with great skill. At Camp Perry, he won the national championship with the Thompson gun.

Many men have asked Mr. Jones why he took a chance with a desperado like Bailey. They wondered why he had not pressed the trigger of his Tommy gun on sight. Nothing in the record of Gus Jones indicates that he believes in dealing gently with criminals, nor does it show that, if the necessity arises, he minds shooting one or more of them. He further realized that if the positions had been reversed, Bailey would have killed him without hesitation. Those who chided him for not opening fire on the kidnapper said, "Nobody would know." "I would know," replied the ex-Ranger.

The success of the campaign was due in a large measure to the planning and leadership of Mr. Jones. The first earmark of his early training was the fact that the men in charge took the lead. He used the old Ranger adage of "come on boys" rather than "go on boys." The traditional hour to round up criminals was also invoked, and they closed in at daybreak. The way of the transgressor is hard, and criminals do not enjoy peaceful, tranquil sleep. After a restless night of tossing, their vitality is at its lowest ebb in the cold, gray dawn.

Among the greatest admirers of Gus Jones are some of the desperate criminals he has brought to justice. For each of them a split second spelled difference between life and death. Harvey Bailey once said to him, "Mr. Jones, I'm sure glad that it was you instead of a shaky man who held that Tommy gun under my nose at Boss Shannon's place in Wise County. A scared man would have squeezed the trigger as soon as he recognized me." Dewey Hunt and Hugh Gant expressed the same sentiments. The ex-Ranger used a 351 semi-automatic Winchester to arrest this pair. At different times, Bailey, Hunt and Gant each enjoyed the dubious honor of being public enemy number one.

Upon completion of the maximum security prison at Alcatraz, the task of transferring its select list of Federal convicts to their new quarters was entrusted to Gus T. Jones. The most hardened criminals in the country had to be picked up from scattered jails, and transported by rail to "The Rock". The Texan planned the dangerous trips with great care, and worked out every detail in advance. He used several special trains in the movement, and his desperados were so well guarded that not a single one of them tried to escape. Among his charges were Al Capone and several other public enemies of the same stripe.

Although the sneak attack on Pearl Harbor did not occur until late in 1941, military men and other informed people realized as early as 1939 that we would be drawn into another world war. It was highly important to keep the German and Japanese agents from becoming active in Mexico, and to avoid the trouble we experienced with them in World War I. The attitude of the Mexican people was friendly toward us, but it could change if the United States was represented by the wrong people. Gus T. Jones understood the temperament of the Mexicans, spoke their language and had earned their confidence. He was detached from the Federal Bureau of Investigation and ordered to Mexico City as civil attache to the American Embassy. No more prudent move could have been made.

While serving in this capacity, he took the lead in assisting the Mexican Government to break up the Nazi gestapo in their country. All its members were arrested, and either jailed or deported. He also assisted the Mexicans in establishing the first police radio patrol in Latin America. For this work, he was made honorary chief of the Secret Service of Mexico, being the only American to achieve this distinction.

In 1940 he was permanently assigned to the Foreign Service as attache in Mexico City. He assisted the Mexican authorities in locating and apprehending Gerhard Wilhelm Kunze, former head of the German-American Bund in the United States, who had fled to Mexico. Kunze was turned over to the American authorities and given a long sentence in prison for his subversive activities in this country.

In 1943, Mr. Jones served as liaison officer with the British Intelligence in the West Indies. He received commendation from both the American and British officials for his outstanding service. While holding these positions, he was as much at home wearing the striped trousers and formal attire of a diplomat as he was in the garb of a Texas Ranger.

During World War II, one of my assignments was that of military intelligence officer for the Southern Land Frontier. This sector comprised the Mexican border from the Gulf of Mexico to the state line of Arizona. I had served in the same territory during World War I. The difference in the attitude of Mexico toward the United States in the two wars was amazing. While they were decidedly hostile in the first conflict, they were friendly and cooperative in the second one. This was due largely to the work of men like Gus T. Jones. His valuable service along this line may not have appeared in any official report, but I could feel it in every one of my dealings with the Mexicans.

One item in particular, although little known, was of vast importance to the war effort. An acute shortage of mercury existed in both Germany and Japan. It is used in the manufacture of percussion caps. Our enemy nations received a large part of their supply from the quicksilver mines of Mexico. Their agents worked frantically to get it to the homelands. A high official of a major oil company was a Nazi sympathizer, and until detected, did his dirty work out of Tampico. He lightered the mercury on fishing boats from the mouth of the Soto la Marina River, and transferred it to cargo submarines. In this way it reached Germany. The Japanese sent theirs by the same method, from Tiburon in the Gulf of California. The Mexican authorities, largely through the efforts of Gus T. Jones, cut off this supply, thereby shortening the war. They also interned a man who had been a U-boat commander in the First World War, and who had subsequently married into a prominent Mexican ranching family near the border.

In 1944 Mr. Jones retired from active service with the Federal Bureau of Investigation. He was an agent-in-charge for twenty-seven years, longest tenure of any agent in that position. Major industrial plants with security problems had no intentions of allowing his vast amount of experience and ability to go to waste. He serves as consultant for several of them, and travels all over the country in his work. Large ranchmen in the United States and Mexico also avail themselves of his services. He lives in a beautiful part of San Antonio, and is one of its most revered citizens. At the age of seventy-five, he is still going strong. While by no means living in the past, he is never too busy to talk to an old comrade about his service in the Texas Rangers.

Chapter 44
SHELY FAMILY

PRACTICALLY every organization has its "First Family". In the Texas Rangers, this distinction unquestionably belongs to the Shelys. Six men who bore that honorable name have been in the Service. They were Captain Josephus, Lorenzo Dow, Warren Washington, Abraham Lincoln, William Ysidro and his son, William Almond Shely.

The eldest brother, Josephus, was appointed first lieutenant of Company F on December 1, 1883. He succeeded Charles B. McKinney, who resigned to run for sheriff of La Salle County. McKinney, a veteran of McNelly's famous company, was killed and S. V. (Pete) Edwards was wounded by outlaws while holding that office. On May 1, 1884, at the age of thirty, Lieutenant Shely was promoted to the rank of captain.

He made a great record in various parts of the state, especially in troubled spots of La Salle and De Witt Counties. His activity is evidenced by an excerpt from the 1884 report of Adjutant General W. H. King. A State senator in the northeastern portion of the state complained that the money spent on maintaining the Rangers was wasted. The general declared:

I could exhibit hundreds of private and official letters speaking in terms of honest praise for the Rangers; I could show the proceedings of citizens' meetings and large stock conventions all over the border in which formal and open recognition was given in favor of this frontier force and its valuable service to the people; I could cite you the constant and earnest efforts, and the moving appeals made for years past, by the legislators from the western and southwestern parts of the State, to have this force kept in the field, as the only sure defense of the orderly, honest and law-abiding citizens of the frontier against the criminal classes. As an evidence of the positive good from this force, I may say that one company alone, of the six in the field, captured and put into the hands of the law, in April and May, 109 men charged with various crimes, mostly stealing and murder. This company serves in Southwest Texas and is commanded by Captain Jos. Shely.

The vast size of Texas and the wide diversity of interests between citizens of its unlike sections had made their impact on the scope of Ranger operations by the early eighties. The Frontier Battalion was wholly dependent for its maintenance on appropriations made by the legislature. The East Texas members were reluctant to grant funds for its support. When they grudgingly traded out with western legislators, it was with the understanding that the Rangers would be used only in the northern and western portions of the state. These short-sighted politicians asserted, in fiery speeches designed for home consumption, that no help from Austin was needed in their piney woods bailiwicks.

This ill advised attempt to restrict the Rangers' territory, however, proved to be an example of the fable, "It all depends on whose ox is gored," paraphrased Texas style into, "It all depends on whose cattle are being stolen". When the night riders started swinging their wide loops on the Coastal Plain, livestock owners there were just as eager to accept Ranger aid as any ranchman on Devil's River.

In the summer of 1884, a group of stockmen in Chambers County appealed to Governor John Ireland to send them a detachment of Rangers. They charged that an organized band of cattle thieves was preying on the herds of legitimate ranchmen. The petitioners did not mince words, and called the ringleaders by name. The Governor was further informed that the local officers were powerless to stop the wholesale thefts, or to arrest the guilty parties. In response to this plea, Captain Joe Shely with six members of Campany F, including John A. Brooks and John H. Rogers, were dispatched to Chambers County.

Ex-Ranger W. W. (Wash) Shely while serving as Sheriff of Starr County.

Their arrival in the historic town of Anahuac on August 11, 1884, in all probability, marked the first time Rangers were used in East Texas.

The dashing Captain Shely had seen extensive service against cow thieves around his station in Cotulla, which at that time might well be called the rustler capital of the world. The denizens of the cactus flats were past masters in the furtive art of re-burning brands and altering earmarks. Compared to the brush poppers with whom he had been dealing in the dense chaparral between the Nueces River and the Rio Grande, the Chambers County boys were rank amateurs.

450

By dint of hard riding and Ranger tactics, Captain Shely soon put a stop to the gang's depredations. The service rendered by his company was highly satisfactory to all honest cowmen in that part of the state. Several of them joined the county judge in writing a letter to the Governor. It was couched in glowing terms, and strongly commended the work of the Rangers during their tour of duty in Chambers County.

Warren W. (Wash) Shely attained the rank of sergeant in Company F. He was a colorful figure, and engaged in many battles with border bandits. On May 9, 1884, he and Ranger S. V. (Pete) Edwards attempted to arrest Pedro Reyes and Pancho Salinas. A running fight ensued. Reyes was killed and Salinas was wounded. On September 11 of the same year, Sergeant Shely killed Juan Posada, under the same circumstances. In each case, the justice of the peace who held the inquest ruled that the Rangers acted in the discharge of their duty. After retiring from the Service, Wash Shely became sheriff of Starr County, and for many years was a political power along the border.

While holding this office, he was a staunch ally of the Rangers. The horde of border outlaws that dodged back and forth across the Rio Grande tried to avoid all contact with this one of the Shelys. They invariably regretted meeting him and the results were usually fatal for the *bandido*.

Bonifacio Martinez was a Mexican citizen who had crossed over into the United States and killed one of his fellow countrymen. The dead *hombre* was a political refugee who had fled Mexico to escape the wrath of President Diaz. He underestimated the long arm of Don Porfirio, and Bonifacio had a murder charge hanging over his head in Texas.

Emboldened by his success, the assassin organized a band of his own, and became a noted border raider. One day he and a dozen or more of his *companeros* rode into Roma. Sheriff Shely enjoyed the confidence of the people, and was well liked by most of them. He had established an efficient information system and was immediately notified when the famous bandit came into his bailiwick. The ex-Ranger did not summon a posse to assist in the arrest, but hitched up his buckboard and went to the scene by himself. He drove directly up to Bonifacio, stuck a six-shooter in his middle and ordered him to get in the vehicle. Martinez was plucked from the midst of his followers and they were warned by Shely that any hostile demonstration would result in the instant death of their leader. Bonifacio was safely jailed in Rancho Davis, which was an early name for Rio Grande City.

Probably the worst border character killed by Wash Shely was a Mexican known as Mangas de Agua. He had been a revolutionist with Catarino Garza and had escaped to this side a few jumps ahead of the *Rurales*. Mangas repaid the country that offered him asylum by becoming a bandit, and made his headquarters in Duval County. He was extremely cruel, and seemed to enjoy torturing his victims. The wily *bandido* had escaped from several posses, and became the object of especial attention from the Rangers. One of his worst crimes was the ambush murder of a prominent San Diego citizen, County Clerk Rufus Glover.

Ranger Will Shely was at that time in Company E under Captain J. S. McNeel. He was sure he could effect the capture or death of Mangas de Agua if the captain would allow him to select his partner, and if they were given a free rein. Permission was readily granted and to aide him on this important scout, Will Shely picked Ranger Henry Perkins.

These two Rangers knew that Mangas de Agua sometimes holed up in a brushy spot near Soledad, a ranch in Duval County. They hoped to jump him there. Ex-Ranger Captain Oglesby lived at Los Americanos Ranch. He was glad to furnish Shely and Perkins with fresh horses. They also secured the services of one of the best trailers in the country, Jorge Alaniz, who lived at Las Animas.

When the three came within a quarter of a mile of the hideout, Jorge was instructed to ride on in. If he saw anybody, he was to tell them he was hunting stray horses. He would also signal the Rangers if Mangas was there, and they would make the arrest. The trailer soon returned leading a saddled horse. He reported that Mangas was not at the house. A *vaquero* there said that the riderless horse came in to the ranch soon after he had heard some shooting. He knew that something was wrong, but he had been afraid to go out and investigate. The Rangers hurried to the ranch and started to backtrack on the horse's trail. In a short time, they found the body of Rufus Glover, where he had been shot from his horse.

Rangers Shely and Perkins took the body to San Diego, where they got the details of the tragedy. Late in the afternoon of the previous day, Glover and two other men had been combing the chaparral for Mangas de Agua. Just about dusk they rode into a small, semi-circular clearing. They saw two men on the other side riding into a *sendero* hewed through the dense brush. Glover and his companions spurred after them, and were perfect targets for an ambush. Beside the trail was a big rock that further aided the bushwhackers. Mangas and his accomplice secreted themselves behind this natural breastwork, and Glover was killed without having the slightest chance to put up a fight. The two men with him escaped with their lives, although one horse was killed.

Upon information furnished through the efforts of his brother, the sheriff of Starr County went to a ranch where Mangas and a *companero* would spend the night. Wash Shely was accompanied by two Seminole Indians who were formerly Army scouts. The wanted men were camped under a large mesquite tree. When he called on them to surrender, Mangas opened fire with a Winchester, and wounded all three of them. Wash Shely was armed with a big bore shotgun, loaded with buckshot. He fired both barrels, and the blast ended the evil career of Mangas de Agua.

Even in that early day, there were sinister happenings in Duval County. In 1890, a county judge, treasurer and others from San Diego petitioned the adjutant general to station a company of Rangers there "to prevent a recurrence of murders such as T. C. Weidenmueller who was burned to death by turpentine". One rumor had it that County Clerk Rufus Glover, who was becoming a man of influence, was marked for slaughter by rival politicians. Mangas de Agua made a convenient and willing tool for their machinations.

In his *The West from a Car Window,* Richard Harding Davis was fascinated by an exhibition of fancy pistol shooting staged for his benefit by William Y. Shely. The eminent war correspondent stated: "A board about one foot wide and two feet high was placed some sixty feet off in the prairie. Sheriff Shely, who had resigned from the Rangers to get married, whipped out his revolver, turning it in the air and shooting with the sights upside down, emptied it into the impromtu target." The 45 Colt single action Peacemaker used by ex-Ranger Will Shely lends itself to this shot, which was a favorite stunt for expert users of that incomparable old weapon. Davis also mentioned that "Will was a brother of Joe Shely, one of the best Captains the Rangers ever had."

William Y. Shely, member of the First Family of the Texas Rangers. He and a brother, Lorenzo Dow Shely, founded the "Traveller" line of Quarter Horses. Photograph taken while he was serving as Sheriff of Nueces County.

In the early nineties, Will Shely was serving as a deputy sheriff of Nueces County. One morning Henry Allen, who was in charge of the horses on Laureles Ranch, then owned by a British syndicate, galloped up to the courthouse and reported that a *vaquero* had stolen two of his best saddle horses. He also stole a Winchester and "lit a shuck" for the Rio Grande. Shely started out after him alone, although he certainly could have used a partner. The fugitive had about twelve hours' start, but as he was riding one horse and leading the other, his trial was easy for an expert tracker like Shely to follow. He took down the fence between the Laureles and the King Ranch, and passed to the southeast of Santa Gertrudis. The trail turned west, and passed near Los Ebanitos, bossed by Wesley Stevens. He hated horse thieves, and gladly loaned Shely one of the best saddle animals on the ranch. With due pride in the Running W, Stevens assured the deputy that he would "take you there and bring you back." In making this statement the ranchero did not care how many miles had to be covered on the ride.

Freshly mounted, Shely followed the trial through the King Ranch fence until it crossed the road to Hidalgo. Here the fugitive turned south in the direction of Mexico. Shely followed his track until late at night when the road forked. He struck matches to find the one taken by the fleeing *vaquero,* and rode on until daylight. Coming to a windmill, he stopped to rest and water his horse. About four o'clock in the afternoon he rode out on a mesa and saw a *jacal.* Two horses were grazing nearby. He rode up within a short distance of the house, and staked his horse. Winchester in hand, he walked up to the house. Looking in at the door, he saw his man, asleep on the floor, with his rifle beside him. Shely stepped inside, picked up the gun, awakened the sleeping horse thief, and snapped the handcuffs on him.

Shely had been on the trail for thirty hours and was very tired. He tied the prisoner to a mesquite tree, and laid down for a short rest. Just before dark, he unloosed him and made him saddle one of the stolen horses. The other was tied to the tail of the one he rode. The cavalcade started out for Alice. About eight o'clock Shely began to get sleepy and decided to camp for the night.

The country had not grown up in brush at that time and Texas riders did not carry picket pins like the cavalrymen. They used a method that is known by few people of this generation. When they wanted to secure their horses for the night on the prairie, they "holed" them. This was done by digging a hole in the ground with their knives. Several knots were tied in the end of the stake rope which was buried and the ground tightly tamped. A hard pull straight up would dislodge it, but as a grazing horse pulls horizontally, it would serve the purpose.

After the horses were attended to, Shely placed all the guns at a safe distance and handcuffed the prisoner to him. Using their saddles for pillows, he tried to get some shut-eye. Before daylight next morning he awoke with a start. All early day border Mexicans smoked corn shuck cigarettes. In fact, one of the nicknames given them by Americans was "Shuck". Shely's prisoner had poked some of the shucks that he was allowed to keep under the manacle and had almost slipped it from his wrist when the deputy awoke. They saddled up again and rode into La Cabra, the ranch of Don Andres Canales. This *caballero* was a proven friend of Rangers, and he furnished guards for the prisoner. After being relieved of this responsibility, Shely got some much needed rest. Don Andres was the father of J. T. Canales, prominent attorney who for many years represented his district in the Texas Legislature.

Will Shely accomplished many constructive things. One of these was the founding of the Traveller family of quarter horses. He and his brother, Lorenzo Dow Shely, kept this outstanding stallion on their ranch in what is now Jim Wells County. Both the brothers were excellent judges of horseflesh, and each assembled a band of carefully selected brood mares. Mating them with Traveller, they produced some of the finest "short" horses in history. Among these were Little Joe, who sired Zantanon, the "Man of War of Mexico," Texas Chief, Blue Eyes, Lady S and many others. The fabulous Waggoner Ranch followed the Shely bloodlines by purchasing Texas Chief. In 1912, I was with a shipment of Lasater cattle destined for Fort Worth. At Alice, Will Shely loaded him on our train. I was glad to look after this grand old stallion on his ride to North Texas. Shortly after arriving at the ranch, he was killed in a storm. Many years later, they purchased a three times removed grandson of Traveller, who won many championships for the Three Dees. They named him Poco Bueno.

The last public service performed by Will Shely was of incalculable value to Texas and the Nation. This could have been accomplished only by a man thoroughly familiar with the Mexican border. While serving

Colonel William Almond Shely mounted on Texas Chief. The Shely family maintain that this horse was the greatest son of Traveller. They believe that if he had not been accidentally killed at an early age, Chief would have surpassed the record of his half brother, Little Joe.

as sheriff of Nueces County, he noticed that a great deal of marihuana was coming into Corpus Christi and that the number of addicts, especially young ones, was increasing at an alarming rate. He started an investigation, sending his deputies southward to locate the source of supply. They found one large field near Raymondville, and another near Bishop in his own county. He immediately notified the Department of Public Safety of his findings, and Captain Will McMurray of the Rangers joined in the campaign against the diabolical weed. The United States Customs and narcotic divisions also gave full cooperation and several thousand acres were destroyed. The entire drive was the result of initiative on the part of ex-Ranger Will Shely.

The only one of the famous brothers that I personally knew was William Y. Shely. I met him in 1912, and we were warm friends until his passing in 1939. He told me some of his experiences in the Rangers, and identified many pictures in my collection. His widow, Mrs. Josephine Almond Shely, with his daughters, Mrs. Elizabeth Shely Newman and Mrs. Dorothy Shely McElroy, are among my dearest friends. At my wedding, his son, the late Colonel William Almond Shely, was one of my groomsmen. The other was Arnold Shary. In his youth, Colonel Shely was a Ranger, and served during the Bandit War of 1915. He resigned to accept a commission in the United States Army, and was awarded the Legion of Merit.

It is unlikely that any other family will ever equal the Ranger record of the Shelys.

Chapter 45
KING RANCH

No book dealing with the Texas Rangers would be complete if it did not contain a chapter on the King Ranch. Captain King believed in the Rangers, and the Rangers believed in him. The owners of the ranch, as well as their employees, both Anglo and Latin, have been my friends for many years. As a captain in the Rangers, I have scouted over the greater part of their lands, and have ridden many of their horses. I have known five generations of the family. Personally and politically, all my sentiments are those of a *Puro Kineño*.

A magnificent two volume history of this cattle empire has just been completed. Nationally known researchers have made an exhaustive study of the subject, and it would be difficult to add anything to their findings. My brief sketch will merely touch on a few incidents of which I have personal knowledge, or ones that have been passed on to me by word of mouth. These will be supplemented by excerpts from reports of former adjutant generals of Texas.

Captain King came to the Rio Grande in 1847, as a steamboat pilot. In 1852, he made a journey on horseback from Brownsville to Corpus Christi. He was deeply impressed by the grasses that grew on the level prairie. After crossing the Arroyo Colorado, only one strip of *encinal* was encountered, the balance being a treeless plain. The sight of so much natural feed turned the twenty-eight year old sea faring man's fancy from ships to ranching. He established the domain bearing his name in 1853. In some manner that has defied the efforts of researchers, Captain King became crippled in one leg. The Mexicans always referred to him as *El Cojo Keen*.

After his lands reached the proportion of an empire, Captain King was forced to employ a company of private rangers. They worked in the dual capacity of fighting men and cowhands. I was well acquainted with one of the best members of this carefully selected group, a Dane named E. R. Jenson. His blue eyes, square jaw and flowing mustache combined to make him the perfect picture of a Viking. Although he was never regularly enlisted by McNelly, he rode many miles with his company. Mr. Jenson revered the names of Captains King and Mc-Nelly. He loved to talk about them. From numerous conversations with him, my role being that of a listener, I was never able to decide which of these great men occupied first place in his memories. One of the pastures in the Santa Gertrudis division of the King Ranch is known as the Jenson.

Around the turn of the century, Jenson left the employ of the Kings and established a ranch of his own in Starr County. Taking up four sections of State land, he later acquired several other tracts by purchase. For a headquarters he built a two-story house and painted it green. This gave his ranch the name of Casa Verde. When Brooks County was organized in 1912, it was included in the new sub-division, and Mr. Jensen became a county commissioner. His duties in this capacity often brought him to Falfurrias, and I met him through Captain Brooks.

He took his official work very seriously, and bought himself a copy of the Revised Statutes. I used to go to his room at the Park Hotel and help him study up on the law as it applied to county commissioners. He was never without his six-shooter, and on one occasion it went off by accident. The wild bullet passed through the wooden wall, and created a sensation among the guests.

Mr. Jenson often spoke of Captain King's fondness for liquor. He recalled that somebody reported one of the captain's trail foremen for being drunk in Dodge City. "Nothing wrong with that," replied Captain King. "I've been drinking whiskey for thirty years." "By nature

Captain King was a kindly man," E. R. Jenson told me. "He used to tell us 'I have to make them think I'm a man-eater or they'll kill me'." In common with everybody else on the ranch, the young Dane soon learned to recognize the *patron's* danger signal. When they saw him stride out on the gallery with one pants leg in his boot and one out, the watchword was *"mucho cuidado"*.

E. R. Jenson's belief that Captain King was a kindly man at heart is borne out by a story related to me by Mrs. Elizabeth Shely Newman, daughter of ex-Ranger and Quarter Horse Breeder William Y. Shely. Her mother was a daughter of Joseph Almond, pioneer ranchman of Southwest Texas. Mrs. Shely was one of my best friends, and I was privileged to pay my last sad respects to this gracious lady by serving as a pallbearer at her funeral. Mrs. Newman said, "Mother always liked and admired Captain King. She often told us children about her first meeting with him, and she considered it one of her most pleasant childhood memories. When Mother was in her early teens, she and her sister, accompanied by their father, were going to Laredo on the Texas-Mexican Railroad. The train was slow, the track rough and the wood burning locomotive poured clouds of smoke on the passengers. They would not reach their destination until far into the night, and the journey was very tiresome. At Collins, a long-since abandoned station east of Alice, Captain King boarded the train. He was attended by a *mozo* whom he called his "toddy boy." The Almond sisters were seated together, and they shared a single pillow. This fact was instantly noted by the cattle king, and he dispatched his man post haste to bring additional pillows from his personal baggage. Notwithstanding his widely publicized thirst, the gallant Captain saw to the comfort of the young ladies before inviting their father into the next car for a drink."

Lieutenant Lee (Red) Hall sent Captain King a fighting man named Pablino Coy. He came from a scrapping family. When Ben Thompson and King Fisher were killed in San Antonio, his brother, Jacobo Coy, was among those present, and could hardly be classed as an innocent bystander. One of Pablino's running mates was a colorful Kentuckian called Colonel Crump. He stood over six feet in height and loved any kind of excitement, from running hounds to fighting bandits.

The picturesque colonel was not employed by the King Ranch. He called himself a free lance, and made his headquarters at Lagarto. Several stockmen of Live Oak and adjoining counties employed him to act as a range rider or stock detective. Each of them contributed a share of his salary, and his function was to protect them against stealing. He hated any kind of a rustler, and did not like to be bothered with prisoners.

Late one afternoon Colonel Crump was scouting with Pablino Coy, and they captured two men suspected of being horse thieves. The next morning the captives were found hanged to a mesquite tree. The colonel reported that he and Coy had been attacked by a mob, who seized their prisoners and strung them up. By way of proving the story, Crump exhibited his hat, which had a bullet hole through the crown. "But Colonel," observed a citizen, "if the bullet had taken that course, it would have blown your brains out." "That would appear to be the case," replied the old fox, "but you see when they started shooting at us, I got so scared that my hair stood straight up. That raised my hat high enough for the bullet to miss my head."

Captain King later sent Crump to Dodge City and several other terminal trail towns. His orders were to meet all incoming herds and cut out any cattle branded Running W.

Pablino Coy had another bravo brother named Emmett. His Spanish speaking friends sometimes called him Emmeterio and sometimes called him Emilio. He was a large, heavy set man of fierce countenance and forbidding manner. Bonifacio Perez was much smaller in size, and weighed around one hundred and thirty pounds. He owned a store at El Lucero (Morning Star). This beautiful *motte* of large, gnarled live-oaks was formerly in Hidalgo County, but since 1911 had been in Brooks County. Bad blood existed between the two men, said to have been originally caused by Coy's attentions to Perez's wife, Maria. This trouble was aggravated by a dispute over an account. One day early in 1900, Emmeterio rode up to the store. Before he could dismount, the merchant started shooting at him with a Winchester. Coy made no attempt to return the fire, but put spurs to his fast gray horse and took cover in a nearby thicket.

Several weeks later the Gunter and Jones outfit were gathering cattle for shipment to the Indian Territory. Emmett Coy was one of the cowboys. They had stopped at a grove of liveoaks called Lucero Viejo. Bonifacio Perez rode out to the camp. Old timers and local historians disagree on the reason for this visit. Some say that Coy had invited Perez out to have dinner with him, in the hope that their quarrel could be settled. A fat calf had been butchered, and plenty of fresh meat placed on the fire. The head was buried and covered with coals to make a *barbicoa*. After a good bait of this cow camp delicacy, the most bitter enemies would feel like burying the hatchet. Other *paisanos* still living in Encino and El Lucero declare that Perez went to collect a debt from Coy.

Be that as it may, Bonifacio rode up and tied his horse at a discreet distance from the chuck wagon. This rule is strictly and often profanely enforced by camp cooks in every part of the cow country. He carried a Winchester in his saddle scabbard, but left it there when he dismounted. Perez walked up and joined the cowhands, who were seated on the ground eating their dinner. As soon as they had finished their meal and gotten up, Coy began cursing and abusing Perez. He kicked him down and then started shooting at the fallen man with a forty-five calibre six-shooter. Coy also had a large knife in his other hand. Bonifacio landed on his all fours and started crawling away. From this position he drew a 38 calibre, bone handled pistol. Some old timers state that he was carrying it in one of his boots. Pancho Garza, noted border character known as El Chinchillo, was fourteen years old at the time of the killing. He declared that Bonifacio had the weapon in the waistband of his trousers, wrapped up in a cloth. He further says that when the gun was pulled, the wrapping came out with it. In any event, Perez fired three shots at his assailant, and hit him every time. One of the bullets struck Coy in the forehead and cut his hat band. It was a glancing shot and only marked the skin. This gave rise to the legend that Perez had hit him squarely between the eyes, when actually the fatal

wounds were the ones in his body. Coy also shot three times but only two of them took effect. Perez died clutching his pistol and still trying to get off another shot.

Ignacio Zarate jumped on his horse and raced to El Lucero with the tragic news. Wiley Seago was foreman of Dillard Fant's Candelaria Ranch. He, with Juvenico Garcia, Vivian de Luna and other *vaqueros* from the Gunter and Jones outfit, buried Coy. They used a large cypress water trough for a coffin. He and another man were interred side by side. Some say that Bonifacio Perez is in the other grave, while others declare he is buried at El Lucero. The site of these graves is a shady spot in the *encinal,* fittingly called Los Muertos (The Dead Men).

Macario Ramirez was justice of the peace in Precinct No. 8 of Hidalgo County. His son, Juan Ramirez of Encino, found Judge Ramirez's official report of the Coy-Perez fight in an old trunk, where it had been for fifty-eight years, and loaned it to me. A copy of it is produced here, with the translation by Professor E. E. Mireles of the Corpus Christi school system.

It is worthy of note that in Hidalgo County at the turn of the century even official documents were written in Spanish.

On this the 20th day of May, 1900, I was called by special messenger of Tom Jones to go and hold an inquest after a fight that had taken place at the old Lucero where, near a camp or about ten steps from it, I found two dead men in whom I recognized the person of Emilio Coy and the person of Bonifacio Perez. After Mr. Jones and J. L. Phillips and Wiley Seago, the manager of the Candelaria Ranch were present, I examined Emilio and found three shots. One entered his left side and went through to his right side destroying the bone of his right arm, one shot hit him on his left shoulder and pierced his neck and the other on his forehead, going through his hat band and grazing his skin. There was a big open knife underneath and a new bone handled .45 calibre gun with three empty shells.

At a distance of a yard from the first was the second one whom I recognized and he had two shots, one over the navel and with the bullet in his skin. He had the other shot over his right breast and out through his underarm. In his right hand, which was almost closed, he held a used .38 calibre, bone handled pistol with three empty shells. When I arrived at the camp there was only an American man who did not understand Spanish and the Mexican cook, both of whom declared that they did not know the reason for the fight, that they heard the noise of the shots and that when they saw the two men, they were lying on the ground. Mr. Jones and Mr. Phillips, who were near, catching horses from the remuda, went to see them and they were already dead.

I hereby affix my official signature on this the 20th day of May, 1900.

> MACARIO RAMIREZ
> Justice of the Peace,
> Precinct No. 8
> Hidalgo County, Texas.

This report of Judge Ramirez clears up several disputed points about the fight at El Lucero.

Border folk love to compose verses, or *corridos,* about any unusual event, particularly tragedies. The Coy-Perez duel to the death inspired this one:

Año de Mil Novecientos	In the year nineteen hundred,
Esta fecha la que doy	This is the date I give,
Fué la muerte de Bonifacio	When the death of Bonifacio
Con Emilio Coy.	and Emilio Coy took place.

El día 20 de Mayo,	It was on the twentieth of May,
Según dice el cocinero,	According to the cook,
Se matan a balazos,	Two men kill each other
Dos hombres en El Lucero	at the Lucero.

Coy le dijo a Bonifacio	Coy said to Bonifacio
Quiero hablar contigo solo,	I want to speak to you alone,
y salieron para afuera,	And they went out by themselves,
Dando manos a las pistolas	Taking their guns in their hands,

Bonifacio mal herido	Bonifacio, badly wounded,
Ya con dos tiros de muerte,	Already with two fatal shots,
Uno le pegó en el cuello,	One hitting him in the neck,
Otro le pegó en la frente	The other on his forehead.

Adios, mi esposa María,	Goodbye my wife, Maria,
Los dos nos dimos la muerte,	We both killed ourselves,
y vas a mi tumba un día,	And you go to my grave someday,
y llorar mi triste suerte.	To cry your sorrow over my death.

When I was bossing a cow outfit for Ed C. Lasater, the former owner, we often camped at Los Muertos. There were twenty *vaqueros* in the *corrida* and I was the only man in it who could speak English. Around the fire at night and through countless corn shuck cigarettes, the details of the Coy-Perez fight were rehashed. I recall that on my twenty-first birthday, our camp was at Los Muertos. It is now on the Encino division of the King Ranch.

On October 1, 1889, Sheriff S. A. Brito of Cameron County appealed to Adjutant General W. H. King for a company of Rangers "to suppress cattle thieving from Mexico, and Mexican bandits, outlaws and marauders, which cannot be taken care of by the county authorities." On October 22, R. J. Kleberg in person, accompanied by District Attorney D. McNeil Turner, made application for Rangers on the same grounds as those outlined by Sheriff Brito. A squad of Special Rangers was appointed.

Following the assassination of District Judge Stanley Welch in Rio Grande City on the night of November 5, 1906, and the ensuing Ranger fight at Las Casitas, Governor Lanham ordered National Guardsmen to the scene. Adjutant General John A. Hulen, Colonel P. C. Townsend, Assistant Quartermaster General Albert E. Devine, Major Thomas

C. Fryar, surgeon, and Troop D of the First Texas Calvary, from Corsicana, commanded by Captain W. H. Murphy, were dispatched to Rio Grande City. The terminus of the railroad was at Sam Fordyce, twenty-four miles from their destination, and the balance of the journey had to be made on horseback. Arrangements were made with Robert J. Kleberg to furnish mounts for the command. They were sent from Kingsville to Sam Fordyce by special train. The horses were classed as "gentle" by the *vaqueros*, but they were somewhat suspicious of the unfamiliar McClellan saddles and the accouterments of the soldiers. Several of the cavalrymen walked part of the way and led their horses, while others rode double on the more gentle ones. It was typical of the King Ranch that they could, on short notice, mount an entire troop of cavalry. Few others in the United States could have duplicated this feat.

Shortly after the termination of the bandit trouble, a politician correctly described by Representative J. T. Canales as an "intriguer" was made senior captain of the Rangers. His advent constituted the lowest blow dealt to the Service by an administration other than those of the Fergusons. He was able to worm his way into this position through the weakness of an adjutant general. This fellow, who brought nothing but discredit on the organization, sought to ingratiate himself with the King Ranch. He called on R. J. Kleberg, Sr. In the familiar language of a gangster, he said, "If you want any of these *hombres* bumped off, just let me know." His offer met with a stern rebuke. "Nothing like that must happen on this ranch," warned Mr. Kleberg. "We don't want anybody killed."

When Captain McNelly came to the border with his picked company, the State armed them with Sharp's carbines. These old smoke poles were 50 calibre, single shot weapons, entirely unsuited for combat service. Shooting the black powder cartridges of that day, they would heat after a few rounds. Captain King had no intentions of allowing this first class fighting force to be handicapped by the lack of the best and most modern guns. He furnished the entire company with the Model 1873, 44-40 calibre Winchesters. These repeating rifles increased McNelly's fire power nearly ten fold. While their range was not as great as the 50 Sharp's long barreled buffalo guns, it compared favorably with that of the short one, and was far superior in every other

467

hoy dia 20 de mayo de 1900
fui llamado por el Sr Tom Jon
con un correo para que fuera a
dar fé de un pleito en el Rancho
del Lucero Bajo donde alli cerca
de un campo de corrida como a
dies pasos de distancia encontre
dos hombres muertos en los que se
conocí la persona de Emilio
Coy y la persona de Bonifacio
Peres despues de ya estar alli
presentes el Sr Jon y C. L. Phillips
y Guale el administrador de la casa
de Candelaria Examine a Emilio
y le alle trestiros uno lo atrabeso
del costado esquierdo a el costado
derecho trosandole el gueso del
Braso derecho, un tiro le pego sobre
el hombro esquierdo le atrabeso el
pesqueso y otro tiro tenia en la
frente trosandole la sinta del som
brero Rallandole poco el cutes alli
debajo estaba una nabaja grande
abierta y una pistola de piano de
gueso nueba calibre 45 con tres
casquillos descargados,
a distancia de una Yarda del primero estaba
el segundo lo reconocí y tenia

dos tiros uno arriba del ombligo lo atraveso y le quedo la bala entre el cutis en el cuadril esquierdo tenia el otro tiro abajo de la tetilla derecha y le salio debajo del sobaco, en la mano derecha casi serrada tenia una pistola puño de gueso usada de calibre 38. tenia la pistola tres casquillos descargados, en el canpo cuande lle que no abia mas que un honbre Americano que no intendia castellano y el cosinero mexicano losque declararon no aber sabido la causa de la disputa olleron la detonacion de los tiros y cuando los vieron lla estaban tirados en tierra el Sr Fon y el Sr Phillipss que estaban cerca agarrando unos caballos para resmudar binieron a berlos y lla estaban bien muertos.

Testigo mi firma oficial este dia 20 de Mayo de 1900

Macario Ramirez
J. de P. P. Nro 8 Hidalgo Cnn Texas

Report of Inquest held over the bodies of Emilio Coy
and Bonifacio Perez by Juez de Paz Macario Ramirez

way. Captain McNelly could not have made his great record on the lower Rio Grande without the contribution from Captain King.

When Captain McNelly died on September 4, 1877, at the age of thirty-three years, he was buried in a private cemetery near Burton, Washington County, Texas. A splendid monument was erected over his grave by Captain King. It is sixteen feet high, and is made of red Texas granite. On one side are his lodge emblems, on another a Confederate cannon, on another his name, and on the fourth side is a

quotation from William Collins' ode, "How Sleep the Brave." There is no reference to his Ranger service nor to the donor of the statue. In 1956, I had a replica of the monument made for Robert C. Wells, public relations director of the King Ranch.

The late George Durham was one of McNelly's youngest Rangers. After leaving the Service, he became a foreman on El Sauz, a division of the King Ranch. Two of his sons, and a grandson, have succeeded him in this position, although the ranch has passed into the hands of other heirs of Captain King. Ex-Ranger Durham often said, "When I die, I want to be buried at the feet of Captain McNelly."

During the years Company D was stationed in Falfurrias, my family and I often visited Santa Gertrudis. It was before the influx of sightseers forced them to adopt the policy of conducting guided tours, and no hospitality could equal the brand dispensed by the King Ranch. One afternoon Mrs. R. J. Kleberg, Sr., Mrs. Sterling, our six year old daughter Inez, and I went for a walk around the grounds. We accompanied Mr. Kleberg, whose nurse pushed him in his wheel chair. At the edge of the spacious yard, my little girl saw a buttercup. With the instinct of a child, she picked the pretty flower and brought it to Mr. Kleberg. His eyes filled with tears as he patted her hand.

In the late nineteen twenties, I saw the largest herd of cattle I have ever seen, or ever expect to see again in Texas. The ranch was working the country between Santa Gertrudis and the coast, and had thrown together around fourteen thousand head. They were held in the Telephone pasture. With four outfits cutting on the edges, the herd was so big that the cattle in the center were not disturbed. The significance of this cannot be appreciated by those whose knowledge of separating cattle has been limited to watching cutting horse contests in rodeos. Here some of these ring tailed tooters make a farce of actual range work in which both horse and rider combine their talents to form an efficient team. Tom T. East, Jr., great-grandson of Captain Richard King, and peerless cowman in his own right, was with his father, the late T. T. East, when this herd was being worked. Although a young lad at the time, he recalls all the details perfectly.

The late Richard Mifflin Kleberg was considered the "patron saint" of Southwest Texas cowboys. He was a marvelous horseman, and

471

In the photo, handwritten: To Bill & Zora with Affectionate regards Dick

Richard Mifflin Kleberg. Horseman par excellence and true friend.

his arrival at any rodeo was hailed with delight by the contestants. With either pistol or rifle, he was an expert marksman and a great hunter. He served his district for many years in Congress, where he proved himself a statesman rather than a politician. A gifted orator when the occasion demanded, he was also a famous raconteur, and his fund of cowboy stories was practically inexhaustible.

For many years the late Tom T. East, son-in-law of R. J. Kleberg, Sr., operated the vast Wells Ranch in Starr County. There was no telephone at Rincon de en Medio, the headquarters, which was eighteen miles from our ranch. We acted as a sort of liaison between this outpost and Santa Gertrudis. When an important message had to be delivered, we were glad to send it out to our neighbor. They also shipped their cattle from our pens on the San Benito & Rio Grande Valley Railroad, commonly called the "Spiderweb." Several bucks bearing the King

Ranch earmark, the Hole and Split, were killed on our ranch. They had been caught in roundups on the Norias division, where the *vaqueros* had roped them for sport. After cutting the *Kineño senal* in both ears, they turned them loose. The decorated deer had decided to change their range.

The last time R. J. Kleberg, Sr., was in San Antonio, he and Caesar Kleberg were eating dinner in the St. Anthony Hotel, I was seated at a nearby table, and arose to pay my respects to them. In front of the elder gentleman was a large bowl of salad. In a sad tone of voice he said, "Isn't this awful? I own as many cattle as any man in Texas, and here they force me to eat rabbit food." It is a source of great satisfaction to those of us who are getting old, that the doctors have now learned that the best diet for older people is plenty of good beef.

Both Captains King and Kenedy were sailors. The love of the sea cropped out in some of their descendants. In 1931, Richard M. Kleberg and John G. Kenedy had a fine gaff rigged sloop constructed especially for local waters. She was made by the veteran Rockport boat builder, Chick Roberts. In honor of the owners and their wives, she was named the *Four Friends*. Before the railroad was built to Brownsville, practically all of the freighting from that area was done by coastwise schooners. Therefore, a breed of men developed that Dick Kleberg called "half cowboy and half sailor." I learned to sail when a small boy, and first came to Corpus Christi on the old *Katie M.* I was also on the old three masted schooner, *Olga,* owned by the Woodhouse family of Brownsville. When we moved to Corpus Christi in 1938, Mr. Kleberg let me have the *Four Friends.* Numerous people enjoyed outings on her, and many boys of the city learned to sail on this grand old boat. After I returned from World War II, we took many of the Navy personnel out and taught them to sail. Several young men who belonged to the most prominent families in the nation stayed on the *Four Friends* during their tour of duty at the naval air training station. One of the national pictorial magazines published an article on the half-cowboy, and half-sailor men, and showed a picture of me going down in the cabin wearing cowboy boots and coming out in a yachting cap.

In the fall of 1938, the Greatest Show on Earth came to Corpus Christi. The owners, John Ringling North and Henry Ringling (Buddy)

Caesar Kleberg at the old Norias Ranch house, with one of his favorite bird dogs.

North, made their private box available to me for a circus party. Mrs. R. J. Kleberg, Sr., her grandson Belton Johnson, Congressman and Mrs. Richard M. Kleberg, Mr. and Mrs. John G. Kenedy, Jr., together with my wife and two daughters made up the group. At the conclusion of the afternoon performance, Mr. Kleberg invited his hosts to visit the King Ranch. We went in the circus car, a huge sixteen cylinder Cadillac. The back road was chosen, in order that the North brothers could see more of the ranch country. It soon become apparent that the liveried chauffeur was not used to driving on rural, unpaved roads. Dick Kleberg took the wheel. He was soon making more than a hundred miles an hour and the circus people declared that the Big Top did not offer a more hair raising spectacle. As a result of their first visit to Santa Gertrudis, the North brothers have purchased many fine quarter horses from the King Ranch. These intelligent animals are easily trained, and quickly learn the circus routines.

During his last campaign, R. M. Kleberg and I went to Palo Alto Ranch to call on Mrs. Clara Driscoll. She was National Democratic Committeewoman for Texas and affectionately known as the "Savior of the Alamo." Mr. Kleberg's opponents were claiming that she was not supporting him, and we decided to call on her and ascertain the facts. Mrs. Driscoll indignantly said, "Richard, who could have made such a statement? After all that our families have meant to each other throughout the years, how could you think such a thing? Of course, I am for you to the limit." Mrs. Driscoll, who owned over a hundred thousand acres of land, was an individualist in her own right and would not play second fiddle to anybody. When asked by a friend in the East if she joined the King Ranch, she is reputed to have answered, "The King Ranch joins me."

I traveled with Dick Kleberg in his campaign, and between towns in which he had speaking engagements I would not let him talk. He told friends that he was in the hands of a tyrant and nicknamed me "Muldoon." I was on terminal leave from World War II, and had determined never again to take part in politics. Mrs. R. J. Kleberg, Sr., and Caesar Kleberg asked me to accompany him, and I was glad to perform this service for them.

Many persons, including a nationally known author, have asked me how the neighbors feel toward the King Ranch. They seemed to be

surprised and disappointed at my answer. Even some supposedly intelligent people get their concept of a large ranch from the movies or
television. In these make-believe media, the big ones oppress and intimidate the little ones. Where Santa Gertrudis is concerned the opposite
is true. They offer every assistance to adjoining ranchmen. In my varied
capacities of ranch owner, ranch manager and Ranger captain, and
through a period of half a century, I have found the King Ranch to be
the personification of "Good Neighbor."

Chapter 46
SAM BASS

Indiana has produced her full share of good as well as famous men. They have made valuable contributions to the welfare and culture of the nation. Numerous statesmen, industrialists, agriculturists, poets and authors were born there. Few early Texans knew very much about these worthy Hoosiers. Many of them, however, will always remember the name of one of her wastrel, law flaunting sons. Cowboy troubadours with their twanging "gitfiddles" are constant reminders of his birthplace, the early age at which he began to wander, and his destination. The ballad declares:

> Sam Bass was born in Indiana,
> It was his native home.
> At the early age of seventeen
> Young Sam began to roam.
>
> At first he came to Texas,
> A cowboy for to be.
> A kinder hearted fellow,
> You'll seldom ever see.

Along with most every man in Texas at that time, Sam was a fancier of race horses. He acquired a fleet-footed mare. She was highly regarded by the sporting citizens of North Texas, who gave her the name of the owner's home town. This honor has been bestowed on noted speedsters at different times, in various parts of the state, as is evidenced by Belton Queen, Karnes City Jim, the Hallettsville Mare, and others of their class. Bass' sorrel filly, unlike the Old Gray *Yegua,* has lost none of the vigor she had in the days of yore. As the years go by, she has made some remarkable gains in both speed and fame.

> Sam used to deal in race stock,
> He bought the Denton Mare.
> He matched her in scrub races,
> And took her to the fair.

Young Bass had found employment with Sheriff "Dad" Egan of Denton County, although he did not serve as a deputy. The boss laid down the law to him. "Either get rid of that mare and stop trying to be a race horse man or get you another job," he said. Sam quit and rode to San Antonio.

Far to the southwest of Denton, in the historic old town of Goliad, another young man made his home. His environment was entirely different from that of the youth from Indiana. Member of an old and highly respected family, he was bred to the occupation of a ranchman. Handsome and dashing, he loved to engage in games of chance or to take part in any other pastime that offered plenty of excitement.

In speaking of him, my mother-in-law told me of a circumstance that happened in her early life. She said, "My father, John Harlan Blackwell, raised good horses in a country that was famed for its fine horseflesh. Our ranch was on the Guadalupe River in the edge of De Witt and Gonzales Counties. His stock of horses enjoyed a widespread reputation. They had lots of stamina or 'bottom' and plenty of cow sense. He proudly declared that any one of them 'would carry a man all day in a lope and bring him back to the ranch that night.' One day, when I was a little girl I went down to the corrals to watch my father and the hands brand some colts. I was peeping through the fence unnoticed when a fine looking young man rode up, shook hands with Father and engaged him in conversation. I was able to catch these words: 'Uncle John (the term did not denote relationship but is borrowed from the Mexicans who call a respected older man *Tio*),

I am in a bad fix. I have had an unfortunate love affair at home. I want to buy a good horse, and get with an outfit that is going up the Trail. I'll pay you for him when I get back.' 'All right, Joel, I'll let you have one,' replied my father. The young man put his saddle on the newly purchased horse and rode away toward San Antonio. His name was Joel Collins."

In the seventies, San Antonio was the mecca of drovers and cow-hands who participated in the annual movement of cattle up the Big Trail. It was also the banking center and clearing house of many beef barons. They could make financial arrangements here for the purchases of their herds, wages for the hands and expenses for supplies. The profits made in successful seasons were so great that steer men were willing to pay as high as twenty per cent interest on their loans. Early in 1877, the trails of Joel Collins, drover looking for hands, and Sam Bass, cowboy looking for a season's work, crossed in the Alamo City.

Collins had both cow sense and ability, and soon qualified as a foreman. After bossing several years for prominent owners, he decided to branch out and drive a herd to the northern markets on his own. Many volumes have been written about the accumulation of cattle in Texas during and directly after the Civil War. This surplus of beef and the opening of the Chisholm Trail resulted in many drovers entering the business, some on a huge scale. The panic of 1873 ruined all but the strongest of them, and curtailed the operations of others. For this reason, a responsible, energetic man who owned a good *remuda,* a chuck wagon and enough money to provision and pay wages for the trip could buy his herd on credit. The ranchmen were willing to wait for their money until the cattle were sold, and the buyer returned to Texas. Moral risk was a prime factor in transactions of this kind and Joel Collins, because of his good family background, was accepted as a trustworthy man. He arranged to put up his herd in Uvalde and ad-joining counties. Several of the local ranchmen pooled their cattle and sold him the required number on deferred payment. Collins went by San Antonio to recruit additional hands and among those hired was Sam Bass. Now, as the head of a trail outfit, Collins received the cattle, tallied the various brands and gave the owners a memorandum showing the amount due each of them. The herd was then road branded and started north with the grass. Collins and his hands overcame all hazards of the trail and arrived safely in Deadwood, South Dakota. The cattle were sold, and the saddle-weary cowboys, with the boss still taking the lead, started out to look for the diversions offered in that notorious frontier town. What began as a harmless frolic turned into a protracted carousal. When Collins sobered up, all the money he owed to his creditors in Texas had been squandered. Filled with remorse, he determined to stop at nothing to get the money needed to pay off his debts. Collins, with Sam Bass and several others, robbed a few stage coaches around Deadwood but their loot was not a drop in the bucket compared to the sum required to square him at home. He, Sam Bass and four others, held up a Union Pacific train at Big Springs, Nebraska. Their loot was $60,000 in freshly coined twenty dollar gold pieces that were being shipped from the San Francisco mint. Each double eagle was stamped with the year it was made, 1877, and as these were the only ones of that vintage, they were easy to identify.

The money was split three ways and the six train robbers divided into pairs. Collins and Bill Heffridge started back to San Antonio, carrying their part of the booty on a pack horse. They were killed by United States soldiers at Buffalo Springs, Kansas.

Cattlemen of that day were given to turning current events, both good and bad, into jokes. When it became an established fact that Collins had proved recreant to his trust, his creditors received the news with mingled feelings of sorrow, disappointment and anger. On learning of the Union Pacific robbery, one chaparral humorist explained, "Joel was too honest to beat a debt. He held up a train to pay his obligations."

After dividing the spoils near Ogalalla, Bass and his partner, Jack Davis, made their way back to Denton, Texas, in a buggy. The sack containing the $20,000 in gold coins was carelessly tossed in the foot of the rig, where it lay unnoticed by the soldiers and others who were searching for the train robbers. Their disguise was perfect. The various posses figured that no self respecting outlaws would travel in such an humble vehicle. Train robbers worthy of the name would be riding fiery steeds.

Sam and Jack chatted amiably with the soldiers at their camp and exchanged the news of the day. The bandits kept their ears open and their mouths closed. They learned from the troopers that Collins and

Hefferidge had been killed, and that the officers had descriptions of each participant in the Union Pacific holdup. The apparent stupidity of the boys in blue was not their fault. They had no railroad agent to point out their quarry, as the others did in the case of Collins and Hefferidge. Furthermore, they had enlisted to be soldiers rather than detectives.

Bass and Davis made the trip back to Denton in safety where they joined their old cronies. By free use of the stolen gold pieces, the train robbers were able to remain undetected in the bottoms of Elm, Hickory and Mustang Creeks. They learned that their names had been placed in the Texas Fugitive List, that dreaded "Black Book" of the Rangers. In it Bass was described as:

> Twenty-five to twenty-six years old, 5 feet 7 inches high, black hair, dark brown eyes, brown mustache, large white teeth, shows them when talking, has very little to say.

In another circular, he is described as having a "Jewish" appearance. Davis realized that there were only three ways to get off this roll of dishonor. They were death, capture, or flight. He decided to hightail it to some distant point, and reputedly went to South America via New Orleans. In any event, he was never again heard of in Texas, and he faded out of the picture.

The fact that the gold pieces could be identified by date was widely circularized by the railroad and express companies. Everybody watched for the easily recognized coins. One of the far-reaching consequences of the Union Pacific holdup was that it started Sam Bass on his career as an outlaw. It is claimed that after a dog gets his first taste of raw mutton, he becomes a sheep killer. Apparently, this is what happened to Sam Bass. The success that crowned his initial effort at Big Springs, Nebraska, caused him to take up train robbery as a profession.

He surrounded himself with a gang of kindred spirits, and began a series of holdups in North Texas. The whole country was aroused, and the most noted man in those parts was Sam Bass. He and his marauders ranged as far west as Stephens County. They seemed to delight in outwitting and harassing local posses. During the oil boom in Breckenridge, a rabble rousing politician was wont to regale any listeners he could corner with tales of his exploits against Sam Bass. From his hirsute adornment and fiesty ways, he was sometimes called "Airdale."

He always left the impression that he had run Sam Bass out of the county. An old timer named Hood was well versed in local history. He also enjoyed quite a reputation as a humorist. His version of the chase went like this: "Yes, it's a fact that Whiskers ran Sam Bass out of Stephens County. But he was in the lead. The outlaws were camped in a cedar brake on Big Caddo Creek. When the posse rode up, Sam's men opened fire on them with Winchesters. Airedale and his bunch turned tail and burned the breeze for home. His gallant attack turned out to be a charge in reverse."

The Bass gang became so bold that the railroads and express companies, as well as the general public, demanded that the State take drastic action to halt their depredations. The commander of the Frontier Battalion, Major John B. Jones, who would soon be appointed adjutant general, was dispatched to Dallas with orders to plan a campaign of extermination against Bass.

Both as a Confederate Army officer and as a Ranger, Jones had seen the value of experienced, seasoned men in combat. He would have preferred to use one of the regular companies on this assignment, but he was overruled by Adjutant General Steele. Even at that early date, the political angle was considered. Opposition to the use of the Frontier Battalion in the interior of the state had already developed in the legislature and in the larger towns. Although the outlaws had ridden up to several saloons in the edge of Dallas and openly disported themselves, the inhabitants of that metropolis felt that they had outgrown the need of rural officers.

Major Jones was instructed to organize a detachment of Rangers in Dallas. After canvassing the field and conferring with prominent local citizens, he decided that the best available man to head the unit would be former City Marshal June Peak. He was given the rank of lieutenant, and told to proceed with the selection of his men. They were recruited among the town officers, and were as inexperienced in Ranger tactics as was their leader. Bass and his gang led them on many wild chases. The only time they made contact with the outlaws was on Salt Creek in Wise County, where Arkansas Johnson, member of the gang, was killed.

The awkward efforts of this green company gave rise to another verse of the song about Sam Bass which averred:

Sam Bass

> They whipped the Texas Rangers,
> And ran the boys in blue.

One night while my family and I were guests of Captain and Mrs. James B. Gillett at the camp meeting in the Davis Mountains, a cowboy singer was rendering ballads for our entertainment. When he came to the part dealing with the defeat of the Rangers by Bass, Captain Gillett interrupted him. "Hold up there, young man," he said. "You've got your facts all wrong. Every time the Rangers caught up with the gang, one of them was killed. Sam himself died from a Ranger bullet. I wouldn't exactly call that 'whipping the Texas Rangers'."

Texas was now aroused against Bass, and he decided to pull out and try to reach Mexico. By this time, a spy had been planted in his ranks. Jim Murphy, a member of the gang, agreed to keep Major Jones posted on their movements. In return for this information, he was promised immunity from prosecution. Bass and Barnes became suspicious of Murphy, and would have killed him if another one of the band, Frank Jackson, had not intervened. Jackson and Murphy were cousins. They started their journey southward, and determined to finance their sojourn in Mexico by robbing a bank in Texas. The one selected was in Round Rock. As soon as Bass announced this fact to his companions, Murphy began to watch for a chance to mail a letter to Major Jones in Austin.

I have always been interested in the southbound ride of the bandits. Bass' remark in a Waco saloon as he paid for the drinks, "There goes the last of the Union Pacific gold pieces, and a lot of good they have done me," has been widely quoted. It might be called the 1878 version of the adage "crime does not pay." The next leg of this trip, a distance of about forty miles, took the outlaws to a camp site near my birthplace. It is about two miles from Belton, not far from the Leon River. As a boy I often hunted rabbits around this place, and we looked with awe at the large liveoak under which they camped. We called it "the Sam Bass tree."

After leaving Waco, the bandits stole a mare from a breeder of fine horses who had the misfortune to live by the side of the road they traveled. Providing themselves with suitable mounts was a vital detail in the lives of outlaws, and they never overlooked an opportunity to annex a good piece of horseflesh. This theft gave them an extra pony, and they decided to sell him in Belton. The appearance of Bass was not one to inspire confidence, and the buyer demanded a bill of sale. While this was being prepared, Murphy seized the opportunity to write and mail a letter to the officers. It stated that Bass intended to rob the bank at Round Rock on the following Saturday.

Upon receipt of the long awaited information, Major Jones made careful plans to end the criminal careers of Sam Bass and his gang. In accomplishing this task, he could not risk further bungling by the recruits from Dallas. He decided to utilize Rangers who were capable of carrying out his objective. Orders could be delivered to Peak by telegraph, and his detachment could ride the train to Round Rock. Company E was at San Saba, and there was no wire communication with that frontier town. Nevertheless, the Major chose to order them to the scene of action, even though it involved many miles of hard riding on horseback, most of it at night.

A squad of Rangers were camped on the capitol grounds, in charge of Corporal Vernon Wilson. Shortly before dark, Major Jones dispatched him to San Saba with orders directing Lieutenant Reynolds to proceed with all possible speed to Round Rock. Wilson made the sixty-five mile ride to Lampasas by sunup, and caught the stage to San Saba, where he delivered the message. The work of the Austin Rangers entailed very little riding, and their horses were hog fat. Wilson's gallant mount was in no condition for such a hard ride, and died just as they reached Lampasas. Vernon Wilson was a nephew of Governor Richard Coke. He later became a famous officer in California, and was killed there in line of duty.

Major Jones' next step was to send Rangers Ware, Connor and Harrel, the other members of the capitol squad, to Round Rock. They rode there on horseback, and were instructed to keep out of sight until he joined them. The following morning the Major took Morris Moore, an ex-Ranger who was a deputy sheriff of Travis County, and went by train to Round Rock. With due official courtesy, Major Jones called on Deputy Sheriff Grimes of Williamson County, and briefed him on the impending action. Grimes was informed that the Rangers were on their way, and was cautioned not to make a move until they arrived.

Ranger Vernon Coke Wilson, nephew of Governor Richard Coke. He made the sixty-five mile ride from Austin to Lampasas in one night.

Bass had set Saturday, July 20, as the date to rob the bank. The outlaws arrived in the vicinity several days in advance, made camp, and planned to give their horses a good rest. Early Friday afternoon, Sam Bass, Frank Jackson, Jim Murphy and Seaborn Barnes decided to ride to town, buy some supplies, and make a final check of the situation. They also wanted to figure out the best escape route, as their departure was sure to be hasty, and in all probability would be under fire. At Old Round Rock, Murphy dropped out, with the explanation that he needed to buy some horse feed. Bass did not object, as no action was expected that day. The informer knew what might happen at any time, and he wanted no part of it.

The other three rode on into Round Rock, tied their horses in an alley, walked around to the front of Kopperel's Store and entered.

Deputies Grimes of Williamson County and Moore of Travis County noticed that the strangers were armed. Completely disregarding Major Jones' instructions, they attempted to search them and the shooting started. The opening of the battle in Round Rock has always been a source of particular interest to me, as I have heard it related many times by a man who was there. My uncle, William Warren Chamberlain, for whom I was named, lived on the old Chamberlain Ranch near Davilla. He and his brother George happened to be in town. According to him, when Deputy Grimes approached Bass, he asked, "Have you got a pistol?" To which Sam replied, "Yes, I've got several of them." All three outlaws jerked out their guns, killed Grimes and shot Moore through the lungs. The outlaws ran to their horses, and the sound of the shooting brought the Rangers. Dick Ware was in a barber shop, and he rushed out just as they were rounding the corner. All three of the outlaws shot at him. One bullet struck a post and filled his face with splinters. He returned the fire and soon was joined by his comrades. Major Jones was at the telegraph office, and he rushed into the fight. The new double action Colt Light Model had just come out in 38 and 41 calibres, and he carried one of them. He was a small man in stature, and he probably bought the little six-shooter to wear around the office, or to use as a "Sunday" gun. No doubt he sorely missed his long barreled forty-five in Round Rock. Rangers Connor and Harrell opened up on the fleeing bandits. Sebe Barnes was killed and Sam Bass mortally wounded. Frank Jackson was unwounded and in the clear, but he came back and assisted his chief to the saddle. They rode away in a shower of bullets. My uncle said one of Bass' hands was disabled, but that he held the bridle reins in his teeth and shot with the other one until his pistol was empty. They galloped out past Old Round Rock and into the country. When Bass could stand the pain no longer, they stopped under the shade of a large oak tree, and Jackson helped his wounded chief to dismount.

Corporal Wilson arrived at the Ranger camp near San Saba about sundown on July 18. The men had just finished supper when he delivered the message from Major Jones. Company E was commanded by Lieutenant N. O. (Mage) Reynolds, described by a Lampasas County feudist as "the bravest man in the world." He had been accorded the unparalleled privilege of picking his company from the entire Frontier Battalion. Small wonder that Major Jones wanted this crack outfit to deal with the gang headed by Sam Bass.

Lieutenant Reynolds ordered a detail of eight Rangers to be ready in thirty minutes. It was to be composed of men whose horses were best suited for a long, fast ride. Among the detachment was Corporal James B. Gillett, who in his later life became one of my best friends. Reynolds was sick, and unable to make the scout on horseback. Under no circumstances would he miss the prospective fight, and he traveled in a buckboard drawn by a pair of wiry Spanish mules that were ordinarily used as pack animals.

The Rangers rode all night at a long trot, and when Reynolds called a halt on the north fork of the San Gabriel River at daylight, they had covered sixty-five miles. He allowed them thirty minutes by his watch to make coffee and fry some bacon. The horses and mules were watered and given a quick feed of sheaf oats. It was still forty-five miles to their destination, and the hot July sun would have to be endured, but neither man nor beast fell out. The detachment reached the vicinity of Round Rock early in the afternoon, and went into camp on Brushy Creek. Lieutenant Reynolds drove on into town to report to Major Jones. He came within five minutes of meeting Bass and Jackson as they fled after the fight.

The balance of the afternoon was spent in resting the men and horses. Early next morning the Rangers took up the trail. They had only gone a short distance when they rode up on a man lying under a tree. He called out that he was Sam Bass and that he was badly wounded. They took him to town where he received medical attention. His wound was a fatal one and he died the next day. He talked freely to Major Jones and the Rangers, but would give no information about his accomplices.

A controversy arose over the Ranger who fired the shot that killed Bass. Some claimed it was George Harrel and others maintained that it was Dick Ware. Captain Gillett states that it was Ware. He was present at the death of Bass, and was an unimpeachable Ranger historian. Bass said on his deathbed, "The man with the lather on his face shot me." Ware was in the barber shop getting a shave.

In 1952, I received a letter from Charles B. McNelly, a nephew of Captain L. H. McNelly. He was born and reared in Uvalde County and graduated from Texas A. & M. College. He moved to Illinois many years ago, but had never lost his interest in Texas history, particularly where it concerned the Rangers. McNelly stated that the Sam Bass story always fascinated him and he had been over the ground several times. He went to Indiana and talked to some of the relatives of Sam Bass. One of them showed him two letters from young Sam, written at Denton, Texas, and mailed in 1872. They gave a clue to his early education. According to my correspondent, "They were rather well written."

Sam Bass is buried in the little cemetery near Round Rock. Souvenir hunters have chipped away most of his headstone. I went there with Captain James B. Gillett, who gave me all the details of the Sam Bass affair. Upon reading the inscription on the tombstone, my heart went out to Sam's sister. She had the monument erected and it bears these words: "A brave man reposes in death here. Why was he not true?"

Chapter 47

FRANK JACKSON

Among all the participants in the Ranger-outlaw battle at Round Rock, regardless of which side they were on, one man stands out in bold relief. In the estimation of those who admire courage and loyalty, wherever it may be found, he occupies an exalted position. Naturally, we regret that these cardinal virtues were not utilized in a just cause. Nowhere in the annals of Western gunfighting can his feat in the alley in that Central Texas town be duplicated. This man's name was Frank Jackson.

Mrs. Leota Gillett Wilson, daughter of Captain James B. Gillett, owns her father's copy of the first Fugitive List. It is believed to be the only one in existence, and it contains this description of Jackson: "22 years old 6 ft. high slender spare made Keen and active dark swarthy complex black curley hair blue or grey eyes smooth face."

His birthplace and early life are of little importance to this brief sketch. He was only twenty-two years old when he and his cousin, Jim Murphy, joined up with Sam Bass. In the Salt Creek brush with the Rangers, Arkansas Johnson was killed and three members of the gang were captured. Among the prisoners was Jim Murphy. In exchange for immunity, he agreed to keep Major Jones posted on the movements of the outlaws, and to furnish information that would lead to their arrest.

Bass became suspicious of Murphy, and would have killed him if Jackson had not taken his part. In this case, Frank showed a fair sample of the nerve he later displayed at Round Rock. He defied the bandit chief, telling him that only over his dead body could he kill Murphy. Although sided by Sebe Barnes, another member of the gang, Bass did not feel lucky enough to engage in a pistol duel with the younger man.

The ill advised attempt to search the outlaws, which resulted in the death of one deputy and the wounding of another, brought on the battle of Round Rock. At the sound of the first shots, Major Jones and his Rangers sprang into action. They killed Sebe Barnes and fatally wounded Sam Bass. At this point Frank Jackson staged his unparalleled exhibition. His escape from the hail of bullets bears out the fatalistic theory that a man will never die until his number is up.

Not even with the aid of marihuana could a writer of wild West fiction dream up a situation comparable to the one faced by Frank Jackson in that alley at Round Rock. The more a man knows about horses and guns, the more marvelous his feat becomes. The din of rapid shots from .45 calibre six-shooters loaded with black powder cartridges, and the reverberations against the rock walls created a scene that beggared description. It was in the days before smokeless powder, and there was no "crack of a pistol." Those old guns went "Ker-bloom" and filled the air with acrid smoke. As a boy I heard several of them go off in the neighboring town of Belton, and can testify that they sound like cannon. Adding to the confusion in the inferno were the half-wild, rearing and terrified horses. Four Rangers, whose occupation demanded good marksmanship, and several townspeople, poured a heavy fire on the fleeing outlaws.

None of these men scored a hit on Jackson. He went through their storm of lead unscathed. When Bass was wounded, he spurned the opportunity to escape, and turned back to help his stricken comrade. The gallant youth untied both of their horses, helped Bass into his saddle and convoyed him out of the jaws of death.

They left town in a dead run, and rode about two miles before Bass was compelled to stop. Jackson picked up a Winchester he had hidden in the woods, and offered to stay with Bass to the finish. The shelling he had just undergone took none of the fight out of him. He declared himself a match for the whole bunch. Bass realized that he was done for, and urged his faithful follower to save himself. After making the wounded man as comfortable as he could under the circumstances, Jackson rode away from Round Rock into the realm of mystery and legend.

Fifty-three years later, when Frank Jackson would have been about seventy-five years old, I was serving as Adjutant General of Texas. In common with every other Ranger, I had always been deeply interested in the saga of Frank Jackson. From time to time, rumors of his whereabouts and the reformed life he was leading drifted into the office. The Rangers of my day did not look on him as a hated enemy, but rather as a man who had made a mis-step in his youth. To us, his bravery atoned for all his sins. If he were still alive, I wanted to get him back, not as a prisoner but as a man who could clear up some historical facts about the fight at Round Rock.

In order to further this wish, I called in the foremost living authority on the subject, Captain James B. Gillett. As a corporal in Lieutenant N. O. Reynolds' Ranger company, he was present at the death of Sam Bass. He later served as a deputy under United States Marshal Dick Ware, the slayer of Bass. We decided to make a project out of clearing up the mystery of Frank Jackson, and to combine forces in achieving this objective.

Captain Gillett had entered the Ranger Service in 1875 under Captain Dan Roberts. Captain Roberts' niece had married Governor J. F. Hinkle of New Mexico. The eminent Western author, Eugene Manlove Rhodes, was a friend of Governor Hinkle, and they were both reputed to be friends of Frank Jackson. Once, while visiting in Austin, Mrs. Hinkle agreed to take up the Jackson case with her husband on her return to Santa Fe. On April 26, 1932, ex-Governor Hinkle wrote me as follows:

> . . . Some two or three years ago I had quite a lot of correspondence in regard to this with someone connected with your office or a captain in the ranger service. This came about by someone in Roswell informing me that he knew where Jackson was and that he was willing to surrender on assurance of protection. I had considerable correspondence about this with Mr. Rhodes and several others, but the person who first told me about it failed to give me Jackson's whereabouts. I have come to the conclusion that they were all wrong in the first place and I do not think Jackson is alive at this time.

We were determined to run down every lead that might shed light on the ex-outlaw. My plan was to have Captain Gillett and Frank Jackson, the last surviving participants, meet at my office in Austin. Then we would drive to Round Rock and go over every phase of the battle on the ground. Governor Sterling, who loved anything pertaining to Texas history, was sympathetic and cooperative. At the inquest held over the body of Deputy Sheriff Grimes in 1878, it was ruled that he came to his death from gunshot wounds at the hands of Frank Jackson. No doubt this was done because he was the only survivor. Sam Bass was the one Grimes attempted to search, and in all probability it was he who killed the deputy. In any event, all the witnesses were long since dead, and it would have been impossible to convict Jackson. I agreed to give him a safe conduct in and out of Texas. We would keep his visit a secret, if he so desired. The rumor was that he had become a respected citizen, and had reared a family. We had no desire to bring any unpleasant notoriety on them.

Captain Gillett and I began to sift the various rumors and clues. They came from all parts of the West. About this time, by a coincidence, T. S. (Stonewall) Jackson, a brother of Frank who lived in Lubbock, wrote a letter to Gene Rhodes stating that he, Jackson, had heard that Rhodes knew the whereabouts of Frank, and asking for help in seeing his brother once more. The Jackson from Lubbock wrote me:

> I recd a letter from Eugene M Rhodes of California giving me your address Telling me you might give me the information I would like to have if in your power I am and the youngest and only brother of Frank Jackson living Having been separated for 55 years and never once heard from him and have tried all these years to locate him and we are getting old if you can't give me his location on secret grounds let me know if he is living and greatly oblige an old man.

It was written with a pencil, and is quoted verbatim. My answer was:

> I have your letter of recent date, and was very glad to hear from you. I have always admired the great bravery of your brother, and have had the deepest sympathy for him. In those days, a boy was likely to get into trouble through being a victim of circumstances and through no fault of his own. I have been trying for nearly a year to find out if your brother was still alive,

and to get him to come to Texas as my guest and a guest of the State, so I could straighten out, historically, some of the facts connected with the Round Rock affair. I will get him absolute immunity from prosecution, and will keep his visit a secret, if he so desires. Even if the authorities were inclined to prosecute him, they would absolutely have no case as there are no witnesses living nor any facts on which to prosecute him. Capt. James B. Gillett, retired Ranger, of Marfa, Texas, is the only living Ranger, who was present at the death of Sam Bass. I am anxious to have Capt. Gillett and your brother meet at Round Rock, and go over the facts of the Round Rock raid. There have been so many hundreds of pages of false stories written about Round Rock that I am anxious for these two gentlemen to get together for the sake of history.

I assure you that I am keeping no secrets from you in regard to your brother, and if I succeed in finding him, will be glad to notify you and have you come down here with us, if you so desire. It would be a fine thing indeed if we could unite two brothers after fifty-five years of separation.

Write to me at any time, as I will always be glad to hear from you.

Charles Siringo, who was a stock detective and author of several books, states: "There is no doubt that Jim T—, who owns a horse ranch in Montana, is the Frank or Dad Jackson who got away after the attempted bank robbery at Round Rock where Sam Bass was killed." Author Siringo confused Frank Jackson with Dad Underwood, who had left the gang before Round Rock. Jackson was only twenty-two years old, and could hardly rate the appellation of "Dad."

Captain Frank Rynning, a former head of the Arizona Rangers, states in his book *Gun Notches* that a convict going under the name of Downing, who died in the Yuma penitentiary, was Frank Jackson, Captain Rynning served as warden of that penal institution after his Ranger days. He stated further that Dick Ware visited him and also talked to Downing.

On May 13, 1932, Captain Gillett wrote me as follows:

I have sketched through Rynning's book pretty well and sized up what he says about Frank Jackson. I read and re-read the last chapter in his book and am satisfied that he is just guessing that the convict, Downing, is Frank Jackson. I would just as soon believe Rhodes' story about Jackson as to believe Rynning's story. It is a mystery what became of Frank Jackson. I am sure Mr. Rynning read my book and made some notes of my description of the Bass fight at Round Rock. I doubt if Dick Ware was ever a guest of Rynning at the prison in Arizona. I was deputy all the time Ware was United States marshal in El Paso, and never heard him say that he visited the prison. In my opinion, if Rynning had talked to Downing in Ware's presence, Dick would have told the story to me.

Captain Gillet also wrote, always in his own handwriting:

I was on my way to the American Royal Stock show, and a gentleman from Denton shared my section in the Pullman. He said he knew Sam Bass and all his men personally. I asked him what became of Frank Jackson, and he replied that the officers in Denton county had word from Frank's relatives in Wise county, that he had been killed in Montana, a few years after Round Rock. So it is still a mystery.

The Montana part lends some credence to Charlie Siringo's account.

In another letter from Captain Gillett, he wrote that he did not believe that anybody could produce the real Frank Jackson, and in his opinion, the ex-bandit was dead. Gillett knew the tendency of outlaws or other men who wanted to be surrounded by an air of mystery. If they were about the age of Jackson, each one would assume a faraway look, probably wink an eye, and leave the impression, particularly when a newspaper man propounded the question, that they had a very interesting past. This tendency is illustrated by the acts of an old man in recent years, who went by the name of Bob Dalton. He professed to be Jesse James, and even went into court in the effort to get the claim substantiated.

Captain Gillett also suggested that I write to Eugene Manlove Rhodes, the fabulous Western author and cowboy. Rhodes was a man who admired Jackson's gameness, and would be glad to help him in his fight to beat back, so it was entirely possible that he might know the ex-bandit. It was also a dead moral certainty that Gene would guard the confidence of a friend with his life. Therefore, our first step was to convince him that we were sincere in our promise to protect Jackson, in the event he agreed to come to Texas. Pursuant to this thought, I asked Governor Sterling if he would issue a pardon to Jackson, which he readily agreed to do. Captain Gillett also joined in the guarantee of good faith, knowing full well that the only object was to clear up some historical points, and that Jackson would not be subjected to any form of embarrassment.

Frank Jackson

Eugene Manlove Rhodes answered my letter promptly, although he was a very sick man. I treasure his letter, written in longhand and it is reproduced here in full:

> I have been (and still am) all too sick to write. Else I would write at some length that—as the record stands. Frank Jackson has little to be ashamed of who was loyal against all odds criminal or not. Some of us would not be proud of that big hour of his. Too much to write.
>
> I can only say again. If you will write to Jim Hinkle (Hon. J. F. Hinkle) Santa Fe he can give you Russell's address. Then you can write to Russell. If he sees fit he can forward your letter to Jackson. Then what will Jackson do? I dunno, I dunno. You see it was the name of Frank Hamer and the Texas Rangers that did not reassure him before. Nor is Adjutant General reassuring sound to his case. I dunno, I dunno. Also it is altogether likely that the man is dead. If not he is going on 73 - 74 - 75? Listen if I can get well I will write for you and for the annals—the Unneeded Defense of Frank Jackson. Very brief. I have not time to be brief now.
>
> In defense of Jim Murphy who intended to betray them and did betray them betrayed where he was trusted. Jackson very quietly and without "registering" defied Sam Bass and Barnes "You can't kill Murphy till you have killed me first," he said, and Bass and Barnes didn't hate Jackson for that. They liked him better for that. Against their better judgement they let Jackson have his way. Then at Round Rock Barnes dead and Bass shot up no faltering no fine speeches. Lifted Bass on horse. Shucks. You know all this. Wouldn't you be proud to have done this yourself. I would. And your grand children proud of you? A heedless boy not 20 at Round Rock. An honorable and useful life since. For myself I rather think he is right to shun the red fire and the spot light—It is his own life and he should have the say. I don't think his children will ever know that "Dad" was Frank Jackson.

Circumstances continued to pile up against our hoped-for meeting. Eugene Manlove Rhodes' illness became more acute. The depression was on; it was an election year, and I had to postpone all historical and other pleasant matters.

So in spite of all efforts, the mystery of Frank Jackson will remain unsolved. At the Last Roundup, I believe that the Boss of the riders, who forgave the thief on the Cross, will cut Frank Jackson into the bunch with the brave and the true regardless of which side of the law he rode on here below.

Chapter 48

GREGORIO CORTEZ

THE Adjutant General of Texas, who at that time was ex-officio commander of the Texas Rangers, included in one of his biennial reports the following item: "On June 22, 1901, Captain Rogers captured Gregorio Cortez, who had killed Sheriff Morris of Karnes County and Sheriff Glover and Deputy Sheriff Schnabel of Gonzales County, in resisting arrest. He made for Mexico overland and had been followed by officers and citizens from nearly every county in the Southwest, many of whom were exhausted in the chase which lasted about ten days. Captain Rogers caught him in about eight or ten miles from the Rio Grande."

This tersely worded official communication wrote the final chapter to a unique and spectacular manhunt. With one possible exception, it was the longest drawn out hue and cry in the annals of Texas. The only comparable one was the game of hare and hounds that Sam Bass and his long riders played with the Dallas Rangers in 1877-78.

In the hunt for Gregorio Cortez, the quarry was one lone man instead of a gang. Nevertheless, the chase continued for ten days, traversed eight counties and covered over three hundred miles. Several hundred heavily armed men participated in it. Most of the riders changed their mounts several times and the number of horses used in the campaign probably exceeded a thousand head.

496

Company "F," Frontier Battalion, Texas Rangers, 1882. 1—J. W. Buck; 2—Pete Edwards; 3—Capt. Joe Shely; 4—George Farrer; 5—Brack Morris; 6—Charlie Norris; 7—Wash Shely; 8—Tom Mebry; 9—Bob Crowder; 10—Ceailio Charo. Brack Morris later became Sheriff of Karnes County and was killed by Gregorio Cortez.

Before the advent of automobiles and tractors, the most pernicious crime that plagued Texas ranchmen, farmers and even townspeople was theft of their horses and mules. The state was infested with organized gangs of thieves who operated what were known as "lines." In carrying on their depredations, they would steal livestock in one locality and pass it down the line to a distant county, where it would be sold by a local accomplice. At the point of delivery the night riders would rest for a few days, then reverse the vicious circle and make a pay load both ways. In 1933 the Fergusons appointed an old time line runner captain of their Rangers. He reflected due credit on the administration, as he was subsequently convicted of a felony and sentenced to eight years in the penitentiary.

Gregorio Cortez and his brother Romaldo, who was sometimes called Roman, were born in Mexico but they grew up in Texas. The Cortez family was well represented in the nefarious occupation of thievery. Another brother, Tomas, was convicted of horse theft and sentenced to five years in prison. Gregorio and Romaldo rode one of the lines from the central part of the state to the Mexican border. Their route was frequently changed by the vigilance of sheriffs and outraged farmers who made it too hot for them on their accustomed trails. They were both wanted for horse theft in Williamson, Atascosa, Hays, and Gonzales counties, and all Southwest Texas officers had been alerted to apprehend them.

On June 12, 1901, the sheriff of Atascosa County telephoned Sheriff W. T. (Brack) Morris that the Cortez brothers were headed toward Karnes county in a narrow tread buggy. Vehicles of that day came in two different axle widths, and as the wide gauge type was used locally, the Cortez rig left an easily noted track. Sheriff Avant, whose posse had turned back at the county line, informed his brother officer of the telltale sign, knowing that it would lead him to the culprits.

Sheriff Morris knew that the brothers would go to the Thulemeyer Ranch, which is located about ten miles south of Karnes City. Here they had planted a crop which they used as a blind to cover up their real occupation. Accompanied by two other men, he drove out to this place in a double seated hack. There were two tenant houses on the ranch, about three miles apart. Not knowing which one of these the horse thieves would be in, Sheriff Morris stationed his best man at the fork of the road. He kept the other one with him. This fellow had been brought along mainly to act as interpreter. They drove on to the second house, where they found both Cortez brothers. The sheriff got out and walked inside the yard, leaving his companion seated in the hack.

Gregorio Cortez came to the front door. Morris, who did not speak much Spanish, started talking to him, partly through the interpreter. The house stood about three feet off the ground, resting on short mesquite posts. Through this space, the man in the hack saw a pair of moving feet. He warned Morris that someone was approaching from the left. At that moment, Romaldo Cortez came around the corner. He was a large, powerful man and he crouched to jump on Morris, who drew his six-shooter and shot him in the mouth. Witnesses disagree on whether or not Romaldo had a pistol but all agree that he made a hostile advance on the sheriff.

Gregorio, from where he stood in the doorway, immediately fired on Morris and hit him in the right arm, knocking the gun from his hand. The sheriff reached down to pick it up with his other hand, but a second bullet in the left shoulder caused him to again drop the

499

weapon. The game ex-Ranger then tried to raise the pistol with both hands, but his arms were paralyzed from the shock of the heavy 45 calibre slugs. He continued the struggle to get on his feet but received another bullet in the stomach, the dreaded "gut shot" from which he died several hours later, alone and unattended. The fatally wounded sheriff dragged himself to a windmill nearly half a mile away in an effort to get the drink of water he craved, and was not found until three o'clock in the morning.

The man in the hack, who always claimed that he was unarmed at the time, left that slow vehicle and carried the news of the shooting to his companion at the crossroad. This man wanted to go back and help the wounded sheriff, but the interpreter insisted that there were too many Cortez people at the house, so they went to Kenedy and spread the alarm. Here a posse was hastily organized and its members spared neither quirt nor spur in reaching the scene of the shooting.

On the road to the ranch the rescue party met a wagon partly loaded with hay, and driven by two of the Cortez women. The badly wounded Romaldo Cortez lay hidden under the straw, and by this ruse they succeeded in getting him to the home of a relative in Kenedy. He was later found in a small house on the outskirts of town where he was taken into custody and given medical attention. Romaldo was then lodged in jail at the county seat where he died about ten days later from the wound inflicted by Sheriff Morris.

After the fatal shooting, Cortez helped the women hide his brother in the hay wagon, and then took to the brush. He stayed there until nightfall, and later went to the house of a friend near Kenedy. Here he inquired about Romaldo's condition, and then rode off in the darkness. Gregorio took a northeasterly course, which would lead him toward the interior, and farther away from the border.

To one who has not lived among those inscrutable people, it may seem strange that immediately after killing Sheriff Morris, Cortez did not head for Mexico. Several other criminal charges against him were pending in the state. Notwithstanding this fact, he made for one of his old haunts in Gonzales County, where he had friends and relatives. He chose this destination because he was reared in Texas and Gregorio knew that his *paisanos* here would harbor him more readily than those who spoke the same language south of the Rio Grande.

Sheriff Dick Glover of Gonzales County was outraged by the murder of his boyhood friend, Brack Morris. The Cortez brothers had committed many depredations in his bailiwick. Upon receipt of the news from Karnes County, he placed a close watch on Gregorio's relatives and soon received information that the wanted man was bedded down for the night on the Schnabel farm. Henry Schnabel, who owned the place, was referred to in the adjutant general's report as a deputy sheriff, but probably joined the posse mainly in the capacity of guide.

Sheriff Glover and his party made an ill planned and badly executed attempt to arrest the fugitive. Their effort had all the earmarks and results of what was known among old time Rangers as a "wild sashay." They surrounded the house in which Cortez was thought to be hidden, and charged it on horseback. All were yelling and shooting their pistols. The statement has been made by those in position to know the facts, that John Barleycorn was a prominent member of the posse. This would be the only plausible explanation of the injudicious action that cost the lives of two good men.

When the officers rode up, Cortez was not even in the house. He was far too crafty to sleep indoors while on the dodge, and most of his adult life had been spent in that state. The night rider had made down his bed some distance from the dwelling. When the posse launched their mad assault, Cortez was in perfect position to shoot into the mass of riders with no danger to himself. He later maintained that in their unorganized rush, the officers killed each other. This is quite possible, for the possemen were certainly in danger of becoming victims of their own cross fire. In my own experience, I always dreaded guns in the hands of untrained, wrought up volunteers more than I did the fire of the outlaws. This is true even when all hands are perfectly sober.

In any event, Cortez, with the blood of one sheriff already on his hands, knew that he would be blamed for the murder of Glover and Schnabel, regardless of who had actually fired the fatal shots. He decided that his best chance for escape would be to make a dash for the Mexican border. Gregorio still had the horse he had ridden from Karnes County, and while at the Schnabel farm, he provided himself with a file. It was used as a wire cutter as long as he was on horseback.

On countless nocturnal forays in the past, Cortez had been guided by the stars. In the present desperate situation, his long use of the cowboys' compass stood him in good stead, and he "lit a shuck" across country. He was prepared to cut any fences that might impede his travel in a straight line. By roughly holding a southwesterly course, he would strike the Rio Grande somewhere between Eagle Pass and Laredo. From some obscure point in this practically uninhabited region, the fugitive planned to slip into Mexico at one of the unguarded fords or "blind crossings" used by smugglers.

During a widespread manhunt, even the air seems to be charged with excitement. This state of near hysteria usually produces some amusing incident in that otherwise serious business. The Cortez case provided more than its share of grim jokes. One of them concerned two young lovers who were enjoying an evening buggy ride a few miles from the scene of the double homicide. They were blissfully unaware of the aroused countryside, and did not know that everybody in the community had joined the search for Cortez. Suddenly a group of armed men appeared out of the darkness and halted their buggy. In the absence of either flash or headlights, the young folks were almost scared out of their wits before they could convince the posse that the occupants of the rig did not include Gregorio Cortez.

When the officers sought to catch Gregorio on a public thoroughfare, they grossly underestimated his cunning. This mistake cost them a great deal of valuable time. The old *bandido* was steeped in every wile known to a professional horse thief. He did not intend to be fenced in, and had far too much coyote in him to be trapped in a barbed wire lane. The hunted man carefully avoided all roads, knowing that the tracks made by his horse might be picked up by some sharp-eyed member of the posse.

All accounts of the Glover-Schnabel killing agree that Cortez was barefooted when the shooting started, and some have it that he ran back to his bed and retrieved his shoes. An old timer who lived near the Schnabel farm told me that the fugitive fashioned a pair of sandals out of a woolen vest, and discarded them after he crossed the Guadalupe River near Belmont. Some sympathetic *amigo* along the line must have furnished him with the needed shoes, for he had on a pair when captured by Captain Rogers at Las Mesas. Bigger Poole of Cotulla, who was a member of the La Salle County posse, said that during the time Cortez was walking, a hole in one shoe sole plainly marked his track.

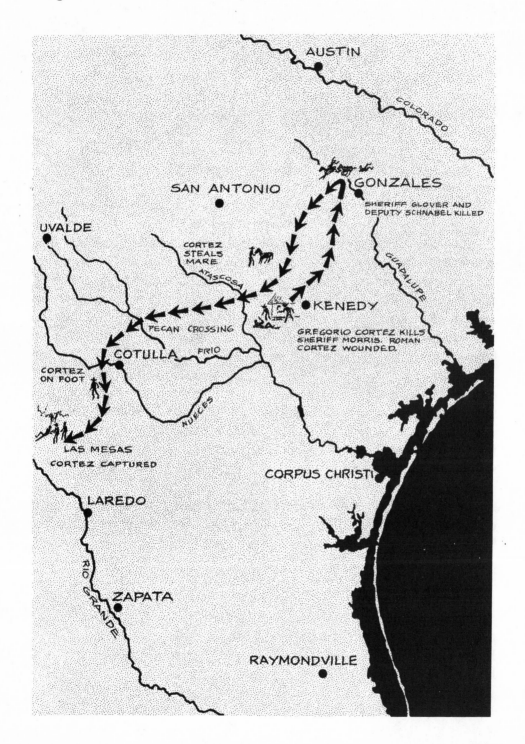

The first tangible evidence of the outlaw's whereabouts and direction of his flight was disclosed when his horse played out in Wilson County. He quickly stole another one. James M. Allen owned a farm about four miles south of Floresville. His son Harry, who now lives in Christine, was a small boy when the hunted man rode up to their place on a jaded sorrel horse. He recalled that the worn out animal had a bad fistula. Harry Allen witnessed both the arrival and departure of Cortez. He also saw him steal the little brown mare whose fame has been perpetuated in a lengthy song.

The fugitive's choice of a getaway mount has been a source of lasting pride to fanciers of quarter horses. They were sixteen horses in the Allen pasture, many of them larger and better looking than the one selected for the all out ride. Nevertheless, with the chips down and life itself dependent upon his judgment, Cortez picked from this *remuda* the small, bulldog type quarter mare. What he had to have was an animal with plenty of stamina combined with great speed in a dash. His knowledge of horseflesh told him that she could fill the bill on both counts.

The mare at that time was about eight years old and stood a little over fourteen hands high. She was raised by Will Adams, a Floresville blacksmith, who raced her some and then sold her to the Allens. The elder Allen was a very religious man, who would not permit horse racing for fear it would lead to gambling. Harry (Red) Allen saw no reason for letting the mare's speed go to waste. He and the other boys often slipped her out and met all comers at any distance up to a quarter of a mile. Before going home they would carefully curry her and dry off all signs of sweat, in order to keep their father from finding out that she had been raced.

Cortez committed what proved to be his last horse theft late one afternoon. At daylight the following morning Jeff Peeler and W. M. Dabney saw him when he crossed the Atascosa. As the crow flies, the distance between the two places is thirty-three miles. He actually traveled a great deal farther, for in his efforts to confuse the trailer, he doubled back and circled many times. Peeler and Dabney had a load of sheep in their wagon, and paid no particular attention to the stranger. They took him to be a transient *vaquero* looking for work. Upon their return to the Peeler ranch, they learned that the lone rider had become the object of a widespread search. He was the notorious Gregorio Cortez.

Young Graves Peeler, who later achieved fame as a combination Ranger and Texas and Southwestern Cattle Raisers Association brand inspector, rode a fast horse to Campbellton. He carried word to the townspeople that the fugitive had been sighted. The village was crowded with prospective possemen, whose mounts were tied to trees, posts and hitching racks. The over-all state of alarm in Southwest Texas during the Cortez chase may be measured by the impact of Peeler's message on the local warriors. One of them was so eager to get started that he leaped in the saddle, applied both quirt and spurs, but forgot to untie his horse.

Still bearing to the southwest, Cortez rode to a point between the Hall and Lewis Ranches, where he crossed the fresh trail of five hundred cattle. They belonged to the Griffith brothers, and the outfit driving them was bossed by Fayette (Slim) Easterling. Gregorio followed this herd until he came in sight of the cowhands, who had stopped for dinner, then backtracked for several miles.

It did not take Manuel Tom long to figure out this maneuver. He readily picked the mare's tracks out of the maze of hoof prints. This painstaking work took time, however, and enabled the fugitive to keep ahead of the posse. He used similar ruses throughout the chase, knowing that it was much easier to make tracks than to follow them. Unlike his pursuers, he was not forced to stop at night.

Gregorio's elusiveness during the protracted chase gave rise to a fantastic tale. The rumor got out that Cortez had nailed the shoes on his mare backwards, thereby making a track that would baffle any trailer. Clyde Allen of Kingsville, whose uncle owned the Cortez mare, said that he heard this yarn in his youth.

Four factors should have kept the Southwest Texans, most of whom were stockmen, from giving the slightest credence to this story. First, their horse sense. Second, Cortez had neither the time nor the means to do any fancy blacksmithing. Third, Emanuel Tom would not have been fooled by the trick, even if the shoes had been nailed on sideways. Fourth, the poor pony would have gone lame in less than a mile, if she had been shod in this impossible manner.

When a fence barred his way, Cortez did not go through the gate.

The file he had carried since fleeing Gonzales County was used to make the required openings. He would cut the top wires, then jump the nimble animal over the bottom strands. When the mare was later placed on exhibition at the International Fair in San Antonio, the result of these forced hurdles could be plainly seen. Her hocks were badly scarred by barbed wire cuts.

Cortez stopped at a small store in La Parrita, a Mexican settlement in Atascosa County, where he procured some sardines and crackers. Continuing his westward course, he crossed the San Miguel near Hindes. He forded the Frio River at Pecan Crossing and rode on to Millett, arriving there late at night. Here the hungry man robbed a store and secured a fresh supply of groceries.

He was now on the west side of the I. & G. N. Railroad and in La Salle County. Cortez turned south and crossed the Nueces River not far from Cotulla. Some of the old timers believe that he mistook this stream for the Rio Grande. Their surmise is probably incorrect, for he certainly did not stop after reaching the south side.

Sheriff Will Hill, a brush popper of the old school, headed the La Salle County posse. His red headed brother, Jack, whose skill as a steer roper had won the admiration of Will Rogers, rode at the sheriff's side. Bigger Poole, of Cotulla, is a surviving member of that hard riding band.

After a week of the most grueling travel a saddle animal ever had to endure, the gallant little mare gave out. The spot of her collapse is in La Salle County, about twenty miles south of the Nueces River, near the railroad station of Atlee. This was the headquarters of a fabulous cattleman and political leader of that day, Thomas Atlee Coleman.

Cortez was now in a ranch country. Pastures were larger and horses harder to catch, as they had to be roped. He was not able to procure another mount, and made the balance of his journey on foot. Gregorio again changed direction, and started walking due west.

The sheriff of Atascosa County and his deputies acted as communication officers throughout the manhunt. They made good use of the limited number of telephones in the area and sent many telegrams. These were often delivered by courier. Numerous wild rumors were circulated. They caused a great deal of confusion, and in most cases proved to be false. On the border all Federal, State and county officers cooperated in the effort to head off the fleeing outlaw.

When the sheriffs of Karnes and Gonzales Counties were killed, Company C of the Texas Rangers was stationed at Laredo, under the command of Captain John H. Rogers. One of its best men, Will L. Wright, who later became a famous captain, was visiting at his home in Floresville, Wilson County.

He immediately joined the posse, and throughout the Cortez pursuit rode at the side of Emanuel Tom. While tracking desperados, the trailer is powerless to defend himself against ambushers. His entire attention as well as his eyes must be focused on the hoof prints below. Only a man who has trailed bandits in a brushy country can fully appreciate a trustworthy comrade who will "side" him in this hazardous duty. Pioneers and frontiersmen referred to unwavering friends as their "side kicks" or "side pardners."

Captain Rogers was thoroughly familiar with his border district, and knew the habits of people like Cortez, particularly when they were on the dodge. He figured that the fugitive could be intercepted somewhere in that strip of ranch country between the Nueces River and the Rio Grande. The captain further reasoned that he would stop for food and rest at some goat or sheep camp. An isolated spot of this kind would be less likely to have prying visitors than a more pretentious ranch, for none but the sorely distressed would risk their digestions on the crude fare of a *pastor*. Both Rangers and river guards made long scouts over the area, and kept a close watch on all trails by which Cortez might make his escape into Mexico.

Captain Rogers' planning and vigilance soon were rewarded. He spent the night of June 21, 1901, at Las Tiendas Ranch. This place adjoined Don Abran de la Garza's sheep and goat ranch, called Las Mesas. It is situated in the northwestern part of Webb County, about ten miles from the Rio Grande.

The captain had paired off for the day's scout with Customs Inspector Bill Merriman. They had just mounted their horses when they were hailed by Jesus Gonzales. This *vaquero* bore the nickname of "El Teco" because he was from Bustamente, Mexico, home of a tribe of Indians by that name. In addition to doing regular ranch work he trained game roosters for the cockpit, and was a noted character in those parts. He reported that a tired, hungry man had walked into the goat camp at Las Mesas, only a short while ago. El Teco felt sure that the footsore traveler was Gregorio Cortez. In order to detain him as long as possible, he invited the stranger to have some breakfast and take a nap. This offer was eagerly accepted.

Captain Rogers and Inspector Merriman rode to the *majada* expecting to meet with desperate resistance from the man who had killed three officers. On their arrival, however, they found that Cortez had reached the limit of his almost superhuman endurance, and was asleep.

Not a shot had been fired since the killing of Glover and Schnabel in Gonzales County. When the officers started off with their prisoner, El Teco ran after them with a *morral* in his hand, yelling that they had forgotten something. The grass bag contained the two pistols that Cortez had used so long and fatally. Before falling asleep, he had hung it up in a huisache tree, where it was found by Gonzales.

Manuel Soto of Encinal was an eyewitness to the arrest of Cortez, and gave me a first hand account of it. He has a natural talent for history, and like most of his *paisanos*, remembers every important event

Gregorio Cortez at the Bexar County jail in San Antonio, seated between Capt. J. H. Rogers and (with rifle) Emanuel Tom.

that has happened during his lifetime. Amador E. Garcia, native of Webb County and a cowman of the old school, went over the ground with me. His cousin, Alfredo Garcia, also furnished me a great deal of authentic data. Alfredo took our artist, Bob Schoenke, and his wife, Pat, to Las Mesas and explained the details of the famous capture to them.

The gnarled old huisache is still filled with fragrant yellow blossoms in the spring, and ruins of the goat corral are visible more than half a century after Cortez was awakened from his troubled sleep by a prodding Winchester in the hands of Captain Rogers.

When he arrived in Laredo with his prisoner, the captain found a telegram from Sheriff Avant advising him that Cortez was headed for a point on the Rio Grande near Dolores. The sender did not know that the fugitive was already in custody, nor that the arrest had been made by the man to whom the dispatch was addressed.

Alfredo Garcia was born and reared in Webb County at Torrecillos, where his father owned a large ranch. He recalled that on a June day in 1901 the few inhabitants of that village, which now bears the name of Oilton, were startled by the unscheduled arrival of a Tex-Mex locomotive pulling a single stock car. This special train passed up the station and stopped at the shipping pens, where three saddled horses were hurriedly unloaded. Three heavily armed men, Porfirio Laurel, Maximino Villareal and Dolores Cano, deputies of Sheriff Luis Ortiz of Webb County, mounted and rode into the chaparral. This was a part of the well organized effort to cut off all escape routes which might be used by Gregorio Cortez.

CORRIDO DE GREGORIO CORTES.
Popular Song.

Transcription by
G. W. Torr

En el Con - da - do del Kar - nes mi -

ren lo queha su - ce - di - do : Mu -

rióel She - ri - fe Ma - yor, Que -

dan - do Ro - mán he - ri do.........

Adjutant General Scurry's report to the governor recites that "Cortez was captured by Captain Rogers" and makes no mention of another man. The omission may be accounted for by the fact that the general was concerned only with State personnel, and Merriman was a Federal officer. Manuel Soto states positively that *"habian dos Rinches"* (there were two Rangers) who made the arrest. The border natives call all mounted officers *Rinches* regardless of whether they are customs inspectors, border patrolmen, county sheriffs or deputies. In the trial at Karnes City, Captain Rogers testified that he and another man captured Cortez. During the trial at Corpus Christi in which Cortez was acquitted for the murder of W. T. (Brack) Morris, it was brought out that Merriman was with Captain Rogers when the defendant was caught.

My version of the Cortez arrest is in no wise intended to detract from the credit that is due Captain Rogers. He would have tackled Gregorio and half a dozen like him single handed if necessity for such an act arose in line of duty. As one who strives to accurately portray

Ranger history, I merely take into account the fact that on scouts of this kind, Rangers practically always rode in pairs. It is a well established principle among border veterans that two men together are equal to five working singly.

Warren W. Downing of Corpus Christi was a spectator at the Cortez trial in Nueces County, and paid careful attention to the proceedings. He states that Mounted Customs Inspector Bill Merriman testified on the witness stand that he took part in the capture of Cortez. This fact was dwelt upon by Samuel Belden, a defense attorney, who asked Merriman what business a Federal officer had to assist in the arrest of a man charged with a State offense. This question may have been technically warranted but it has always been the practice of border officers to work together, regardless of whether they represented the State or Federal Government. I have ridden hundreds of miles along the Rio Grande in company with the Border Patrol, a branch of the Immigration Service, and the river guards, who have the official designation of Mounted Custom Inspectors. A large number of these men received their training in the Rangers.

William Doughty, who was born in Duval County, has lived in Southwest Texas more than seventy-five years, and knows as much of its authentic history as any living man. He and Captain Rogers were attending Sunday school in Alice when a messenger boy came to the church with an urgent telegram for the captain. It stated that one Gregorio Cortez had killed three officers and was making his way across country towards Mexico. The devout Ranger laid down his Bible, and caught the Tex-Mex train for Laredo. On arriving there, he continued his journey to the ranch where he captured Cortez.

Gregorio Cortez was indicted in Karnes County for the murder of Sheriff Morris. When tried for this offense he was given the death penalty. The jury's verdict was reversed by the Court of Criminal Appeals and the case sent to Goliad County on a change of venue. There the trial resulted in a hung jury and the case was again transferred, this time to Nueces County.

B. R. Abernethy of Gonzales, one of Cortez' lawyers, made a written application for a continuance on two grounds. The first was that Gregorio's former wife, who was an eyewitness to the killing of Brack Morris, had now turned against the defendant and was married to another man. The second reason was a minor error in the interpreting to which Abernethy attached great importance. The words are similar in sound, and really amounted to very little at the time of the murder. When Sheriff Morris told Gregorio Cortez through the interpreter that he was under arrest, he replied, *"No me arresta nadie"* (Nobody arrests me; or, nobody can arrest me.). In the Goliad trial the interpreter is alleged to have testified that he said, *"No me arresta nada,"* which Abernethy branded as a meaningless phrase, as *nada* means "nothing" while *nadie* means "nobody."

On the border a majority of the Anglos are practically bilingual but some of the "Mescan" spoken farther up the State is very droll. An example in point is that of a gentleman from Goliad, who bought a ranch near Laredo. While driving a two horse buggy in one of his pastures that was posted and the gates padlocked, he met a Mexican in a wagon drawn by four burros. The ranchman was sorely vexed at the trespasser and wanted to find out who he was. *"Quien soy yo?"* (Who am I?) he shouted. The perplexed hombre replied, *"Pues senor, yo no se"* (Why, sir, I do not know). The stockman, who was rather short tempered, grabbed his Winchester and yelled, "You impudent scoundrel, don't dare tell me you don't know who you are." Fortunately, the boy who had been brought along as gate opener spoke good Spanish. He explained to the boss that he had asked, "Who am I," instead of "Who are you." This is a sample of the mistakes sometimes made by interpreters, and it is entirely possible that *nada* was used instead of *nadie* on that fatal day at the Karnes County ranch. However, there was no mistaking the fact that Gregorio Cortez meant to kill anybody who tried to arrest him, nor that Romaldo was the aggressor.

The Twenty-eighth Judicial District of that day started at Corpus Christi, took in Brownsville and all the sparsely settled Lower Rio Grande Valley, then extended up the river to include Starr County. Honorable Stanely Welch, the one armed jurist who two years later was assassinated in his sleep at Rio Grande City, presided over this court. Judge Welch overruled the defendant's motion for continuance and the case was called for trial April 25, 1904, nearly three years after Sheriff Morris was killed. District Attorney John I. Kleiber, Bell & Brown, Judge James B. Wells, and D. McNeil Turner represented the State. Samuel Belden of San Antonio, B. R. Abernethy of Gonzales and John

Scott of Corpus Christi were the defense lawyers. Attorney Belden had always enjoyed an extensive practice among people of Mexican extraction. One of his later clients was Francisco I. Madero, leader of the revolution that overthrew the Diaz regime in Mexico.

The indictment charging him with the murder of W. T. Morris was read to Cortez, first in English and then in Spanish, to which he pleaded "not guilty." The jury was empaneled and Ernest J. Fivel, who operated a restaurant on Chaparral Street in Corpus Christi served as foreman. The defense was based on the fact that Sheriff Morris did not have a warrant of arrest with him at the time he attempted to take the defendant into custody. Cortez also contended that he did not fire until after the sheriff had shot his brother. The State proved that Cortez rode around the country carrying one or more pistols in a *morral* hung from his saddle horn. Judge Welch, in his charge to the jury, instructed them that under Texas law, anybody traveling from one county to another had a right to carry weapons. The case was given to the jury April 29, 1904, and the following day they returned a verdict of "not guilty."

Gregorio Cortez was being tried for the murder of a popular sheriff. He also stood charged with the slaying of two others. Because of the Alamo, Goliad, the Mexican War and countless incidents along the border, more or less prejudice against his people still existed. Well within the memory of the older jurors, Mexican bandits had made two raids in Nueces County, almost on the outskirts of Corpus Christi. In both of these forays, some of the victims had been tortured and murdered. Despite any personal feelings they may have had about the defendant, the jury rendered their verdict strictly according to the law and evidence as presented to them.

Cortez was indicted in Gonzales County for the murder of Sheriff Dick Glover and Henry Schnabel. He was tried there on the Schnabel charge and sentenced to fifty years in the penitentiary, but this case was also reversed by the Court of Criminal Appeals. For the murder of Sheriff Glover he was tried in Colorado County, and through able prosecution by Sam Hopkins of Gonzales, the jury found him guilty and assessed the penalty at ninety-nine years.

Captains Brooks, Hughes, Rogers and McDonald in their reports for the years of 1903-04 state that each of them furnished Rangers to guard

Cortez as he was transferred from one jail to another between trials. It is worthy of note that in nearly all instances the Rangers were ordered to meet the prisoner and his escort at Yoakum. The adjutant general apparently felt that there would be no danger of Cortez trying to escape or a mob forming to lynch him at any point east of that railroad junction.

An unusual fact about the murder or murders committed by Cortez is that the weapon he used was a six-shooter. Outlaws of his type usually preferred rifles as most of their shooting was done at long range. He probably used the pistol because it was handier to carry on horseback. The day before Sheriff Morris was killed, Graves Peeler saw the Cortez brothers in their buggy. Gregorio had a Winchester across his knees.

After Sheriff Morris was killed, the women on the ranch wrapped his pistol in a grass sack and hid it in a hollow tree. When Cortez was brought back to Karnes County for trial, they showed the officers where the gun had been concealed. It is now used by Harper Morris, the present sheriff of Karnes County and a son of the first officer killed by Gregorio Cortez. He supplied me with the details of his father's death, and much other information about the Cortez case.

Horses used by possemen were left scattered all over Southwest Texas and it took nearly two years to get them back where they belonged. Many ranch housewives were almost eaten out of house and home by large parties of hungry men who would ride up unexpectedly in quest of food. These harassed women were finally forced to adopt the policy of cooking up a batch of bread and telling the riders to kill a calf for meat.

The little brown mare that Cortez had stolen and ridden down was brought to the shipping pens at Atlee. Officials of the I. & G. N. Railroad recognized the tremendous interest that the case had created among the people served by their line and transported her free of charge to San Antonio. She was placed on exhibition at the International Fair, where hundreds of curious people paid two bits apiece to see her. The now famous animal was returned to the Allens who renamed her Fanny Cortez. Emanuel Tom was presented with a fine watch by the citizens of Southwest Texas in recognition of his service as the premier trailer. When the Tom ranch in Atascosa County was burned some years ago, this memento was lost. His son, Dewey Tom, has been my friend since boyhood. He helped me get many facts of this case.

Gregorio Cortez stayed in the penitentiary until he was pardoned by Governor Oscar B. Colquitt. This was done at the instance of Colonel Frank A. Chapa of San Antonio, a member of the Governor's personal staff. It has been erroneously stated that the clemency granted Cortez was in exchange for the pardon of an American prisoner in Mexico. This story, which is generally believed in Southwest Texas, is without foundation of fact. Colonel Chapa at that time was *persona non grata* with the party that controlled the Mexican Government. He had always been on the friendliest terms with General Porfirio Diaz, and a strong supporter of his administration. When this regime was overthrown by Francisco I. Madero, the colonel naturally had no influence with the revolutionary leader, and was in no position to arrange an exchange of pardons.

I am indebted to the present Colonel Frank A. Chapa for correcting the mistaken version of the Cortez clemency. During my term as Adjutant General of Texas, he was a member of my staff. I entrusted numerous important assignments to him, each of which he carried out faithfully. Colonel Chapa told me that as a boy he had often seen Gregorio Cortez in his father's store.

An interesting sidelight on the Cortez case deals with the attitude taken by an Anglo American resident of the border country, as contrasted to that of a Latin American citizen of the same region.

During the hottest part of the pursuit, a posse rode up to a small ranch, located deep in the chaparral. The man they found there will be given the fictitious name of Tracey. One of his near relatives had been taken from a county jail and hanged by a mob. He hated officers and all they represented. When asked by the leader for information about Cortez, Tracey deliberately gave him false directions, and sent the riders on the wrong trail.

Jesus Gonzales, better known as El Teco, had no such ideas and pursued a more law-abiding course. He knew that Gregorio Cortez was a desperate criminal and did not shield him merely because they were of the same blood. A short distance from the ranch on which Cortez was captured is the coal mining town of Dolores. It was inhabited by miners from both sides of the Rio Grande. Many of them sympathized with the fugitive, and hoped he would escape into Mexico. By their mental processes, if any, a man who helped bring one of their number to justice was a traitor. They gave Gonzales his second nickname by calling him *Bocon* (Bigmouth) for informing on Cortez. However, El Teco was as game as the roosters he trained, and all attacks on him were confined to the verbal variety. He passed away peacefully in Laredo.

Judge T. M. Fly succeeded the slain Dick Glover as sheriff of Gonzales County. When Cortez was brought to Gonzales for trial, Sheriff Fly protected him from a group of outraged citizens who sought to make short work of the prisoner. I recently went over the case with this courageous veteran, and checked many of the details with him. He branded as utterly false any claim that Cortez was an inoffensive tenant farmer. "He had the small feet of a man who had spent his life on horseback. His hands showed absolutely no signs of honest toil. He could never have learned to prowl in the brush like a coyote by picking cotton," said the venerable pioneer. Gregorio Cortez could speak better than average English. When it suited his purpose however, he made full use of the old standby *"no sabe."*

Proof that the Schnabel farm was used as a waystation by the line riders is found in the fact that they had built outdoor bunks so that riders arriving in the night could catch some sleep between trips. From the character of their noctural visitors, they seemed to anticipate that the house might be rounded up at any time.

Neither Cortez nor his defenders showed the slightest gratitude toward Sheriff Fly or the Rangers who protected him, although on several occasions they saved him from being lynched. If a similar situation had arisen in Cortez's native land, the offender would have been summarily executed.

Gregorio soon tired of the quiet life in San Antonio. The revolution in Mexico offered many opportunities to a man of his talents. The "inoffensive farm hand" joined forces with Victoriano Huerta, and was a natural for the *Rurales,* whose treatment of prisoners made the worst of the Rangers look like angels of mercy. He came back to this country and was reported to have died on the border. Others believe that he found work on a ranch in Jones County and is buried there. *Quien Sabe?* A *corrido,* or folk song, of some twenty verses has perpetuated his name. Among *paisanos* on both sides of the Rio Grande, a best selling phonograph record is still the one titled "Gregorio Cortez".

Chapter 49
CONCLUSION

JanUary 18, 1933 marked a day of infamy for the Texas Rangers. On that date every member of the old and honored organization was arbitrarily discharged without notice, cause or reason. Each one had been carefully picked for his ability, character and integrity. They were dedicated men whose devotion to the Service was only exceeded by their love for their families. Several of them had enlisted early in the present century, and one, Edgar T. Neal, joined in 1895. The combined service of these veterans would approximate five hundred years. They had served Texas faithfully and well. No hint of graft or corruption marred their record. Coffee, Brooks, Hughes and Gillet united in declaring that the Rangers under Governor Sterling reached the highest point in their history. No finer body of officers was ever assembled in one group. This superb array was not dismissed for any fault or dereliction on their part. Their wealth of experience and judgement was being scrapped in order that an impeached ex-governor might wreak vengeance on those who had brought so many of his henchmen to justice, and that he might pay his debt to the criminal element for their practically solid support of his wife's candidacy.

The incoming adjutant general came from England. His co-conspirator was a Yankee. Between them, they concocted the following un-Texas order: "All leaves of absence and furloughs are revoked, all commissions, regular or special, are cancelled; all enlistments are terminated." The salary of captains was reduced to $150 per month and privates to $115. Many years of effort aimed at attracting high class men to the Service by adequate pay was scrapped by these interlopers. Their foreign handiwork was reflected in the personnel of their crew. The Rangers sank to the lowest level in history.

One fellow, who would not even have had the temerity to come to my office, much less ask me to enlist him, was made a Ferguson Ranger. He rented a house in Austin, and the approach to his garage was through an alley. One day he and a neighbor reached home at the same time. Instead of courteously awaiting his turn, the Fergusonite killed the inoffensive citizen. He was sentenced to the penitentiary, but his crime was made possible by those who voted for the Fergusons.

A Ranger was always placed on duty at night to guard the Governor's Mansion. During our regime, the man who had this assignment was O. C. (Red) Humphries of San Patricio County. He came from a fine family and made a splendid record in the first World War. Mrs. R. S. Sterling invited him to use the kitchen and ice box any time he wanted a midnight lunch.

When the Fergusons moved in, Red asked me if he should stay on. I advised him to remain until a replacement arrived, as the Mansion was State property. About nine o'clock he called to tell me he had left it with them. "What's the trouble?" I asked. "One of the Fergusons," he replied, "come to me and said, 'I understand the Sterlings gave you the run of the kitchen.' Pointing to a room at the end of the back gallery, which also contained the servants' toilet, she said, 'That's where you belong.'" In all their campaigns, the Fergusons had posed as "friends of the working man."

In his official report, the imported adjutant general made a statement that was typical of a Ferguson appointee. Following Jim's tactics, he charged his predecessor with the faults of which he himself was guilty. He said, "There were several hundred Special Rangers serving without pay." The Fergusonite neglected to add that they were among the best people in the country. They included brand inspectors of the

Texas and Southwestern Cattle Raisers Association, special agents of railroads and others engaged in protecting property at the expense of their employers. The number was greatly exaggerated, and I exercised the greatest care in issuing them.

The Fergusons flagrantly abused this practice. Police characters, gamblers, bootleggers and thugs were given Special Ranger commissions. They became badges of dishonor and objects of derision. One of the large newspapers said, "A Ranger commission and a nickel will get you a cup of coffee anywhere in Texas."

The Ranger company stationed in Southwest Texas confiscated the gambling paraphernalia from a dive in Duval County, moved it to an oil field town on the Rio Grande and operated it themselves. A prominent cattleman who owned several ranches met me one day in San Antonio. "Bill," he asked, "what on earth is the matter with the Rangers? My cattle are being stolen and when I asked the captain at Falfurrias to send me a Ranger, he replied, 'I don't have a man who can ride horseback'." I let him finish and then inquired, "You voted for the Fergusons, didn't you?" "Yes," he replied, "but I didn't know that it would affect you or the Rangers. I didn't lose an animal while your company was stationed there." "You got just what you voted for," I reminded him. The captain who failed to help the cowman was later sentenced to eight years in the penitentiary.

Many amazing and unbelievable factors worked against responsible government in Texas. A man I had long considered to be one of my best friends was vice president of a major railway system. I had often traveled in his private car, and was one of his greatest admirers. When the 1932 campaign opened, I was astounded to find that he and his railroad were supporting the Fergusons. Hurrying to Houston, I asked him, "Would you give Jim Ferguson a position of trust on your railroad?" "I wouldn't trust him with the payroll of a section foreman," he replied. "Then why would you vote for him?" I continued. The executive answered, "Because when Ross Sterling was chairman of the highway commission, he began a system of roads that caused the trucks and busses to ruin our business. If we put the Fergusons back in, maybe Jim will wreck it again."

The Ferguson pardon policy made Texas the laughing stock of other states. With them, clemency to a convict was usually a financial transaction rather than an act of mercy. In 1958 a man was picked up in Corpus Christi as an escaped convict. In 1925 he had paid Jim Ferguson's favorite pardon broker something over $3000 for his release, but the record had never been cleared. Jim had authority without accountability. He could take the fees and then have his wife sign the necessary papers. His shameful record in these matters, as well as in those of the highway department and text book board, would fill a book. I have barely scratched the surface.

The height of futility would be to misrepresent any part of the political career of Jim Ferguson. The facts are far more damaging than any distortion that could be dreamed up by a writer of fiction. He is reputed to have complained to an elderly preacher who had known him since boyhood that his enemies were circulating lies about him. "Jim," said the parson, "don't you ever worry about that. What's hurting you is the truth they are telling."

Apologists for the Fergusons like to point out that the only Texas governors removed from office were Sam Houston and Jim Ferguson. This is a fact, but the reasons for their unseating were as far apart as the poles. Sam Houston, who opposed secession, was removed for upholding a principle. Jim Ferguson, who was found guilty of high crimes and misdemeanors, was removed for the lack of principle. Paraphrasing a statement made by Abraham Lincoln on another subject, "While Jim Ferguson has many defenders he has no defense."

Captain Tom R. Hickman is a gentleman who was a credit to the Service. His personal, fraternal and business affiliations are of the best. It is a sad commentary on justice in Texas when it is remembered that his long and faithful service in the Rangers was terminated twice by politicians. In both instances this was done because his honest enforcement of the law offended some of their pets. He was recently appointed to the public safety commission, and his wealth of experience should be of vast benefit to that organization, which now has charge of the Rangers.

In 1932 Captain Hickman and his men raided a large gambling layout in Gregg County. Money amounting to something over five hundred dollars was confiscated. He placed it in a sealed box and refused to turn it over to anybody without a court order. In 1937, I received the following letter from Captain Hickman:

> Herewith enclosed I am sending you a carbon copy of an order that I have just received from Judge Clarence E. McGraw pertaining to the $511 that I confiscated in my "Jelly Bean Raid" on the Palace Hotel during your and Governor Sterling's most efficient administration and direction of the Texas Rangers' activities. You might be interested in knowing that I have exchanged letters with the last three District Attorneys of the 124th Judicial District concerning this confiscated money. They have each tried to get me to turn it over to somebody without an official court order. I have persistently demanded that I have an order from the District Judge and that I have three carbon copies of that order. One of the copies I am sending to Colonel Carmichael, because he was then the Assistant Adjutant General and is now in charge of the activities of the rangers. . . . . (Here it is deemed advisable to delete several sentences.) I would appreciate your writing me immediately your approval of my turning over this cash as directed by Judge McGraw. Please let me hear from you and come to see me whenever you can.

I am intensely proud of being a Texan. Pride and loyalty, however, do not blind me to the fact that my native state is a land of contradictions. The voting pattern of its citizens is unpredictable. In many elections a majority of them have cast their ballots with small intelligence and no consistency.

In 1938 three men ran for Governor of Texas. Two of them, Ernest O. Thompson and William McGraw, were native Texans. In the first World War, both served overseas in the American Expeditionary Force. Thompson received a citation for bravery in battle and was the youngest man to attain the rank of colonel. The third serious candidate was Wilbert L. O'Daniel, who was born in Ohio, grew up in Kansas, and as a flour salesman, landed in Texas. Everything about him was spurious. During the war he stayed at home and was openly charged with being a slacker. He used the name of "Lee" to curry favor with the southern people. Texans should have taken this deception as an affront to the memory of the revered Confederate Commander in Chief. The Peerless Leader was the soul of honor, and spurned all offers to use his name in any form of commercial exploitation. When O'Daniel migrated the last time, he brought with him the word "hillbilly." It does not belong to Texas, and prior to his coming, was rarely heard here. It is indigenous to some of the mountain states in the Old South. The smooth traveling salesman also employed the term "professional politician," to intrigue the voters. Many of them believed that it was original with him. Al Jennings, ex-outlaw who ran for Governor of Oklahoma, had used the expression years before it was copied by O'Daniel. All these deceptions and many others were swallowed by the electorate. In the gubernatorial race, O'Daniel, who was not even a qualified voter, beat both of the ex-soldier natives in the first primary. Over half a million gullible Texans voted for this slicker. Following the election, another weird circumstance was found to exist. Outside of a few job hunters, it was hard to find a person who would admit he or she had voted for O'Daniel.

With the advent of World War II, the state witnessed another incongruity. After turning down their own product for this unwarlike newcomer, Texas sent more than three quarters of a million persons to the armed forces, and was third in voluntary enlistments.

William Sydney Porter (O. Henry) was born in North Carolina and spent many years in Texas. He said that his pet aversion was a "professional Southerner." I feel the same way about a "professional Texan." Many of them are also synthetic. They are as offensive to us as they are to anybody else. Real Texans, especially the cowmen, when traveling in the East or North, wear shoes and a small hat. On the other hand, salesmen, merchants and others who do not wear *sombreros* at home, will buy or borrow one for the journey. They also acquire a pair of cowboy boots to complete their Texas costume. Awkwardly herding their unfamiliar footwear down the sidewalks of New York, they present an amusing spectacle. One afternoon I saw the people turn and stare at a big-hatted figure striding down Fifth Avenue. They thought that he must be either a cattle king or a Texas Ranger. I recognized him and ducked into a doorway, although he probably would not have known me in shoes and a little hat. He was the owner of an ice cream emporium and at home did not wear such an outfit. Some of the newly rich oil men also enjoy displaying their Western finery on many inappropriate occasions.

The Rangers in all things should preserve their individuality. Hays, Walker, McCullough, Ford and McNelly set the pattern. It was followed by every outstanding captain. They would not ape anybody. Each one of them possessed great initiative and originality of thought. When a Ranger so far forgets their example as to emulate Hollywood in either dress or mannerisms, he becomes an imitation instead of the standard. Those who cherish the organization always refer to it as "the Service," and never as a "Force". Captain Brooks said, "Whenever you make a 'constabule' or policeman out of a Ranger, you destroy his usefulness." Imported efficiency experts who know nothing of our traditions endeavor to turn the Rangers into State police. They would lose over one hundred years of prestige by scrapping the name of "Texas Rangers." Their next step will probably be to streamline the Alamo.

I had made extensive plans to raise a pension fund for faithful Rangers. It would not have cost the taxpayers a cent. Will Rogers, Tom Mix, Roxy and others had agreed to put on benefit shows for this purpose. When a Ranger reached an age that he wanted to "take out," he would not be forced to pass his last days as a night watchman in some small town. He could retire on a comfortable annuity.

I also planned to honor these men in their later years, as well as conform to an old custom. In Texas, when a Ranger or sheriff who has made a good record retires from active service, everybody calls him "Captain." Scoffers would say, "Oh, he never was a captain." I planned to organize Company X. A month or so before a Ranger retired, I was going to make him captain of this company. His title would then be official.

The Ranger Service, more than any other organization, is dependent on the quality of its personnel. When composed of good men, it is the best outfit in the world, but when incompetents are enlisted by self-serving politicians, it quickly becomes the worst. I would rather have a good man armed with a muzzle loader than a poor one armed with a machine gun. In these modern times, finger printing, ballistics and the other scientific methods of crime detection are essentials. However, proficiency in their use does not necessarily denote ability. The Army, as well as many successful business firms, has often found that a man's worth cannot be ascertained by means of a questionnaire. Those having the highest grades on their examination papers may be lacking in the other necessary talents that make a good Ranger.

There is no question but that a definite potency exists in the name "Texas Ranger." Take two men of equal size and arm them with identical weapons. Call one of them a deputy sheriff and the other a Ranger. Send each of these officers out to stop a mob or quell a riot. The crowd will resist the deputy, but will submit to the authority of the Ranger. There is also something in the name "Ranger" that makes the wildest cowboy become completely dedicated to his duty the moment he takes the oath of office. He needs no blowing of bugles or flying of flags to make him carry on. He might be out in the chaparral far away from doctors or ambulances and if wounded he would probably, as one old Ranger put it, "lie out there and sour." Nobody would know but he and God, yet he will not flinch or shirk his responsibility.

Any Ranger commander who fails to make full use of these traditions is throwing away a large portion of his efficiency, for without an *esprit de corps* and a heart, the Service becomes a souless robot.

In looking back over my service in the Texas Rangers, I find several sources of pride and satisfaction. Since I first saw Captains Brooks and Rogers as a lad, I have done everything in my power to uplift the Service. One of my most cherished objectives has been its constant improvement, adequate pay to attract better men, and to maintain the Service on a high plane. My efforts were well rewarded by the friendships and remarks of the old comrades who served during my administration. At a recent meeting of the ex-Rangers Association, George Allen said, "The happiest years of my life were the ones I spent in the Ranger Service under your command". Many of my comrades have expressed the same sentiment.

My children are fifth generation Texans, and are descended from a veteran of San Jacinto. God bless Texas. May she ever be well and honestly governed and may she always have reason to be proud of her Rangers.

Bibliography

OFFICIAL DOCUMENTS

Reports of various Adjutant Generals of Texas.
Lists of fugitives from justice.

BOOKS

Aten, Sergeant Ira—*Six and One Half Years in the Ranger Service.*
Cofer, David Brooks—*The Second Five Administrations of Texas A. & M. College.*
Davis, Richard Harding—*The West from a Car Window.*
Deibert, Chaplain Ralph C.—*History of the Third United States Cavalry.*
Gillett, Captain James B.—*Six Years with the Texas Rangers.*
Jennings, N. A.—*A Texas Ranger.*
McKay, S. S.—*Texas Politics 1906-1944.*
Nolen, Oren Warder—*Galloping Down the Texas Trail.*
Paine, Albert Bigelow—*Captain Bill McDonald, Texas Ranger.*
Pennybacker, Anna J. H.—*A History of Texas.*
Pierce, Frank Cushman—*A Brief History of the Lower Rio Grande Valley.*
Sullivan, Sergeant W. J. L.—*Twelve Years in the Saddle for Law and Order.*
Webb, Walter Prescott—*The Texas Rangers.*
Wharton Clarence R.—*History of Fort Bend County.*

NEWSPAPERS

Amarillo *Globe*
Austin *American*
Corpus Christi *Caller*
Dallas *News*
Falfurrias *Facts*
Floresville *Chronicle*
Fort Worth *Star-Telegram*
Houston *Chronicle*
Houston *Post*
Laredo *Times*
San Antonio *Express*
Sterling City *Record-News*
Washington *Post*
Wichita Falls *Record-News*

MAGAZINE

The Cattleman

Index

527